THE COMPLETE HERB BOOK

JEKKA McVICAR

WITH AN INTRODUCTION BY
PENELOPE HOBHOUSE

FIREFLY BOOKS

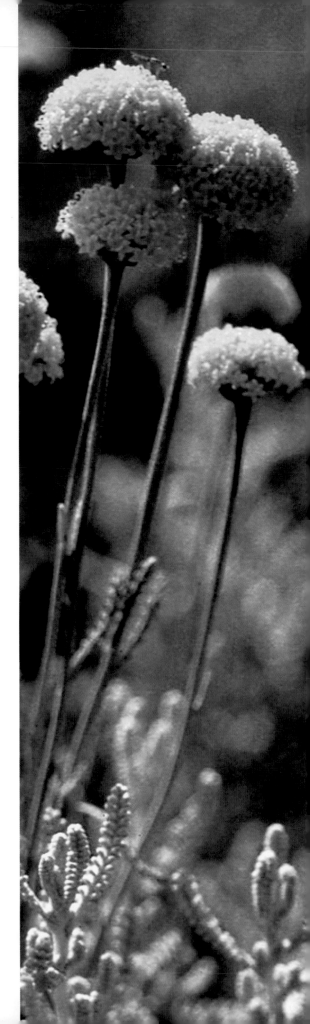

A FIREFLY BOOK

Published by Firefly Books Ltd. 2007

Copyright © 2008 Jekka Enterprises Ltd.
Photographs © 2008 Jekka McVicar
Artwork © 2008 Sally Maltby

Second printing, 2009

Publisher Cataloging-in-Publication Data (U.S.)

McVicar, Jekka.
   The complete herb book / Jekka McVicar ; with an introduction by
Penelope Hobhouse ; in association with the Royal Horticultural Society.
Originally published as: Jekka's complete herb book, London : Kyle Cathie Ltd., 1994.
[304] p. : col. photos. ;   cm.
Includes bibliographical references and index.
Summary: classic gardening book varieties of herb to grow and recipes, bringing together all aspects of an individual herb - history and folklore, species to grow and cosmetic, medicinal and culinary uses. Chapters on propagation, harvesting and making herb oils are complemented with ideas for ten different designs for herb gardens and a unique yearly calendar.
ISBN-13: 978-1-55407-365-8   (pbk.)
ISBN-10: 1-55407-365-0 (pbk.)
1. Herbs. 2. Herb gardening. 3. Cookery (Herbs).
4. Herbs — Therapeutic use. I. Hobhouse, Penelope.
II. Title.
635/.7 dc22   SB351.H5M354 2008

Published in the United States by
Firefly Books (U.S.) Inc.
P.O. Box 1338, Ellicott Station
Buffalo, New York 14205

For Kyle Cathie:
Edited by Jane Simmonds
Index by Helen Snaith
Design by Geoff Hayes
Production by Sha Huxtable and Alice Holloway

Cover Design by Erin R. Holmes

Printed in China

IMPORTANT NOTICE

This book contains information on a wide range of herbs that can be used medicinally. It is not intended as a medical reference book, but as a source of information. Before trying any herbal remedies, the reader is recommended to sample a small quantity first to establish whether there is any adverse or allergic reaction. Remember that some herbs that are beneficial in small doses can be harmful if taken to excess or for a long period. The reader is advised not to attempt to self-medicate for serious long-term problems without consulting a qualified medicinal herbalist or physician. Neither the author nor the publisher can be held responsible for any adverse reactions to the recipes, recommendations and instructions contained herein, and the use of any herb or derivative is entirely at the reader's own risk.

To Mac, Hannah and Alistair

Author's Acknowledgments
With many thanks to Mac for all his support, Kyle for letting me create a new edition, the RHS for endorsing the book, Simon Maughan of the RHS, Penny for her compliments, Jamie for being an inspiration, Jane for wading through my text, Rosemary for getting it all legal, and to all the staff at Jekka's Herb Farm for keeping the plants growing while I wrote.

CONTENTS

INTRODUCTION

In Western civilization ancient herbals, dating back to the *De Materia Medica* of Dioscorides written in the first century AD, described plants for their healing virtues. In his great work the Greek physician named and described 500 plants actually seen by him, as well as how to observe their growth, how to gather and store the "flowers and sweet scented things" in "dry boxes of Limewood" and the moister medicines in more suitable containers. The earliest extant copy of his manuscript, written and illustrated in the sixth century and known as the *Codex Vindobonensis*, is in Vienna. His plants came from the Mediterranean basin and scholars over the centuries have worked to find and identify them.

In the next 1500 years herbals came to include and emphasize the culinary as well as the medicinal uses, sometimes a mixture of fanciful myth and magic, at others the down-to-earth practicalities of culture and preparation. The best known in Britain is John Gerard's *Herbal* written in 1597, much more a treatise on gardening than just a catalogue of plants considered for their "vertues" as medicinal plants or in cooking. It is treasured because of the practical nature of his descriptions, many based on his own personal knowledge of growing them in his garden at Holborn. By 1596, of course, he was growing plants newly arrived from east of the Mediterranean and from the New World, pushing out the frontiers of plant and herb knowledge.

Jekka McVicar grows over 600 varieties of herbs in her nursery. In this very practical book she brilliantly assembles information on species and varieties, their cultivation and garden use, and their medicinal, culinary and cosmetic properties, as well as uses for aromatherapy. For appropriate herbs she provides recipes, her writing evocative of scent and taste.

The old favorites are here but, in addition, for each genus she amplifies the range of species and cultivars to cover those most useful as well as most garden-worthy. For anyone who has seen her stands, set up as decorative herb gardens at Chelsea or Hampton Court, it will be axiomatic that her book is also a guide to growing herbs aesthetically, including plans for herb gardens designed for all occasions. Jekka describes in detail how to sow, propagate from cuttings and how to maintain and grow the herbs – even how to turn them into ornamental topiary subjects. It is a book on herbs which has, without sacrificing plant information, expanded into an encyclopedia on making and enjoying herb gardens, in which their aromatic leaves and scented flowers can be enjoyed by all the senses.

Growing herbs, with their poetic and historical associations, has a connotation of "usefulness" which serves a moral purpose when ordinary decorative gardening can seem too full of display and artistry. Jekka McVicar strikes a happy balance between industry and pleasure, between history — she looks back to the old herbalists for facts and then amplifies these in the light of contemporary knowledge — and modern use. It is particularly good to be reminded of herbal remedies scientifically approved today. She encourages us to know and grow a great number of herbs which are unfamiliar to many of us, and to experiment with them. She leads us through her growing processes with a clarity not always discovered in "how-to" books and her recipes sound practical as well as enticing.

Penelope Hobhouse

AUTHOR'S NOTE

"Excellent herbs had our fathers of old
Excellent herbs to ease their pain."
"Our Fathers of Old" — Rudyard Kipling.

My life in the world of herbs has evolved over the years but my passion and enthusiasm for these plants, which are of so much benefit to man, is as strong as ever. Over 30 years ago I started work on a herb farm in Somerset, England; it was then that my thirst for more knowledge was ignited. During the subsequent years I started, with my husband, a herb farm in South Gloucestershire that was originally wholesale and has now developed into a mail order business with the advent of the Internet. In 1992 we started exhibiting at the Royal Horticultural Society flower shows, where we have been awarded over 60 Gold medals for our herb exhibits.

I wrote the original *Complete Herb Book* because, after exhibiting at the RHS flower shows, I found that I was being overwhelmed with requests for practical information on the growing and the use of each herb. The book stemmed from first-hand knowledge obtained from running my organic herb farm as well as considerable research.

One of the questions I am often asked is "What is a herb?" It can be argued that all useful plants are herbs. The *Oxford English Dictionary* defines them as "plants of which the leaves, stem or flowers are used for food or medicine, or in some way for their scent or flavor." That many herbs do you good is in no doubt, improving your health, appearance or sense of well-being.

This new edition of the *Complete Herb Book,* which includes 38 new herbs, also shows how far organic horticulture has developed during the past decade. What I find exciting is that the development and knowledge of these plants is ever increasing and as I travel throughout the United Kingdom and overseas lecturing I realize that the interest in herbs as part of a movement toward a healthier, greener lifestyle is accelerating, so it is an appropriate time for this updated book.

For a newcomer to the world of herbs the most extraordinary feature of these plants is their incredible versatility. You may think of a particular herb as having mainly culinary or medicinal properties and then discover it has other useful applications. A herb that is greatly valued in cooking may also be of value for its medicinal properties. A plant such as thyme can provide the raw material for cooking, medicines and aromatherapy. I have included many culinary recipes in this book because herbs can transform a meal into a feast; there is nothing more inspiring than walking into a kitchen that is full of the aromas of herbs as their essential oils mingle with the food.

Herbs have been my life for over three decades. In this book I have tried to convey to you just some of the pleasure that working with these remarkable plants can bring.

Please note that the image in the colored box at the beginning of each herb is the first one described in the text.
I'm sure I don't need to remind you, but please don't dig up any wild plants.

HOW TO USE THIS BOOK

This book is comprised of two main sections:

The A–Z of Herbs

The A–Z of Herbs is arranged alphabetically by the botanical Latin name with detailed information for each specific herb such as

Other Names: lists some folk and country names.

Natural Habitat: native country and area of distribution.

Propagation: provides helpful tips for the individual herb that will make all the difference between success and failure. Techniques for seed, cuttings, division and layering are given.

Pests and Diseases: where a particular herb is susceptible to pests or diseases, treatments and any preventative measures are detailed.

Maintenance: a quick checklist of tasks necessary throughout the year season by season.

Garden Cultivation: gives the preferred position and soil type and details specific tasks for maintaining the plant at its best, its likes and dislikes, watering requirements and winter protection needs.

Harvesting: the parts of the plant to harvest, together with the best time for harvesting, depending on the eventual use and method of storing.

Companion Planting: indicates when the herb is thought to be beneficial to another plant if located nearby.

Container Growing: whether indoors or outdoors, I give the preferred compost together with watering and feeding needs.

Uses: known uses for individual herbs, subdivided into culinary, medicinal and other uses, demonstrating the vast number of ways herbs have been used throughout history.

Species: identifying the important species and some other closely related selections displaying unique characteristics. For many species there are so many varieties it would be impossible to name them all.

Warning: this is given if herbs are toxic or have adverse effects. If a plant is particularly poisonous, it is indicated with a symbol next to the relevant plant.

Zones: Indicates the plant's northern hardiness when grown in the United States and Canada.

General Details of Herb Growing

Propagation: what you need to propagate your plant, whether it be by seed, cutting, layering, or division. Detailed step-by-step instructions are provided for each method.

Planning Your Herb Garden: useful tips in planning a herb garden, together with plans for ten herb gardens.

Herbs in Containers: including useful tips for growing herbs successfully in pots, indoors or outdoors.

Harvesting: including instructions on methods of harvesting, drying, storing and freezing.

Herb Oils, Vinegars and Preserves: methods of making delicious produce from the garden.

Natural Dyes: step-by-step instructions on how to dye your own material to natural colors.

Pests and Diseases: the major pests and diseases and the best organic strategies to cure, and prevent reccurrence of, problems.

Yearly Calendar: a checklist of tasks to be performed season by season, and also identifies the herbs available for harvest at different times of the year.

Climate: defines the way that certain terms are used in the book to describe the range of temperatures a plant needs in order to thrive.

Botanical Names: explains the relationship between the family, genus, species and varieties of a given plant.

THE A-Z OF
HERBS

Achillea ageratum

ENGLISH MACE

From the family Asteraceae.

Native to Switzerland, English mace is now cultivated in northern temperate countries. This culinary herb is little known and under-used.

English mace belongs to the (genus) *Achillea*, named after Achilles, who is said to have discovered the medicinal properties of the genus. There is no direct historical record of English mace itself apart from the fact that it was discovered in Switzerland in 1798.

 species

Achillea ageratum
English Mace
Hardy perennial. Ht. 12–18 in. when in flower. Spread 12 in. Clusters of small cream flowers that look very Victorian in summer. Leaves brightish green, narrow and very deeply serrated. Zone 6.

 cultivation

Propagation
Cuttings
This is the best method for the propagation of a large number of plants. Take softwood cuttings in late summer; protect from wilting as they will be very soft. Use a seed compost mixed in equal parts with composted fine bark. When well-rooted, harden off and plant out in the garden 12 in. apart.

Division
If you require only a few plants it is best to propagate by division. Either divide the plant in early spring—it is one of the first to appear—or in the fall. Replant in the garden in a prepared site. As this is a hardy plant it will not need protection, but if you leave division until the frosts are imminent, winter the divided plants in a cold frame or cold greenhouse.

Pests and Diseases
Mace, in most cases, is free from pests and diseases.

Maintenance
Spring Divide established plants.
Summer Cut back flowers. Take softwood cuttings.
Fall Divide established plants if needed.
Winter Does not need protection.

Garden Cultivation
This fully hardy plant, which even flourishes on my heavy soil, prefers a sunny, well-drained site. It starts the season off as a cluster of low-growing, deeply serrated leaves and then develops long, flowering stems in summer. Cut back after flowering for a fresh supply of leaves and to encourage a second flowering crop. When in flower this plant may need staking in a windy, exposed site.

ENGLISH MACE

Achillea ageratum new spring growth

Harvesting

Cut fresh leaves when you wish. For freezing—the best method of preserving—cut before flowering and freeze in small containers.

Pick the flowers during the summer. Collect in small bunches and hang upside down to dry. Both flowers and leaves dry particularly well.

 container growing

For a tall flowering plant this looks most attractive in a terracotta pot. Make sure it has a wide base to allow for its height later in the season. Use a soil-based compost mixed in equal parts with composted fine bark. Water regularly thoughout the growing season and give a liquid feed (according to manufacturer's instructions) in the summer months during flowering. Cut back after flowering to stop the plant from toppling over and encourage new growth. As this plant dies back in winter, allow the compost to become nearly dry, and winter the container in a cold greenhouse or cold frame.

 other uses

Flowers in dried flower arrangements.

 culinary

The chopped leaves can be used to stuff chicken, flavor soups, stews, and to sprinkle on potato salads, rice and pasta dishes. The leaf has a mild, warm, aromatic flavor and combines well with other herbs.

Chicken with English Mace in Foil
Serves 4

4 chicken breasts
2 tablespoons yogurt
2 tablespoons Dijon mustard
Salt and fresh ground black pepper
Bouquet garni herb oil (or olive oil)
6 tablespoons of chopped English mace leaves
Juice of 1 lemon

Preheat oven to 375°F/190°C. Mix the yogurt and mustard together and coat the chicken pieces on all sides. Sprinkle with salt and pepper. Cut 4 pieces of foil and brush with herb or olive oil. Lay the chicken breasts in the foil and scatter a thick layer of English mace on each piece. Sprinkle with lemon juice. Wrap in the foil, folding the ends very tightly so no juices can escape. Lay the packets on a rack in the oven, cook for 30 minutes. Serve with rice and a green salad.

Achillea millefolium

YARROW

Also known as Nosebleed, Millefoil, Thousand leaf, Woundwort, Carpenter's weed, Devil's nettle, Soldier's woundwort and Noble yarrow. From the family *Asteraceae*.

Yarrow is found all over the world in waste places, fields, pastures and meadows. It is common throughout Europe, Asia, and North America.

This is a very ancient herb. It was used by the Greeks to control hemorrhages, for which it is still prescribed in homeopathy and herbal medicine today. The legend of Achilles refers to this property—it was said that during the battle of Troy, Achilles healed many of his warriors with yarrow leaves. Hence the name *Achillea*.

It has long been considered a sacred herb. Yarrow stems were used by the Druids to divine seasonal weather. The ancient Chinese text of prophecy, *I Ching, The Book of Changes*, states that 52 straight stalks of dried yarrow, of even length, were spilled to foretell the future instead of the modern way of using three coins.

It was also associated with magic. In Anglo-Saxon times it was said to have a potency against evil, and in France and in Ireland it is one of the Herbs of St John. On St John's Eve, the Irish hang it up in their houses to avert illness.

There is an old superstition, which apparently still lingers in remote parts of Britain and the United States, that if a young girl tickles her nostrils with sprays of yarrow and her nose starts to bleed, it proves her lover's fidelity:

"Yarrow away, Yarrow away, bear a white blow? If my lover loves me, my nose will bleed now."

Achillea filipendulina 'Gold Plate'

Achillea millefolium

 varieties

Achillea millefolium
Yarrow
Hardy perennial. Ht. 1–3 ft., spread 2 ft. and more. Small white flowers with a hint of pink appear in flat clusters from summer to fall. Its specific name, *millefolium,* means "a thousand leaf," which is a good way to describe these darkish green, aromatic, feathery leaves. Zone 2.

Achillea millefolium 'Fire King'
Hardy perennial. Ht. and spread 24 in. Flat heads of rich, red, small flowers in flat clusters all summer. Masses of feathery dark green leaves. This has an upright habit and is a vigorous grower. Zone 2.

Achillea filipendulina 'Gold Plate'
Hardy perennial. Ht. 4 ft, spread 24 in. Large flat heads of small golden flowerheads in summer that dry well for winter decoration. Filigree green foliage. Zone 3.

Achillea 'Moonshine'
Hardy perennial. Ht. 24 in., spread 20 in. Flat heads of bright yellow flowers throughout summer. Masses of small feathery gray/green leaves. Zone 3.

cultivation

Propagation

Seed

For reliable results sow the very small seed under cool protection in the fall. Use either a proprietary seeder or the cardboard trick (see page 265) and sow into prepared seed or plug trays. Leave the trays in a cool greenhouse for the winter. Germination is erratic. Harden off and plant out in the garden in spring. Plant 8–12 in. apart, remembering that it will spread. As this is an invasive plant, I do not advise sowing direct into the garden.

Division

Yarrow is a prolific grower, producing loads of creeping rootstock in a growing season. To stop an invasion into areas where it is not wanted, divide by digging up a clump and replanting where required in the spring or early fall.

Pests and Diseases

Yarrow is usually free from both.

Maintenance

Spring Divide established clumps.
Summer Deadhead flowers, and cut back after flowering to prevent self-seeding.
Fall Sow seeds. Divide established plants.
Winter No need for protection, very hardy plant.

Garden Cultivation

Yarrow is one of nature's survivors. Its creeping rootstock and ability to self-seed ensure its survival in most soils.

It does well in coastal gardens, as it is drought-tolerant. Still, owners of manicured lawns will know it as a nightmare weed that resists all attempts to eradicate it.

Yarrow is the plant doctor of the garden, its roots' secretions activating the disease resistance of nearby plants. It also intensifies the medicinal actions of other herbs and deepens their fragrance and flavor.

Harvesting

Cut the leaves and flowers for drying as the plant comes into flower.

culinary

The young leaves can be used in salads. Here is an interesting salad recipe:

Salad Made with Three Wild Herbs

Equal parts of yarrow, plantain and watercress leaves
A little garlic
1/2 cucumber
Freshly chopped or dried chives and parsley
1 medium, boiled, cold potato
Salad dressing consisting of lemon and cream, or lemon and oil, or lemon and cream and a little apple juice.

Select and clean herbs. Wash carefully and allow to drain. Cut the yarrow and plantain into fine strips. Cube the cucumber and potato into small pieces. Leave the watercress whole and arrange in a bowl. Add herbs and other vegetables and salad dressing and mix well.

container growing

Yarrow itself does not grow well in containers. However, the hybrids, and certainly the shorter varieties, can look stunning. Use a soil-based potting compost mix and feed plants with liquid fertilizer during the flowering season, following the manufacturer's instructions. Cut back after flowering and keep watering to a minimum in winter. No varietiy is suitable for growing indoors.

medicinal

Yarrow is one of the best-known herbal remedies for fevers. Used as a hot infusion it will induce sweats that cool fevers and expel toxins. In China, yarrow is used fresh as a poultice for healing wounds. It can also be made into a decoction for wounds, chapped skin and rashes, and as a mouthwash for inflamed gums.

warning

Yarrow should always be taken in moderation and never for long periods because it may cause skin irritation. It should not be taken by pregnant women. Large doses produce headaches and vertigo.

other uses

Flowerheads may be dried for winter decoration.

Traditionally the leaves of this unassuming herb were used to accelerate the decomposition of garden waste in a compost bin. The leaves were also used as a copper fertilizer.

Infusion of yarrow

Aconitum napellus
MONKSHOOD

Also known as Friar's cap, Old woman's night-cap, Chariots drawn by doves, Blue rocket, Wolf's bane and Mazbane. From the family Ranunculaceae.

Various species of monkshood grow in temperate regions. They can be found on shady banks, in deciduous woodlands and in mountainous districts. They are all poisonous plants.

One theory for the generic name, *Aconitum*, is that the name comes from the Greek *akoniton*, meaning "dart." This is because the juice of the plant was used to poison arrow tips and was used as such by the Arabs and ancient Chinese. Its specific epithet *napellus* means "little turnip," a reference to the shape of the root. It was the name used by Theophrastus, the Greek botanist (370–285 BC), for a poisonous plant.

This plant has been known throughout history to kill both animals and humans. In the 16th century Gerard commented in his *Herbal* on its "fair and good bluey flowers in shape like helmet which are so beautiful that man would think they were of some excellent virtue." Appearances should not be trusted. One hundered fifty years later, Miller in his garden dictionary wrote, "Monks Hood was in almost all old gardens and not to be put in the way of children less they should prejudice themselves therewith."

As late as 1993 a British flower seller had to be hospitalized after handling monkshood outside pubs in Salisbury and Southampton.

Aconitum napellus flowers

 varieties

☠ ***Aconitum napellus***
Monkshood
Hardy perennial. Ht. 5 ft., spread 1 ft. Tall slender spires of hooded, light blue/indigo/blue flowers in late summer. Leaves mid-green, palm shaped and deeply cut. There is a white flowered form, *A. napellus* 'Albiflorus', which grows in the same way. Zone 4.

☠ ***Aconitum napellus* subsp. *napellus* Anglicum Group**
Monkshood
Hardy perennial. Ht. 5 ft., spread 1 ft. Tall slender spires of hooded, blue/lilac flowers are borne in early/mid-summer. Leaves mid-green, wedged shaped, and deeply cut. One of a few plants peculiar to the British Isles, liking shade or half-shade along brooks and streams. Among the most dangerous of all plants.

MONKSHOOD

 ## cultivation

Propagation
Seed
Sow the small seed under protection either in the fall (which is best) or spring. Use prepared seed or plug trays. Cover with perlite. Germination can be erratic, an all-or-nothing affair. The seeds do not need heat to germinate. In spring, when the seedlings are large enough to handle, plant out into a prepared, shady site 12 in. apart. Wash your hands after handling the seedlings; even better wear thin gloves. The plant takes 2–3 years to flower.

Division
Divide established plants throughout the fall, so long as the soil is workable. Replant in a prepared site in the garden—remember the gloves. You will notice when splitting the plant that the tap root puts out daughter roots with many rootlets. Remove and store in a warm dry place for planting out later.

Pests and Diseases
This plant rarely suffers from pests, and it is usually disease free.

Maintenance
Spring Plant out fall-grown seedlings.
Summer Cut back after flowering.
Fall Sow seeds, divide established plants.
Winter No need to protect. Fully hardy.

Garden Cultivation
In spite of the dire warnings this is a most attractive plant, which is hardy and thrives in most good soils.
   Position it so that it is not accessible. Plant at the back of borders, or under trees where no animals can eat it or young fingers fiddle with it. It is useful for planting in the shade of trees as long as they are not too dense.
   It is important always to teach people which plants are harmful, and which plants are edible. If you remove all poisonous plants from the garden, people will not learn which to respect.

Harvesting
Unless you are a qualified herbalist I do not recommend harvesting.

 ## container growing

Because of its poisonous nature, I cannot whole-heartedly recommend that it be grown in containers, but it does look very attractive in a large container surrounded by heartsease *(Viola tricolor)*. Use a soil-based compost mixed in equal parts with composted fine bark (see page 282), water regularly throughout the summer months. Liquid feed in summer only.

 ## warning

The symptoms of *Aconitum* poisoning are a burning sensation on the tongue, vomiting, abdominal pains and diarrhea, leading to paralysis and death. Emergency antidotes, which are obtainable from hospitals, are atropine and strophanthin.

 ## medicinal

This plant contains one of the most potent nerve poisons in the plant kingdom and is used in proprietory analgesic medicines to alleviate pain both internally and externally. These drugs can only be prescribed by qualified medical practitioners. Tinctures of monkshood are frequently used in homeopathy.

Under no circumstances should monkshood ever be prepared and used for self-medication.

Aconitum napellus in a meadow

Agastache

ANISE HYSSOP

Also known as Giant Hyssop, Blue Giant Hyssop, Fennel Hyssop, Fragrant Giant Hyssop. From the family Lamiaceae.

Anise hyssop is a native of North America. *A. cana*, the Mosquito Plant originates from Mexico and *A. rugosa* is from Korea.

There are few references to the history of this lovely herb. According to Allen Paterson, Past Director of the Royal Botanical Garden in Ontario, it is a close cousin of the bergamots. It is common in North American herb gardens and is certainly worth including in any herb garden for its flowers and scent. The long spikes of purple, blue, and pink flowers are big attractions for bees and butterflies.

 varieties

Agastache foeniculum (Pursh)
Anise Hyssop
Hardy perennial. Ht. 2 ft., spread 1 ft. Long purple flower spikes in summer. Aniseed-scented mid-green oval leaves. Zone 4.

Agastache cana
Mosquito Plant
Half-hardy perennial. Ht. 2 ft., spread 1 ft. Pink tubular flowers in the summer with aromatic oval mid-green toothed leaves. Zone 8.

Agastache rugosa
Korean Mint
Hardy perennial. Ht. 3 ft., spread 1 ft. Lovely mauve/purple flower spikes in summer. Distinctly mint-scented mid-green oval pointed leaves. Zone 5.

Agastache rugosa 'Golden Jubilee'
Anise Hyssop Golden Jubilee
Hardy perennial. Ht. 20 in., spread 1 ft. Lovely mauve/purple flower spikes in summer. Anise-scented golden leaves. Prone to sun scorch, plant in partial shade. Zone 5.

Agastache cana

cultivation

Propagation

Seed
The small fine seeds need warmth to germinate: 65°F (17°C). Use the cardboard method (see page 265) and artificial heating if sowing in early spring.

Use either prepared seed or plug trays or, if you have only a few seeds, directly into a pot of standard seed compost mixed in equal parts with composted fine bark. Cover with perlite. Germinates in 10–20 days.

You can also sow outside in the fall when the soil is warm, but the young plants will need protection throughout the winter months.

When the seedlings are large enough to handle, prick out and pot on using a potting compost mixed in equal parts with propagating bark. In mid-spring, when air and soil temperatures have risen, plant out at a distance of 18 in. apart.

Cuttings
Take cuttings of soft young shoots in spring, when all the species root well. Use a seed compost mixed in equal parts with composted fine bark. After a full period of weaning, cuttings should be strong enough to plant out in the early fall.

Semiripe wood cuttings may be taken in late summer, using the same compost mix. After they have rooted, pot them, and winter in a cold frame or cold greenhouse.

Division
This is a good alternative way to maintain a short-lived perennial. In the second or third year divide the creeping roots in spring, either by the "forks back-to-back" method, or by digging up the whole plant and dividing it into several segments.

Pests and Diseases
This herb rarely suffers from pests or diseases, although seedlings can be prone to "dampening off."

Maintenance
Spring Sow seeds.
Summer Take softwood or semiripe cuttings late in the season.
Fall Tidy up the plants by cutting back the old flower heads and woody growth. Sow seeds. Protect young plants from frost.
Winter Protect half-hardy species (and anise hyssop below –6°C/20°F) with either frost cloth, bark or straw.

Garden Cultivation
All species like a rich, moist soil and full sun, and will adapt very well to most ordinary soils if planted in a sunny situation. All are short-lived and should be propagated each year to ensure continuity.

Anise hyssop, although hardier than the other species, still needs protection below 20°F (–6°C). The Mexican half-hardy species need protection below 26°F (–3°C).

Harvesting

Flowers
Cut for drying just as they begin to open.

Leaves
Cut leaves just before late spring flowering.

Seeds
Heads turn brown as the seed ripens. At the first sign of the seed falling, pick and hang upside down with a paper bag tied over the heads.

 ## container growing

Not suitable for growing indoors. However, anise hyssop and Korean mint both make good patio plants provided the container is at least 10–12 in. in diameter. Use a potting compost mixed in equal parts with fine composted bark (see page 282), and a liquid fertilizer feed only once a year after flowering. If you feed the plant beforehand, the flowers will be poor. Keep well watered in summer.

 ## other uses

Anise hyssop and Korean mint both have scented leaves, which make them suitable for potpourri.

 ## culinary

The two varieties most suitable are:

Anise Hyssop
Leaves can be used in salads and to make refreshing tea. Like borage, they can be added to summer fruit cups. Equally they can be chopped and used as a seasoning in pork dishes or in savory rice.

Flowers can be added to fruit salads and cups giving a lovely splash of color.

Korean Mint
Leaves have a strong peppermint flavor and make a very refreshing tea, said to be good first thing in the morning after a night on the town. They are also good chopped up in salads, and the flowers look very attractive scattered over a pasta salad.

Korean mint tea

Alchemilla

LADY'S MANTLE

From the family Rosaceae.

Lady's mantle is a native of the mountains of Europe, Asia and America. It is found not only in damp places but also in dry shady woods.

The Arab *alkemelych* (alchemy) is thought to be the source of the herb's Latin generic name, *Alchemilla*. The crystal dew lying in perfect pearl drops on the leaves has long inspired poets and alchemists, and was reputed to have healing and magical properties, even to preserve a woman's youth provided she collected the dew in May, alone, in full moonlight, naked, and with bare feet as a sign of purity and to ward off any lurking forces.

In the medieval period it was dedicated to the Virgin Mary, hence lady's mantle was considered a woman's protector, and nicknamed "a woman's best friend." It was used not only to regulate the menstrual cycle and to ease the effects of menopause, but also to reduce inflammation of the female organs. In the 18th century, women applied the leaves to their breasts to make them recover shape after they had been swelled with milk. It is still prescribed by herbalists today.

Alchemilla mollis

 varieties

Alchemilla alpina L.
Alpine Lady's Mantle
Known in America as Silvery lady's mantle.
Hardy perennial. Ht. 6 in., spread 24 in. or more. Tiny, greenish-yellow flowers in summer. Leaves rounded, lobed, pale green and covered in silky hairs. An attractive plant suitable for groundcover, rockeries and dry banks. Zone 3.

Alchemilla conjuncta
Lady's Mantle Conjuncta
Hardy perennial. Ht. 12 in., spread 12 in. or more. Tiny, greenish-yellow flowers in summer. Leaves star-shaped, bright green on top with lovely silky silver hairs underneath. An attractive plant suitable for groundcover, rockeries and dry banks. Zone 3.

Alchemilla mollis
Lady's Mantle (Garden variety)
Hardy perennial. Ht. and spread 20 in. Tiny, greenish-yellow flowers in summer. Large, pale green, rounded leaves with crinkled edges. Zone 3.

Alchemilla xanthochlora (A. vulgaris)
Lady's Mantle (Wildflower variety)
Also known as Lion's foot, Bear's foot and Nine hooks. Hardy perennial. Ht. 6–18 in., spread 20 in. Tiny, bright greenish-yellow flowers in summer. Round, pale green leaves with crinkled edges. Zone 3.

Alchemilla mollis **flower**

LADY'S MANTLE

 ## cultivation

Propagation

Seed

Why is it that something that self-seeds readily around the garden can be so difficult to raise from seed? Sow its very fine seed in early spring or fall under protection into prepared seed or plug trays (use the cardboard method on page 265), and cover with perlite. No bottom heat required. Germination can either be sparse or prolific, taking 2–3 weeks. If germinating in the fall, winter seedlings in the trays and plant out the following spring when the frosts are over, at 18 in. apart. Alternatively, sow in spring where you want the plant to flower. Thin the seedlings to 12 in. apart.

Division

All established plants can be divided in the spring or fall. Replant in the garden where desired.

Pests and Diseases

This plant rarely suffers from pests or diseases.

Maintenance

Spring Divide established plants. Sow seeds if necessary.

Summer To prevent self-seeding, cut off flowerheads as they begin to die back.

Fall Divide established plants if necessary. Sow seed.

Winter No need for protection.

Garden Cultivation

This fully hardy plant grows in all but boggy soils, in sun or partial shade.

This is a most attractive garden plant in borders or as an edging plant, but it can become a bit of a nuisance, seeding everywhere. To prevent this, cut back after flowering and at the same time cut back old growth.

Harvesting

Cut young leaves after the dew has dried for use throughout the summer. Harvest for drying as plant comes into flower.

 ## container growing

All forms of lady's mantle adapt to container growing and look very pretty indeed. Use a soil-based compost, water throughout the summer, but feed with liquid fertilizer (following manufacturer's instructions) only occasionally. In the winter, when the plant dies back, put the container in a cold greenhouse or cold frame, and water only very occasionally. Lady's mantle can be grown in hanging baskets as a centerpiece.

Alchemilla mollis

Leaves laid out for drying

 ## medicinal

Used by herbalists for menstrual disorders. It has been said that if you drink an infusion of green parts of the plant for 10 days each month it will help relieve menopausal discomfort. It can also be used as a mouth rinse after tooth extraction. Traditionally, the alpine species has been considered more effective, although this is not proven.

 ## culinary

Tear young leaves, with their mild bitter taste, into small pieces and toss into salads. Many years ago Marks & Spencer had a yogurt made with lady's mantle leaves! I wish I had tried it.

 ## other uses

Excellent for flower arranging. Leaves can be boiled for green wool dye. They are also used in veterinary medicine for the treatment of diarrhea.

Allium

WELSH & TREE ONIONS

From the family Alliaceae.

These plants are distributed throughout the world. The onion has been in cultivation so long that its country of origin is uncertain, although most agree that it originated in Central Asia. It was probably introduced to Europe by the Romans. The name seems to have been derived from the Latin word *unio*, a large pearl. In the Middle Ages it was believed that a bunch of onions hung outside the door would absorb the infection of the plague, saving the inhabitants. Later came the scientific recognition that its sulfur content acts as a strong disinfectant. The juice of the onion was used to heal gunshot wounds.

Allium fistulosum

 ## varieties

There are many, many varieties of onion; the following information concerns the two that have herbal qualities.

Allium fistulosum
Welsh Onion
Also known as Japanese leek.
Evergreen hardy perennial. Ht. 2–3 ft. Greenish-yellow flowers on second year's growth in early summer. Leaves are green hollow cylinders. This onion is a native of Siberia and extensively grown in China and Japan. The name Welsh comes from *walsch* meaning foreign. Zone 5.

Allium cepa Proliferum Group
Tree Onion
Also known as Egyptian onion, Lazy man's onions. Hardy perennial. Ht. 3–5 ft. Small greenish-white flowers appear in early summer. It grows bulbs underground and then, at the end of flowering, bulbs in the air. Seeing is believing. It originates from Canada. It is very easy to propagate. Zone 5.

 ## cultivation

Propagation
Seed
Welsh onion seed loses its viability within 2 years, so sow fresh in late winter or early spring under protection with a bottom heat of between 60°F (15°C) and 70°F (21°C). Cover with perlite. When the seedlings are large enough, and after a period of hardening off, plant out into a prepared site in the garden at a distance of 10 in. apart. The tree onion is not grown from seed.

Division
Each year the Welsh onion multiply in clumps, so it is a good idea to divide them every 3 years in the spring.
Because the tree onion is such a big grower, it is a good idea to split the underground bulbs every 3 years in spring.

Bulbs
The air-growing bulbils of the tree onion have small root systems, each one capable of reproducing another plant. Plant where required in an enriched soil either in the fall, as the parent plant dies back, or in the spring.

Pests and Diseases
The onion fly is the curse of the onion family especially in late spring and early summer. The way to try and prevent this is to take care not to damage the roots or leaves when thinning the seedlings and also not to leave the thinnings lying around, as the scent attracts the fly.
Another problem is downy mildew caused by cool, wet falls; the leaves become velvety and die back. Another disease is white rot, which can be introduced in contaminated soil. If you have either of the above diseases, burn the affected plants and do not plant in the same position again.

Allium cepa Proliferum Group

Other characteristic diseases are neck rot and bulb rot, both caused by a *Botrytis* fungus that usually occurs as a result of the bulbs being damaged either by digging or hoeing.

Onions are prone to many more diseases but, if you keep the soil fertile and do not make life easy for the onion fly, you will still have a good crop.

Maintenance

Spring Sow the seed, divide 3-year-old clumps of Welsh and tree onions. Plant bulbs of tree onions.
Summer Stake mature tree onions to stop them falling over and depositing the ripe bulbils on the soil.
Fall Mulch around tree onion plants with well-rotted manure. Use a small amount of manure around Welsh onions.
Winter Neither variety needs protection.

Garden Cultivation

Welsh Onions
These highly adaptable hardy onions will grow in any well-drained fertile soil. Seeds can be sown in spring after the frosts, direct into the ground. Thin to a distance of 10 in. apart. Keep well watered throughout the growing season. In the fall give the area a mulch of well-rotted manure.

Tree Onions
Dig in some well-rotted manure before planting. Plant the bulbs in their clusters in a sunny well-drained position at a distance of 12–18 in. apart.

In the first year nothing much will happen (unless you are one of the lucky ones). If the summer is very dry, water well.

In the following year, if you give the plant a good mulch of well-rotted manure in the fall, it grows to 3–5 ft. and produces masses of small onions.

Harvesting

Welsh onions may be picked at any time from early summer onward. The leaves do not dry well but can be frozen like those of their cousin, chives. Use scissors and snip them into a plastic bag. They form neat rings; freeze them.

The little tree onions can be picked off the stems and stored; lay them out on a rack in a cool place with good ventilation.

 culinary

Welsh onions make a great substitute for spring onions, as they are hardier and earlier. Pull and use in salads or stir-fry dishes. Chop and use instead of chives.

Tree onions provide fresh onion flavor throughout the year. The bulbils can be pickled or chopped raw in salads (fairly strong), or cooked whole in stews and casseroles.

Pissaladière (A French Pizza)
Serves 4–6

4 tablespoons olive oil (not extra virgin)
20 tree onions, finely chopped
1 clove garlic, crushed
2 teaspoons fresh thyme, chopped
Salt
Freshly ground black pepper
3/4 lb. once-risen bread dough
1/2 lb. ripe tomatoes, peeled and sliced
2 oz. canned anchovy fillets, drained and
    halved lengthways
16 large black olives, halved and pitted

Heat the olive oil in a heavy frying pan, add the onions, cover the pan tightly and fry, gently stirring occasionally for 15 minutes. Add the garlic and the thyme and cook uncovered for 15 minutes, or until the onions are reduced to a clear purée. Season to taste and leave to cool. Preheat the oven to 400°F/200°C. Roll the bread dough directly on the baking sheet into a circle 10 in. in diameter. Spread the puréed onions evenly over the dough, put the tomato slices on the onions and top with a decorative pattern of anchovy fillets and olives.

Bake for 5 minutes. Reduce the oven temperature to 375°F/190°C and continue to bake for 30 minutes or until the bread base is well risen and lightly browned underneath.

Serve hot with a green herb salad.

 container growing

Welsh onions can be grown in a large pot using a soil-based compost, but make sure the compost does not dry out. Feed regularly throughout the summer with a liquid fertilizer.

Tree onions grow too tall for containers.

other uses

The onion is believed to help ward off colds in winter and also to induce sleep and cure indigestion. The fresh juice is antibiotic, diuretic, expectorant and antispasmodic, so is useful in the treatment of coughs, colds, bronchitis, laryngitis and gastroenteritis. It is also said to lower the blood pressure and to help restore sexual potency that has been impaired by illness or mental stress.

GARLIC
Allium sativum

Also known as Clove garlic. From the family Alliaceae.

Garlic originates from India or Central Asia and is one of the oldest and most valued of plants. In Greek legend, Odysseus used Moly, a wild garlic, as a charm to keep the sorceress, Circe, from turning him into a pig. The Egyptians used it medicinally. Both the slaves constructing the pyramid of Cheops and the Roman soldiers were given garlic cloves daily to sustain their strength. It was probably the Romans who introduced it into Britain. The common name is said to have been derived from the Anglo-Saxon *leac*, meaning "pot herb" and *gar*, "a lance," after the shape of the stem.

The term for leper in the Middle Ages was "pilgarlic" because the leper had to peel his own. During World War I, spaghnum moss was soaked in garlic juice as an antiseptic wound dressing. An old remedy for whooping cough was to put a clove of garlic in the shoes of the whooper.

A tradition still held in rural New Mexico is that garlic will help a young girl rid herself of an unwanted boyfriend.

Garden Cultivation
Plant in full sun, in rich, light and well-drained soil from early fall to early spring. Traditionally garlic cloves are planted on the shortest day of the year and harvested on longest. Split the bulb into the cloves and plant individually, pointed end up, into holes 1 in. deep and 6 in. apart. Keep well watered. They will be well matured in summer when the top growth starts to change color and keel over. Tying the stems in a knot is said to increase the size of the cloves.

Harvesting
Ease the bulbs out of the ground when the leaves die down and lose their greenness (mid- to late summer). Either use immediately (known as wet garlic) or dry in the sun for a few days if possible, but indoors if there is a danger of rain. Hang them up in a string bag, or plait them into a garlic string. Store somewhere cool and airy.

 ## companion planting

Garlic, it is said, helps to prevent leaf curl in trees, especially peaches. Also, when planted next to roses it is said to ward off black spot.

 ## container growing

In the spring place a number of individual cloves in a pot (tip up) and position on a sunny windowsill. Feed with liquid fertilizer regularly and harvest the green leaves as you would chives, or wait until mid- to late summer to harvest the bulbs, which will be smaller than those grown in the soil.

 ## culinary

Garlic is a very pungent but indispensible culinary herb. In spring the flavor is lively, but from summertime onward, cloves should be split in half and the green filaments and sheath enclosing them discarded to make the garlic more digestible. Whole bulbs may be divided into cloves and roasted under a joint of lamb, and slivers of garlic inserted under the surface of meat. The longer garlic is cooked, the milder the flavor. A peeled clove may be left to stand in a vinaigrette and then discarded before the dressing of the salad. Alternatively, rub a clove around the salad bowl. Whole

 ## varieties

Allium sativum
Garlic
Hardy perennial grown as an annual. Ht. 16–24 in. A bulb made up of several cloves (bulblets) enclosed in white papery skin. The cloves vary in color from white to pink. Green leaves. White or pink round flower head. Only flowers in warm climates. Zone 4.

Allium oleraceum
Field Garlic
Hardy perennial, bulbous plant. Ht. up to 33 in. Pink summer flowers. Zone 4.

 ## cultivation

Propagation
Plant the bulbs direct in the ground.

Pests and Diseases
Susceptible to white rot, which causes yellowing of the foliage and white fungal growth on the bulbs. It is also very susceptible to rust. Remove infected plants and avoid using this ground again for garlic.

Maintenance
Spring In no-frost regions plant the first month into spring. Feed with liquid fertilizer.
Summer Potash dress garden plants. Dig up bulbs.
Fall Plant cloves.
Winter Protect if the temperature is below 5°F (−15°C).

cloves can be used to flavor bottles of olive oil or wine vinegar. Garlic butter is a traditional accompaniment to snails.

Many Asians, particularly the Chinese, are great lovers of garlic. Their solution to garlic breath is to offer pods of cardamom seeds to chew at the end of a meal. You may prefer to eat parsley or basil, mint or thyme, all of which reduce the aroma on the breath.

 other uses

Its juice acts as an insect repellent and neutralizes the poisons of bites and stings.

Traditionally crushed garlic cloves rubbed over the surface of glass enables holes to be made cleanly.

 medicinal

Garlic has been shown to reduce blood pressure, and it is useful in guarding against strokes. It has also been successfully used as one of the constituents in controlling diarrhea, dysentry, TB, whooping cough, typhoid and hepatitis. Effective against many fungal infections, it can also be used to expel worms. It has even been shown to lower blood sugar levels, suggesting a use in controlling diabetes. Herbalists consider garlic to be a first-rate digestive tonic and also use it to treat toothache, earache, coughs and colds. A decaying tooth will hurt less if packed with garlic pulp until treatment is obtained. Externally, garlic can be applied to insect bites, boils and unbroken chilblains but it may cause an allergic rash if used for too long.

Garlic tonic

Allium ursinum
WILD GARLIC

Also known as Wood garlic, Ransomes, Ramsons, Devil's posy, Onion flower, Stinkplant and Bear's garlic. From the family Alliaceae.

Wild garlic is a native of Europe and Asia, naturalized in many countries in the Northern hemisphere including Britain and North America.

 varieties

Allium ursinum *Wild Garlic*
Hardy perennial. Ht. 12–18 in. Clusters of white flowers in spring and summer. Zone 5

 cultivation

Propagation
Seed
It is better to sow straight into the garden.

Division
Divide established plants in late summer, when the flowers have died back.

Maintenance
Spring If the plant is getting invasive, dig it up.
Summer Divide plants in late summer, when the plant has died back.
Fall Sow seed.
Winter No need to protect this herb as it is fully hardy.

Garden Cultivation
Plant wild garlic in a moist fertile soil, in either semi-shade or full shade. Wild garlic self-seeds easily; in wet and damp areas it can be invasive. In the fall, sow the seeds into a prepared site, cover lightly with soil. Germination will take place in early spring.

Pests and Diseases
Wild garlic is mostly free from pests and diseases.

 culinary

Pick from late spring for use in salads, soups or as a vegetable.

 other uses

Traditionally, as a liquid household disinfectant.

Allium schoenoprasum
CHIVES

From the family Alliaceae.

Chives are the only member of the onion group found wild in Europe, Australia and North America, where they thrive in temperate and warm to hot regions. Although they are one of the most ancient of all herbs, chives were not cultivated in European gardens until the 16th century.

Chives were a favorite in China as long ago as 3,000 BC. They were enjoyed for their delicious mild onion flavor and used as an antidote to poison and to stop bleeding. Their culinary virtues were first reported to the West by the explorer and traveler, Marco Polo. During the Middle Ages they were sometimes known as rush-leeks, from the Greek *schoinos* meaning "rush" and *parson* meaning "leek."

Allium schoenoprasum f. *albiflorum*

 varieties

Allium schoenoprasum
Chives
Hardy perennial. Ht. 12 in. Purple globular flowers all summer. Leaves green and cylindrical. Apart from being a good culinary herb it makes an excellent edging plant. Zone 3.

Allium schoenoprasum fine-leaved
Extra Fine-Leaved Chives
Hardy perennial. Ht. 8 in. Purple globular flowers all summer. Very narrow cylindrical leaves, not as coarse as standard chives. Good for culinary usage. Zone 3.

Allium schoenoprasum f. *albiflorum*
White Chives
Hardy perennial. Ht. 8 in. White globular flowers all summer. Cylindrical green leaves. A cultivar of ordinary chives and very effective in a silver garden. Good flavor. Zone 3.

Allium schoenoprasum 'Forescate'
Pink Chives
Hardy perennial. Ht. 8 in. Pink flowers all summer. Cylindrical green leaves. The pink flowers can look a bit insipid when planted too close to standard chives. Good in flower arrangements. Zone 3.

Allium tuberosum
Garlic Chives, Chinese Chives
Hardy perennial. Ht. 16 in. White flowers all summer. Leaf mid-green, flat and solid with a sweet garlic flavor when young. As they get older the leaf becomes tougher and the taste coarser. Zone 3.

CHIVES

cultivation

Propagation

Seed
Easy from seed, but they need a temperature of 65°F (19°C) to germinate, so if sowing outside, wait until late spring for the soil to be warm enough. I recommend starting this plant in plug trays with bottom heat in early spring. Sow about 10–15 seeds per 1 in. cell. Transplant either into pots or the garden when the soil has warmed through.

Division
Every few years in the spring lift clumps (made up of small bulbs) and replant in 6–10-bulb clumps, 6 in. apart, adding fresh compost or manure.

Pests and Diseases

Greenfly may be a problem on pot-grown herbs. Wash off gently under the tap or use a liquid insecticidal soap. Be diligent, for aphids can hide deep down low amongst the leaves.

Cool wet falls may produce downy mildew; the leaves will become velvety and die back from the tips. Dig up, split and repot affected plants, at the same time cutting back all the growth to prevent the disease spreading.

Chives can also suffer from rust. As this is a fungus it is essential to cut back diseased growth immediately and burn it. DO NOT COMPOST. If it is very bad, remove the plant and burn it all. Do not plant any chives or garlic in that area.

Maintenance

Spring Clear soil around emerging established plants. Feed liquid fertilizer. Sow seeds. Divide established plants.
Summer Remove the flower stem before flowering to increase leaf production.
Fall Prepare soil for next year's crop. Dig up a small clump, pot, bring inside for forcing.
Winter Cut forced chives and feed regularly.

Garden Cultivation

Chives are fairly tolerant regarding soil and position, but produce the best growth planted 6 in. from other plants in a rich moist soil and in a fairly sunny position. If the soil is poor they will turn yellow and then brown at the tips. For an attractive edging, plant at a distance of 4 in. apart and allow to flower. Keep newly transplanted plants well watered in the spring, and in the summer make sure that they do not dry out, otherwise the leaves will quickly shrivel. Chives die right back into the ground in winter, but a winter cutting can be forced by digging up a clump in the fall, potting it into a loam-based potting compost mixed in equal parts with composted fine bark, and placing it somewhere warm with good light.

Harvesting

Chives may be cut to within 1 in. of the ground 4 times a year to maintain a supply of succulent fresh leaves. Chives do not dry well. Refrigerated leaves in a sealed plastic bag will retain crispness for up to 7 days. Freeze chopped leaves in ice cubes for convenience. Cut flowers when they are fully open before the color fades for use in salads and sauces.

companion planting

Traditionally it is said that chives planted next to apple trees prevent scab, and when planted next to roses can prevent black spot. Hence the saying, "Chives next to roses creates posies."

container growing

Chives grow well in pots or on a windowsill and flourish in a window box if partially shaded. Use a soil-based compost mixed in equal parts with composted fine bark. They need an enormous quantity of water and occasional liquid feed to stay green and succulent. Remember too that, being bulbs, chives need some top growth for strengthening and regeneration, so do not cut away all the leaves if you wish to use them next season. Allow to die back in winter if you want to use it the following spring. A good patio plant, easy to grow, but not particularly fragrant.

medicinal

The leaves are mildly antiseptic and when sprinkled onto food they stimulate the appetite and help to promote digestion.

other uses

Chives are said to prevent scab infection on animals.

culinary

Add chives at the end of cooking or the flavor will disappear. They are delicious freshly picked and snipped as a garnish or flavor in omelettes or scrambled eggs, salads and soups. They can be mashed into soft cheeses or sprinkled onto grilled meats. Add liberally to sour cream as a filling for baked potatoes.

Chive Butter

Use in scrambled eggs, omelettes and cooked vegetables and with grilled lamb or fish or on baked potatoes.

1/2 cup butter, softened
4 tablespoons chopped chives
1 tablespoon lemon juice
Salt and pepper

Cream the chives and butter together until well mixed. Beat in the lemon juice and season. Cover and cool the butter in the refrigerator until ready to use; it will keep for several days.

Ajuga reptans
BUGLE

Also known as Common or Creeping bugle, Bugle weed, Babies' shoes, Baby's rattle, Blind man's hand, Carpenter's herb, Dead men's bellows, Horse and hounds, Nelson's bugle, Thunder and lightning and Middle comfrey. From the family Lamiaceae.

The bugle found in Britain is a native of Europe. It is frequently found in mountainous areas and often grows in damp fields, mixed woodland and meadows. The bugle of North America is a species of *Lycopus* (gypsy weed).

Among the many folk tales associated with bugle is one that its flowers can cause a fire if brought into the house, a belief that has survived in at least one district of Germany.

 ## varieties

Ajuga reptans
Bugle
Hardy evergreen perennial. Ht .1 ft., spread up to 3 ft. Very good spreading plant. Blue flowers from spring to summer. Oval leaves are dark green with purplish tinge. It is this plant that has medicinal properties. Zone 3.

Ajuga reptans 'Atropurpurea'
Bronze Bugle
Hardy evergreen perennial. Ht. 6 in., spread 3 ft. Blue flowers from spring to summer. Deep bronze/purple leaves. Very good for grouncover. Zone 3.

Ajuga reptans 'Multicolor'
Multicolored Bugle
Hardy evergreen perennial. Ht. 5 in., spread 18 in. Small spikes of blue flowers from spring to summer. Dark green leaves marked with cream and pink. Good for groundcover. Zone 3.

 ## cultivation

Propagation
Seeds
Sow the small seed in the fall, or spring as a second choice. Cover only lightly with soil. Germination can be erratic and slow.

Division
This method is easy and the only one suitable for cultivars as bugle produces runners, each one having its own root system. Plant out in the fall or spring. Space 2 ft. apart, as a single plant spreads rapidly.

Pests and Diseases
Nothing much disturbs this plant!

Maintenance
Spring Clear winter debris around established plants. Dig up runners and replant in other areas. Sow seeds.
Summer Dig up runners to control established plants.
Fall Sow seed and dig up runners of established plants. Pot them using a loam-based compost mixed in equal parts with composted fine bark, and winter in a cold frame, alternatively replant into a prepared site in the garden.
Winter No protection needed unless it is colder than −6°F (−20°C).

Garden Cultivation
It will grow vigorously on any soil that retains moisture, in full sun, and it also tolerates quite dense shade. It will even thrive in a damp boggy area near the pond or in a hedgerow or shady woodland area. At close quarters bugle is very appealing and can be used as a decorative groundcover. Guard against leaf scorch on the variegated variety.

Harvesting
For medicinal usage the leaves and flowers are gathered in early summer.

 ## container growing

Bugle makes a good outside container plant, especially the variegated and purple foliage varieties. Use a soil-based compost mixed in equal parts with composted fine bark. Also good in hanging baskets.

 ## culinary

The young shoots of *Ajuga reptans* can be mixed in salads to give you a different taste. Not mine.

 ## medicinal

An infusion of dried leaves in boiling water is thought to lower blood pressure and to stop internal bleeding. Nowadays it is widely used in homeopathy in various preparations against throat irritation, especially in the case of mouth ulcers.

 ## other uses

In some countries it is gathered as cattle fodder.

Ajuga reptans 'Artopurpurea'

Aloe vera

ALOE VERA

From the family Aloaceae.

There are between 250 and 350 species of aloe around the world. They are originally native to the arid areas of Southern Africa. In cultivation they need a frost-free environment. Aloe has been valued at least since the fourth century BC when Aristotle requested Alexander the Great to conquer Socotra in the Indian Ocean, where many species grow.

Flower spike of *Aloe vera* (*Aloe barbadensis*)

varieties

Aloe vera (Aloe barbadensis)
Aloe vera
Half-hardy perennial. Grown outside: Ht. 2 ft., spread 2 ft. or more. Grown as a house plant: Ht. 1 ft. Minimum temperature 50°F (10°C). Succulent gray/green pointed foliage, from which eventually grows a flowering stem with bell-shaped yellow or orange flowers. Zone 10.

Aloe arborescens 'Frutescens'
Half-hardy perennial. Grown outside: Ht. and spread 6 ft. Minimum temperature 45°F (7°C). Each stem is crowned by rosettes of long, blue/green leaves with toothed edges and cream stripes. Produces spikes of red tubular flowers in late winter and spring. Zone 8.

Aloe variegata
Partridge-breasted Aloe
Half-hardy perennial. A house plant only in temperate climates. Ht. 1 ft., spread 4 in. Minimum temperature 45°F (7°C). Triangular, white marked, dark green leaves. Spike of pinkish-red flowers in spring. Zone 10.

cultivation

Propagation
Seed
A temperature of 70°F (21°C) must be maintained during germination. Sow the small seeds in spring onto the surface of a pot or tray, using a standard seed compost mixed in equal parts with sharp horticultural sand, and cover with perlite. Place in a propagator with bottom heat. Germination is erratic—4 to 24 months.

Division
In summer gently remove offshoots at the base of a mature plant. Leave for a day to dry, then pot into 2 parts compost to 1 part sharp sand mix. Water and leave in a warm place to establish. Give the parent plant a good liquid feed when returning to its pot.

Pests and Diseases
Overwatering causes it to rot.

Maintenance
Spring Sow seeds. Give containerized plants a good dust! Spray the leaves with water. Give a good feed of liquid fertilizer.
Summer Remove the basal offshoots of a mature plant to maintain the parent plant. Repot mature plants.
Fall Bring in pots if there is any danger of frost.
Winter Rest all pot-grown plants in a cool room (minimum temperature 40°F/5°C); water sparingly.

Garden Cultivation
Aloes enjoy a warm, frost-free position—the full sun to partial shade—and a free-draining soil. Leave 3 ft. minimum between plants.

Aloe vera leaf

Harvesting
Cut leaves throughout the growing season. A plant of more than 2 years old has stronger properties.

container growing

Compost must be gritty and well drained. Don't over water. Maintain a frost-free, light environment. Ideal for sunny indoor location.

cosmetic

Aloe vera is used in cosmetic preparations, in hand creams, suntan lotions and shampoos.

medicinal

The gel obtained by breaking the leaves is a remarkable healer. Applied to wounds it forms a clear protective seal and encourages skin regeneration. It can be applied directly to cuts and burns, and is immediately soothing.

warning

It should be emphasized that, apart from external application, aloes are not for home medication. ALWAYS seek medical attention for serious burns.

LEMON VERBENA

From the family Verbenaceae.

Lemon verbena grew originally in Chile.

This Rolls Royce of lemon-scented plants was first imported into Europe in the 18th century by the Spanish for its perfume.

 ## varieties

Aloysia triphylla (Lippia citriodora)
Lemon Verbena
Half-hardy deciduous perennial. Ht. 3–10 ft., spread up to 8 ft. Tiny white flowers tinged with lilac in early summer. Leaves pale green, lance shaped and very strongly lemon-scented. Zone 8.

cultivation

Propagation
Seeds
The seed sets only in warm climates and should be sown in spring into prepared seed or plug trays and covered with perlite; a bottom heat of 60°F (15°C) helps. Prick out into 3½ in. pots using a standard seed compost mixed in equal parts with composted fine bark. Keep in pots for the first 2 years before planting specimens in the garden 3 ft. apart.

Cuttings
Take softwood cuttings from the new growth in late spring. The cutting material will wilt quickly so have everything prepared.
   Take semihardwood cuttings in late summer or early fall. Keep in pots for the first 2 years.

Pests and Diseases
If grown under protection you may have whitefly and red spider mite; either use the relevant predators or spray with a liquid horticultural soap, but not both.

Maintenance
Spring Trim established plants. Take softwood cuttings. In warm climates sow seed.
Summer Trim lightly after flowering to remove the flowers. Take semihardwood cuttings.
Fall Protect from excessive wet and frosts.
Winter Keep plants frost free.

Garden Cultivation
Likes a warm humid climate. The soil should be light, free draining and warm. A sunny wall is ideal. It will need protection against frost and wind, and temperatures below 40°F (4°C). If left in the ground, cover the area around the roots with mulching material. In spring give the plant a gentle prune and spray with warm water to help revive it.
   New growth can appear very late in spring so never discard a plant until late summer. Once the plant has started re-shooting, cut back all last years growth to 1½ in. Cut off flowers once flowering has finished.

Harvesting
Pick the leaves any time before they start to wither and darken. Leaves dry quickly and easily, keeping their color and scent. Store in a damp-proof container.

 ## container growing

Choose a container at least 8 in. wide and use a soil-based compost mixed in equal parts with composted fine bark. Place the container in a warm, sunny, light and airy spot. Water well throughout the growing season and feed with liquid fertilizer during flowering. Cut back last year's growth to 1½ in. in the spring only. In winter move the container into a cold greenhouse, and allow the compost to nearly dry out. The plant must be allowed to drop its leaves: this is not a sign that it is dead.

 ## medicinal

A tea last thing at night is refreshing and has mild sedative properties; it can also soothe bronchial and nasal congestion and ease indigestion. However, long-term use may cause stomach irritation.

 ## other uses

The leaves with their strong lemon scent are lovely in potpourri, linen sachets, herb pillows, sofa sacks. The distilled oil made from the leaves is an essential basic ingredient in many perfumes.

 ## culinary

Use fresh leaves to flavor oil and vinegar, drinks, fruit desserts, confectionery, apple jelly, cakes and stuffings. Infuse in finger bowls.
   Add a teaspoon of chopped, fresh leaves to home-made ice cream for a delicious dessert.

Althaea officinalis
MARSH-MALLOW

Also known as Mortification root, Sweet weed, Wymote, Marsh malice, Mesh-mellice, Wimote, and Althea. From the family Malvaceae.

Marsh-mallow is widely distributed from Western Europe to Siberia, from Australia to North America. It is common to find it in salt marshes and on banks near the sea. The generic name, *Althaea*, comes from the Latin *altheo*, meaning "I cure." It may be the *althea* that Hippocrates recommended so highly for healing wounds. The Romans considered it a delicious vegetable, used it in barley soup and in stuffing for suckling pigs. In the Renaissance era the herbalists used marsh-mallow to cure sore throats, stomach trouble and toothache. The soft, sweet marshmallow was originally flavored with the root of marsh-mallow.

 ## varieties

Althaea officinalis
Marsh-mallow
Hardy perennial. Ht. 2–4 ft., spread 2 ft. Flowers pink or white in late summer/early fall. Leaves, gray-green in color, tear-shaped and covered all over with soft hair. Zone 5.

 ## cultivation

Propagation
Seed
Sow in prepared seed or plug trays in the fall.
   Cover lightly with compost and winter outside under glass. Erratic germination takes place in spring. Plant out, 18 in. apart, when large enough to handle.

Division
Divide established plants in the spring or fall, replanting into a prepared site in the garden.

Pests and Diseases
This plant is usually free from pests and diseases.

Maintenance
Spring Divide established plants.
Summer Cut back after flowering for new growth.
Fall Sow seeds and winter the trays outside
Winter No need for protection. Fully hardy.

Garden Cultivation
Marsh-mallow is highly attractive to butterflies. A good coastal plant, it likes a site in full sun with a moist or wet, moderately fertile soil. Cut back after flowering to encourage new leaves.

Harvesting
Pick leaves for fresh use as required; they do not preserve well. For use either fresh or dried, dig up the roots of 2-year-old plants in the fall, after the flowers and leaves have died back.

 ## medicinal

Due to its high mucilage content (35 percent in the root and 10 percent in the leaf), marsh-mallow soothes or cures inflammation, ulceration of the stomach and small intestine, soreness of throat, and pain from cystitis. An infusion of leaves or flowers serves as a soothing gargle; an infusion of the root can be used for coughs, diarrhea and insomnia.
   The pulverized roots may be used as a healing and drawing poultice, which should be applied warm.

Decoction for Dry Hands
Soak 2 tablespoons of scraped and finely chopped root in a ½ cup of cold water for 24 hours. Strain well. Add 1 tablespoon of the decoction to 2 tablespoons of ground almonds, 1 teaspoon of milk and 1 teaspoon of cider vinegar. Beat it until well blended. Add a few drops of lavender oil. Put into a small screwtop pot.

 ## culinary

Boil the roots to soften, then peel and quickly fry in butter.
   Use the flowers in salads. Leaves are also good in salads and may be added to oil and vinegar, or steamed and served as a vegetable..

Amaranthus

AMARANTH

Also known as Pigweed. From the family of Amarathaceae.

This native of South America has been in cultivation as a pot herb since 4000 BC. All parts of the plant are edible; however it is the seeds that are of financial and nutritional value as they are high in protein and fiber. Research into the potential of the grain of the indigenous Mexican variety began in 1970 and, from this research, a number of crops have been developed that are now grown around the world—from Africa, India, Nepal, China to Eastern Europe—where it has become a good source of dietary fiber as well as minerals.

 varieties

The following have the best herbal properties:

Amaranthus hypochondriacus 'Pygmy Torch'
Half-hardy annual. Ht. 16 in. In summer tiny crimson flowers grow in long tassels. Oval to heart shaped scarlet leaves. Warmer zones.

Amaranthus dubius
Known as wild spinach, 'Bhaji' and Zepnia. Tropical annual. Ht. 24–36 in. Spikes of green and white flowers. Oval, occasionally toothed-edged green leaves.

Amaranthus 'Hopi Red Dye'
Half-hardy annual. Ht. 52–64 in. In summer tiny scarlet/crimson flowers grow in long tassels. Oval to heart-shaped scarlet leaves. This herb was used by the Hopi Indians as a source of deep red dye, hence its name. Warmer zones.

 cultivation

Propagation
Seed
Sow the small seeds in spring, into either seed or module plug trays using a standard seed compost mixed in equal parts with perlite. Cover the seeds with

Amaranthus 'Hopi Red Dye'

perlite, place under protection at 68°F (20°C). Germination takes 1–5 days. As soon as the seeds have germinated, remove from the heat to prevent the seedlings growing too fast and therefore weakly, which will make them prone to damping off. Grow until large enough to handle, either pot using a standard peat-free potting compost or, if all threat of frost has passed, plant in the garden in a prepared site, 8 in. apart. Alternatively, once all threat of frost has passed and the nighttime temperature does not fall below 45°F (7°C), sow the seeds into prepared drills in the garden. Cover the row with perlite so you can see the seedlings as soon as they appear.

Pests and Diseases

When propagating amaranth in a cool climate the seedlings and young plants can be prone to damping off, so watch the watering especially when the evening temperature drops below 39°F (4°C). When grown under protection in a greenhouse or polytunnel it can be attacked by aphids. Use an insecticidal soap, mixed with soft water, and spray early morning or evening to prevent leaf scorch.

Maintenance

Spring Sow seeds, pick leaves as required.
Summer Harvest leaf and, in late summer, the seed.
Fall Prepare site for next season's sowing.
Winter Dig up old plants.

Garden Cultivation

Amaranth is so attractive that it looks wonderful in the garden as a spot plant, mixed with the vegetables or grown as a focal point in a small garden. Wherever you choose it will need a warm sheltered spot. If you want it for leaf production then the soil should be fed with well-rotted manure in the previous fall. If you want it for flower and grain, then it should be planted in a less rich soil.

Harvesting

For medicinal use, the whole plant is cut when coming into flower, and dried. Leaves can also be picked as required, young ones for salads, mature ones for cooking. The seed is usually harvested just before it fully matures, otherwise some will be lost during harvesting. The seed will keep best when stored in a tightly sealed container, such as a glass jar in the refrigerator. This will protect the fatty acids from becoming rancid. The seeds should be used within 3 to 6 months.

 container growing

I have grown 'Hopi Red Dye' very successfully in containers; it looked stunning. Plant in a soil-based compost, position the container in a sheltered, warm, sunny spot.

 medicinal

The whole plant is used medicinally; it has astringent, soothing properties and is used to control bleeding. It is taken internally to control diarrhea and used externally to treat wounds and nosebleeds.

 other uses

Green varieties of amaranth produce a yellow and green dye; the red-leaved varieties produce a red and brown dye. All are used in coloring foods and medicines.

 culinary

Young leaves can be added to salads, and mature leaves can be cooked like spinach, but do not use tough leaves because they will have a bitter flavor. The seeds can be combined with wheat and other flours to make cookies and bread. In Mexico the seeds are popped like pop corn: simply add the seeds to a pan and put it on the heat, being careful not to over cook it. Once cooked, toss in salt or sugar or pour into some honey. You can also use the seeds prepared this way to make a form of flapjack.

When you cook the seeds in water they become glutinous, so making a good substitute for oatmeal. To cook the seed of amaranth bring 2¹/₂ cups of liquid, which can be stock or juice of your choice to the boil, stir in 1 cup of seeds, then reduce to a simmer and simmer for 20 minutes until cooked. This then, can be added to soups, or to vegetable stews or curries.

To make a breakfast cereal similar to porridge, boil 3 cups of water, add 1 cup of seeds. To turn it into a yummy breakfast add chopped apple, raisins and nuts and sweeten with honey.

DILL

Anethum graveolens

Also known as Dillweed and Dillseed. From the family Apiaceae.

A native of southern Europe and western Asia, dill grows wild in the cornfields of Mediterranean countries and also in North and South America. The generic name *Anethum* derives from the Greek *anethon*. "Dill" is said to come from the Anglo-Saxon *dylle* or the Norse *dilla*, meaning to soothe or lull. Dill was found amongst the names of herbs used by Egyptian doctors 5,000 years ago and the remains of the plant have been found in the ruins of Roman buildings in Britain.

It is mentioned in the Gospel of St. Matthew, where it is suggested that herbs were of sufficient value to be used as a tax payment—if only that were true today! "Woe unto you, Scribes and Pharisees, hypocrites! for ye pay tithe of mint and dill and cumin, and have omitted the weightier matters of the law."

During the Middle Ages dill was prized as protection against witchcraft. While magicians used it in their spells, lesser mortals infused it in wine to enhance passion. It was once an important medicinal herb for treating coughs and headaches, as an ingredient of ointments and for calming infants with whooping cough—dill water or gripe water is still called upon today. Early settlers took dill to North America, where it was known as the "Meeting House Seed," because the children were given the seed to chew during long sermons to prevent them feeling hungry.

 varieties

Anethum graveolens
Dill
Annual. Ht. 2–5 ft., spread 12 in. Tiny yellow/green flowers in flattened umbel clusters in summer. Fine aromatic feathery green leaves. All zones.

 cultivation

Propagation

Seed
Seed can be started in early spring under cover, using pots or module plug trays. Do not use seed trays, as dill does not like being transplanted, and if it gets upset it will bolt and miss out the leaf-producing stage.

The seeds are easy to handle, being a good size. Place four per plug or evenly spaced on the surface of a pot, and cover with perlite. Germination takes 2–4 weeks, depending on the warmth of the surrounding area. As soon as the seedlings are large enough to handle, the air and soil temperatures have started to rise and there is no threat of frost, plant out 9 in. apart.

Garden Cultivation
Keep dill plants well away from fennel, otherwise they will cross pollinate and their individual flavors will become muddled. Dill prefers a well-drained, poor soil in partial shade. Sow mid-spring into shallow drills on a prepared site, where they will be harvested. Protect seedlings from wind. When the plants are large enough to handle, thin out to a distance of about 8 in. apart to allow plenty of room for growth. Make several small sowings in succession so that you have a supply of fresh leaves throughout the summer. The seed is viable for 3 years.

The plants are rather fragile and it may be necessary to provide support. Twigs pushed into the ground around the plant and enclosed with string or raffia give better results than attempting to stake each plant.

In very hot summers, make sure that the plants are watered regularly or they will run to seed. There is no need to liquid feed, as this only promotes soft growth and in turn encourages pests and disease. The foliage is a food source for Black Swallow Tail Butterfly caterpillars.

Pests and Diseases
Watch out for greenfly in crowded conditions. Treat with a liquid insecticidal soap if necessary. Be warned, slugs love dill plants.

Dill vinegar

Maintenance

Spring Sow the seeds successively for a leaf crop.
Summer Water well after cutting to promote new growth.
Fall (early) Harvest seeds.
Winter Dig up all remaining plants. Make sure all the seed heads have been removed before you compost the stalks, as the seed is viable for 3 years. If you leave the plants to self-seed they certainly will, and they will live up to their other name of Dillweed.

Harvesting

Pick leaves fresh for eating at any time after the plant has reached maturity. Since it is quick-growing, this can be within 8 weeks of the first sowing. Although leaves can be dried, great care is needed and it is better to concentrate on drying the seed for storage.

Cut the stalks off the flower heads when the seed is beginning to ripen. Put the seed heads upside down in a paper bag and tie the top of the bag. Put in a warm place for a week. The seeds should then separate easily from the husk when rubbed in the palm of the hand. Store in an airtight container and the seeds will keep their flavor very well.

 ## container growing

Dill can be grown in containers, in a sheltered corner in partial shade. However, it will need staking. The art of growing it successfully is to keep cutting the plant for use in the kitchen. That way you will promote new growth and keep the plant reasonably compact. The drawback is that it will be fairly short-lived, so you will have to do successive sowings in different pots to maintain a supply. I do not recommend growing dill indoors — it will get leggy, soft and prone to disease.

 ## medicinal

Dill is an antispasmodic and calmative. Dill tea or water is a popular remedy for an upset stomach, hiccups or insomnia, for nursing mothers to promote the flow of milk, and as an appetite stimulant. It is a constituent of gripe water and other children's medicines because of its ability to ease flatulence and colic.

 ## culinary

Dill is a culinary herb that improves the appetite and digestion. The difference between dill leaf and dill seed lies in the degree of pungency. There are occasions when the seed is better because of its sharper flavor. It is used as a flavoring for soup, lamb stews and grilled or boiled fish. It can also add spiciness to rice dishes, and be combined with white wine vinegar to make dill vinegar.

Dill leaf can be used generously in many dishes, as it enhances rather than dominates the flavor of many foods.

Before it sets seed, add one flowering head to a jar of pickled gherkins, cucumbers and cauliflowers for a flavor stronger than dill leaves but fresher than seeds. In America these are known as dill pickles.

Gravlax (Salmon marinaded with dill)

This is a traditional Scandinavian dish of great simplicity and great merit. Salmon treated in this way will keep for up to a week in the fridge.

1 1/2-2 lb. salmon, middle or tail piece
1 heaped tablespoon sea salt
1 rounded tablespoon superfine sugar
1 teaspoon crushed black peppercorns
1 tablespoon brandy (optional)
1 heaped tablespoon fresh dill

Have the salmon cleaned, scaled, bisected lengthways and filleted. Mix remaining ingredients together and put some of the mixture into a flat dish (glass or enamel) large enough to take the salmon. Place one piece of salmon skin side down on the bottom of the dish, spread more of the mixture over the cut side. Add the second piece of salmon, skin

 ## other uses

Where a salt-free diet must be followed, the seed, whole or ground, is a valuable replacement. Try chewing the seeds to clear up halitosis and sweeten the breath. Crush and infuse seeds to make a nail-strengthening bath.

up, and pour over the remaining mixture. Cover with foil and place a plate or wooden board larger than the area of the salmon on top. Weigh this down with weights or heavy cans. Put in the refrigerator for 36–72 hours. Turn the fish completely every 12 hours or so and baste (inside surfaces too) with the juices.

To serve, scrape off all the mixture, pat the fish dry and slice thinly and at an angle. Serve with buttered rye bread and a mustard sauce called Gravlaxsas:

4 tablespoons mild, ready-made Dijon mustard
1 teaspoon mustard powder
1 tablespoon superfine sugar
2 tablespoons white wine vinegar

Mix all the above together, then slowly add 6 tablespoons of vegetable oil until you have a sauce the consistency of mayonnaise. Finally stir in 3 to 4 tablespoons of chopped dill. Alternatively, substitute a mustard and dill mayonnaise.

ANGELICA

Angelica

Also known as European angelica, Garden angelica and Root of the Holy Ghost. From the family Apiaceae.

Angelica in its many forms is a native of Europe, Asia and North America. It is also widely cultivated as a garden plant. Wild angelica is found in moist fields and the countryside throughout Europe. American angelica is found in similar growing conditions in Canada and north-eastern and northern central states of America.

Angelica probably comes from the Greek *angelos*, meaning "messenger." There is a legend that an angel revealed to a monk in a dream that the herb was a cure for the plague, and traditionally angelica was considered the most effective safeguard against evil, witchcraft in particular. Certainly it is a plant no self-respecting witch would include in her brew.

Angelica is an important flavoring agent in liqueurs such as Benedictine, although its unique flavor cannot be detected from the others used. It is also cultivated commercially for medicinal and cosmetic purposes.

 varieties

Angelica archangelica
Angelica
Monocarpic (will live until it has successfully flowered and set seed). Ht. 3–8 ft., spread 3 ft. in second year. Dramatic second-year flowerheads late spring through summer, greenish-white and very sweetly scented. Bright green leaves, the lower ones large and bi- or tri-pinnate; the higher, smaller and pinnate. Rootstock varies in color from pale yellowish-beige to reddish-brown. Zone 4.

Angelica atropurpurea
American Angelica
Also known as Bellyache root, High angelica, Masterwort, Purple angelica and Wild angelica. Biennial. Ht. 4–5 ft. Flowers resemble those of *A. archangelica*—white to greenish white, late spring through summer. Leaves large and alternately compound. Rootstock purple. The whole plant delivers a powerful odor when fresh. Zone 5.

Angelica gigas
Korean Angelica
Monocarpic. Ht. up to 4 ft., spread 3 ft. in second year.

Beautiful second or third year spherical deep red umbels with tiny white flowers in late summer. Palmate green foliage. Zone 5.

Angelica polymorpha var. sinensis (Angelica sinensis)
Chinese Angelica. Also known as Dang Gui, Women's Ginseng. Zone 9.
Monocarpic. Ht. up to 3 ft., spread 28 in. Umbels of small green and white flowers in summer. Palmate green foliage. Zone 9.

 cultivation

Propagation
Seed
The fresh seeds are only viable for 3 months from harvest. Sow in early fall, either where you want it to grow next year, or into plug trays that are placed outside to get the weather. There is no need to protect the seedlings from frost. Plant out in the following spring. If you cannot sow the seed fresh, mix them with horticultural sand and put them in to a plastic bag and then into the fridge. Once the seeds start to germinate in the bag, approximately 2–6 weeks, sow the seeds in groups of three into a prepared site in the garden 3 ft. apart. This plant cannot be

Angelica gigas

successfully transplanted once the tap root has developed, so choose your site with care.

Pests and Diseases
Remove blackfly easily with liquid insecticidal soap

Maintenance
Spring Clear ground around existing plants. Plant out fall seedlings. Put old seed in refrigerator.
Summer Cut stems of second-year growth for crystallizing. Cut young leaves before flowering to use fresh in salads or to dry for medicinal or culinary uses.
If in summer the leaves turn a yellowish-green, it is usually a sign that the plant needs more water.
Fall The ideal seed sowing time.
Winter No need for protection.

Garden Cultivation
Angelica dislikes hot humid climates and appreciates a spot in the garden where it can be in shade for some part of every day. But it can be a difficult plant to accommodate in a small garden, as it needs a lot of space. Site at the back of a border, perhaps near a wall where the plant architecture can be shown off. Make sure that the soil is deep and moist. Add well-rotted compost to help retain moisture. Note that angelica dies down completely in winter but green shoots appear quickly in the spring. Angelica forms a big clump of foliage in the first summer and dramatic flowers the second or third, dying after the seed is set. A plant will propagate itself in the same situation if allowed to self-seed.

Harvesting
Harvest leaves for use fresh from spring onward for culinary and medicinal; for drying, from early summer until flowering. Dry flowers in early summer for flower arrangements. Collect seeds when they begin to ripen. Harvest roots to dry for use medicinally in the second fall immediately after flowering.

 medicinal

It is used to treat indigestion, anemia, coughs and colds; it has antibacterial and antifungal properties. It is said that a tea made from the young leaves is good for reducing tension and nervous headaches and that a decoction made from the roots is soothing for colds and other bronchial conditions. Reputedly crushed leaves freshen the air in a car and may help travel sickness.

 culinary

Candied Angelica

Angelica is now best known as a decorative confectionery for cakes. There is a bright emerald, apparently plastic, specimen sold commercially as angelica, which cannot compare with home-made, pale green candied angelica; this tastes and smells similar to the freshly bruised stem or crushed leaf of the plant.

Angelica stems
Granulated sugar
Water
Superfine sugar for dusting

Choose young tender springtime shoots. Cut into 3–4 in. lengths. Place in a saucepan with just enough water to cover. Simmer until tender, then strain and peel off the outside skin. Put back into the pan with enough water to cover and bring to the boil, strain immediately and allow to cool.

When cool, weigh the angelica stalks and add an equal weight of granulated sugar. Place the sugar and angelica in a covered dish and leave in a cool place for 2 days.

Put the angelica and the syrup which will have formed back into the pan. Bring slowly to the boil and simmer, stirring occasionally, until the angelica becomes clear and has good color.

Strain again discarding all the liquid, then sprinkle as much superfine sugar as will cling to the angelica. Allow the stems to dry in a cool oven (200°F/100°C). If not thoroughly dry they become moldy.

Store in an airtight container between sheets of greaseproof paper.

Stewed Rhubarb
If when you cook rhubarb or gooseberries you add young angelica leaves, you will need to add less sugar. Angelica does not sweeten the fruit but its muscatel flavor cuts through the acidity of the rhubarb.

2 lb. rhubarb
1 cup angelica stems
juice and rind of one orange
2/3 cup water
1/4 cup sugar

 container growing

Angelica is definitely not an indoor plant, though if the container is large enough it can be grown as such. Do not over-fertilize and be prepared to stake when in flower. Be wary of the pot toppling over as the plant grows taller.

 warning

Large doses first stimulate and then paralyze the central nervous system. The tea is not recommended for those suffering from diabetes.

Anthriscus cerefolium
CHERVIL

From the family Apiaceae.

Native to the Middle East, South Russia and the Caucasus, chervil can be cultivated in warm temperate climates. It is now occasionally found growing wild.

Almost certainly brought to Britain by the Romans, chervil is one of the Lenten herbs, thought to have blood-cleansing and restorative properties. It was eaten in quantity in those days, especially on Maundy Thursday.

Gerard, the Elizabethan physician who superintended Lord Burleigh's gardens, wrote in his *Herbal* of 1597, "The leaves of sweet chervil are exceeding good, wholesome and pleasant among other salad herbs, giving the taste of Anise seed unto the rest."

cultivation

Propagation
Seed
The medium-size seed germinates rapidly as the air and soil temperatures rise in the spring provided the seed is fresh (it loses viability after about a year). Young plants are ready for cutting 6–8 weeks after sowing, thereafter continuously providing leaves as long as the flowering stems are removed.

Sow seed in prepared plug module trays if you prefer, and cover with perlite. Pot into containers with a minimum 5 in. diameter. But, as a plant with a long tap root, chervil does not like being transplanted, so keep this to a minimum. It can in fact be sown direct into a 5 in. pot, growing it, like mustard and cress, as a "cut and come again" crop.

Pests and Diseases
Chervil can suffer from greenfly. Wash off gently with a liquid insecticidal soap. Do not blast off with a high-pressure hose, as this will damage the soft leaves.

Maintenance
Spring Sow seeds.
Summer A late sowing in this season will provide leaves through winter, as it is very hardy. Protect from midday sun.
Fall Cloche fall-sown plants for winter use.
Winter Although chervil is hardy, some cloche protection is needed to ensure leaves in winter, except in frost zones, where it is not possible to have foliage in winter.

Garden Cultivation
The soil required is light with a degree of moisture retention. Space plants 9–12 in. apart. Semishade is best, because the problem with chervil is that it will burst into flower too quickly should the weather become sunny and hot and be of no use as a culinary herb. For this reason some gardeners sow between rows of other garden herbs or vegetables or under deciduous plants to ensure some shade during the summer months.

Harvesting
Harvest leaves for use fresh when the plant is 6–8 weeks old or when 4 in. tall, and all the year round if you cover with a cloche in winter. Otherwise, freezing is the best method of preservation, as the dried leaves do not retain their flavor.

varieties

Anthriscus cerefolium
Chervil
Hardy annual (some consider it to be a biennial). Ht. 12–24 in., spread 12 in. Flowers, tiny and white, grow in clusters from spring to summer. Leaves, light green and fern-like, in late summer may take on a purple tinge. When young it can easily be confused with cow parsley. However, cow parsley is a perennial and eventually grows much taller and stouter, its large leaves lacking the sweet distinctive aroma of chervil. All zones.

Anthriscus cerefolium 'Crispum'
Chervil curly leafed
Hardy annual. Grows like the ordinary chervil except that, in my opinion, the leaf has an inferior flavor. All zones.

Anthriscus cerefolium—a cut and come again plant

 ## container growing

When grown inside in the kitchen chervil loses color, gets leggy and goes floppy, so unless you are treating it as a "cut and come again" plant, plant outside in a large container that retains moisture and is positioned in semishade.

Chervil looks good in a window box, but be sure that it gets shade at midday.

 ## medicinal

Leaves eaten raw are rich in Vitamin C, carotene, iron and magnesium. They may be infused to make a tea to stimulate digestion and alleviate circulation disorders, liver complaints and chronic lung congestion, and fresh leaves may be applied to aching joints in a warm poultice.

 ## other uses

An infusion of the leaf can be used to cleanse skin, maintain suppleness and discourage wrinkles.

 ## culinary

It is one of the traditional *fines herbes*, indispensable to French cuisine and a fresh green asset in any meal, but many people elsewhere are only now discovering its special delicate parsley-like flavor with a hint of aniseed.

This is a herb especially for winter use because it is easy to obtain fresh leaves and, as every cook knows, French or otherwise, "Fresh is best."

Use its leaf generously in salads, soups, sauces, vegetables, chicken, white fish and egg dishes. Add freshly chopped toward the end of cooking to avoid flavor loss.

In small quantities it enhances the flavor of other herbs. Great with vegetables.

Chervil with broad beans

Apium graveolens

CELERY LEAF

Also known as Wild celery, Smallage, Ajmud. From the family Apiaceae.

Wild celery has been used in both medicine and food for thousands of years. Seeds from this herb were found in the tomb of Tutankhamun (1327 BC). Today it can be found growing wild in marshy ground and by rivers in Europe and northern Africa. The whole plant strongly smells of celery—root, leaves and seed—hence the latin *graveolens,* which means "strong-smelling." The salad celery, *Apium graveolens* var. *dulce* was originally bred in the 17th century from this wild form.

 varieties

Apium graveolens
Celery Leaf
Hardy biennial. Ht. 12 in.–3¹/₂ ft., spread 6–12 in. Umbels of tiny green white flowers early in the second summer followed by ridged gray-brown seeds. The bright, aromatic, mid-green, cut leaves are very similar to its cousin French parsley, with which, when young, it is often confused. Warmer zones.

 cultivation

Propagation
Seed
Sow the fresh seed in early spring into pots or plug modules using a standard seed compost. Cover with perlite, place under protection at 60°F (15°C). Germination takes 2–3 weeks. Alternatively sow seeds in late spring when the air temperature does not drop below 45°F (7°C) at night into a well-prepared site that has been fed in the previous fall with well-rotted manure.

Pests and Diseases
Some years this herb has no problems at all then, in other years, it gets attacked by everything. If you see brown tunnel marks on the leaf, this is caused by the celery leaf miner. As soon as you see affected leaves remove them and burn them. If you have a bad infestation cut the plant back to 1¹/₄ in. above the ground and make sure you remove all debris. Like parsley, it can be attacked by carrot fly in early summer. This fly attacks the roots and stem bases. To prevent this, cover the crop with a frost cloth, and only thin the seedlings in the early morning before the temperature rises. Cover immediately after thinning with a frost cloth to prevent the fly laying its eggs.

Maintenance
Spring Sow seeds under protection.
Summer Sow seeds into a prepared site. Remove flowers to maintain growth if seed not needed. Liquid feed plants.
Fall Harvest seeds. Feed the soil for next season's crops.
Winter Pick leaves. Only protect if temperatures fall below 23°F (−5°C).

Garden Cultivation

Celery leaf is a hungry plant: it likes a good deep soil that does not dry out in summer. Always feed the chosen site well in the previous fall with well-rotted manure. If you wish to harvest celery leaf all year round have two different sites prepared. For summer supplies, a western or eastern border is ideal because the plant needs moisture and prefers a little shade.

For winter supplies a more sheltered spot will be needed in a sunny position, for example against a sunny wall.

Harvesting

Pick the new young shoots throughout the growing season. Harvest the seeds in the late summer once they are fully ripe and start falling from the seed head. If you are saving the seed for sowing the following year be aware that celery is prone to disease and this can be harbored in the seed. So, for propagation, collect from healthy plants only. Dig up the roots of the second-year growth for use medicinally.

 ## companion planting

It is said that this herb helps repel the cabbage white fly from Brassicas.

 ## container growing

Celery leaf is ideal for containers. It can adapt to any deep container as it has a long tap root. Use a soil-based compost. In summer place the container in partial shade to prevent the leaves from becoming tough. Feed and water regularly throughout the growing season.

 ## medicinal

The whole plant is used medicinally: roots, stem, leaf and seeds. It is used to treat osteoarthritis, rheumatoid arthritis and gout. Externally it is used to treat fungal infections. In the East it is used in Ayurvedic medicine to treat asthma, bronchitis and hiccups.

 ## other uses

The essential oil made from the seed is used in perfumery and to make celery salt.

 ## warning

If the plant is infected with the fungus *Sclerotinia sclerotiorum*, contact with the sap can cause dermatitis in sensitive skin. Never take medicinally when pregnant.

Apium graveolens

 ## culinary

The young leaves are delicious in salads or when added to mashed potato. They are also great added to soups or sweated down with onions. In my opinion the mature, tough leaves are inedible. The seeds are also very useful: grind them in a pestle and mortar or add them whole to stews, casseroles and soups. They are also lovely added to dough for flavorsome bread. In India it is an important minor spice.

Celery Seed Bread
Serves 4

3 ¾ cups wholewheat flour
2 teaspoons of sunflower oil plus some extra for the griddle
1 tablespoon of finely chopped young celery leaves
1 pinch of salt
2 teaspoons celery seeds
Water to make the dough

Make a soft dough with the flour, sunflower oil, celery leaves and celery seeds. Add water sparingly as you work the dough. Once the dough is easy to handle, divide into 4 equal-sized balls. Cover a board or surface with a dusting of flour, roll out each ball into a flat disc, adding a further dusting of flour if it sticks. By keeping the dough moving as you roll, you will prevent this happening.

Heat a griddle to hot. Place the bread on the griddle, reduce the heat and cook until the bread is covered in bubbles. Brush the upper surface with oil and turn over. Cook until bubbles appear on the surface. Cook the three remaining breads, serve warm with soups, pickles or yogurts.

Armoracia rusticana

HORSERADISH

From the family Brassicaceae.

Native of Europe, naturalized in Britain and North America. Originally the horseradish was cultivated as a medicinal herb. Now it is used as a flavoring herb. The common name means a coarse or strong radish, the prefix "horse" often being used in plants to denote a large, strong or coarse plant. In the 16th century it was known in England as Redcol or Recole. In this period the plant appears to have been more popular in Scandinavia and Germany, where they developed its potential as a fish sauce. For some, horseradish is considered the perfect condiment for roast beef.

Armoracia rusticana 'Variegata'

 ## varieties

Armoracia rusticana (Cochlearia armoracia)
Horseradish
Hardy perennial. Ht. 24–35 in., spread indefinite! Flowers white in spring (very rare). Leaves large green oblongs. The large root, which is up to 24 in. long, 2 in. thick and tapering, goes deep into the soil. Zone 3.

Armoracia rusticana 'Variegata'
Hardy perennial. Ht. 24–35 in., spread also indefinite. Flowers white in spring (rare in cool climates). Leaves large with green/cream variegation and oblong shape. Large root which goes deep into the soil. Not as good flavor as *A. rusticana*. Zone 3.

 ## cultivation

Propagation
Root Cuttings
In early spring cut pieces of root 6 in. long. Put them either directly into the ground, at a depth of 2 in., at intervals of 12 in. apart, or start them off in individual pots. These can then be planted when the soil is manageable and frosts have passed.

Division
Divide established clumps in spring. Remember small pieces of root will always grow, so do it cleanly, making sure that you have collected all the little pieces of root. Replant in a well-prepared site.

Pests and Diseases
Cabbage white caterpillars may feed on the leaves during late summer. The leaves may also be affected by some fungus diseases, but this should not be a problem on vigorous plants and leaves should be simply removed and burnt.

Maintenance
Spring Plant cuttings in garden.
Summer Liquid feed with seaweed fertilizer.
Fall Dig up roots if required when mature enough.
Winter No need for protection, fully hardy.

Garden Cultivation
Think seriously if you want this plant in your garden. It is invasive. Once you have it, you have it. It is itself a most tolerant plant, liking all but the driest of soils. But for a good crop it prefers a light, well-dug, rich, moist soil. Prepare it the fall before planting with lots of well-rotted manure. It likes a sunny site but will tolerate dappled shade.

If large quantities are required, horseradish should be given a patch of its own where the roots can be lifted and the soil replenished after each harvest. To produce strong, straight roots I found this method in an old gardening book. Make holes 15 in. deep with a crow bar, and drop a piece of horseradish 2–3 in. long with a crown on the top into the hole. Fill the hole up with good rotted manure. This will produce strong straight roots in 2–3 years, some of which may be ready in the first year.

Harvesting
Pick leaves young to use fresh, or to dry.

If you have a mature patch of horseradish then the root can be dug up any time for use fresh. Otherwise dig up the roots in the fall. Store roots in sand and make sure you leave them in a cool dark place over the winter.

Alternatively, wash, grate or slice and dry. Another method is to immerse the whole washed roots in white wine vinegar.

 ## companion planting

It is said that when grown near potatoes it improves their disease resistance. However, be careful that it does not take over.

Horseradish dye

other uses

Chop finely into dog food to dispel worms and improve body tone.

Traditionally, spray made from an infusion of the roots protects apple trees against brown rot.

The roots and the leaves produce a yellow dye for natural dyeing.

Slice and infuse in a pan of milk to make a lotion to improve skin clarity.

medicinal

Horseradish is a powerful circulatory stimulant with antibiotic properties.

As a diuretic it is effective for lung and urinary infections. It can also help with coughs and sinus congestion. It can also be taken internally for gout and rheumatism, containing as it does potassium, calcium, magnesium and phosphorus.

Grate into a poultice and apply externally to chilblains, stiff muscles, sciatica and rheumatic joints, and to stimulate blood flow.

warning

Overuse may blister the skin. Do not use it if your thyroid function is low or if taking thyroxin. Avoid continuous dosage when pregnant or suffering from kidney problems.

culinary

The reason horseradish is used in sauces, vinegars, and as an accompaniment rather than cooked as a vegetable is that the volatile flavoring oil which is released in grating evaporates rapidly and becomes nothing when cooked. Raw it's a different story. The strongest flavor is from root pulled in the fall. The spring root is comparatively mild. Fresh root contains calcium, sodium, magnesium and vitamin C, and has antibiotic qualities that are useful for preserving food.

It can be used raw and grated in coleslaw, dips, pickled beetroot, cream cheese, mayonnaise and avocado fillings.

The young leaves can be added to salads for a bit of zip.

Make horseradish sauce to accompany roast beef, and smoked oily fish.

Avocado with Horseradish Cream

Fresh horseradish root (approx. 6 in. long); preserved horseradish in vinegar can be substituted. If it is, leave out the lemon juice.
1 tablespoon butter
3 tablespoons fresh breadcrumbs
1 apple
2 teaspoons yogurt
1 teaspoon lemon juice
Pinch of salt and sugar
1 teaspoon chopped fresh chervil
1/2 teaspoon each of fresh chopped tarragon and dill
3–4 tablespoons heavy whipping cream
2 avocados (ripe) cut in half, pits removed

Peel and grate the horseradish. Melt the butter and add the breadcrumbs. Fry until brown, and add grated horseradish. Remove from heat and grate the apple into the mixture. Add yogurt, lemon juice, salt, sugar and herbs. Put aside to cool. Chill in refrigerator. Just before serving gently fold the cream into the mixture and spoon into the avocado halves. Serve with green salad and brown toast.

Arnica chamissonis
ARNICA

Also known as Mountain tobacco, Leopards bane, Mountain arnica, Wolfsbane and Mountain daisy. From the family Asteraceae.

It is found wild in the mountainous areas of Canada, North America, and in Europe, where it is a protected species. Bees love it.

The name *Arnica* is said to be derived from the word *ptarmikos*, Greek for "sneezing." One sniff of arnica can make you sneeze.

The herb was known by Methusalus and was widely used in the 16th century in German folk medicine. Largely as a result of exaggerated claims in the 18th century by Venetian physicians, it was, for a short time, a popular medicine.

 ## varieties

Arnica chamissonis
Arnica
Hardy perennial. Ht. 1–2 ft., spread 6 in. Large, single, scented yellow flowers throughout summer. Oval, hairy, light green leaves. Zone 4.

 ## cultivation

Propagation
Seed
Sow the small seed in spring or fall in either a pot, plug module or seed tray, and cover with perlite. Place trays in a cold frame as heat will inhibit germination. The seed is slow to germinate, even occasionally as long as two years! Once the seedlings are large enough, pot them and harden them off in a cold frame.

You can get a more reliable germination if you collect the seed yourself and sow no later than early fall. After potting, winter the young plants under protection. They will die back in winter. Plant in the following spring, when the soil has warmed up, 1 ft. from other plants.

Division
Arnica's root produces creeping rhizomes, which are easy to divide in spring. This is much more reliable than sowing seed.

Pests and Diseases
Caterpillars and slugs sometimes eat the leaves.

Maintenance
Spring Sow seeds. Divide creeping rhizomes.
Summer Deadhead if necessary. Harvest plant for medicinal use.
Fall Collect seeds and either sow immediately or store in an airtight container for sowing in the spring.
Winter Note the position in the garden because the plants die right back.

Garden Cultivation
Being a mountainous plant, it is happiest in a sandy acid soil, rich in humus, and in a sunny position. Arnica is a highly ornamental plant with a long flowering season. It is ideally suited for large rock gardens, or the front of a border bed.

Arnica chamissonis

Harvesting
Pick flowers for medicinal use in summer, just before they come into full flower. For drying, pick in full flower, with stalks.

Collect leaves for drying in summer before flowering.

Dig up roots of 2nd/3rd year growth after the plant has fully died back in late fall/early winter for drying.

 ## medicinal

Arnica is a famous herbal and homeopathic remedy. A tincture of flowers can be used in the treatment of sprains, wounds and bruises, and also to give relief from rheumatic pain and chilblains, if the skin is not broken. Homeopaths say that it is effective against epilepsy and sea sickness, and possibly as a hair growth stimulant. It has also been shown to be effective against salmonella.

⚠ warning

Do not take arnica internally except under supervision of a qualified herbalist or homeopath. External use may cause skin rash or irritation. Never apply to broken skin.

 ## other uses

Leaves and roots smoked as herbal tobacco, hence the name Mountain tobacco.

Artemisia abrotanum
SOUTHERNWOOD

Also known as Lad's love and Old man. From the family Asteraceae.

This lovely aromatic plant is a native of southern Europe. It has been introduced to many countries and is now naturalized widely in temperate zones.

The derivation of the genus name is unclear. One suggestion is that it honours Artemisia, a famous botanist and medical researcher, sister of King Mausolus (353 BC). Another is that it was named after Artemis or Diana, the Goddess of the Hunt and Moon.

In the 17th century, Culpeper recommended that the ashes of southernwood be mingled with salad oil as a remedy for baldness.

 ## varieties

Artemisia abrotanum
Southernwood
Deciduous or semi-evergreen hardy perennial. Ht. and spread 3½ ft. Tiny insignificant clusters of dull yellow flowers in summer. The abundant olive green feathery leaves are finely divided and carry a unique scent. Zone 5.

 ## cultivation

Propagation
Seed
It rarely flowers and sets seed, unless it is being grown in a warm climate.

Cuttings
Take softwood cuttings in spring from the lush new growth, or from semihardwood cuttings in summer. Use a standard seed compost mixed in equal parts with composted fine bark. Roots well. It can be wintered as a rooted cutting, when it sheds its leaves and is dormant. Keep the cuttings on the dry side, and in early spring slowly start watering. Plant 2 ft. apart after the frosts have finished.

Pests and Diseases
It is free from the majority of pests and diseases.

Maintenance
Spring Cut back to maintain shape. Take cuttings.
Summer Take cuttings.
Fall Trim any flowers off as they develop.
Winter Protect the roots in hard winters with mulch.

Garden Cultivation
Southernwood prefers a light soil containing well-rotted organic material in a sunny position. However tempted you are by its bedraggled appearance in winter (hence its name, Old man) NEVER cut hard back as you will kill it. This growth protects its woody stems from cold winds. Cut the bush hard in spring to keep its shape, but only after the frosts have finished.

Harvesting
Pick leaves during the growing season for use fresh. Pick leaves for drying in midsummer.

 ## medicinal

It can be used for expelling worms and to treat coughs and bronchial congestion. A compress helps to treat frost bite, cuts and grazes.

 ## culinary

The leaves can be used in salads. They have a strong flavor, so use sparingly. It also makes a good aromatic vinegar

 ## other uses

The French call it Garde Robe, and use it as a moth repellent. It is a good fly deterrent, too—hang bunches up in the kitchen, or rub it on the skin to deter mosquitoes.

 ## warning

No product containing southernwood should be taken during pregnancy.

Artemisia absinthium

WORMWOOD

Artemisia absinthium

Also known as Absinthe and Green ginger. From the family Asteraceae.

A native of Asia and Europe, including Britain, it was introduced into America as a cultivated plant and is now naturalized in many places. Found on waste ground, especially near the sea in warmer regions.

Legend has it that as the serpent slithered out of Eden, wormwood first sprang up in the impressions on the ground left by its tail. Another story tells that in the beginning it was called *Parthenis absinthium*, but Artemis, Greek goddess of chastity, benefited so much from it that she named it after herself—*Artemisia absinthium*. The Latin meaning of *absinthium* is "to desist from," which says it all.

Although it is one of the most bitter herbs known, it has for centuries been a major ingredient of aperitifs and herb wines. Both absinthe and vermouth get their names from this plant, the latter being an 18th-century French variation of the German *wermut*, itself the origin of the English name wormwood.

Wormwood was hung by the door where it kept away evil spirits and deterred nighttime visitations by goblins. It was also made a constituent of ink to stop mice eating old letters.

It was used as a strewing herb to prevent fleas, hence:

"White wormwood hath seed, get a handful or twaine,
to save against March, to make flea to refrain.
Where chamber is sweeped and wormwood is strewn,
no flea for his life, dare abide to be knowne."

This extract comes from Thomas Tusser's *Five Hundred Pointes of Good Husbandrie*, written in 1573.

Finally, wormwood is believed to be the herb that Shakespeare had in mind when his Oberon lifted the spell from Titania with "the juice of Dian's bud," Artemis being known to the Romans as Dian or Diana.

 varieties

Artemisia absinthium
Wormwood
Partial-evergreen hardy perennial. Ht. 3 ft., spread 4 ft. Tiny, yellow, insignificant flowerheads are borne in sprays in summer. The abundant leaves are divided, aromatic and gray/green in color. Zone 5.

Artemisia absinthium 'Lambrook Silver'
Evergreen hardy perennial. Ht. 32 in., spread 20 in. Tiny, gray, insignificant flowerheads are borne in long panicles in summer. The abundant leaves are finely divided, aromatic and silver/gray in color. May need protecting in exposed sites. Zone 6.

Artemisia pontica
Old Warrior
Evergreen hardy perennial. Ht. 24 in., spread 12 in. Tiny, silver/gray insignificant flowerheads are borne on tall spikes in summer. The abundant, feathery, small leaves are finely divided, aromatic and silver/gray in color. This can, in the right conditions, be a vigorous grower, spreading well in excess of 12 in. Zone 5.

Artemisia 'Powis Castle'
Evergreen hardy perennial. Ht. 36 in., spread 4 ft. Tiny, grayish-yellow insignificant flowerheads are borne in sprays in summer. The abundant leaves are finely divided, aromatic and silver/gray in color. Zone 6.

WORMWOOD

cultivation

Propagation

Seed
Of the species mentioned above, only wormwood is successfully grown from seed. It is extremely small and best started off under protection. Sow in spring in a prepared seed or plug tray, using a standard seed compost mixed in equal parts with composted fine bark. Cover the seeds with perlite and propagate with heat, 60–70°F (15–21°C). Plant when the seedlings are large enough to handle and have had a period of hardening off.

Cuttings
Take softwood cuttings from the lush new growth in early summer; semihardwood in late summer. Use a seed compost mixed in equal parts with perlite.

Division
As they are all vigorous growers, division is a good idea at least every 3 to 4 years to keep the plant healthy, to stop it becoming woody and to prevent encroaching. Dig up the plant in spring or fall, divide the roots and replant in a chosen spot.

Pests and Diseases
Wormwood can suffer from a summer attack of blackfly. If it gets too bad, use a liquid insecticidal soap, following manufacturer's instructions.

Maintenance
Spring Sow seeds. Divide established plants. Trim new growth for shape.
Summer Take softwood cuttings.
Fall Prune back semihardwood cuttings to within 6 in. of the ground. Divide established plants.
Winter Protect in temperatures below 23°F (−5°C). Cover with a frost cloth, straw, bark, anything that can be removed in the following spring.

Garden Cultivation
Artemisias like a light well-drained soil and sunshine, but will adapt well to ordinary soils provided some shelter is given. Planting distance depends on spread.
   Wormwood is an overpoweringly flavored plant and it does impair the flavor of dill and coriander so do not plant nearby.

Harvesting
Pick flowering tops just as they begin to open. Dry. Pick leaves for drying in summer.

container growing

Artemisia absinthium 'Lambrook Silver' and *Artemisia pontica* (old warrior) look very good in terracotta containers. Use a soil-based compost mixed in equal parts with composted fine bark. Only feed in the summer; if you feed too early the leaves will lose their silvery foliage and revert to a more green look. In winter keep watering to the absolute minimum and protect from hard frosts.

other uses

Wormwood can produce a yellow dye.

Antiseptic Vinegar

This vinegar is known as the "Four Thieves" because it is said that thieves used to rub their bodies with it before robbing plague victims.

1 tablespoon wormwood
1 tablespoon lavender
1 tablespoon rosemary
1 tablespoon sage
4 1/2 cups vinegar

Put the crushed herbs into an earthenware container. Pour in the vinegar. Cover the container and leave it in a warm sunny place for two weeks. Strain into bottles with tight-fitting, nonmetal lids. This makes a very refreshing tonic in the bath, or try sprinkling it on work surfaces in the kitchen.

Moth-Repellent

Wormwood or southernwood can be used for keeping moths and other harmful insects away from clothes. The smell is sharp and refreshing and does not cling to your clothes like camphor moth-balls. Mix the following ingredients well and put into small sachets.

2 tablespoons dried wormwood or southernwood
2 tablespoons dried lavender
2 tablespoons dried mint

medicinal

True to its name, wormwood expels worms, especially round- and thread- worms.

warning

Not to be taken internally without medical supervision. Habitual use causes convulsions, restlessness and vomiting. Overdose causes vertigo, cramps, intoxication and delirium. Pure wormwood oil is a strong poison, although with a proper dosage there is little danger.

Artemisia dracunculus
TARRAGON

Also known as Estragon. From the family Asteraceae.

A native of southern Europe, tarragon is now found in dry areas of North America, Southern Asia and Siberia.

***Dracunculus* means "little dragon." Its naming could have occurred (via the Doctrine of Signatures) as a result of the shape of its roots, or because of its fiery flavor. It was certainly believed to have considerable power to heal bites from snakes, serpents and other venomous creatures. In ancient times the mixed juices of tarragon and fennel made a favorite drink for the Kings of India.**

In the reign of Henry VIII, tarragon made its way into English gardens, and the rhyme, "There is certain people, and certain herbs, that good digestion disturbs," could well be associated with tarragon. I love, too, the story that Henry VIII divorced Catherine of Aragon for her reckless use of tarragon.

 cultivation

Propagation

Seed

Only the Russian and wild varieties produces viable seed. A lot of growers are propagating and selling it to the unsuspecting public as French tarragon. If you really want Russian tarragon, sow the small seed in spring, into prepared seed or plug module trays, using a standard seed compost mixed in equal parts with composted fine bark. No extra heat required. When the young plants are large enough to handle, transfer to the garden, 24 in. apart.

Cuttings

Both French and Russian tarragon can be propagated by cuttings.

Dig up the underground runners in spring when the frosts are finished; pull them apart, do not cut. You will notice growing nodules: these will reproduce in the coming season. Place a small amount of root (3–4 in.) each with a growing nodule, in a 3 in. pot, and cover with compost. Use a seed compost mixed in equal parts with perlite and place in a warm, well-ventilated spot. Keep watering to a minimum. When well rooted, plant out in the garden after hardening off, 24 in. apart.

It is possible to take softwood cuttings of the growing tips in summer. Keep the leaves moist, but

Artemisia dracunculus

 varieties

Artemisia dracunculus—French
French Tarragon
Half-hardy perennial. Ht. 3 ft., spread 18 in. Tiny, yellow, insignificant flowerheads are borne in sprays in summer but rarely produce ripe seed sets except in warm climates. The leaves are smooth dark green, long and narrow, and have a very strong flavor. Zone 3.

Artemisia dranunculus—Russian
Russian Tarragon
Hardy perennial. Ht. 4 ft., spread 18 in. Tiny, yellow insignificant flowerheads borne in sprays in summer. The leaves are slightly coarser and green in color, their shape long and narrow. This plant originates from Siberia, which explains why it is so hardy. Zone 3.

TARRAGON

Artemisia dracunculus

the compost on the dry side. It works best under a misting unit with a little bottom heat 60°F (15°C).

Division
Divide established plants of either variety in the spring.

Pests and Diseases
Recently there has been a spate of rust developing on French tarragon. When buying a plant, look for tell-tale signs—small rust spots on the underneath of a leaf. If you have a plant with rust, dig it up, cut off all foliage carefully, and bin the leaves. Wash the roots free from soil, and pot into fresh sterile soil. If this fails, place the dormant roots in hot water after washing off all the compost. The temperature of the water should be 111°F (44°C); over 114°F (46°C) will damage the root. Leave the roots in the hot water for 10 minutes then replant in a new place in the garden.

Maintenance
Spring Sow Russian tarragon seeds if you must. Divide established plants. Take root cuttings.
Summer Remove flowers.
Fall Pot pieces of French tarragon root as insurance.
Winter Protect French tarragon. As the plant dies back into the ground in winter it is an ideal candidate for either a frost cloth, straw or a deep mulch.

Garden Cultivation
French tarragon has the superior flavor of the two and is the most tender. It grows best in a warm dry position, and will need protection in winter. It also dislikes humid conditions. The plant should be renewed every 3 years because the flavor deteriorates as the plant matures.

Russian tarragon is fully hardy and will grow in any conditions. There is a myth that it improves the longer it is grown in one place. This is untrue, it gets coarse. It is extremely tolerant of most soil types, but prefers a sunny position, 2 ft. away from other plants.

Harvesting
Pick sprigs of French tarragon early in the season to make vinegar.

Pick leaves for fresh use throughout the growing season. For freezing it is best to pick the leaves in the midsummer months.

 ## container growing

French tarragon grows well in containers. Use a soil-based compost mixed in equal parts with composted fine bark. As it produces root runners, choose a container to give it room to grow so that it will not become pot bound. At all times make sure the plant is watered, and in the daytime, not at night. It hates having wet roots. Keep feeding to a minimum: overfeeding produces fleshy leaves with a poor flavor, so be stingy. In winter, when the plant is dormant, do not water, keep the compost dry and the container in a cool, frost-free environment.

medicinal

No modern medicinal use. Formerly used for toothache. Traditionally, a tea made from the leaves is said to overcome insomnia.

 ## culinary

Without doubt French Tarrogan is among the Rolls Royces of the culinary herb collection. Its flavor promotes appetite and complements so many dishes — chicken, veal, fish, stuffed tomatoes, rice dishes, and salad dressings, and of course is the main ingredient of sauce béarnaise.

Chicken Salad with Tarragon and Grapes
Serves 4–6

4 1/2 cups cooked chicken
2/3 cup mayonnaise
1/3 cup heavy whipping cream
1 heaped teaspoon fresh chopped tarragon
   (1/2 teaspoon dried)
3 spring onions, finely chopped
1/2 cup green grapes (seedless or de-pitted)
1 small lettuce
A few sprigs watercress
Salt and pepper

Remove the skin from the chicken and all the chicken from the bones. Slice the meat into longish pieces and place in a bowl.

In another bowl mix the mayonnaise with the cream, the chopped tarragon, and the finely chopped spring onions. Pour this mixture over the chicken and mix carefully together. Arrange the lettuce on a dish and spoon on the chicken mixture. Arrange the grapes and the watercress around it. Serve with baked potatoes or rice salad.

Atriplex hortensis
ORACHE

Atriplex hortensis var. rubra

From the family Chenopodiaceae.

The garden species of orache, *Atriplex hortensis*, originated in Eastern Europe and is now widely distributed in countries with temperate climates. In the past it was called mountain spinach and grown as a vegetable in its own right.

The red form, *Atriplex hortensis* var. *rubra*, is still eaten frequently in Continental Europe, particularly with game, and was used as a flavoring for breads.

The common orache, *Atriplex patula*, was considered a poor man's pot herb, which is a fact worth remembering when you are pulling out this invasive annual weed.

 varieties

Atriplex hortensis
Orache
Hardy annual. Ht. 5 ft., spread 12 in. Tiny greenish (boring) flowers in summer. Green triangular leaves. All zones.

Atriplex hortensis var. rubra
Red Orache
Hardy annual. Ht. 4 ft., spread 12 in. Tiny reddish (boring) flowers in summer. Red triangular leaves. All zones.

Atriplex patula
Common Orache
Hardy annual. Ht. 3 ft., spread 12 in. Flowers similar to orache, the leaves more spear shaped and smaller. All zones.

 cultivation

Propagation
Seed
For an early supply of leaves, sow under protection in early spring, into prepared plug module trays. Cover with perlite. When the seedlings are large enough and after hardening off, plant into a prepared site 10 in. apart. Alternatively, in late spring, when the soil has started to warm and all threat of frost has passed, sow

Atriplex hortensis

Artemisia dracunculus

the compost on the dry side. It works best under a misting unit with a little bottom heat 60°F (15°C).

Division
Divide established plants of either variety in the spring.

Pests and Diseases

Recently there has been a spate of rust developing on French tarragon. When buying a plant, look for tell-tale signs—small rust spots on the underneath of a leaf. If you have a plant with rust, dig it up, cut off all foliage carefully, and bin the leaves. Wash the roots free from soil, and pot into fresh sterile soil. If this fails, place the dormant roots in hot water after washing off all the compost. The temperature of the water should be 111°F (44°C); over 114°F (46°C) will damage the root. Leave the roots in the hot water for 10 minutes then replant in a new place in the garden.

Maintenance

Spring Sow Russian tarragon seeds if you must. Divide established plants. Take root cuttings.
Summer Remove flowers.
Fall Pot pieces of French tarragon root as insurance.
Winter Protect French tarragon. As the plant dies back into the ground in winter it is an ideal candidate for either a frost cloth, straw or a deep mulch.

Garden Cultivation

French tarragon has the superior flavor of the two and is the most tender. It grows best in a warm dry position, and will need protection in winter. It also dislikes humid conditions. The plant should be renewed every 3 years because the flavor deteriorates as the plant matures.

Russian tarragon is fully hardy and will grow in any conditions. There is a myth that it improves the longer it is grown in one place. This is untrue, it gets coarse. It is extremely tolerant of most soil types, but prefers a sunny position, 2 ft. away from other plants.

Harvesting

Pick sprigs of French tarragon early in the season to make vinegar.

Pick leaves for fresh use throughout the growing season. For freezing it is best to pick the leaves in the midsummer months.

 ## container growing

French tarragon grows well in containers. Use a soil-based compost mixed in equal parts with composted fine bark. As it produces root runners, choose a container to give it room to grow so that it will not become pot bound. At all times make sure the plant is watered, and in the daytime, not at night. It hates having wet roots. Keep feeding to a minimum: overfeeding produces fleshy leaves with a poor flavor, so be stingy. In winter, when the plant is dormant, do not water, keep the compost dry and the container in a cool, frost-free environment.

medicinal

No modern medicinal use. Formerly used for toothache. Traditionally, a tea made from the leaves is said to overcome insomnia.

 ## culinary

Without doubt French Tarrogan is among the Rolls Royces of the culinary herb collection. Its flavor promotes appetite and complements so many dishes — chicken, veal, fish, stuffed tomatoes, rice dishes, and salad dressings, and of course is the main ingredient of sauce béarnaise.

Chicken Salad with Tarragon and Grapes
Serves 4–6

4½ cups cooked chicken
⅔ cup mayonnaise
⅓ cup heavy whipping cream
1 heaped teaspoon fresh chopped tarragon
 (½ teaspoon dried)
3 spring onions, finely chopped
½ cup green grapes (seedless or de-pitted)
1 small lettuce
A few sprigs watercress
Salt and pepper

Remove the skin from the chicken and all the chicken from the bones. Slice the meat into longish pieces and place in a bowl.

In another bowl mix the mayonnaise with the cream, the chopped tarragon, and the finely chopped spring onions. Pour this mixture over the chicken and mix carefully together. Arrange the lettuce on a dish and spoon on the chicken mixture. Arrange the grapes and the watercress around it. Serve with baked potatoes or rice salad.

Atriplex hortensis
ORACHE

Atriplex hortensis var. *rubra*

From the family Chenopodiaceae.

The garden species of orache, *Atriplex hortensis*, originated in Eastern Europe and is now widely distributed in countries with temperate climates. In the past it was called mountain spinach and grown as a vegetable in its own right.

The red form, *Atriplex hortensis* var. *rubra*, is still eaten frequently in Continental Europe, particularly with game, and was used as a flavoring for breads.

The common orache, *Atriplex patula*, was considered a poor man's pot herb, which is a fact worth remembering when you are pulling out this invasive annual weed.

 varieties

Atriplex hortensis
Orache
Hardy annual. Ht. 5 ft., spread 12 in. Tiny greenish (boring) flowers in summer. Green triangular leaves. All zones.

Atriplex hortensis var. rubra
Red Orache
Hardy annual. Ht. 4 ft., spread 12 in. Tiny reddish (boring) flowers in summer. Red triangular leaves. All zones.

Atriplex patula
Common Orache
Hardy annual. Ht. 3 ft., spread 12 in. Flowers similar to orache, the leaves more spear shaped and smaller. All zones.

 cultivation

Propagation
Seed
For an early supply of leaves, sow under protection in early spring, into prepared plug module trays. Cover with perlite. When the seedlings are large enough and after hardening off, plant into a prepared site 10 in. apart. Alternatively, in late spring, when the soil has started to warm and all threat of frost has passed, sow

Atriplex hortensis

in rows 2 ft. apart, thinning to 10 in. apart when the seedlings are large enough. As this herb grows rapidly and the leaves can become tough, it is advisable to sow a second crop in midsummer to ensure a good supply of young tender leaves.

Pests and Diseases

Mostly pest and disease free, but it can suffer from leaf minor damage; bin or burn all affected leaves.

Maintenance

Spring Sow seeds.
Summer Cut flowers before they form.
Fall Cut seeds off before they are fully ripe to prevent too much self-seeding.
Winter Dig up old plants.

Garden Cultivation

This annual herb produces the largest and most succulent leaves when the soil is rich. So prepare the site with well-rotted manure. For red orache choose a site with partial shade as the leaves can scorch in very hot summers. Water well throughout the growing season. Red orache looks very attractive grown as an instant hedge or garden divide. Remove the flowering tips as soon as they appear. This will help to maintain the shape and, more importantly, prevent the plant from self-seeding. If you wish to save some seed for the following season, collect before it is fully ripe, otherwise you will have hundreds of orache babies all over your garden and next door.

Harvesting

Pick young leaves to use fresh as required. The herb does not dry or freeze particularly well.

 ## container growing

The red-leaved orache looks very attractive in containers; don't let it get too tall. Nip off the growing tip and the plant will bush out, and do not let it flower. Use a good potting compost. Keep the plant in semi-shade in high summer and water well at all times. If watering in high sun be careful not to splash the leaves as they can scorch, especially the red variety.

 ## medicinal

This herb is no longer used medicinally. In the past it was a home remedy for sore throats, gout and jaundice.

 ## culinary

The young leaves can be eaten raw in salads, and the red variety looks most attractive. The old leaves of both species ought to be cooked as they become slightly tough and bitter. It can be used as a substitute for spinach or as a vegetable, served in a white sauce. It is becoming more popular in Europe, where it is used in soups.

Red Orache Soup

1 lb. potatoes
1 cup young red orache leaves
1/4 cup butter
3 1/2 cups chicken stock
1 clove garlic, crushed
Salt and black pepper
4 tablespoons sour cream

Peel the potatoes and cut them into thick slices. Wash the orache and cut up coarsely. Cook the potatoes for 10 minutes in salted water, drain. Melt the butter in a saucepan with the crushed garlic and slowly sweeten; add the red orache leaves and gently simmer for 5–10 minutes until soft (if the leaves are truly young then 5 minutes will be sufficient).

Pour in the stock, add the parboiled potatoes and bring to the boil; simmer for a further 10 minutes. When all is soft, cool slightly then purée in a blender or food processor.

After blending, return the soup to a clean pan, add salt and pepper to taste and heat slowly (not to boiling). Stir in the sour cream, and serve.

Ballota nigra

BLACK HOREHOUND

Also known as Stinking horehound, Dunny nettle, Stinking Roger and Hairy hound. From the family Lamiaceae.

Black horehound comes from a genus of about 25 species mostly native to the Mediterranean region. Some species have a disagreeable smell and only a few are worth growing in the garden. Black horehound is found growing wild on roadsides and in the countryside throughout most of Europe, Australia and America.

***Ballota nigra*, the black horehound, was originally called *ballote* by the ancient Greeks. It has been suggested that this comes from the Greek word *ballo*, which means "to reject," "cast," or "throw," because cows and other farm animals with their natural instincts reject it. The origin of the common name is more obscure, it could come from the Anglo-Saxon word *har*, which means "hoar" or "hairy."**

 cultivation

Propagation
Seed
Sow the seeds directly into the prepared garden in late summer, thinning to 16 in. apart.

Division
Divide roots in mid-spring.

Pests and Diseases
Rarely suffers from any pests or diseases.

Maintenance
Spring Dig up established plants and divide; replant where required.
Summer When the plant has finished flowering, cut off the dead heads before the seeds ripen, if you wish to prevent it from seeding itself in the garden.
Fall Sow seed.
Winter No need to protect.

Garden Cultivation
Black horehound will grow in any soil conditions, though it prefers water-retentive soil—in fact I have seen it growing in the countryside throughout England. In the garden, place it in a border. The bees love it and the flowers are attractive. Make sure it is far enough back so that you do not brush it by mistake because it does stink.

Harvesting
As this is a herbalist's herb, the leaves should be collected before flowering and dried with care.

 container growing

Not recommended, as it is such an unpleasant-smelling plant.

 varieties

Ballota nigra
Black Horehound
Hardy perennial. Ht. 16–40 in., spread 12 in. Purple-pink attractive flowers in summer. The leaves are green and medium-sized, rather like those of the stinging nettle. All parts of the plant are hairy and have a strong, disagreeable smell and taste. Zone 4.

Ballota pseudodictamnus
Half-hardy perennial. Ht. 24 in., spread 12 in. White flowers with numerous purple spots in summer. Leaves white and woolly. This plant originated from Crete. The dried calyces look like tiny furry spinning tops; they were used as floating wicks in primitive oil lamps. Zone 7.

 medicinal

Black horehound was used apparently in the treatment of bites from mad dogs. A dressing was prepared from the leaves and laid on the infected part. This was said to have an antispasmodic effect. This is not a herb to be self-administered. Professionals use it as a sedative, antiemetic and to counteract vomiting in pregnancy.

Bellis perennis

ENGLISH DAISY

Also known as Bruisewort, Eye of the day, Common daisy and Barinwort. From the family Asteraceae.

This humble, attractive flower, beloved by generations of children, was traditionally used medicinally by eminent herbalists such as Gerard who, in the 17th century, called it bruisewort and used it as a cure for wounds and disorders of the liver. Currently its medicinal properties as a treatment for bruising are being researched.

varieties

Bellis perennis
Daisy
Hardy perennial. Ht. and spread 6–8 in. Numerous small flowers with yellow centers, white petals with a pink blush to the tips. Basal rosette of spoon-shaped, scalloped mid-green leaves. Zone 3.

Bellis perennis 'Alba Plena'
Double-flowered Daisy
Hardy perennial. Ht. and spread 6–8 in. Numerous small flowers with yellow centers, double white petals, which often have a pink blush. A basal rosette of spoon-shaped, scalloped mid-green leaves. Zone 3.

cultivation

Propagation
Seed
Sow fresh seed in summer into prepared trays or plug modules, using a standard seed compost. Cover with perlite, no extra heat is needed. Germination takes 10–20 days. Once the seedlings are large enough, pot using loam-based compost. Alternatively plant into a prepared site in early fall. They will flower in their second season.

The double varieties of the species are, in the majority of cases, sterile and can only be grown by division.

Division
Divide the creeping rhizomes in spring or fall. Once divided, either pot into loam-based compost or replant into a prepared site in the garden.

Pest and Diseases
Rarely suffers in the garden from any pest or disease. Can be prone to powdery mildew in containers, this is usually caused by the compost drying out then being overwatered to compensate.

Maintenance
Spring Divide established plants.
Summer Sow fresh seed, deadhead flowers to maintain flowering.
Fall Divide established plants.
Winter No need for protection, fully hardy.

Garden Cultivation
This is a most tolerant plant; it will survive in most soils. When grown in an ideal situation it requires a loam that does not totally dry out in summer, in full sun to partial shade. When it is planted in the lawn it can be happily mown; this will encourage it to continue flowering.

Harvesting
Pick the leaves when young for using in salads. Pick the flowers in bud or just opening for use in salads and desserts. Dig up the roots for medicinal use in the fall.

container growing

Daisies look very attractive in a container. Use a soil-based compost so that it does not totally dry out on hot summer days.

culinary

New young leaf shoots can be eaten raw or cooked. The flowering buds and flowers, just as they open, can be added to salads; they have a light, honey bitter flavor which combines well with lettuce. They look most attractive in fruit salads.

medicinal

An ointment made from the leaves can be applied to external wounds and bruising. A decoction made from the roots can ease the irritation of eczema. It is also used in homeopathic remedies to treat bruising.

other uses

Traditionally, an insect-repellent spray was made from an infusion of the leaves.

Bellis perennis

Beta vulgaris
BEETS

Also known as Mangel and Mangel-wurzel. From the family Chenopodiaceae.

Historically, beets have been eaten and used medicinally since prehistoric times when the leaves were used as a pot-herb. During the medieval era, beet roots remained long, thin and white. One of the earliest records of a swollen root was in the mid-16th century. Our present red beets started being produced in the 17th century. In the 19th century, Robinson wrote the *Family Herbal*, where he prescribed sniffing beet juice up the nose to promote sneezing and as a cure for toothache!

Spring Sow seeds and second sowing in late spring.
Summer Start eating.
Fall Harvest the rest of the beets. Feed soil with well-rotted manure.
Winter Dig over plot.

Garden Cultivation
Beets prefers a deep rich moist soil that has been mulched with well-rotted manure the previous fall. It dislikes being grown in shade or dry soil. In drought, the leaves become tough and the roots become small and woody. To avoid any check in growth, water regularly, from spring until late summer. However do not overwater because this will produce extra leaf growth and small roots. If you know your soil is prone to drying out or there is a threat of drought, mulch with 2 in. of well-rotted compost or leaf mold. The red-leafed varieties can look very attractive planted in a

Beta vulgaris 'Bulls Blood'

varieties

Beta vulgaris subsp. *vulgaris*
Beet
Hardy biennial grown as an annual Ht. 11–15 in. Round or long purple roots. Green leaves. All zones.

Beta vulgaris 'Bulls Blood'
Hardy biennial grown as an annual. Ht. 11–15 in. Round purple roots. Deep red leaves. All zones.

Beta vulgaris 'Boltardy'
Hardy biennial grown as an annual. Ht. 11–15 in. Round smooth-skinned, purple roots. Green leaves with red veins. Early cropper, good in containers. All zones.

Beta vulgaris 'Barbietola di Chioggia'
Hardy biennial grown as an annual Ht. 11–15 in. Round, smooth-skinned pale pink/purple roots, which, when sliced, reveal unusual whiter internal rings. Green leaves. Great in salads, turns pale pink when cooked. A mild, traditional, Italian variety. All zones.

cultivation

Propagation
Seed
Sow seeds in early spring into pots or plug modules using a seed compost. Before sowing, place the seeds in a sieve and rinse thoroughly under cold running water. This removes the chemicals that inhibit germination, so sow immediately and cover with perlite or vermiculite. Germination takes 7–10 days.

Alternatively, sow washed seed in late spring when the soil temperature is above 45°F (7°C) into prepared open ground at a distance of 8inch apart in drills 12 in. apart. Germination takes 2–3 weeks.

Pests and Diseases
Downy mildew can be a problem, resulting in either or both of the following: yellow patches on the leaves and gray mold on the under surfaces. This is caused by overcrowding and bad drainage. Remove any diseased leaves, and thin the crop to give more space and air.

Maintenance

mixed border. If you grow them among other plants, and wish to crop them, bear in mind their watering requirements in summer.

Harvesting

Pick the leaves when they are young and soft for use in salads. When you see the roots swelling, and reaching golf-ball size, pull up alternate plants; leave the others to reach maturity. Harvest these when no bigger than a baseball. Finish harvest before it gets too wet and before the frosts set in. Store the roots in a cool frost-free room. A plastic bin is ideal. Place some seed compost at the bottom, then place the roots on the compost not touching each other, cover with seed compost, repeat in layers, finishing with a layer of compost on the top.

 container growing

Beets can be successfully grown in large containers. I recommend the following varieties of beet that both adapt well: *Beta vulgaris* 'Boltardy' and *Beta vulgaris* 'Bulls Blood'. The latter looks wonderful interplanted with parsley. Use a loam-based potting compost. Position the container in partial shade to protect the container from overheating in the height of summer; however do not put in full shade as this will produce small roots. Water regularly throughout the growing season and liquid feed monthly following the manufacturer's instructions.

 medicinal

Historically, beets were used to cleanse the digestive system, and this is now becoming fashionable again. It makes a spectacular-looking healthy juice, being high in vitamin C and fiber. Beets contain about twice the amount of natural sugars as carrots which is why their juice is so sweet. However, because the sugars are integral to the cells in the beet, the sugars are absorbed quite slowly by the body, giving the body sustained energy rather than a sugar burst. Recent research has shown that drinking one glass of beet juice a day is very beneficial.

The leaves of the beet are high in beta carotene, which has antioxidant properties. They also contain a useful amount of fiber and vitamin C.

 other uses

The color from the beet root is due to a pigment called betalain, which is used to make the red food coloring, E162.

 culinary

Beets have been a part of my kitchen since childhood. My mother used to cook all the parts, the leaf like spinach and the root grated in salads, savory jellies, pickled, cooked whole and served in a white sauce, roasted in the oven or turned into soups.

Beets and Marjoram in a White Sauce

8 whole baby beets

White sauce
1¼ cups milk
2 tablespoons butter
2 tablespoons flour
1 tablespoon sweet marjoram leaves chopped.
1 tablespoon oregano flowers (broken up into individual florets, with no green bits attached)
Salt and freshly ground black pepper
Extra oregano flowers for decoration

First prepare the beets by cutting off the tops, leaving about ¾ in. of stem. Wash them in cold water, taking care not to pierce the skin, otherwise the beets will "bleed" when cooking. Put the beets into a pan of boiling water and cook for 30–45 minutes, longer if they are large. Alternatively cook in a pressure cooker by covering the beets generously with water, but take care not to fill the pressure cooker more than three-quarters full. Bring the water up to the boil and cook on the highest pressure for 10 minutes. With either method, check to see if the beets are ready by pressing gently with your fingers. If the skin slips off easily, the beet is cooked. Peel and place on a serving dish. Make the white sauce by melting the butter, adding the flour, the chopped sweet marjoram and the oregano flowers and the milk, stirring all the time. Cook until the sauce becomes thick and smooth, season to taste with salt and freshly ground black pepper and pour over the beets. Put in the oven at 350°F/180°C for 10 minutes. When ready to serve, sprinkle some more oregano flowers over the top.

Borago officinalis
BORAGE

Also known as Bugloss, Burrage, and Common bugloss. From the family Boraginaceae.

Borage is indigenous to Mediterranean countries, but has now been naturalized in Northern Europe and North America. In fact you can find escapees growing happily in the wild.

The origin of the name is obscure. The French *bourrache*, is said to derive from an old word meaning "rough" or "hairy," which may describe the leaf, but the herb's beautiful, pure blue flowers are its feature and are supposed to have inspired the painting of the robes of the Madonna, and charmed Louis XIV into ordering the herb to be planted at Versailles. The herb's Welsh name translates as "herb of gladness"; and in Arabic it is "the father of sweat," which we can accept as borage is a diaphoretic. The Celtic word *borrach* means "courage," however, and in this we have an association more credible by far. The Greeks and Romans regarded borage as both comforting and imparting courage, and this belief so persisted that Gerard was able to quote the tag, *Ego borage gaudia semper ago* in his Herbal. It was for courage, too, that borage flowers were floated in stirrup cups given to the Crusaders. Clearly, the American Settlers also thought sufficiently highly of borage to take the seed with them on their long adventure. Records of it were found in a seed order of an American in 1631, where it was called burradge.

Borago officinalis 'Alba'

varieties

Borago officinalis
Borage
Hardy annual (very occasionally biennial). Ht. 36 in. with hollow, bristly branches and spreading stems. The blue or purplish star-shaped flowers grow in loose racemes from early summer to mid-fall. The leaves are bristly, oval or oblong. At the base they form a rosette; others grow alternately on either side of the stem. All zones.

Borago officinalis 'Alba'
White Borage
Hardy annual. Ht. 36 in. White star-shaped flowers from late spring through summer. Bristly, oval, oblong leaves. Can be used in the same way as *B. officinalis*. All zones.

cultivation

Propagation
Seed
Borage is best grown directly from seed, sown in spring and summer in its final position, as it does not like having its long tap root disturbed. But for an early crop it is as well to start the seeds under protection. In early spring sow singly in small pots. Transplant to final position as soon as possible after hardening off, when the seedling is large enough and all threat of frosts is over.

Pests and Diseases
Blackfly. If you are growing borage as a companion plant this will not worry you, but if it is becoming a nuisance then spray with liquid insecticidal soap.

A disease that can be unsightly at the end of the season, is a form of mildew. Dig the plant up and burn.

Maintenance

Spring Sow seeds. They germinate quickly and plants are fully grown in 5–6 weeks.

Summer Sow seeds. Look out for flower heads turning into seeds—collect or destroy if you do not want borage plants all over the garden. Deadhead flowers to prolong flowering season.

Fall As the plants begin to die back collect up the old plants. Do not compost the flower heads or next year you will have a garden full of unwanted borage.

Winter Borage lasts until the first major frost, and some years it is the last flowering herb in the garden.

Garden Cultivation

Borage prefers a well-drained, light, rather poor soil of chalk or sand, and a sunny position. Sow borage seeds 2 in. deep in mid-spring and again in late spring for a continuous supply of young leaves and flowers. Thin seedlings to 36 in. apart and from other herbs, as they produce lots of floppy growth.

I have used borage as an exhibit plant at flower shows, and have found that by continuously deadheading the flowers you can maintain a good supply of flowers for longer.

Harvesting

Pick flowers fresh or for freezing or drying when they are just fully opened. Cut the young leaves fresh throughout summer. They do not dry or freeze very successfully. Collect seed before the plant dies back fully. Store in a light-proof container in a cool place.

 ## companion planting

Borage is a good companion plant. The flower is very attractive to bees, helping with pollination, especially for runner beans and strawberries. Borage also attracts blackfly to itself, theoretically leaving the other plants alone. Equally, if planted near tomatoes it is said to control tomato worm.

 ## container growing

It is not suitable for container-growing indoors. However, when planted outside in large containers (like a half barrel), borage can be very effective combined with other tall plants like oxeye daisies, poppies and cornflowers.

 ## culinary

Be brave, try a young leaf. It may be hairy, some would say prickly, but once in the mouth the hairs dissolve and the flavor is of cool cucumber. Great cut up in salads, or with cream cheese, or added to yogurt, or even in an egg salad sandwich.

They give a refreshing flavor to summer cold drinks. Finally fresh leaves are particularly good to use in a salt-free diet as they are rich in mineral salts. Try them combined with spinach or added to ravioli stuffing.

The flowers are exciting tossed in a salad, floated on top of a glass of sweet liqueur, or crystallized for cake decoration. Also excellent as garnish for savory or sweet dishes, and on iced soups.

 ## medicinal

In the 1980s borage was found to contain GLA, gamma linoleic acid, an even more valuable medicinal substance than evening primrose oil. But cultivation problems coincided with a dramatic slump in prices when waste, blackcurrant pulp, provided a cheaper and richer source of GLA. So hopes for the future of borage as a commercial crop have diminished recently, but it deserves more medicinal research.

Borage tea is said to be good for reducing high temperatures when taken hot. This is because in inducing sweat—it is a diaphoretic—it lowers the fever. This makes it a good remedy for colds and flu especially when these infect the lungs as it is also good for coughs. Leaves and flowers are rich in potassium and calcium and therefore good blood purifiers and a tonic.

Borage Tea

Small handful of fresh leaves
2 cups of boiling water

Simmer for 5 minutes.

Natural Night-cap

3 teaspoons fresh borage leaves
1 1/8 cups boiling water
1 teaspoon honey
1 slice lemon

Put the roughly chopped borage leaves into a warmed cup and pour over the boiling water. Cover with a saucer and leave the leaves to infuse for at least five minutes. Strain and add the lemon slice and honey. Drink hot just before retiring to bed.

 ## other uses

Dried flowers add color to potpourri. Children enjoy stringing them together as a necklace. Add to summer flower arrangements.

As a novelty burn the whole plant—nitrate of potash will emit sparks and little explosive sounds like fireworks.

Facial Steam for Dry, Sensitive Skin

Place 2 large handfuls of borage leaves in a bowl. Pour over 5 cups of boiling water. Stir quickly with a wooden spoon. Using a towel as a tent, place your face about 12 in. over the water. Cover your head with towel. Keep your eyes closed and maintain for about 10–15 minutes. Rinse your face with tepid cool water. Use a yarrow infusion dabbed on with cotton wool to close pores.

 ## warning

Prolonged use of borage is not advisable. Fresh leaves may cause contact dermatitis.

Brassica juncea
BROWN MUSTARD

Also known as Juncea, Brown mustard, Indian mustard, Mustard greens and Chinese mustard. From the family *Brassicaceae*.

This herb is mentioned more than once in the Bible; it has been used for thousands of years both medicinally and for culinary purposes.

Historically the Romans used the brown mustard as a pungent salad vegetable and the seeds of black mustard as a spice. The English name "mustard" is said to derive from the Latin, *mustem ardens*, which translates as "burning wine," a reference to the heat of mustard and the French practice of mixing unfermented grape juice with the ground seeds.

Brassica juncea 'Rubra'

 varieties

Brassica alba
White Mustard, Yellow Mustard
Hardy annual. Ht. 12–24 in. Pale yellow flowers in summer followed by long seed pods with pale yellow seeds. Rough, bristly, oval, deeply lobed green leaves. All zones.

Brassica juncea
Brown Mustard
Hardy annual. Ht. 16–40 in. Clusters of pale yellow flowers in summer followed by long seed pods with brown seed. Oval, lobed olive green leaves with pale green veins with crinkled edges. All zones.

Brassica juncea 'Rubra'
Red Mustard
Hardy annual. Ht. 12 in. Yellow flowers in summer. Oval red, purple tinted leaves with indented edges, pungent mustard flavor. Good in salads and sandwiches. All zones.

Brassica juncea 'Red Frills'
Mustard Red Frills
Hardy annual. Ht. 6 in. Yellow flowers in summer. Attractive dark red, narrow indented leaves with a mild mustard flavor, great for salads. All zones.

Brassica nigra
Black Mustard
Hardy annual. Ht. 16–40 in. Pale yellow flowers in summer followed by long seed pods with dark brown seeds. Rough, bristly, oval lobed green leaves. All zones.

 cultivation

Propagation
Seed
Sow seeds in the spring for seed and leaf production and the fall for leaf, into pots or plug modules using a standard seed compost. Cover with perlite and place under protection at 60ºF (15ºC). Germination is in 5–10 days. Plant after hardening off at a distance of 8 in. apart.

Alternatively sow seeds in late spring or early fall into prepared open ground, when the air temperature does not go below 45°F (7°C) at night. Germination takes 2–3 weeks. Once the seedlings are large enough, thin to 8 in. apart.

Pests and Diseases
All mustards can be attacked by flea beetle, which is a tiny shiny dark blue beetle that hops from plant to plant. A tell-tale sign that the plants are being attacked are small round holes on the leaves, which turn pale brown, making the leaves look unattractive. The adult beetles overwinter in leaf litter, emerging in the spring to attack lush seedlings. The other major attack comes in summer when there is a significant migration of adult beetles from oilseed rape fields into gardens; these can come in such numbers that they attack mature plants. The best organic method is to put a frost cloth over the plants so the beetles cannot attack the leaves.

Maintenance
Spring Sow seeds.
Summer Pick leaves and flowers.
Fall Harvest seeds, sow fall crop.
Winter Prepare ground for next season's crop.

Brassica juncea 'Red Frills'

BROWN MUSTARD

Brassica juncea

Garden Cultivation

All brassicas like to feed well, and mustard is no exception. However do not become too enthusiastic and give them too much nitrogen, because this will make them soft and flabby and prone to attack from pests. Try and prepare your plant plots the fall before planting. Give the site a good feed of well-rotted manure and compost in the fall prior to sowing in the spring.

Harvesting

Pick young leaves as required and the flowers just as they open. The seed pods are harvested as they change color. Dry the pods in a light airy room until totally dried, remove from the pods and store in clean, dry jars which have a tight-fitting top.

 ## companion planting

Mustard is a good companion plant because it germinates quickly so can be sown next to slow germinators, for example parsley, to indicate the row.

There is some evidence that mustard can be grown as a green manure. It is said to be effective in reducing soil-borne root diseases in pea crops.

 ## container growing

Mustard can successfully be grown in a container, using a standard potting compost. Place the container in partial shade. Water and feed regularly from spring until early fall.

 ## medicinal

Mustard has been and is still used to ease muscular pain, and treat respiratory tract infections. It is a warming stimulant with antibiotic effects. In China the leaves are eaten to ease bladder inflammation. In Korea, the seeds are used in the treatment of abscesses, colds, lumbago, rheumatism, and stomach disorders. Current research has found that mustard seeds inhibit the growth of cancerous cells in some animal studies.

 ## culinary

The mustard leaves have a distinctive, warm peppery taste; the flowers also have a mild mustard flavor. Both are great in salads, stir-fry dishes and they can transform a sandwich into a delight. Try a red mustard and ham sandwich.

Mustard seeds only get their pungency when they are crushed. When the seed is mixed with water and allowed to stand, the strength of flavor increases. If you mix the seed directly with vinegar or salt without previously soaking in water, you kill the flavor and if you boil the seed it will become bitter. The easiest and best way to use mustard seed is to make your own mustard. Use a combination of the black, brown and white seeds. This mustard is very versatile, complementing many dishes and enhancing the flavors of cheese, vegetables, poultry, red meat and fish. The seeds are also great added to salad dressings or sauces. When adding mustards to food, remember that the pungency of mustard is destroyed by heat, so add it to finished sauces or stews. Mustards are particularly good when combined with crème fraîche or cream cheese as dips for vegetables or pretzels.

Dill Mustard

1/3 cup black mustard seeds
2 tablespoons white mustard seeds
1/2 cup English mustard powder
2 cups water
2/3 cup cider vinegar
1/4 cup light brown sugar

 ## other uses

Mustard seeds have been suggested as a possible source of biodiesel in Australia.

 ## warning

Mustard seeds have been known to cause an allergic reaction. Prolonged contact with the skin can cause blistering.

1 1/2 teaspoons salt
1 1/2 teaspoons turmeric
1/4 cup chopped dill, or any other herb of your choice

Place the mustard seed in a china or glass bowl, add in 2 cups water and soak for 24 hours prior to use. The next day add the mustard powder, vinegar, salt and turmeric. When thoroughly mixed, place the bowl over a saucepan containing water, ensuring the water does not touch the bottom of the bowl. On a very low heat gently cook the mustard seed for 4 hours, stirring occasionally. Check from time to time that the water has not evaporated and never boil the mixture as the mustard will loose its flavor and become bitter. Once cooked allow to cool, then add the chopped dill. Cover the herb mustard and keep in the refrigerator.

AFRICAN BULBINE

Bulbine frutescens

Also known as Burn jelly plant, Snake flower, Cat's tail, Bulbinella, Ibhucu (Zulu) and Rooiwortel (Afrikaans). From the family *Asphodelaceae*.

This attractive drought-resistant herb is a native of South Africa and can be found growing wild in the desert grasslands of the Northern, Western and Eastern Capes. Indigenous plants play a pivotal role in Africa for traditional healing; this herb has been used by the Zulu for hundreds of years not only to cure rashes, to stop bleeding and as an antidote to poison, but also to treat their sick livestock.

 varieties

Bulbine frutescens
African Bulbine
Frost-tender, evergreen perennial. Ht. 24 in., spread 40 in. Attractive star-shaped yellow or orange single flowers, which grow in a linear cluster around the stem appearing sequentially throughout the summer. The flower has a characteristic hairy stamen. The leaves are succulent, cylindrical, narrow and varying in length. They are glutinous when broken. Zone 9.

Bulbine latifolia (Bulbine natalensis)
Broad-leaved Bulbine
Frost-tender, evergreen perennial. Ht. 24 in., spread 40 in. Attractive star-shaped yellow flowers which grow on 24 in. flowering spikes throughout the summer. Dark green, aloe like, pointed succulent triangular leaves which form a basal crown. Zone 9.

 cultivation

Propagation
Seed
Sow fresh seed in spring, into prepared seed trays or module plugs, using a seed compost mixed in equal parts with perlite. Place under protection at 68°F (20°C). Germination takes 10–20 days; however it is erratic as, like many herbs, it will happily self seed in a warm garden but, in a controlled situation, it sometimes will not perform. During germination, make sure that the compost does not dry out. Once the seedling is well rooted, pot using a seed compost mixed in equal parts with river sand. Grow until the plant has at least four well-developed leaves before either planting in warm climates into a prepared site in the garden or potting in cold climates to grow as a container plant.

Cuttings
This is the easiest method of propagation in a cold climate. Cuttings can be taken from early spring for plants raised under protection or in late spring for plants grown outside. By looking at the plant you will note that it puts down roots where the clusters of leaves touch the soil. Using a sharp knife, take the cutting, removing some root at the same time. Put the cuttings into a small pot or large module plug, using a

Bulbine frutescens Yellow form

seed compost mixed in equal parts with composted fine bark. Place the container in a warm position. It will root very quickly. Once the plant is established, either pot using a loam-based compost mixed in equal parts with river sand or, in warm climates, plant into a prepared site in the garden.

Division
This plant grows rapidly in a container or garden and benefits from being divided. In spring or early summer, before dividing, remove all the flowering stems; this will make it easier to handle and also to see what you are doing. Divide established garden plants by using the two forks back to back method, replanting immediately into a prepared site. Container-raised plants will need to be removed from the pot, then, either using hands or two hand forks, tease the plant apart, repotting into a loam-based potting compost mixed in equal parts with river sand.

Pests and Diseases
This herb is rarely troubled by pests or disease, with the exception of vine weevil if pot grown. There are two methods of getting rid of vine weevil organically. Either repot all the containers, checking each one for vine weevil grubs or, alternatively, watering the containers with a natural predator called *Steinernema krauseii* in late summer, early fall, when the night

temperature does not fall below 50°F (10°C) and before the vine weevil grubs have grown large enough to cause serious damage. This predator is a nematode, a microscopic worm, which infects the weevil grubs with a fatal bacterial disease. Prior to using this nematode, make sure the compost in the containers is moist all the way down by watering well a few hours before you intend to add the biological control.

Maintenance
Spring In early spring remove flowering spikes, sow fresh seeds and divide established clumps.
Summer Remove flowering spikes that have finished flowering, take cuttings.
Fall Remove flowering spikes.
Winter Do not overwater, but do not allow the compost to become totally dry. Protect when temperatures drop below 32°F (0°C).

Garden Cultivation
This herb is a good drought-loving plant; it can be planted out in cold climates in the early summer and then lifted before the frosts. Plant in a well-drained fertile soil that was fed with well-rotted manure in the previous spring. Position in full sun or semishaded and protected from cold winds.

Harvesting
The leaves can be picked for use throughout the year.

 ## container growing

This useful attractive herb, which can flower all year round, is ideal for growing in a warm sunroom as it requires a good light. Pot using a loam-based potting compost mixed in equal parts with river sand. Water regularly, and feed monthly, from spring until fall, with a liquid fertilizer following the manufacturer's instructions.

 ## medicinal

The leaves are filled with a clear gel similar in appearance and consistency to *Aloe vera*. This gel can be used directly on minor burns, wounds, cuts, abrasions, stings, and rashes. It can also be used to treat eczema, cracked lips and herpes. An infusion or tincture made from the roots of *Bulbine latifolia* is taken to quell sickness and diarrhea, and it is also

used to treat urinary complaints and rheumatism. Currently the medicinal properties of this herb are under research, and the leaf gel is being used to aid the healing of postoperative scars.

 ## other uses

A red dye can be obtained from the roots of *Bulbine latifolia*.

 ## warning

Do not take internally when pregnant.

Bulbine frutescens Yellow form

BOXWOOD

Also known as Box and Bushtree. From the family Buxaceae.

Boxwood is a native plant of Europe, Western Asia and North Africa. It has been cultivated widely throughout the world and is found in North America along the Atlantic coast, especially as an ornamental and hedging plant.

The common name, box, comes from the Latin *buxus*, which is in turn derived from the Greek *puxus*, meaning "a small box." At one time, boxwoods were widespread in Europe but the demand for the wood, which is twice as hard as oak, led to extensive felling. Its timber is close-grained and heavy, so heavy in fact that it is unable to float on water. The wood does not warp and is therefore ideal for boxes, engraving plates, carvings, and musical and navigational instruments.

It is not used medicinally now but the essential oil from box was used for the treatment of epilepsy, syphilis and piles, and also as an alternative to quinine in the treatment of malaria. A perfume was once made from its bark and a mixture of the leaves with sawdust has been used as an auburn hair dye.

When it rains, box gives off a musky smell evocative of old gardens, delicious to most people, but not Queen Anne who so hated the smell that she had the box parterres in St James Park (planted for her predecessors, William and Mary, in the last years of the 17th century) torn out.

 varieties

Buxus balearica
Balearic Boxwood
Half-hardy evergreen. Ht. 6 ft., spread 4½ ft. Suitable for hedging in mild areas. Has broadly oval, bright green leaves. Planting distance for a hedge 12–16 in. Zone 8.

Buxus microphylla
Small-leaved Boxwood
Hardy evergreen. Ht. 3 ft., spread 4½ ft. Forms a dense mass of round/oblong, dark green, glossy leaves. Attractive cultivar 'Green Pillow,' which is good for formal shaping. Planting distance for a hedge 6–9 in. Zone 5.

Buxus sempervirens
Common Boxwood
Hardy evergreen. Ht. and spread 15 ft. Leaves glossy green and oblong. Good for hedges, screening, and topiary. Planting distance for a hedge 15–18 in. Zone 5.

***Buxus sempervirens* 'Elegantissima'**
Variegated Boxwood
Hardy evergreen. Ht. and spread 3 ft. Good variegated gold/green leaves. Susceptible to scorch in hard winter. Trim regularly to maintain variegation. Very attractive as a center hedging in a formal garden or as specimen plants in their own right. Planting distance for a hedge 12–16 in. Zone 5.

***Buxus sempervirens* 'Latifolia Maculata'**
Golden Boxwood
Hardy evergreen. Ht. and spread 3 ft. The new growth is very golden, and as it matures it becomes mid-green. Planting distance for a hedge 12–16 in. Zone 5.

***Buxus sempervirens* 'Suffruticosa'**
Dwarf Boxwood
Hardy evergreen. Ht. and spread 18 in. Evergreen dark shrub that forms tight, dense mass. Slow grower. This is the archetypal edging in a formal herb garden for patterns and parterres of the knots. It is trimmed to about 6 in. in height when used for hedging. Planting distance for hedge 6–9 in. Zone 5.

Buxus sempervirens 'Latifolia Maculata'

Buxus sempervirens 'Suffruticosa'

Buxus wallichiana
Himalayan Boxwood
Hardy evergreen. Ht. and spread 6 ft. Slow growing. Produces long narrow, glossy, bright green leaves. Planting distance for a hedge 12–16 in. Zone 6.

 ## cultivation

Propagation
Cuttings
Boxwood is cultivated from cuttings taken in spring from the new growth. Use a standard seed compost mixed in equal parts with composted fine bark. Keep the cuttings moist but NOT wet, and in a cool place, ideally in shade. They will take 3–4 months to root. If you have a propagator then they will take 6–8 weeks at 70°F (21°C). Use a spray to mist the plant regularly. When rooted, pot the young plants using a soil-based compost or plant , as per the distances mentioned under varities.

Alternatively, take semiripe cuttings in summer, using the same compost mix as above. Rooting time is approximately 2 months longer than for the softwood cuttings, but only 3–4 weeks longer with heat.

Pests and Diseases
Boxwood can be attacked by the green box sucker nymph, which is noticeable by a white deposit and curled leaves. Cut back the plant, then spray with insecticidal soap. Box blight, *Cylindrocladium buxicola* is a fungal disease that can cause serious defoliation. There is no reliable organic remedy. However, I know of one gardener who cut his boxwood plants back,

then fed weekly with an organic fertilizer for 1 year and it recovered.

Maintenance
Spring Take stem cuttings. Trim fast growers such as *Buxus sempervirens* 'Latifolia Maculata'.
Summer Take semiripe cuttings. Trim hedges to promote new growth.
Fall Trim if needed but not hard.
Winter Does not need protection.

Garden Cultivation
Known for its longevity, it is not uncommon for it to live 600 years. Boxwood flourishes on limestone; it prefers an alkaline soil. But it is very tolerant of any soil provided it is not waterlogged. Boxwood is also fairly tolerant of position, surviving sun or semishade.

Boxwood hedges are a frame for a garden, outlining, protecting and enhancing what they enclose. Because you will be planting the boxwood plants closer together than when planting individual plants it is important first to feed the soil well by adding plenty of well-rotted manure or garden compost. Width of bed for a boundary hedge should be 24 in.; for small internal hedges 12 in. wide. Planting distances vary according to variety (see above).

If using common boxwood or golden boxwood, the more vigorous growers, trim in spring and prune at the end of summer or, in mild climates, in early fall. A late cut may produce soft growth that could be damaged by frost, which would then look ugly in winter. The slower varieties need a cut only in the summer. In general the right shape for a healthy, dense hedge is broad at the base, tapering slightly toward the top, rounded or ridged but not too flat, to prevent damage from heavy snow.

 ## container growing

Boxwood, especially the slow-growing varities, lends itself to topiary and looks superb in containers. *Buxus sempervirens* 'Elegantissima' looks very attractive in a terracotta pot. They are very easy to maintain. Use a soil-based compost. Feed with a liquid fertilizer in spring; water sparingly in winter.

 ## other uses

Boxwood is a favorite timber with cabinet makers, wood engravers and turners because it has a non-fibrous structure.

A mahogany box with boxwood detailing

 ## medicinal

It is advisable not to self-administer this plant; it should be used with caution. Boxwood is used extensively in homoeopathic medicines; a tincture prepared from fresh leaves is prescribed for fever, rheumatism and urinary tract infections.

 ## warning

Animals have died from eating the leaves. All parts of the plant, especially the leaves and seeds, are poisonous. It is dangerous to take internally and should never be collected or self-administered. Symptoms of poisoning are vomiting, abdominal pain and bloody diarrhea.

CALAMINT

Calamintha

From the family Lamiaceae.

Calamintha **originated in Europe. It is now well established throughout temperate countries, but sadly it is still not a common plant. Calamint has been cultivated since the 17th century. Herbal records show that it used to be prescribed for women.**

Calamintha nepeta

 varieties

Calamintha grandiflora
Calamint
Hardy perennial. Ht. 15 in., spread 12 in. Square stems arise from creeping rootstock. Dense whorls of lilac pink flowers appear midsummer to early fall above mint-scented, toothed, oval green leaves. Zone 5.

Calamintha grandiflora 'Variegata'
Hardy perennial. As *C. grandiflora* but with cream variegated leaves. Zone 6.

Calamintha nepeta
Lesser Calamint
Perennial. Ht. 12–24 in., spread 12 in. Small purple/white flowers from summer to early fall. Stems and leaves pale gray and covered in fine downy hairs. Its wonderful aromatic scent attracts butterflies and bees. Zone 5.

Calamintha nepeta

Calamintha sylvatica subsp. ascendens
Mountain Balm, Mountain Mint
Hardy perennial. Ht. 12 in., spread 8 in. Pale purple flowers in dense whorls from late summer to early fall. Leaves mid-green, oval, finely toothed and mint scented. A tisane can be made from the leaves. Zone 5.

 cultivation

Propagation
Seed
Sow calamint's fine seeds in spring or fall, either in their eventual flowering position or in trays, using a standard seed compost mixed in equal parts with composted fine bark and covered lightly with perlite. If fall sowing in trays, leave them outside to overwinter, covered with a sheet of glass. As germination can be tricky, fall sowing is sometimes more successful because subjecting the seeds to all weathers—thereby giving the hot and cold treatment—can trigger the process (stratification, see pages 264–265). When the seedlings are large enough to handle, prick out and plant into pots, using a potting compost mixed in equal parts with propagating bark. Alternatively plant them directly into the chosen site in late spring after hardening off.

Cuttings
Take cuttings of young shoots in spring. This is an especially good method for the variegated *C. grandiflora*. They take easily, but keep in the shade until fully rooted and do not allow to dry out. Plant in their final position when fully hardened off.

Division
Once the plants are established they can be divided in the spring or fall, either by lifting the whole plant or by the double fork method. Replant immediately either into a prepared site or into pots using a potting compost mixed in equal parts with propagating bark. If this method is chosen in the fall, keep in a cold frame all winter.

Pests and Diseases
Rarely suffers from pests or diseases.

Maintenance
Spring Sow seeds. Take cuttings from new growth.
Summer Cut back after first flowering and keep the plant tidy. Give a feed of liquid fertilizer, which can promote a second flowering.
Fall Sow seeds. Cut back new growth after second flowering.
Winter Protect new growth in frosts below 25°F (−4°C). Use a frost cloth, bracken, straw, or pine needles.

Garden Cultivation
These plants are indigenous to the limestone uplands and like a sunny position in well-drained soil that is low in nutrients. The leaves of *Calamintha grandiflora* 'Variegata' scorch easily and need some shade.

Harvesting
Pick leaves either side of flowering for use fresh or dried.

 container growing

Unsuitable for growing indoors, but can look good in containers outside. Use a potting compost mixed in equal parts with propagating bark and a container with a diameter no less than 5 in. *Calamintha grandiflora* 'Variegata' looks particularly striking in a terracotta pot.

 culinary

The young minty leaves of the lesser calamint can be added to salads and used to make a refreshing tea.

 medicinal

Infuse dried leaves as a tea for colic, and an invigorating tonic. Use fresh leaves in a poultice for bruises.

Calomeria amaranthoides

INCENSE PLANT

From the family Asteraceae.

This fascinating, highly aromatic herb is a native of Australia. Historically this plant came to England via the famous plant collector Sir Joseph Banks who gave some seed to Lady Hume, hence its former name *Humea elegans,* **which was only changed in 1993 to** *Calomeria amaranthoides.* **Sadly it is now rarely grown in parks or large private gardens because of its tendency to cause skin irritation and because of its high pollen count, which can cause asthma attacks.**

Pests and Diseases

As a container-grown plant, it suffers from greenfly and red spider mite. Keep an eye out for these and use an insecticidal liquid soap as soon as they appear.

Maintenance

Spring Prick out first year's plants. Pot second year's.
Summer Feed and water regularly. Collect seeds off second year's plants and sow immediately.
Fall Protect first year's plants.
Winter Protect plants from frost. Keep watering to a minimum.

Garden Cultivation

Do not plant outside until the night temperature no longer falls below 40°F (4°C). Plant in an area protected from the wind; even here, a stake is recommended. It prefers a light soil and a sunny position. All in all, it makes a better indoor plant, where the marvelous scent can be enjoyed.

Harvesting

Collect flowers for drying in summer.

 container growing

The incense plant is very ornamental and is the ultimate pot plant, growing to over 5 ft. It is, however, rarely seen because it needs a good deal of attention and protection.

Use a good peat-free potting compost mixed in equal parts with composted fine bark. Regularly repot one size up at a time and regularly liquid feed throughout its short life until a pot size of 12 in. in diameter is reached. Place in full sun and water regularly throughout the growing season.

other uses

Use in potpourri.

 varieties

Calomeria amaranthoides (Humea elegans)
Incense Plant
Tender biennial (sometimes annual). Ht. up to 6 ft., spread 3 ft. Tiny, delicate, coral flower bracts, very numerous on large branches. Large, oblong mid-green leaves. Zone 9.

 warning

Leaves can cause irritation and the same kind of burns as rue (see page 208). The scent can cause breathing difficulties and when in flower, it has a high pollen count and can trigger asthma attacks.

 cultivation

Propagation
Seed
Being a biennial, this is grown from the small seed, which is viable for only a short time. Collect from the plants in the summer, when ripe, and sow immediately into prepared seed or plug module trays using a standard seed compost mixed in equal parts with composted fine bark. Leave the seeds uncovered. Overwinter in a cold frame and cover the seed tray with glass or plastic wrap. Germination is lengthy and very erratic. Pot on seedlings as soon as they appear, taking care not to injure the roots. Grow young plants in a cool, frost-free environment, and keep the roots almost dry through winter. In spring gradually encourage growth by watering and repotting.

Calendula officinalis

MARIGOLD

Also known as Souci, Marybud, Bulls eye, Garden marigold, Holligold, Pot marigold and Common marigold. From the family Asteraceae.

Native of the Mediterranean and Iran. Distributed throughout the world as a garden plant.

This sunny little flower—the "merrybuds" of Shakespeare—was first used in Indian and Arabic cultures, before being "discovered" by the ancient Egyptians and Greeks. The Egyptians valued the marigold as a rejuvenating herb, and the Greeks garnished and flavored food with its golden petals. The botanical name comes from the Latin *calendae*, meaning "the first day of the month."

In India wreaths of marigold were used to crown the gods and goddesses. In medieval times they were considered an emblem of love and used as chief ingredient in a complicated spell that promised young maidens knowledge of whom they would marry. To dream of them was a sign of all good things; simply to look at them was thought to drive away evil humors.

In the American Civil War, marigold leaves were used by the doctors on the battlefield to treat open wounds.

Calendula officinalis

 varieties

Calendula officinalis
Marigold
Hardy annual. Ht. and spread 24 in. Daisy-like, single or double flowers, yellow or orange: from spring to fall. Light green, aromatic, lance-shaped leaves. All zones.

Calendula officinalis Fiesta Gitana Group
Hardy annual. Ht. and spread 12 in. Daisy-like, double flowers, yellow and/or deep orange: from spring to fall. Light green, lance-shaped leaves. All zones.

 cultivation

Propagation
Seeds
Sow in the fall under protection, directly into prepared pots or singly into plug module trays, in a standard seed compost mixed in equal parts with composted fine bark, covering lightly with compost. Plant in the spring after any frost, 12–18 in. apart. Alternatively in spring sow direct onto a prepared site in the garden.

Pests and Diseases
Slugs love the leaves of young marigolds. Keep night-time vigil with a flashlight and a bucket, or lay beer

Calendula officinalis Fiesta Gitana Group

traps. In the latter part of the season, plants can become infested with blackfly. Treat in the early stages by brushing them off and cutting away the affected areas, or later on by spraying with an insecticidal soap. Very late in the season the leaves sometimes become covered with a powdery mildew, which should be removed and burnt.

Maintenance
Spring Sow seeds in the garden.
Summer Deadhead to promote more flowering.
Fall Sow seeds under protection for early spring flowering.
Winter Protect young plants.

Garden Cultivation
Marigold is a very tolerant plant, growing in any soil that is not waterlogged but prefers, and looks best in, a sunny position. The flowers are sensitive to variations of temperature and dampness. Open flowers forecast good weather. Encourage continuous flowering by deadheading. It self-seeds abundantly but seems never to become a nuisance.

Harvesting
Pick flowers just as they open during summer, both for fresh use and for drying. Dry at a low temperature. Pick leaves young for fresh use; they are not much good preserved.

Dried flowers make a colorful oil

 container growing

Marigolds look very cheerful in containers and combine well with other plants. Well suited to window boxes, but not so in hanging baskets, where they will become stretched and leggy.

Use a standard potting compost mixed in equal parts with composted fine bark. Pinch off the growing tips to stop the plant from becoming too tall and leggy. Deadhead flowers to encourage more blooms.

 medicinal

Marigold flowers contain antiseptic, antifungal and antibacterial properties that promote healing. Make a compress or poultice of the flowers for burns, scalds, or stings. Also useful in the treatment of varicose veins, chilblains and impetigo. A cold infusion may be used as an eyewash for conjunctivitis, and can be a help in the treatment of thrush.

The sap from the stem has a reputation for removing warts, corns and calluses.

 other uses

There are many skin and cosmetic preparations that contain marigold. Infuse the flowers and use as a skin lotion to reduce large pores, nourish and clear the skin, and clear up spots and pimples. The petals make a pale yellow dye (see pages 288–289).

culinary

Flower petals make a very good culinary dye. They have been used for butter and cheese, and as a poor man's saffron to color rice. They are also lovely in salads and omelettes, and make an interesting cup of tea.

Young leaves can be added to salads.

Sweet Marigold Muffins
Makes 18

1/2 cup softened butter
1/2 cup superfine sugar
2 large eggs
1/2 cup self-raising flour
1 teaspoon baking powder
2 tablespoons fresh marigold petals

Put the butter, sugar, eggs, sifted flour and baking powder into bowl, and mix together until smooth and glossy. Fold in 1 1/2 tablespoons of marigold petals. Pour the mixture into greased muffin tins. Sprinkle a few petals onto each muffin with a little sugar. Bake in an oven 325°F/160°C for approximately 25–30 minutes.

CAPER

Capparis spinosa

Also known as Caper bush, Kapparis, Tápara, Umabusane. From the family Capparaceae.

This trailing evergreen shrub is now native in the Mediterranean but probably originated in the Middle East. It can be seen in the most unlikely places, from the ruins of ancient walls to the rubble alongside a newly built hotel. The Greek name *kapparis* is from the Persian *kabar*, hence "caper." The first recorded use of the caper bush was for medicinal purposes in 2000 BC by the Sumerians. Since then it has been used not only medicinally, but also as a useful condiment in the kitchen.

 varieties

Capparis spinosa
Caper

Tender evergreen shrub. Ht. up to 3 ft., spread up to 4½ ft. Masses of green buds (it is these that are pickled) are followed by very pretty solitary white, four-petalled flowers with long pink/purple stamens from early summer until fall. Leaves are oval, mid-green with a hint of brown, with two spines at the base of the leaf. The leaves grow on long stems which have been known to reach over 4½ ft. in length. Zone 9.

Capparis spinosa var. inermis
Spineless caper

Tender evergreen shrub. Ht. and spread up to 4½ ft. Masses of edible green buds followed by solitary white four-petalled flowers with long pink/purple stamens from early summer until fall. Leaves are oval, mid-green with a hint of brown. Zone 9.

 cultivation

Propagation

Seed

Caper seeds are miniscule, and once germinated they take a long time to grow into transplantable seedlings. Fresh caper seeds germinate readily—but only in low percentages. Once the seeds dry they become dormant and are notably more difficult to germinate, so patience is required. Start by immersing the dried seeds in hot water, 105°F (40°C), and leave to soak for 1 day. Carefully remove the seeds. Place them on some damp white kitchen towel, which makes them easier to see. Then put them into a sealed container and keep in the refrigerator for 2–3 months. After refrigeration, soak the seeds again in warm water overnight and then sow into prepared modules or plug trays, filled with a seed compost mixed in equal parts with perlite. Sow the seeds on the surface of the compost and cover with perlite. Keep warm at a minimum of 50°F (10°C). Plants raised from seed will not flower until their fourth or fifth year.

Cuttings

The best and most reliable method is to raise plants from cuttings. Take cuttings from the new spring

Capparis spinosa var. *inermis*

growth. Put them into prepared modules or plug trays filled with seed compost mixed in equal parts with composted fine bark for extra drainage. Put the tray on a heated propagator at 65°F (18°C), making sure the cuttings do not dry out. Once well rooted, pot using a loam-based compost mixed in equal parts with propagating bark.

Pests and Diseases

This herb is rarely attacked by pests. Young cuttings and seedlings can keel over if the watering is too much or too little.

Maintenance

Spring Take cuttings.
Summer Harvest flowering buds.
Fall Sow fresh seed.
Winter Protect from excessive wet in winter.

Garden cultivation

A simple rule of thumb is that the caper bush can be planted where the olive tree grows. It will thrive in lean, well-drained soil in a hot, sunny location with little or no water. It hates damp, cold, wet winters so if you live in that climate you will need to grow it in a container and place the container in a sheltered position for the winter. As an ornamental plant, caper bushes can be an attractive loose groundcover, a specimen small shrub can be used as an espalier, which presents the flower buds well for picking. The caper bush is salt-tolerant and will flourish along shores. As flowers are borne on first-year branches, cut back plants annually in the fall. It tolerates the cold down to 18°F (−7°C), however the growing tips can be damaged even in slight frost. The damaged growing tips can be cut off in the spring.

Harvesting

The flower buds are picked early in the morning for pickling and salting. The roots are dug up in the fall, the bark is then stripped from the roots and dried prior to use.

 ## container growing

If the plant is pruned well in the fall it will look wonderful growing in a container. For ease and self-preservation, I advise growing the spineless variety, *Capparis spinosa* var. *inermis*. Pot using a loam compost mixed in equal parts with horticultural grit.

 ## culinary

Throughout the Mediterranean you can buy fresh capers from the vegetable markets and stores from early summer for a few months. They are bright green tightly closed flower buds, the smallest having the best flavor. However when eaten fresh they do not taste particularly good; the flavor comes only after they have been pickled. This is due to the development of an organic acid called capric acid, which is an important flavoring in the kitchen. When you buy capers fresh they will still have the stems attached, so remove them, place the capers on a plate or tray, cover with sea salt and each time you pass the plate, give it a shake. After 2 days place them in a colander and rinse well under running water. Pack the capers into jars, add a few fennel seeds to each jar and a few immature flowers. Fill the jar up with white wine vinegar and seal with a nonmetallic top. Leave for a month before use.

 ## medicinal

The parts used medicinally are the bark from the roots and the flower buds. The bark is used to treat diarrhea and rheumatism. In South Africa the roots are reputedly used to treat insanity, snake bites, chest pains, jaundice and malaria. The buds are used to treat coughs.

 ## warning

Capparis spinosa has incredibly sharp spikes: wear gloves when handling this plant.

The attractive stamens of *Capparis spinosa*

Carum carvi

CARAWAY

From the family Apiaceae.

Caraway is a native of Southern Europe, Asia and India and thrives in all but the most humid warm regions. It is commercially and horticulturally cultivated on a wide scale, especially in Germany and Holland.

Both the common name and specific epithet stem directly from the ancient Arabic word for the seed, *karawya*, which was used in medicines and as a flavoring by the ancient Egyptians. In fact fossilized caraway seeds have been discovered at Mesolithic sites, so this herb has been used for at least 5,000 years. It has also been found in the remains of Stone Age meals, Egyptian tombs and ancient caravan stops along the Silk Road.

Caraway probably did not come into use in Europe until the 13th century, but it made a lasting impact. In the 16th century when Shakespeare, in *Henry IV*, gave Falstaff a pippin apple and a dish of caraways, his audience could relate to the dish, for caraway had become a traditional finish to an Elizabethan feast. Its popularity was further enhanced 250 or so years later when Queen Victoria married Prince Albert, who made it clear that he shared his countrymen's particular predilection for the seed in an era celebrated in England by the caraway seed cake.

No herb as ancient goes without magical properties of course, and caraway was reputed to ward off witches and also to prevent lovers from straying, a propensity with a wide application—it kept a man's doves, pigeons and poultry steadfast too!

 varieties

Carum carvi
Caraway
Hardy biennial. Ht. in first year 8 in., second year 24 in.; spread 12 in. Flowers white/pinkish in tiny umbellate clusters in early summer. Leaves feathery, light green, similar to carrot. Pale thick tapering root comparable to parsnip but smaller. This plant is not particularly decorative. Zone 4.

 cultivation

Propagation
Seed
Easily grown; best sown outdoors in early fall when the seed is fresh. Preferred situation full sun or a little shade, in any reasonable, well-drained soil. For an acceptable flavor it must have full sun.

If growing caraway as a root crop, sow in rows and treat the plants like vegetables. Thin to 8 in. apart and keep weed free. These plants will be ready for a seed harvest the following summer; and the roots will be ready in their second fall. Caraway perpetuates itself by self-sowing and can, with a little control, maintain the cycle.

If you want to sow in spring, do it either direct in the garden into shallow drills after the soil has warmed, or into prepared plug module trays to minimize harmful disturbance to its tap root when potting up. Cover with perlite. Pot when seedlings are large enough to handle and transplant in the early fall.

Pests and Diseases
Caraway occasionally suffers from carrot root fly. The grubs of these pests tunnel into the roots. The only organic way to get rid of them is to pull up the plants and bin them. To prevent the fly laying the eggs in the first place cover the crop with a frost cloth.

Caraway seeds

Maintenance

Spring Weed well around fall-sown young plants. Sow seeds.
Summer Pick flowers and leaves.
Fall Cut seed heads. Dig up second-year plants. Sow seeds.
Winter Does not need much protection unless it gets very cold.

Garden Cultivation

Prepare the garden seedbed well. The soil should be fertile, free draining and free of weeds, not least because it is all too easy to mistake a young caraway plant for a weed in its early growing stage. Thin plants when well established to a distance of 8 in.

Harvesting

Harvest the seeds in summer by cutting the seed heads just before the first seeds fall. Hang them with a paper bag tied over the seed head or over a tray in an airy place. It was once common practice to scald the freshly collected seed to rid it of insects and then dry it in the sun before storing. This is not necessary. Simply store in an airtight container.

Gather fresh leaves when young for use in salads. They are not really worth drying.

Dig up roots in the second fall as a food crop.

 container growing

Caraway really is not suitable for growing in pots.

 other uses

Pigeon fanciers claim that tame pigeons will never stray if there is baked caraway dough in their coot.

An infusion of caraway seeds

 medicinal

The fresh leaves, roots and seeds have digestive properties. Chew seeds raw or infuse them to sharpen appetites before a meal, as well as to aid digestion, sweeten the breath, and relieve flatulence.

An infusion can be made from 3 teaspoons of crushed seeds with 1/2 cup of water.

 culinary

When you see caraway mentioned in a recipe it is usually the seed that is required. Caraway seed cake was one of the staples of the Victorian tea table. Nowadays caraway is more widely used in cooking, and in savories as well as sweet dishes. The strong and distinctive flavor is also considered a spice. It is frequently added to sauerkraut, and the German liqueur, Kummel, contains its oil along with cumin.

Sprinkle over rich meats, goose, Hungarian beef stew—as an aid to digestion. Add to cabbage water to reduce cooking smells. Add to apple pies, cookies, baked apples and cheese.

Serve in a mixed dish of seeds at the end of an Indian meal to both sweeten the breath and aid the digestion.

Caraway root can be cooked as a vegetable, and its young leaves chopped into salads and soups.

Caraway and Cheese Potatoes
Serves 4

4 large potatoes
1/2 cup grated Gruyère cheese
2 teaspoons caraway seeds

Scrub but do not peel the potatoes. Cut them in half length-wise. Wrap in a boat of greaseproof foil and sprinkle each half with some of the grated cheese and a little caraway. Preheat the oven to 350°F/180°C and cook for 35–45 minutes, or until the potatoes are soft.

Carlina acaulis

CARLINE

Also known as Carline thistle, Stemless thistle, Dwarf thistle. From the family Asteraceae.

This native herb of the Mediterranean is steeped in history. It is said that Charlemagne had a vision that the plant would ward off the plague, and in medieval times it was considered a good antidote to poisons. Today, in France, it is still known as *baromètre* because the flower closes at the approach of rain.

 varieties

Carlina acaulis
Carline
Short-lived hardy perennial. Ht. 2–4 in., spread up to 6 in. Stemless, large solitary, creamy white flower, which is surrounded by creamy pointed flower bracts in late summer of the second season. Oblong, dark green pinnate prickly leaves. Zone 5.

Carlina vulgaris
Carline Thistle
Biennial. Ht. 8–24 in., spread up to 6 in. Groups of two to five yellow to purplish-brown flowers each surrounded by cream, linear, stiff pointed bracts in the summer of the second season. Leathery dark green, narrow oblong, prickly leaves. Native to Britain and northwest Europe. Traditionally used as a purgative and in magical incantations. All zones.

 cultivation

Propagation
Seed
Sow fresh seed in the fall into pots or plug modules using a standard loam-based seed compost. Cover lightly with compost, place in a cold frame. Germination takes 4–6 months. Plant in spring once the seedlings are large enough to handle.

Division
Wearing gloves for protection from the prickles, divide plants in the second spring prior to flowering, using two small hand forks back to back. Replant in a prepared sunny site in the garden.

Pests and Diseases
Rarely suffers from pests and diseases.

Maintenance
Spring Divide first-year plants.
Summer Pick flowers for drying.
Fall Sow seeds.
Winter No need for protection, hardy to −4°F (−20°C).

Garden Cultivation
This drought-tolerant, very hardy plant needs to be planted in full sun in a low-nutrient, free-draining soil. In the right conditions it will self-seed. It is now endangered in many Mediterranean countries; do not take from the wild.

Harvesting
Dig up the root of the second-year plant in early fall for making decoctions or drying. Pick the flower buds before they open for use in the kitchen. Pick the flowers when just opening for drying. Wear gloves to protect your hands.

Carlina vulgaris are popular in dried flower arrangements (right)

 container growing

This herb looks most attractive when flowering. Use a loam-based potting compost mixed in equal parts with horticultural grit. Place the container in full sun.

 medicinal

A salve made from the root can be used to treat several skin complaints including acne. Today the roots are used in veterinary medicine to stimulate the appetite of cattle.

 other uses

The plant is popular in dried flower arrangements as the dried heads keep their appearance indefinitely.

 culinary

It may seem unbelievable when you look at this plant that the flower bud is quite edible. It is eaten in the same manner as the globe artichoke (*Cynara scolymus*).
   In Southern Italy there is a recipe for stuffing the small bud with cheese and eggs before it is fried. Before cooking the prickles are brushed off with a stiff brush.

 warning

If the root is taken in large doses it is emetic and a purgative. Wear gloves when handling this plant.

Catha edulis

KHAT

Also known as Bushman's tea, Qat, Chat and Miraa. From the family Celastraceae.

This herb is indigenous to East Africa. Historically the ancient Egyptians considered the khat plant a "divine food," which was capable of releasing humanity's divinity. The generic name *Catha* is derived from the Arabic name for this plant, *Khat*, and the specific epithet *edulis* is a Greek word meaning "edible."

 varieties

Catha edulis
Khat
Evergreen tropical and subtropical shrub or small tree. Ht. up to 4 in. Clusters of minute creamy-white to greenish flowers in spring. These are followed by three-lobed capsules, which split in late summer to release one to three narrowly winged seeds. Dark green shiny leaves with a dull underside. Zone 10.

 cultivation

Propagation
Seed
If you are able to obtain fresh seed, which is rarely available outside of Africa, sow in spring. Place the tray under protection at 68°F (20°C); germination takes 4–6 weeks. Once the seedling is established, pot using a potting compost mixed in equal parts with river sand. Grow in a container for two years before planting into a prepared site in the garden or, in cold climates, potting as a container plant.

Cuttings
In early summer take cuttings from the nonflowering shoots and insert into small pots or plug module trays using a seed compost mixed in equal parts with propagating bark. Once well rooted, pot using a soil-based compost mixed in equal parts with river sand. Grow for 2 years before planting into a prepared site. In cold climates grow as a container plant.

Pests and Diseases
Rarely suffers from pests or diseases in warm climates. When grown as a container plant it can be prone to scale and red spider mite. To treat, either use the relevant predators or insecticidal soap following the manufacturers' instructions. Do not use both.

Maintenance
Spring In warm climates sow seed.
Summer Take cuttings from new growth.
Fall Cut back after flowering. Protect from excessive wet and cold weather.
Winter Protect from frost.

Garden Cultivation
In hot climates this herb can make an attractive garden plant, giving height in the border and all-year-round interest. Plant in full sun in a well-drained soil.

Harvesting
In early summer pick the new shoots as required for using fresh.

Bunches of khat shoots

 container growing

Khat can be grown successfully in a container using soil-based compost mixed in equal parts with river sand. Water and feed with a liquid fertilizer regularly throughout the growing season. Protect from frost and cold rains from the fall onward and reduce watering; do not allow the compost to totally dry out. In spring reintroduce watering once the night temperature does not drop below 41°F (5°C). Place the container outside in a warm, sunny, sheltered position once the night temperature is over 50°F (10°C).

 medicinal

In Africa this herb is used to treat chest complaints, asthma and coughs. It is taken in old age to stimulate and improve mental functions and communication skills. However as with many beneficial medicinal herbs, this can, and has been abused; see the warning.

 other uses

The bark is used as an insect repellent.

 warning

This herb has been banned in many countries. In 1980 the World Health Organization classified khat as a drug of abuse that can produce mild to moderate psychic dependence. Overuse can cause aggression and develop personality problems. It should never be taken when pregnant or breastfeeding.

Cedronella canariensis

BALM OF GILEAD

Also known as Canary balm. From the family Lamiaceae.

Although this herb originates from Madeira and the Canary Islands, as indicated by its specific epithet, balm of Gilead is now established in many temperate regions of the world. Many plants have been called balm of Gilead, the common link being that they all have a musky, eucalyptus, camphor-like scent.

The Queen of Sheba gave Solomon a balm of Gilead, which was *Commiphora opobalsamum*, an aromatic desert shrub found in the Holy Land. Today this plant is rare and protected, its export prohibited.

The balm of Gilead mentioned in the Bible ("Is there no balm in Gilead; is there no physician there?") was initially held to be *Commiphora meccanensis*, which was an aromatic shrub. However some now say it was oleo-resin obtained from *Balsamodendron opobalsamum*, a plant now thought to be extinct. Whatever is the case, the medicinal balm of Gilead is *Populus balsamifera*. This is balsam poplar, a tree found growing in several temperate countries, which smells heavenly in early summer, while the herb now known as balm of Gilead is *Cedronella canariensis*. This is said to have a similar scent to the Biblical shrubs, perhaps the reason for its popular name.

Cedronella canariensis

varieties

Cedronella canariensis (Cedronella triphylla)
Balm of Gilead
Half-hardy perennial, partial evergreen. Ht. 3 ft., spread 2 ft. Leaves with strong eucalyptus scent, three lobes and toothed edges, borne on square stems. Pink or pale mauve, two-lipped flowers throughout summer. Black seed heads. Zone 10.

cultivation

Propagation
Seed
The fairly small seeds should be sown in spring directly on the surface of a prepared pot, plug or seed tray. Use a standard seed compost mixed in equal parts with composted fine bark. Cover with a layer of perlite. It is a temperamental germinator, so bottom heat of 68°F (20°C) can be an asset. If using heat, remember not to let the compost dry out, and only water with a fine spray when needed. The seedlings will appear anytime between 2 and 6 weeks. When

2 leaves have formed, prick out the seedlings and plant them in position 3 ft. apart.

Cuttings
More reliable than seed. They take readily either in early summer before flowering from new growth or in early fall from the semiripe wood. Use a standard seed compost mixed in equal parts with composted fine bark.

Pests and Diseases
Since it is aromatic, aphids and other pests usually leave it alone, but the seedlings are prone to damping off.

Maintenance
Spring Sow seeds under protection. In a warm garden a mature plant can self-seed; rub the leaves of any self-seedlings to see if it is balm of Gilead or a young nettle (but don't get stung!). At this stage their aroma is the only characteristic that tells them apart. Plants overwintered in containers should be repotted if root-bound and given a liquid feed.
Summer Cut back after flowering to keep it neat and tidy, and also to encourage new growth from which late cuttings can be taken.
Fall Take stem cuttings. Collect seed heads.
Winter Protect from frost.

Garden Cultivation
Balm of Gilead grows happily outside in sheltered positions. Plant in a well-drained soil in full sun, preferably against a warm, wind-protecting wall. The plant has an upright habit but spreads at the top, so planting distance from other plants should be approximately 3 ft.

It is a tender plant that may need protection in cooler climates. If you get frosts lower than 29°F (−2°C) protect the plant for the winter, either by bringing it into a cool greenhouse or sunroom or by covering in a frost cloth.

Harvesting
Pick leaves for drying before the flowers open, when they will be at their most aromatic.

Either pick flowers when just coming into bloom and dry, or wait until flowering is over and collect the black flower heads (good for winter arrangements).

Seeds are ready for extraction when you can hear the flower heads rattle. Store in an airtight container to sow in the spring.

container growing

Balm of Gilead makes an excellent container plant. A 9–10 in. pot will be required for a plant to reach maturity. Use a soil-based compost mixed in equal parts with composted fine bark. Liquid feed a mature plant monthly throughout summer.

When grown in a sunroom, the scent of the leaves perfumes the air, especially when the plant is watered or the sun shining on it. Flowers are long lasting and give a good show during the summer. Keep watering to the absolute minimum in the winter months.

medicinal

Crush the leaves in your hand and inhale the aroma to clear your head.

Rub the leaves on skin to prevent mosquito bites.
Said to be an aphrodisiac when applied....
no comment.

other uses

Dried leaves combine well in a spicy or woody potpourri with cedarwood chippings, rosewood, pine needles, small fir cones, cypress oil and pine oil.

Add an infusion of the leaves to bath water for an invigorating bath.

Centella asiatica

GOTU KOLA

Also known as Indian Pennywort, Spadeleaf, Brahmi, Tiger herb, Tiger grass. From the family Apiaceae.

This herb is indigenous to the subtropical and tropical areas of India, where it is known as Tiger herb. This is because it is said that wounded tigers roll in the leaves, to help themselves heal. It can also be found in marshlands and alongside rivers in Pakistan, Sri Lanka, South Africa, Hawaii and Florida. It has been an important Ayurvedic medicinal herb for thousands of years, and its Ayurvedic name is Brahmi, or "knowledge." It was traditionally used to promote wound healing and slow the progress of leprosy, senile decay and loss of memory. It was also reputed to prolong life; for example, a Sinhalese proverb says, "Two leaves a day keep old age away." In China, Gotu kola is one of the reported "miracle elixirs of life." This was attributed to a healer named Li Ching Yun who reputedly lived 256 years by taking a tea brewed from Gotu kola and other herbs. It did not become important in Western medicine until the 1800s.

 varieties

Centella asiatica
Gotu Kola
Tender perennial creeping plant. Ht. 3in., spread indefinite. The tiny magenta flowers in summer are surrounded by green bracts, which grow in small umbels near to the soil surface. Bright green kidney-shaped leaves with indented margins. Zone 8.

 cultivation

Propagation
Seed
In warm climates this herb will happily self-seed. However, in cool climates it rarely sets seeds and, when you propagate from the seeds, the germination is very spasmodic. So it is much easier to raise plants from cuttings.

Cuttings
As this plant tends to root where the stems touch the ground, and it is prolific when growing in damp conditions, it is easy to propagate any time during the growing season from spring until early fall. Separate the plantlet from the main plant by cutting the stem above the ground, and then gently tease the small roots from the ground. You can then, depending on the size of the root, either pot into small pots or trim the roots and ease them into a plug tray using a seed compost mixed in equal parts with vermiculite. Once rooted, which takes place very quickly in summer, pot using a loam-based compost mixed in equal parts with vermiculite, and winter in a frost-free environment.
Division
Divide established plants in summer, either replanting into a prepared site in the garden or repotting using a loam-based compost mixed in equal parts with vermiculite.

Pests and Diseases
When grown as a container plant it can be prone to red spider mite. If this is the case introduce *Phytoseiulus persimilis*, its natural predator, or treat regularly with insecticidal soap following the manufacturer's instructions. Do not use both.

Centella asiatica leaves

Centella asiatica **flowers**

Maintenance
Spring Take cuttings and repot container-raised plants.
Summer Take cuttings. Do not allow the plants to dry out at this time of year.
Fall Protect young plants and container-grown plants from frost.
Winter Cut off any damaged leaves to prevent the spread of disease.

Garden Cultivation
This plant will only grow successfully outside all year round in tropical or subtropical climates. For those in cooler and cold climates it will tolerate temperatures as low as 50°F (10°C); below this it must be grown under protection. Its appearance changes, depending on growing conditions. In shallow water, the plant puts forth floating roots and the leaves rest on top of the water. In dry locations, it puts out numerous small roots and the leaves are small and thin.

Harvesting
Pick the leaves to use fresh from spring until late summer. Pick the leaves for drying in late spring.

 container growing

It will adapt happily to being grown in containers, and looks very interesting in a hanging basket where it will cascade. Plant in a loam-based compost mixed in equal parts with vermiculite. Place the container in partial shade, not full sun. Water and feed regularly from early spring until early fall with a liquid fertilizer following the manufacturer's instructions. This is especially important if you are picking the leaves regularly.

 medicinal

This is one of the most important medicinal herbs I grow. It is a rejuvenating, diuretic herb that clears toxins and reduces inflammation. It is being used in the treatment of rheumatism and rheumatoid arthritis. In 1987 the Indian Council of Medical Research carried out a double-blind clinical test on 30 mentally challenged children to study the effect of the drug on their general mental ability. The results, after a 12-week period, indicated a significant improvement in both general ability and behavioral patterns. It is commonly used to treat depression, but be warned that it has been reported to also cause depression in well-adjusted individuals.

 other uses

As a beauty aid, Gotu kola stimulates the production of collagen and this helps improve the tone of veins near the surface of the skin. It is now being used in face creams that claim to be antiwrinkle and skin-firming.

 warning

Excessive use of this herb taken internally or externally can cause itching, headaches and even unconsciousness. Avoid Gotu kola if you are pregnant or breastfeeding, using tranquillizers or sedatives, or have an overactive thyroid.

 culinary

When picking leaves for use in the kitchen, choose the new young tender leaves; the mature ones are dry and tough, especially if grown in dry conditions. Add the young leaves to salads, sandwiches and stir-fry dishes where the dry, slightly spicy flavor combines well with fish and vegetables.

Eastern Herb Salad
Serves 4

1 cucumber, peeled, deseeded and cut into
    ½ inch dice
Salt and freshly ground black pepper
3 tablespoons extra virgin olive oil
3 pita breads, toasted and broken into small
    pieces, or five slices of white bread, toasted then
    cut into strips
2 cloves of garlic, crushed
Juice of 1 lemon
2 tablespoons young Gotu kola leaves, roughly
    chopped
4 tablespoons purslane leaves, removed from the
    stalks and lightly chopped
2 tablespoons flat leaf parsley, roughly chopped
2 tablespoons coriander leaves, roughly chopped
2 tablespoons mint, roughly chopped
1 red onion, finely chopped
5 ripe tomatoes, peeled, deseeded and
    roughly chopped.

Place the diced cucumber in a colander, sprinkle with salt and leave to drain for 20 minutes. Toast the bread. In a large bowl, mix together the garlic, lemon juice and the olive oil to make a dressing. Add the herbs, the diced vegetables, the pieces of bread and toss well to coat with the dressing. Season with salt and pepper, serve immediately. This salad does not keep.

Centaurea cyanus

CORNFLOWER

Also known as Blue bottle, Bachelors buttons. From the family Asteraceae.

Cornflowers are the national flower of Estonia. Historically it is said that Chiron, an ancient Greek Centaur, taught mankind the healing value of this herb. It was regarded as a good remedy against the poison of scorpions and also as a healing wash for wounds. This pretty traditional European flower is better known as a wild flower, which nearly became extinct in the U.K. due to the introduction of chemical weed controls in farming.

companion planting

The blue flowers reputedly attract pollinating insects more than other colors, which is beneficial for increasing yield in the vegetable garden.

container growing

They can be grown in large containers using a soil-based potting compost. They look stunning on their own, or mixed with other tall wild flowers like oxeye daisies or poppies. When growing in a container it is worth tying some dark green sewing thread around the established plants to hold them in place and to minimize the damage from high winds or heavy rain.

culinary

The petals of the flowers are edible; they look lovely scattered over green salads or over cold rice dishes.

medicinal

The flower is the part used medicinally; it is considered a tonic and stimulant. The famous French eyewash Eau de Casselunettes was traditionally made from the distilled flowers because of their eye-brightening properties.

other uses

The juice extracted from the petals makes a good blue ink which, when mixed with alum-water, can be used in watercolor paintings. It also makes a very good fabric dye. The dried flowers make up for their lack of scent by looking striking in arrangements or when added to potpourri.

varieties

Centaurea cyanus
Cornflower
Hardy annual. Ht. 12–32 in., spread 6 in. Stunning single and double blue, daisy-like flowers in summer. Lanced-shaped, gray-green leaves. The lower leaves are often toothed and covered in fine cotton. There are hybrids with pink, white or purple flowers. All zones.

cultivation

Propagation
Seed
In early spring sow seeds into prepared module plug trays using standard seed compost. Place the tray in a warm position; extra bottom heat is not required. Germination takes 14–21 days. Be careful not to overwater as the seedlings are prone to damping off. Pot or plant when all threat of frost has passed. Alternatively, for the best results, sow in spring where you want the plant to grow and when the air temperature does not go below 50°F (10°C) at night.

Pests and Diseases
Rarely suffers from pests or diseases.

Maintenance
Spring Sow seeds.
Summer Pick flowers for display and drying.
Fall Harvest seeds.
Winter Prepare garden for next season's sowing.

Garden Cultivation
Plant in a well-drained soil in a sunny position. If you wish to create a meadow effect, in the fall prior to sowing, prepare the ground well by clearing all the grass and weeds in a 12 in. square area for each plant. Sow 15 seeds per patch, thinning to preferably 2 plants. In the fall, allow the plants to die back and self-seed naturally.

Harvesting
For use in the kitchen or for drying, pick the flowers in summer when they are just half open, before the center stems are visible. When drying tie into small bunches of about 10 flowers per bunch and dry fast, otherwise the color will fade and the heads will start to crumble.

Centaurea cyanus

Centranthus ruber
RED VALERIAN

Also known as American Lilac, Bloody butcher, Bouncing Bess and Bouncing Betsy. From the family Valerianaceae.

A native of central and southern Europe, cultivated widely in temperate climates and has now become widely naturalized. This cheerful plant was a great ornament in Gerard's garden, but he described it in 1597 as "not common in England." However, by the early 18th century it had become well known.

butterflies. As an ornamental, it thrives in poor, well-drained, low fertile soil, especially on limestone. It likes a sunny position and self-seeds prolifically.

 ## container growing

Make sure the container is large enough and use a soil-based compost. No need to feed, otherwise you will inhibit its flowers. Position the container in a sunny spot and water regularly.

 ## culinary

Very young leaves are eaten in France and Italy. They are incredibly bitter.

 ## medicinal

A drug is obtained (by herbalists only) from the root, which looks like a huge radish and has a characteristic odor. It is believed to be helpful in cases of hysteria and nervous disorders because of its sedative and anti-spasmodic properties.

 ## warning

Large doses or extended use may produce symptoms of poisoning. Do not take for more than a couple of days at a time, without seeking medicinal advice.

 ## varieties

Centranthus ruber
Red Valerian
Perennial. Ht. 2–3 ft., spread 18–24 in. Showy red fragrant flowers in summer. They can also appear in all shades of white and pink. Fleshy, pale green, pointed leaves. Zone 5.

cultivation

Propagation
Seed
Sow the small seeds in early fall in seed or plug module trays, using a standard seed compost mixed in equal parts with composted fine bark. Cover lightly with compost and leave outside over winter, covered with glass. As soon as you notice it germinating, remove the glass and place in a cold greenhouse. Prick the seedlings out when large enough to handle and pot using the same mix of compost. Leave the pots outside for the summer, maintain watering until the fall. No need to feed. Plant 2 ft. apart.

Pests and Diseases
This plant does not suffer from pests or diseases.

Maintenance
Spring Dig up self-sown seedlings and replant if you want them.
Summer Deadhead to prevent self-seeding.
Fall Sow seeds. Plant previous year's seedlings.
Winter A very hardy plant.

Garden Cultivation
Red valerian has naturalized on banks, crumbly walls, rocks and along coastal regions. It is very attractive to

Centranthus ruber

CHAMOMILE

Chamaemelum nobile

From the family Asteraceae.

"I am sorry to say that Peter was not very well during the evening. His mother put him to bed and made some chamomile tea and she gave a dose of it to Peter, one tablespoon full to be taken at bedtime."–The Tale of Peter Rabbit by Beatrix Potter

Chamomile grows wild in Europe, North America, and many other countries. As a garden escapee, it can be found in pasture and other grassy places on sandy soils.

The generic name, *Chamaemelum*, is derived from the Greek *khamaimelon*, meaning "earth apple" or "apple on the ground."

summer. Finely serrated aromatic foliage. The main use of this chamomile is medicinal. All zones.

 cultivation

Propagation

Seed
Dyers, Roman and German chamomiles can be grown from seed. In spring, sow onto the surface of a prepared seed or plug tray. Use a standard seed compost mixed in equal parts with composted fine bark. Cover with perlite. Use bottom heat 65°F (19°C). Harden off and plant or pot.

Cuttings
Double-flowered chamomile and chamomile Treneague can only be propagated by cuttings and division. Take cuttings in the spring and fall from the offsets or clusters of young shoots. They are easy to grow as they have aerial roots.

Division
All perennial chamomiles planted as specimen plants will benefit from being lifted in the spring of their second or third year and divided.

Pests and Diseases
As all the chamomiles are highly aromatic they are not troubled by pests or diseases.

 varieties

Chamaemelum nobile
Roman Chamomile
Also known as garden chamomile, ground apple, low chamomile and whig plant. Hardy perennial evergreen. Ht. 4 in., spread 18 in. White flowers with yellow centers all summer. Sweet smelling, finely divided foliage. Ideal for groundcover. Can be used as a lawn, but because it flowers it will need constant cutting. Zone 4.

Chamaemelum nobile 'Flore Pleno'
Double-flowered Chamomile
Hardy perennial evergreen. Ht. 3in., spread 12 in. Double white flowers all summer. Sweet-smelling, finely divided, thick foliage. Good for groundcover, in between paving stones and lawns. More compact habit than Roman chamomile, and combines well with chamomile Treneague. Zone 4.

Chamaemelum nobile 'Treneague'
(Athemis nobile 'Treneague')
Chamomile Treneague
Also known as lawn chamomile. Hardy perennial evergreen. Ht. 2¹/₂ in., spread 6 in. Non-flowering. Leaves are finely divided and very aromatic. Ideal for groundcover or mow-free lawn. Plant in well-drained soil, free from stones, 4–6 in. apart. Zone 4.

Anthemis tinctoria
Dyers Chamomile
Also known as yellow chamomile. Hardy perennial evergreen. Ht. and spread 3 ft. Yellow daisy flowers in the summer. Leaves are mid-green and fern like. Principally a dye plant. Zone 4.

Matricaria recutita
German Chamomile
Also known as scented mayweed, wild chamomile. Hardy annual. Ht. 24 in., spread 4 in. Scented white flowers with conical yellow centers from spring to early

Chamaemelum nobile 'Flore Pleno'

CHAMOMILE

Maintenance

Spring Collect offshoots, sow seeds. Fill in holes that have appeared in the chamomile lawn. Divide established plants. Give a liquid fertilizer feed to all established plants.

Summer Water well. Do not allow to dry out. In the first season of a lawn, trim the plants to encourage bushing out and spreading. In late summer collect flowers from the dyers chamomile and cut the plant back to 2¹/₂ in. to promote new growth.

Fall Take cuttings. Divide if they have become too invasive. Cut back to promote new growth. Give the final feed of the season.

Winter Only protect in extreme weather.

Garden Cultivation

All the chamomiles prefer a well-drained soil and a sunny situation, although they will adapt to most growing conditions.

As a lawn plant, chamomile gets more credit than it deserves. Chamomile lawns are infinitely less easy to maintain in good condition than grass lawns. There is no selective herbicide that will preserve chamomile and kill the rest of the weeds. It is a hands-and-knees job with no short-cuts.

Prepare the site well, make sure the soil is light, slightly acid, and free from weeds and stones. Plant young plants in plug form. I use a mix of double-flowered and Treneague chamomile at a distance of 4–6 in. apart. Keep all traffic off it for at least 12 weeks, and keep it to the minimum during the whole of the first year.

If all this seems daunting, compromise and plant a chamomile seat. Prepare the soil in the same way and do not sit on the seat for at least 12 weeks. Then sit down, smell the sweet aroma and sip a cool glass of wine. Summer is on hand...

Harvesting

Leaves
Gather in spring and early summer for best results. Use fresh or dry.

Flowers
Pick when fully open, around midsummer. Use fresh or dry. Dyers chamomile flowers should be harvested in summer for their yellow dye.

 ## companion planting

Chamomile is said to be the plants' physician because when it is planted near ailing plants, it apparently helps them to revive. Roman Chamomile, when planted next to onions, is said to repel flying insects and improve the crop yield.

Traditional Chamomile Infusion

Bring 2 cups water to the boil. Add a handful of chamomile leaves and flowers. Cover and let it stand for half a day. This infusion was traditionally used as a spray to prevent dampening off. It was also added to the compost heap as an activator to accelerate decomposition.

 ## container growing

I would not advise growing chamomiles indoors, as they get very leggy, soft and prone to disease. But the flowers can look very cheerful in a sunny window box. Use chamomile 'Flore Pleno,' which has a lovely double flower head, or the nonflowering chamomile Treneague as an infill between bulbs, with a standard potting compost mixed in equal parts with composted fine bark.

 ## cosmetic

Chamomile is used as a final rinse for fair hair to make it brighter. Pour 3¹/₂ cups boiling water over one handful of chamomile flowers and steep for 30 minutes. Strain, cover and allow to cool. It should be poured over your hair several times.

 ## medicinal

German chamomile's highly scented dry flower heads contain up to 1 percent of an aromatic oil that possesses powerful antiseptic and anti-inflammatory properties. Taken as a tea, it promotes gastric secretions and improves the appetite, while an infusion of the same strength can be used as an internal antiseptic. It may also be used as a douche or gargle for mouth ulcers and as an eye wash.

An oil for skin rashes or allergies can be made by tightly packing flower heads into a preserving jar,

Chamomile tea

covering with olive oil and leaving in the sun for three weeks. If you suffer from overwrought nerves, add five or six drops of chamomile oil to the bath and this will help you relax at night.

Chamomile Tea

1 heaped teaspoon chamomile flowers (dried or fresh)
1 teaspoon honey
Slice of lemon (optional)

Put the chamomile flowers into a warm cup. Pour on boiling water. Cover and leave to infuse for 3–5 minutes. Strain and add the honey and lemon, if required. Can be drunk either hot or cold.

 ## other uses

Dyers chamomile can be used as a dye plant. Depending on the mordant, its color can vary from bright to olive/brown yellow (see pages 288–289).

German and double-flowered chamomile are best for herb pillows and potpourri.

 ## warning

When taken internally, excessive dosage can produce vomiting and vertigo.

Chenopodium bonus-henricus

GOOD KING HENRY

Also known as All good, Good King Harry, Good neighbor, Wild spinach, Lincolnshire asparagus and Mercury. From the family Chenopodiaceae.

Good King Henry comes from a genus *(Chenopodium)* that is distributed all over the world and is found growing in all climates. This species *(C. bonus-henricus)* is native to Europe.

Good King Henry was popular from Neolithic times until the 19th century. Its curious name is not taken from the English king, Henry VIII, as might be expected, but from King Henry IV of Navarre, and to distinguish it from the poisonous Bad Henry *(Mercurialis perennis)*.

Gerard in the 16th century observed that Good King Henry grew in untilled places and among rubbish near common ways, old walls, hedges and fields, and it still does—colonies of the herb can be found on many medieval sites.

 varieties

Chenopodiaceae, the goosefoot family, includes 1,500 rather unattractive plants, some of them important edible plants, for example, spinach and beet.

Chenopodium bonus-henricus
Good King Henry
Perennial. Ht. 24 in., spread 18 in. Tiny greenish-yellow flowers in early summer. Leaves green and arrow-shaped. Very occasionally a variegated form is found; but the yellow variegation will be difficult to maintain. Zone 5.

Chenopodium album
Fat Hen
Also known as lambs' quarters, white goosefoot, common pigweed, all good and muckweed. Annual. Ht. 2–3 ft. Flowers small, greenish-white, summer to mid-fall. Green lance-shaped leaves. Its seeds have been identified at Neolithic villages in Switzerland and in the stomach of the Iron Age Tollund Man. Rich in fat and albumen, it appears to have been a food supplement for primitive man. All zones.

☠ Chenopodium ambrosioides
American Wormseed
Also known as Mexican tea, and in China as fragrant tiger bones. Annual. Ht. 2–4 ft. Small greenish flowers from late summer to late fall. Green lance-shaped leaves. This is native to tropical Central America. Introduced through Mexico, it has become naturalized as far north as New England in the United States. It was introduced into Europe in the 18th century. Mexican Tea was once included in the United States pharmacopoeia but is now restricted to American folk medicine and mainly used for its essential oil, Chenopodium oil, against roundworm and hookworm. All zones.

Warning: *Chenopodium ambrosioides* is poisonous. Use under strict supervision. It causes deafness, vertigo, paralysis, incontinence, sweating, jaundice and death.

GOOD KING HENRY

 ## cultivation

Propagation

Seeds
Sow the fairly small seeds early in spring in prepared seed or plug trays for an early crop. Use a standard seed compost mixed in equal parts with composted fine bark and cover with perlite. No extra heat required. When the seedlings are large enough to handle and after hardening off, plant in the garden 10 in. apart. Can be sown direct into prepared soil in the garden in late spring in ½ in. drills. Allow 18 in. between rows. Cover the seeds with ¼ in. soil. Germination in warm soil, 10–14 days. When large enough to handle, thin to 10 in. apart.

Division
Divide established plants in the spring. You will find even small pieces will grow.

Pests and Diseases

Does not usually suffer from these.

Maintenance

Spring Lift and divide established plants. If you wish to grow as an asparagus, blanch the shoots from early spring onward. As they emerge, earth up with soil. Divide and repot container-grown plants.
Summer Liquid feed if a second crop of leaves is desired.
Fall Cut back dying foliage and give the plant a mulch of compost.
Winter No need for protection.

Garden Cultivation

Good King Henry will tolerate any soil, but if planted in a soil rich in humus, dug deep and well drained in a sunny position, the quality and quantity of the crop will be much improved. Sow directly.

Keep well-watered in dry months. In the fall cover beds with a thin layer of manure. Beds should be renewed every 3 to 4 years.

Harvesting

Allow plants one year to develop before harvesting. From mid-spring the young shoots can provide an asparagus substitute crop. They should be cut when they are about 6 in. long. Harvest the flowering spikes as they begin to open. Later in the season gather the larger leaves as a spinach substitute as required. Freeze only when used as an ingredient in a cooked dish.

 ## container growing

Can be grown outside in a large container, in a soil-based potting compost mixed in equal parts with composted fine bark. Needs to be kept well watered throughout the summer and fed once a week to maintain a supply of leaves.

Divide each spring and repot the divisions in fresh compost.

 ## medicinal

The seeds have a gentle laxative effect, making them

suitable relief for a slightly constipated condition. A poultice (or ointment) cleanses and heals skin sores.

 ## other uses

Good King Henry is a cough remedy for sheep. The whole plant is used to fatten poultry. Seed is used commercially in the manufacture of shagreen, an artificially granulated untanned leather, often dyed green.

The whole plant of fat hen can be used as a red or golden dye (above).

⚠ warning

Sufferers of kidney complaints or rheumatism should avoid medicinal preparations containing extracts from this plant.

 ## culinary

The leaves of good King Henry and fat hen are rich in iron, calcium and vitamins B1 and C, and are particularly recommended for anemic subjects.

Like all low-growing leaves, good King Henry must be washed with great care; the slightest suspicion of grit in the finished dish will ruin the meal. Use 2 or 3 changes of water.

Eat young leaves raw in salads. Alternatively, cook in casseroles, stuffings, soups and purées and savory pies. The leaves are more nutritious than those of spinach or cabbage.

Steam flower spikes and toss in butter before serving, like broccoli.

To blanch the shoots, dip in hot water, rinse immediately in cold water. Alternatively, cut shoots 6 in. long. Steam or boil very quickly. Peel if necessary. Serve hot with melted butter, or cold with a vinaigrette.

The seed of fat hen can be ground into flour and used to make a gruel.

Cichorium intybus

CHICORY

Also known as Blue endive, Bunks, Strip for strip, Blue sailors, Succory, Wild chicory and Wild succory. From the family Asteraceae.

Chicory grows throughout Europe in fields and on the roadside. In England and Wales it settles on lime-rich soils, although it is rarely found in Scotland and Ireland. In Australia and the United States it has been naturalized and is found on roadsides and field edges.

Chicory was an important medicinal herb, vegetable and salad plant in ancient Egypt, and in Greek and Roman times. Among the many delightful folk tales about the blue flowers we hear that the flowers are the transformed eyes of a lass weeping for her lover's ship, which never returned. Another from German folklore says that a young girl who could not stop weeping for her dead lover by the side of the road was turned into a flower called wegwort (chicory).

Careful English wives grew chicory among their herbs. It was good for purging and for the bladder. It was a principle of white magic that water distilled from the round blue flowers worked against inflammation and dimness of sight.

Chicory was grown in floral clocks because of the regular opening and closing of its flowers—they open to the sun and close about five hours later—and some gardeners, who have noticed that chicory leaves always align with North, credit the herb with metaphysical significance.

Since the 17th century, dried, roasted and ground roots of chicory have been used to make a drink. Two centuries later, Dickens described in his magazine *Household Words* the extensive cultivation of chicory in England as a coffee substitute.

 varieties

Cichorium intybus
Chicory
Hardy perennial. Ht. 3 ft., spread 1 ft. Clear blue flowers from midsummer to mid-fall. Leaves mid-green, hairy underneath, and coarsely toothed. Zone 3.

Among the many varieties of chicory are

'Magdeburg' or 'Brunswick'
The best for producing roots which can be used as a coffee substitute.

'Pain de Sucre' (Sugar Loaf)
Looks like lettuce and can be used in the same way. Does not require blanching.

'Red Verona'
Crimson red foliage, good in salads.

'Witloof' (Brussels chicory)
This is the one grown for the chicons (see opposite).

Cichorium intybus

CHICORY

 cultivation

Propagation

Seeds

Sow the small seed thinly, either in spring or late summer in prepared pots, plug module or seed trays, and cover with perlite. For rapid germination (7–10 days), sow when freshest, in late summer. Winter the young plants under cover in a cold greenhouse, or on a cold windowsill. Plant these young plants in the spring, 18 in. apart. The seed can also be sown direct into the garden in spring.

Pests and Diseases

Fairly trouble free; watch for earwigs in the chicons.

Maintenance

Spring Sow seed under protection for herb garden. Prepare site for outside sowing for chicons.
Summer Sow seeds in situ for chicons.
Fall Dig up roots for forcing, also dig up and dry for coffee. Cut back flowers of plants in herb garden.
Winter Dig in manure or compost where next year's chicon crop is to be grown.

Garden Cultivation

Grows easily. Sow in a sunny and open site with a light, preferably alkaline, soil. If you plan to harvest the roots prepare the site well, digging deeply. Thin the seedlings to 6–8 in. apart in mid- to late summer. Transplant if necessary in the spring, remembering that chicory grows fairly tall and looks well at the back of a border or against a fence, and needs to get the early morning sun as its flowers open at sunrise.

Harvesting

Roots can be dug up throughout the summer, but are usually left until the fall. Lift the root. Shorten to 8 in. Remove all side shoots and leaves, and stack in dry sand in the dark. Dry roots for use as a coffee substitute.

Gather leaves when young for fresh use. Pick before flowering for drying. Collect flowers in early summer either fresh or to dry.

Chicons

These are produced by forcing the roots in warmth and darkness, which blanches the new growth.

Prepare the soil, choosing a part of the garden that is rich in manure and well cultivated. Do not plant in recently manured land because this can cause forking in the roots.

In June sow the seeds. If you sow too early the plants may run to seed in the warm weather. Sow in ½ in. drills, 12 in. apart. Thin the seedlings. Keep the area well-watered in dry weather and weed free.

In late fall or early winter, begin carefully to dig up a few roots for forcing. Cut off the tops just above the crown. Plant the roots close together in a box of loamy soil with the crowns of the roots at soil level. Water and cover with another box. These must remain in total darkness if they are not to become bitter. Put the box where the temperature does not go below 50°F (10°C).

In 4–6 weeks the chicons will be 6–8 in. long and ready to harvest. If you break the chicons off carefully, instead of cutting, a second crop will appear. They will be smaller and looser but just as tasty.

The whole process can be repeated. When the remaining plants have died back, dig up the roots, trim, and store in sand in a frost-proof room, and force as required. One word of warning: do not pick the chicons before you need them because even after an hour in the light they will become limp.

 container growing

As chicory grows so tall it is not ideally suited to container growing.

 medicinal

Chicory, like dandelion, is a gentle but effective, bitter tonic, which increases the flow of bile. It is also a specific remedy for gall stones, and for this reason Galen called it "friend of the liver." Like dandelion it has diuretic properties and can be used for treating rheumatism and gout, because it eliminates uric acid from the body. The roots, in the form of syrup or succory, make an excellent laxative for children.

 culinary

Add young leaves and flowers to summer salads, use forced leaves as a winter salad. Toss chicons in salads, or braise in butter as a vegetable dish.

Roasted chicory roots are still widely used as an excellent substitute or adulterant for coffee. Wash, slice and dry in gentle heat . Roast and grind.

When young the root can be dug up, boiled and served with a sauce.

 other uses

Boil the leaves to produce a blue dye. Grow crop for animal fodder.

 warning

Excessive and continued use may impair the function of the retina.

Convallaria majalis

LILY OF THE VALLEY

Also known as Our Lady's Tears, Fairy's Bells, May Lily, Ladder to Heaven and May Bells. From the family Convallariaceae.

Lily of the valley is a native of Europe, North America and Canada and has been introduced throughout the world in moist cool climates.

According to European folk tales, lily of the valley either originated from the Virgin Mary's tears, shed at the foot of the Cross, or from those shed by Mary Magdalen when she found Christ's tomb.

From the Middle Ages onward the flowers form the traditional part of a bride's bouquet and are associated with modesty and purity.

In the 16th century they were used medicinally and called Convall Lily. The Elizabethan physician Gerard has this amazing recipe: "Put the flowers of May lilies into a glass and set it in a hill of ants, firmly closed for 1 month. After which you will find a liquor that when applied appeaseth the paine and grief of gout."

 varieties

💀 *Convallaria majalis*
Lily of the Valley
Hardy perennial. Ht. 6 in., spread indefinite. White, bell shaped, scented flowers, late spring to early summer. Mid-to dark green oval shaped leaves.
Zones 3–7.

💀 *Convallaria majalis* 'Flore Pleno'
Double Flowered Lily of the Valley
Hardy perennial. Ht. 9–12 in., spread indefinite. Creamy white double, bell shaped, scented flowers that are larger than the species, late spring to early summer. Mid to dark green oval shaped leaves.
Zones 3–7.

💀 *Convallaria majalis* 'Fortin's Giant'
Fortin's Giant Lily of the Valley
Hardy perennial. Ht.18 in., spread indefinite. White, larger than the species, bell shaped, scented flowers, late spring to early summer. Mid- to dark green wide oval shaped leaves. A robust growing form of the Lily of the Valley. Widely thought to be a triploid form.
Zones 3–7.

💀 *Convallaria majalis* var. *rosea*
Pink Lily of the Valley
Hardy perennial. Ht. 6 in., spread indefinite. Pale pink, bell shaped, scented flowers, late spring to early summer. Mid- to dark green oval shaped leaves.
Zones 3–7.

💀 *Convallaria majalis* 'Vic Pawlowski's Gold'
Vic Pawlowski's Gold Lily of the Valley
Hardy perennial. Ht. 6 in., spread indefinite. White, bell shaped, scented flowers, late spring to early summer. Mid- to dark green oval shaped leaves with attractive thin golden strips running the length of the leaves. This has a more consistent and better variegation than *Convallaria majalis* 'Albostriata.'
Zones 3–7.

LILY OF THE VALLEY

 ## cultivation

Propagation

Seeds
Ripe seeds are seldom formed, and the scarlet berries are highly poisonous, so better to propagate by division.

Division
The plant produces crowns on creeping rhizomes. Divide in the fall after the plant has finished flowering and the leaves have died back.

Pests and Diseases
Lily of the valley is free from most pests and diseases.

Maintenance
Spring In very early spring, bring pots into the house for forcing.
Summer Do nothing!
Fall When the plant has died back fully dig up the rhizomes for splitting. Pot crowns for forcing.
Winter No need for protection.

Garden Cultivation
Unlike its name, it should be grown not in an open valley but in partial shade. Ideal for growing under trees or in woodlands or in the shade of a fence provided there is not too much competition from other plants.

To get the best flowers, prepare the site well. The soil should be deeply cultivated with plenty of well-rotted manure, compost or leaf mold. Plant in the fall, 6 in. apart, before the frosts make the soil too hard. Place the crowns upright in the prepared holes with the tips just below the soil.

Harvesting
Pick the flowers when in full bloom for drying so that they can be added to potpourri.

 ## container growing

This plant can be happily grown in pots as long as it is kept in the shade and watered regularly. Use a loam based compost mixed in equal parts with propagating bark. Feed with liquid fertilizer only during flowering. In winter let the plant die down, and keep it in a cool place outside.

Convallaria majalis

 ## medicinal

This plant, like the foxglove, is used in the treatment of heart disease. It contains cardiac glycosides which increase the strength of the heartbeat while slowing and regularizing its rate, without putting extra demand on the coronary blood supply.

 ## culinary

None—all parts of the plant are poisonous.

 ## warning

Lily of the Valley should only be used as prescribed by a qualified practitioner and it is restricted. All parts of the plant are poisonous.

 ## other uses

The flowers of the Lily of the Valley are often used in bridal arrangements not only for their wonderful scent but also because in the language of flowers they signify a "return to happiness." I did not know this fact when I married over 30 years ago where I wore a wreath of Lily of the Valley flowers in my hair and carried them as my bouquet.

An essential oil is obtained from the flowers and used in the perfumery industry.

The leaves can be used to make a natural dye. The young leaves in spring will give a green dye and the mature fall leaves will give a yellowish brown dye.

Lily of the Valley soap and cream

Coriandrum sativum
CORIANDER

Also known as Chinese parsley, Yuen sai, Pak chee, Fragrant green, Dhania (seed), Dhania pattar and Dhania sabz (leaves). From the family Apiaceae.

A native of southern Europe and the Middle East, coriander was a popular herb in England up until Tudor times. Early European settlers in America included seed among the beloved items they took to the New World, as did Spaniards into Mexico.

Coriander has been cultivated for over 3,000 years. Seeds have been found in tombs from the 21st Egyptian Dynasty (1085–945 BC). The herb is mentioned in the Old Testament—"when the children of Israel were returning to their homeland from slavery in Egypt, they ate manna in the wilderness and the manna was as coriander seeds"—and it is still one of the traditional bitter herbs to be eaten at the Passover when the Jewish people remember that great journey.

Coriander was brought to Northern Europe by the Romans who, combining it with cumin and vinegar, rubbed it into meat as a preservative. The Chinese once believed it bestowed immortality and in the Middle Ages it was put in love potions as an aphrodisiac. Its name is said to be derived from *koris,* Greek for "bedbug," since the plant smells strongly of the insect.

 varieties

Coriandrum sativum
Coriander
Tender annual. Ht. 24 in. White flowers in the summer. The first and lower leaves are broad and scalloped, with a strong, strange scent. The upper leaves are finely cut and have a different and yet more pungent smell. The whole plant is edible. This variety is good for leaf production. Warmer zones.

Coriandrum sativum 'Leisure'
Tender annual. Ht. 24 in. Much as *C. sativum;* whitish flowers in summer; also suitable for leaf production. Warmer zones.

Coriandrum sativum 'Morocco'
Tender annual. Ht. 28 in. Flowers white with a slight pink tinge in summer. This variety is best for seed production. Warmer zones.

 cultivation

Propagation
Seed
Coriander is grown from seed. Thinly sow its large seed directly into the soil in shallow drills. Lightly cover with fine soil or compost, and water. Look for results after a period of between 5 and 10 days. Seed sowing may be carried out as often as required between early spring (under glass), and late fall. When large enough to handle, thin out the seedlings to leave room for growth.

Sowing into seed trays is not recommended because coriander plants do not transplant well once the tap root is established. If they get upset they bolt straight into flower, missing out the leaf production stage altogether.

If a harvest of fresh leaves is required, space the plants 2 in. apart; if of seed, 9 in. apart.

Pests and Diseases
Being a highly aromatic plant, coriander is usually free from pests. In exceptional circumstances it is attacked by greenfly. If so, do not be tempted to pressure hose the pests off, as this will destroy the leaves. Either wash off gently under the tap, and shake the plant carefully to remove excess water on the leaves, or use a liquid insecticidal soap.

culinary

The leaves and ripe seeds have two distinct flavors. The seeds are warmly aromatic, the leaves have an earthy pungency.

Coriander seeds are used regularly in garam masala (a mixture of spices) and in curries. Use ground seed in tomato chutney, ratatouille, frankfurters, curries, also in apple pies, cakes, cookies and marmalade. Add whole seeds to soups, sauces and vegetable dishes.

Add fresh lower leaves to curries, stews, salads, sauces and as a garnish. Delicious in salads, vegetables and poultry dishes. A bunch of coriander leaves with a vinaigrette dressing goes particularly well with hard boiled eggs.

Mushrooms and Coriander
Serves 2

1 lb. button mushrooms
2 tablespoons cooking oil
2 teaspoons coriander seeds
1 clove garlic
2 tablespoons tomato purée
1 cup dry white wine
Salt and pepper
Coriander leaf for garnish

Wipe mushrooms and slice in half. Put the oil, wine, coriander seeds and garlic in a large saucepan. Bring to the boil and cover and simmer for 5 minutes. Add the mushrooms and tomato purée. Cook for 5 minutes, by which time the vegetables should be tender. Remove the mushrooms and put in a serving dish. Boil the liquid again for 5 minutes and reduce it by half. Pour over the mushrooms. When cool, sprinkle with some chopped coriander leaf.

Coriandrum sativum

Maintenance
Spring Sow seeds.
Summer Sow seeds, cut leaves.
Fall Cut seed heads. Sow fall crop in mild climates. Dig up old plants.
Winter Once the seed heads have been collected, the plant should be pulled up.

Garden Cultivation
Coriander grows best in a light, well-drained soil, in semishade and a dry atmosphere. In fact it is difficult to grow in damp or humid areas and needs a good dry summer at the very least if a reasonable crop is to be obtained. However do not allow the soil to dry out because this will cause the plant to bolt.

When the plant reaches maturity and the seed sets and begins to ripen, the plant tends to loll about on its weak stem and needs staking. On ripening, the seeds develop a delightful orangey scent, and are used widely as a spice and a condiment. For this reason alone, and because the flavor of home-grown seeds is markedly superior to those raised commercially, coriander deserves a place in the garden. If you live in a mild, frost-free climate, sow in the fall for an overwinter crop; but make sure the plants are in full sunlight.

Harvesting
Pick young leaves any time. They should be 4 in. in height and bright green.

Watch seed heads carefully, as they ripen suddenly and will fall without warning. Cut the flower stems as the seed smell starts to become pleasant. Cover bunches of about 6 heads in a paper bag. Tie the top of the bag and hang upside down in a dry, warm, airy place. Leave for 10 days. The seeds should come away from the husk quite easily and be stored in an airtight container. Coriander seeds keep their flavor well.

container growing

Coriander can be grown in containers inside with diligence, but the plants produced will be weak and straggly. It is ideal for growing in large, deep pots outside, in partial shade on a patio or by a kitchen door. Fill the container with a standard potting compost mixed in equal parts with composted fine bark, water well, then sow the seeds thinly and cover lightly with compost. Once the leaves are large enough, start cropping. To maintain a supply prepare another large container and sow 20 days later. Water your containers regularly in the morning, not at night, as like many other herbs, coriander does not like having wet feet. Do no allow the compost to dry out because this will cause the plant to bolt to seed.

medicinal

Coriander is good for the digestive system, reducing flatulence, stimulating the appetite and aiding the secretion of gastric juices. It is also used to prevent gripe caused by other medication such as senna or rhubarb. Bruised seed can be applied externally as a poultice to relieve painful joints and rheumatism.

Crambe maritima
SEA KALE

Also known as Sea cabbage. From the family Brassicaceae.

Sea kale is a classic "pot herb" that was once abundant along the coastlines and was traditionally harvested from the wild. The Romans used to gather it from the wild and preserve it in wooden barrels for use during long voyages. In Victorian times the blanched forced shoots were considered a delicacy and it was widely cultivated. Only recently has it come back in favor in the kitchen garden.

 varieties

Crambe maritima
Sea Kale
Herbaceous perennial. Ht. up to 30 in., spread 24 in. Clusters of honey-scented white flowers in summer. Attractive fleshy gray-green leaves with crinkled edges. Zone 6.

 cultivation

Propagation
Seed
In the fall sow fresh seed into prepared small pots or module plug trays using a seed compost mixed in equal parts with river sand. If the seed is uncleaned, put a nick into the outer cork-like casing with a sharp knife to aid germination. Place the container in a cold frame; germination will occur in the following spring. Alternatively, in late spring, sow the cleaned flat dark brown seed direct into a well-prepared site; germination takes 24–36 days.

Cuttings
In the fall, when the leaves have died back, take root cuttings from the side shoots; these are called "thongs." Either store in sand to prevent them drying out, prior to planting in the garden in the spring, or pot using a loam-based compost mixed in equal parts with river sand. When buying "thongs" from a nursery, make sure that the crown has been marked so you know which way up to plant them.

Pests and Diseases
Cover crops with horticultural mesh in early summer to prevent them from being attacked by flea beetle. Sea kale can catch club root, so never plant it in infected beds.

Maintenance
Spring Sow cleaned seed, plant "thongs."
Summer Water regularly, do not allow the plant to dry out. Collect seeds.
Fall Take root cuttings. Sow seeds. Force plants.
Winter Protect the crowns with a thick covering of straw when temperatures go below 30°F (–1°C).

Garden cultivation
Sea kale prefers a well-drained light soil in a sunny position. Prior to planting or direct sowing in the previous fall, feed the soil well with well-rotted manure because this plant will remain in position for up to 5 years.

Forcing
In the fall cut back the old foliage of a two-year-old or older plant. Cover the crown with straw, and in addition put a layer of well-rotted manure around with the plant. From late fall until early spring place a bucket or a terracotta forcing jar over the crown. When the blanched sprouts are 3–8 in. long, cut them with a sharp knife. Stop harvesting in late spring, uncover the plant, cut back and feed well. Do not allow the plant to dry out in summer.

Harvesting
Pick new young growth in late spring; pick forced growth from the fall until spring. Pick the young flowerheads before flowering from early summer on.

 container growing

Sea kale adapts to being grown in large containers; use a loam-based compost mixed in equal parts with river sand. Do not allow the container to dry out in summer.

 culinary

Sea kale is very versatile in the kitchen. The blanched stems are delicious and in summer the young flower-heads, when in bud, can be cooked like cauliflower.

 medicinal

Sea kale is rich in vitamin C and magnesium. Traditionally a broth was made from the tender new growth in spring to help cure colds and as a tonic.

Crambe maritima leaves

Crithmum maritimum
SEA FENNEL

Also known as Samphire, Crest marine, Krítamo. From the family Apiaceae.

This native of the Atlantic, Mediterranean and Black Sea is mentioned in Shakespeare's *King Lear*, where it is referred to as that "dreadful trade" of the samphire gatherer. Rock samphire was at one time cultivated in English gardens for its seed pods and sold in London, where it was called crest marine.

 varieties

Crithmum maritimum
Sea Fennel
Hardy perennial. Ht. 12 in., spread 8 in. Flat umbels of tiny white-green flowers in summer. Aromatic, succulent sea-green, triangular leaves with long rounded linear lance-shaped segments which grow in small groups along the branch. Zone 7.

 cultivation

Propagation
Seed
In the fall, sow fresh seeds into prepared small pots or module plug trays, using a seed compost mixed in equal parts with river sand, under protection at 50ºF (10ºC). Germination takes 2–3 weeks; if there is no germination within this period, place the container in a refrigerator for 4 weeks, then return to 50ºF (10ºC). Germination should occur within 4–6 weeks. Once the seedlings are large enough, pot using a loam-based compost mixed in equal parts with horticultural grit. Winter seedlings in a frost-free environment. Plant out in the following spring.

Division
Divide established plants in spring. In the garden, dig up the whole plant, then divide. Once divided, replant into a well-prepared site. Container-raised plants can be divided gently so as not to destroy the crown, and repotted into a loam-based compost mixed in equal parts with horticultural grit.

Pests and Diseases
These plants, being aromatic, are not prone to pest damage. However in cold wet winters, when grown in soil that does not drain well, they can be prone to rot.

Maintenance
Spring Divide established plants. Pick young leaves.
Summer Pick leaves until it starts to flower.
Fall Sow fresh seeds.
Winter Protect from hard frosts below 26°F (–3°C).

Garden Cultivation
As this is a coastal plant that grows literally in the crevices between rocks, it is essential to prepare the site well, making sure it is well drained, adding extra grit if necessary. Plant in a sunny position and protect from cold winds. In winter cover the crown with straw, not mulch or compost, which would cause it to rot.

Harvesting
In early summer pick the leaves either to use fresh or to pickle.

 container growing

Sea fennel will grow happily in containers. Use a soil-based compost mixed in equal parts with grit. Place in a sheltered, sunny position.

 medicinal

This herb is very high in vitamin C; it also has digestive and purgative properties. It is under research for treating obesity and is in a number of herbal products.

 culinary

The leaves can be eaten fresh or cooked. Prior to cooking, remove any leaves that have begun to turn slimy and any hard parts of the stalk. The leaves have an aromatic salty flavor which combines well in salads or cooked in butter. They can also be used to make sauces and aromatic pickles.

 other uses

The seeds produce a fragrant oil which is widely used in modern perfumery and medicine. A number of leading manufacturers of face creams purport to having included this herb for hydrating the skin.

Curcuma longa

TURMERIC

Also known as Indian saffron, Haldi, Haridra. From the family **Zingiberaceae.**

Of all the herbs I grow, this is one of the most traditional and versatile. The exact origin of turmeric is not known. It most probably came from western India where records show it has been used for at least 2,500 years. The yellow and yellow-orange colors obtained from the roots are sacred and auspicious. It is important in Hindu and Buddhist ceremonies, being associated with fertility and prosperity, and brings good luck if applied to a bride's face and body as part of the purification ritual before a wedding. The roots may be given as a present on special occasions, such as a visit to a pregnant woman. The use of turmeric is prohibited in a house of mourning.

 varieties

Curcuma longa
Turmeric

Tropical, subtropical, herbaceous perennial. Ht. 3 ft., spread indefinite. The yellow/white flowers, with pink tinges to the tips of the petals, appear surrounded by pale green bracts in spring on a single stem. The flowers are sterile and do not produce viable seed. Aromatic, long, up to 2 ft., mid-green, oval leaves. The root is a large rhizome. Zone 9.

 cultivation

Propagation
Cuttings

A word of warning before you start taking root cuttings: wear gloves and an apron because, once the root is cut, it produces a yellow sap which will stain your fingers and can permanently stain cloth.

Unless you live in the tropics, the best source for fresh turmeric root is from Asian and Caribbean stores. However be aware that the quality can be variable. Often, after it has been air-freighted, the cold temperatures have killed the growth, alternatively it may have been treated with chemicals to inhibit sprouting. Choose a fresh, plump, juicy-looking root which has a tooth bud growing on one side. Choose a shallow container not much larger than the root; fill with a seed compost mixed in equal parts with horticultural grit. Place the root in the container with the tooth bud facing up, and cover the roots with compost making sure the tooth bud is peeping through the compost. Place the pot in a plastic bag, seal, and place in a warm place or in a propagator at 68°F (20°C). The shoots should emerge in 3–4 weeks but may take longer depending on the warmth. Once the shoots emerge, remove the plastic bag. Keep the container in a warm place, minimum temperature 64°F (18°C), but not in direct sunlight until fully established.

Only repot one size up, using a potting compost mixed in equal parts with horticultural grit when the plant looks as if it is bursting out of the container; it likes being pot bound.

Division

If you live in the tropics, or have a plant raised in a container, it can be divided in the spring. In the garden use two forks back to back to divide the rhizome. Once

Curcuma longa flower with its green bracts

divided replant into a prepared site in the garden. Pot-raised plants should be lifted from the container and excess compost removed so you can see the rhizome. Choose a section of rhizome with a growing bud; slice the root using a sharp knife. Pot the cutting into a small container which just fits the cutting using a seed compost mixed in equal parts with horticultural grit.

Pests and Diseases

Red spider mite can be an occasional problem on older plants when grown under glass; regular misting and keeping the leaves well-washed will reduce this. If it gets out of hand use an insecticidal soap spray following the manufacturer's instructions.

Maintenance

Spring Divide rhizomes.
Summer Pick leaves as required.
Fall Cut back on watering of container plants.
Winter Grow at a minimum of 64°F (18°C).

Garden Cultivation

This herb can only be grown outside in the tropics. It requires a minimum temperature of 64°F (18°C) at night. It is suitable for growing in a sunroom, heated greenhouse or a well-lit east- or west-facing window, not in direct midday sun, as this will cause leaf scorch.

Harvesting

Outside the tropics, this only produces a small amount of fresh rhizome, so is most usefully used medicinally or as a cosmetic. Harvest the rhizome in late summer/early fall. Only turmeric rhizome, when cured commercially, has the aroma and color necessary for cooking. The leaves can be used as a flavoring; pick as required throughout the growing season.

 ## container growing

Turmeric is ideal for growing in a container in cool and cold climates. However you will not be able to harvest much useful root from your plant, although you will be able to use the leaves for flavoring. Pot using a loam-based potting compost mixed in equal parts with horticultural grit. Be conservative with the container size; do not over pot, as this can cause the rhizome to rot in cool climates. In summer, place the plant in partial shade, water and liquid fertilize regularly. In dry weather plants will benefit from a daily light misting with rainwater. In the fall cut back on the watering, keeping the compost fairly dry. Keep the plant frost free at a minimum of 64°F (18°C).

 ## medicinal

Turmeric has been used medicinally for thousands of years; it is an important Ayurvedic herb used to treat inflammation, coughs and gastric disorders. It is also a very good first-aid remedy in the home; a paste can be used as a quick household antiseptic, for cuts, grazes and minor burns. It is also used as a decoction to calm the stomach and can be applied externally to remove hair and alleviate itching.

 ## other uses

Turmeric has been used as dye for centuries, it is used to color medicine, confectionery, paints, varnishes, silk and cotton.

 ## warning

If the roots are cut, the yellow sap will stain fingers or cloth indelibly.

 ## culinary

Turmeric is an essential ingredient in Indian cuisine. It is used in virtually every Indian meat, vegetable and lentil dish with the exception of greens because when cooked with green vegetables, it turns them gray and bitter. Turmeric has been known as poor-man's saffron as it offers a less expensive alternative yellow coloring. The flavor of the cured turmeric can vary, and this is dependent on how it is used. When added to oil before the main ingredient, the flavor is pungent, when added after the main ingredient it is more subtle.

The leaves have a warm rich sweet aroma and can be used fresh to wrap fish or sweets before steaming.

Cymbopogon citratus

LEMON GRASS

Also known as Fever grass, Bhustrina and Takrai. From the family Poaceae.

This important culinary and medicinal herb, which can be found throughout the tropics, is indigenous to Southeast Asia where it is used extensively to produce an essential oil. It is also a snake repellent and a versatile garden plant. There are records showing that the Persians were using it as a tea in the first century BC. I have been lucky enough to see it growing and flowering naturally in the Caribbean where they primarily use it for reducing fevers.

 varieties

Cymbopogon citratus
Lemon Grass
Half-hardy perennial, evergreen in warm climates. Ht. 4½ ft., spread 3 ft. Lax panicles of awnless spikelets appear throughout the summer. However it rarely flowers in cold climates or in cultivation. Lemon-scented linear, gray/green leaves up to 3 ft. in length. Robust cream/beige cane-like stems. Zone 9.

Cymbopogon nardus
Citronella Grass
Half-hardy perennial, evergreen in warm climates. Ht. 5 ft. and spread 3 ft. Lax panicles of awnless spikelets appear throughout the summer. However it rarely flowers in cold climates. Lemon-scented drooping, flat, blue/gray/green leaves up to 2 ft. in length. This species is cultivated for its medicinal and insect-repellent properties. It is also grown around buildings in Africa, as a snake repellent. The oil is used to perfume soaps. Zone 9.

Cymbopogon martini var. *motia*
Palmarosa, Rosha, Indian Geranium
Half-hardy perennial, evergreen in warm climates. Ht. 4½ ft. and spread 3 ft. Lax panicles of awnless spikelets appear throughout the summer. However it rarely flowers in cold climates. Rose-scented linear gray/green leaves up to 20 in. in length. The oil made from this species is used to perfume cosmetics and soap. It is also used in Ayurvedic medicine to treat fevers and infectious diseases. Zone 9.

 cultivation

Propagation
Seed
In spring, sow seeds into prepared seed or module plug trays and place under protection at 68°F (20°C). Germination takes 15–25 days. Once the seedlings are large enough, pot using a loam-based compost and grow until well established. Either plant in the garden in warm climates or, in cool climates, grow as a container plant.

Cuttings
Take cuttings, in spring, from a plant that is more than a year old, which has an established crown. Gently remove the swollen lower stems from the crown. Remove any grass from the stem and cut the stem back to 4 in. Place in a prepared module plug tray or a very small pot using a seed compost; do not be tempted to over pot the cutting as this will cause it to rot. Place under protection or in a warm position away from cold draughts. Once rooted, pot into a small pot using a loam-based compost.

Division
In the garden use two forks back to back and gently tease the plant apart, replanting immediately into a prepared site. Divide container plants either with your fingers, or two small forks, teasing the crown apart, repotting into a pot which fits snugly around the roots. This plant is happiest when pot bound. Use a loam-based potting compost.

Pests and Diseases
Outside the tropics this herb can be prone to rot and mildew. To prevent this, in winter, keep container-grown plants nearly dry and in a well-ventilated, frost-free room.

94 THE COMPLETE HERB BOOK

LEMON GRASS

Lemon grass stems

Maintenance

Spring Sow seeds. Divide or take root cuttings of established plants. Feed container-raised plants regularly.
Summer Do not allow the plants to dry out. Maintain feeding until late summer.
Fall In cool climates, to prevent disease, cut back the grass leaving the stems.
Winter Protect from frost. Keep watering to the minimum.

Garden Cultivation

Lemon grass can be grown outside where the night temperature does not fall below 48°F (8°C). Plant in any soil, including a heavy soil, as long as the summers are hot and wet and the winters are warm and dry. In low light levels the plant can become dormant. In spring, prune back all the old growth and thick stalks to 4 in.

Harvesting

The fresh leaves and lower stems can be cut throughout the summer to use fresh or to dry. The stems can be stored whole in the refrigerator in a plastic bag for up to 2 weeks. Alternatively the stems and the leaves can be frozen for use within 5 months.

 ## container growing

An excellent container plant. Use a loam-based compost which should not be allowed to dry out in summer. In winter, bring the plant into a frost-free environment of 40°F (5°C) minimum. When the light levels and night temperatures drop the plant will go "dormant," the grass gradually turns brown and the outside leaves shrivel. Reduce the watering to a minimum and cut back the grass to 4 in. above the stems. In early spring, as the day lengthens and the temperatures rise you will notice new grass starting to grow. Cut off all dead growth. repot if necessary and liquid feed weekly.

 ## medicinal

A tea made from fresh leaves is very refreshing as well as being a stomach and gut relaxant. It is also a good antidepressant and helps lift the spirits if you are in a bad mood. The essential oil is antiseptic, antibacterial, antifungal and deodorizing.

 ## other uses

Valued for its exotic citrus fragrance, it is commercially used in soaps, perfumes and as an ingredient in sachets. Also used as an insect repellent.

 ## warning

Do not take the essential oil internally without supervision.

 ## culinary

The fresh leaves and stalks have been traditionally used in Thai, Vietnamese and Caribbean cooking. The lemon flavor complements curries, seafood, garlic and chilies.

Vegetable and Lemon Grass Soup
Serves 4

2 tablespoons of light olive oil
1 large onion, finely chopped
2 cloves of garlic, finely sliced
*4 carrots, scrubbed then finely sliced or, if in a
  hurry, grated.*
²/₃ cup button mushrooms, sliced
*4–6 stems of lemon grass, cut into 1 ¹/₂ in.
  lengths and bruised*

1 tablespoon very finely chopped lemon grass leaves
1 teaspoon of ginger, finely grated
3 ¹/₂ cups chicken stock or vegetable stock
Salt to taste

Heat the oil in a heavy-bottomed saucepan, add the onions, garlic and carrots, stir-fry for 3 minutes, stirring all the time. Add the mushrooms and stir-fry for a further minute. Pour in the water, stir and add the lemon grass stems, ginger and salt to taste. Bring to the boil, then reduce the heat, cover and simmer for about 4–7 minutes until all the vegetables are cooked but still crunchy.

With a slotted spoon, remove the lemon grass stalks, add the very finely chopped lemon grass leaves, stir and serve.

CARDOON

From the family Asteraceae.

Cardoon is structurally a magnificent herb; it is indigenous in the Mediterranean and North Africa where it has been in cultivation for thousands of years as a vegetable and as a gentle laxative. The Romans considered it a prized vegetable and they took it with them as part of their wagon train as they marched through Europe and North Africa. It is currently having a lot of attention paid to it in Australia, where it has been considered as a weed. Research is on-going regarding its potential as a vegetable, winter fodder for stock, a vegetable oil (extracted from the seed) and an environmentally friendly biofuel.

 ## varieties

Cynara cardunculus
Cardoon
Perennial. Evergreen in warm climates. Ht. 6 ft., spread 4 ft. Lovely large thistle-like blue/violet flowers in summer. Thick fibrous stems, downy, silver/gray/green deeply cut leathery leaves which have a silver underside. Some forms of cardoon have very spiny leaves especially the French varieties. Zone 7.

 ## cultivation

Propagation
Seeds
The seeds are large and easy to handle. In early spring sow under protection at 65ºF (18ºC) either individually into prepared plug modules or three seeds in a 3 in. pot using a standard seed compost. Germination takes 5–10 days. Alternatively, sow seeds in late spring into prepared open ground, when the air temperature at night does not fall below 45ºF (7ºC). Germination takes 2–3 weeks.

Division
In spring or fall, using a spade, remove the suckers (side shoots) from the main stem, pot using a soil-based compost and winter in a cold frame or cold greenhouse. Plant in the spring once all threat of frost has passed.

Pests and Diseases
Slugs: I have been stunned at how quickly a gang of slugs can destroy the young shoots of this plant. This is worse in early spring especially if it is damp. Night patrol with a flashlight and hand picking the pests off the plant is the best method. Alternatively try slug traps made with beer or milk. Black fly can cause a problem especially around flower buds; spray with insecticidal soap.

Caterpillars in late summer can also strip the leaves. So, as soon as you see damage, remove the pests by hand. Powdery mildew can be a problem if the plant is in a container or growing against a wall. Remove damaged leaves, make sure that the ground or compost has not dried out, water as necessary.

Maintenance
Spring Sow seeds under cover or in late spring in the ground. Divide established plants.

The dramatic structure of a *Cynara cardunculus*

Summer Feed and water regularly, remove any damaged leaves, check for slugs.

Fall In early fall blanch leaves. Feed mature plants.

Winter In excessive cold, protect with straw or bracken.

Garden Cultivation

Plant in a sunny situation in a well-drained, deep, fertile soil, that has been well fed the previous fall with well-rotted manure. Space plants 3 ft. apart. Cardoon can become inedible when grown under hot conditions, the leaves and stalks become pithy and tough, the flower bud hard. So mulch well in early spring with either leaf mold, composted bark, or well-rotted compost and maintain a constant, uniform supply of water throughout the growing season. In the fall, when the plant has died back, feed with well-rotted manure.

To blanch the leaves, which are a culinary delight, choose a sunny day in late summer or early fall to prepare the plant for blanching. The plant, including the crown, needs to be totally dry. Tie the outer mature leaves together near the top, wearing gloves and long sleeves for protection if you have grown the spiny variety. Wrap the whole plant in sacking, straw, or paper and earth up. Do not use plastic wrap because it will make the plant sweat and rot the leaves and crown. Leave for 4–5 weeks, not longer, because this can cause rot. When blanched, cut just below the crown, trimming off excess loose foliage, leaving the trimmed blanched heart. Use as soon as possible. Once harvest is finished, protect the remaining trimmed blanched heart with straw until the new growth reappears.

Harvesting

Pick the flower buds before the bracts start to open. Pick flowers in summer, just as they open, for drying. Collect seeds in early fall as the flowers start to drop. Again, wear gloves and beware of the prickles on certain species.

Harvest the blanched stems from early winter onwards.

 ## container growing

This herb, despite its size, can be grown successfully in large containers and can look stunning. Use a soil-based compost; this will help prevent the soil from drying out in summer. Protect from the midday sun and once in flower protect from high winds. Water regularly throughout the year. Make sure, especially in summer, that the container does not dry out. Liquid feed weekly from spring until late summer.

 ## medicinal

Cardoons are a good source of potassium, calcium and iron.

A decoction made from the leaves is used as a detoxifier; it is said to help the liver regenerate and is a good stimulant for the gall bladder in exactly the same way as its cousin the dandelion (*Taraxacum officinale*).

 ## other uses

The leaves yield a good yellow woollen and cotton dye. A decoction made from the leaves can be used as a substitute for rennet in the making of cheese.

 ## culinary

The blanched leaves, ribs and stalks are used chiefly as a winter vegetable. To prepare, remove the tough outer ribs, cut the inner blanched ribs into 3 in. slices and soak in water that has either the juice of a lemon squeezed into it or a couple of tablespoons of white wine vinegar; this prevents the lovely creamy white stems browning. After soaking for 20 minutes the prepared ribs can then be either eaten raw, boiled, braised or baked depending on your recipe. Personally I love eating them raw with an olive oil, garlic and anchovy dip. This is called *bagna cauda* in Italy.

The flower buds are occasionally eaten but I consider them to be inferior to globe artichoke (*Cynara scolymus*).

Dianthus
PINKS

Dianthus gratianopolitanus

Also known as Clove pink and Gillyflower. From the family Caryophyllaceae.

Dianthus comes from the words *dios,* meaning "divine," and *anthos,* meaning "flower." Both the Romans and Greeks gave pinks a place of honor and made coronets and garlands from the flowers. In the 17th century it was recognized that the flowers could be crystallized, and the petals started being used in soups, sauces, cordials and wine.

 varieties

Dianthus deltoides
Maiden Pink
Evergreen hardy perennial. Ht. 6 in., spread 12 in. Small cerise, pink or white flowers are borne singly all summer. Small, narrow, lance-shaped, dark green leaves. Zone 5.

Dianthus gratianopolitanus
Cheddar Pink
Evergreen hardy perennial. Ht. 6 in., spread 12 in. Very fragrant pink/magenta flat flowers are borne singly all summer. Small, narrow, lance-shaped, gray/green leaves. This variety is protected in the UK. Zone 5.

Dianthus plumarius
Pinks
Evergreen hardy perennial. Ht. 6 in., spread 12 in. Very fragrant flowers, white with dark crimson centers, are borne singularly all summer. Loose mats of narrow, lance-shaped, gray/green leaves. This species is related to the Cheddar pink and the origin of the garden pink. Zone 5.

 cultivation

Propagation
Seed
Sow the small seeds when fresh in the fall into prepared seed or plug module trays using a standard seed compost, and cover with perlite. Winter seedlings in a cold frame, prior to planting out in the following spring 12 in. apart. Pinks raised from seed can be variable in height, color and habit.

Cuttings
Take stem cuttings in spring and heel cuttings in early fall. Place the cuttings into prepared plug module trays or a small pot using a seed compost mixed in equal parts with fine composted bark. Do not overwater the cuttings while they are rooting as this will cause them to rot.

Division
Established plants can be divided in early fall after flowering.

Layering
Established plants can be layered in late summer and then lifted in the following spring.

Pests and Diseases
During propagation young plants can be prone to rot; this is usually caused by fungus due to the compost being too wet. Infected plants must be removed as soon as this is spotted as it can spread to other plants very quickly. Aphids can be a problem; spray with insecticidal soap.

Maintenance
Spring Lift layers. Take stem cuttings.
Summer Deadhead flowers.
Fall Take heel cuttings. Divide established plants. Sow seed. Layer established plants.
Winter No need for protection.

Garden Cultivation
Pinks prefer to be planted in a well-drained soil, which does not become waterlogged in winter, and in full sun.

Harvesting
Pick the flowers just as they open for either using the petals fresh or for crystallizing.

 container growing

Pinks grow well in containers. Use a soil-based compost mixed with 25 percent composted fine bark and 25 percent fine horticultural grit.

 culinary

Before eating the petals, they must be removed individually from the flower. You will notice that each petal has a white heel (see below); this must also be removed as it is very bitter. The prepared petals can be added to salads, sandwiches, and fruit pies. They can be used to flavor jams, sugars and syrups. The crystallized petals can be used to decorate cakes and desserts.

 medicinal

An excellent nerve tonic can be made from the petals, either as a cordial or infused in white wine.

 other uses

Add dried petals to potpourri, scented sachets and cosmetic products.

Dianthus flowers, showing the bitter-tasting white heel

FOXGLOVE

Digitalis purpurea

Also know as Fairy fingers, Fairy gloves and Deadmen's bells. From the family Scrophulariaceae.

Foxgloves are a common wild flower in temperate climates throughout the world, seeding freely in woods and the countryside. The principal common name is probably derived from the Anglo-Saxon *foxglue* or *foxmusic* after the shape of a musical instrument. In 1542 Fuchs called it Digitalis after the finger-like shape of its flowers, but he considered it a violent medicine. It was not until the late 18th century, after William Withering used foxglove tea in Shropshire as an aid for dropsy, that its reputation as a medicinal herb grew.

Digitalis purpurea f. *albiflora*

 ## varieties

☠ ***Digitalis purpurea***
Foxglove, wild, common
Short lived perennial, grown as a biennial. Ht. 3–5 ft., spread 2 ft. Flowers all shades of pink, purple and red in second summer. Rough, mid- to dark green leaves. Zone 4.

☠ ***Digitalis purpurea* f. *albiflora***
White Foxglove
Short-lived perennial, grown as a biennial. Ht. 3–5 ft., spread 2 ft. Tubular white flowers all summer in the second season. Rough, mid-to dark green leaves. Zone 4.

 ## cultivation

Propagation
Seed
For the best germination, sow the very fine seeds in the fall, using the cardboard method (see page 265), either directly onto the prepared ground, or into pots or plug module trays, which have been filled with a standard seed compost. Sow on the surface and do not cover the seeds with compost. Place the container in a cold frame, cold greenhouse or under the eaves of the house. Winter the seedlings in the containers, only protecting if temperatures fall below 14°F (−10°C). In the following spring either prick out or plant in the garden 18 in. apart. They will flower in the second season.

Pests and Diseases
Foxgloves rarely suffer from pests or diseases.

Maintenance
Spring Thin seedlings from fall sowing.
Summer If self-seeding is not required, remove flowering spikes after flowering.
Fall Sow fresh seeds. Dig up self-sown seedlings for potting or replanting.
Winter No need for protection.

Garden Cultivation
This is one of the most poisonous plants in the flora, so choose its position with care. Foxgloves will grow in most conditions, even dry exposed sites, but do best in semishade and a moist but well-drained acid soil enriched with leaf mold. Water well in dry weather and remove the center spike after flowering to increase the size of the flowers on the side shoots.

Harvesting
Do not harvest unless you are a trained herbalist or pharmacist.

 ## container growing

Foxgloves are not ideally suited for growing in containers mainly because of their flowering spike, which can be damaged in high winds. If you do wish to grow them in a container use a soil-based compost and water regularly throughout the summer months.

 ## medicinal

Foxgloves are grown commercially for the production of a drug, the discovery of which is a classic example of a productive marriage between folklore and scientific curiosity. Foxgloves contain glycosides which are extracted from the second-year leaves to make the heart drug digitalis. For more than 200 years digitalis has provided the main drug for treating heart failure. It is also a powerful diuretic.

 ## warning

The whole plant is poisonous; seeds, leaves and roots. Even touching the plant can cause rashes, headaches and nausea. DO NOT USE without medical direction.

ECHINACEA

Also known as Coneflower, Purple coneflower and Black Sampson. From the family Asteraceae.

Echinacea is a herb that has been used by the Native American Indians for hundreds of years for everything from snake bites and wounds to respiratory infections. Its generic name *Echinacea* comes from the Greek *echinos*, "hedgehog," referring to the central golden cone, which becomes more pointed and prickly as the flower matures. It is only in the past decade that modern research has confirmed its medicinal properties; however there is still some argument over its validity. Despite this, it remains in much demand. This has had a major impact on the wild species, which has now become endangered due to over collection.

Echinacea purpurea

 varieties

Echinacea angustifolia

Narrow-leafed Purple Coneflower, Black Sampson
Hardy herbaceous perennial. Ht. 2 ft., spread 12 in.
Single flowers with long, thin, purple or, rarely, white petals and a spiky central cone, borne throughout the summer until early fall. Mid-green linear leaves. In its natural habitat this echinacea has become an endangered species. The Native American Indians regarded this herb as a cure all. Zone 4.

Echinacea pallida

Echinacea, Pale Coneflower
Hardy herbaceous perennial. Ht. 32 in., spread 18 in.
Single flowers with long mauve/pink, narrow, drooping petals and a spiky central cone, throughout the summer until early fall. The leaves are oval, narrow, dark green and veined. Zone 4.

Echinacea purpurea

Echinacea, Purple Coneflower
Hardy herbaceous perennial. Ht. 4 ft., spread 18 in.
Single honey-scented flowers with long mauve/pink, narrow, drooping petals and a spiky central cone,

Echinacea pallida

throughout the summer until early fall. The leaves are oval, narrow, dark green and deeply veined. This species is cultivated for its medicinal properties. Zone 3.

 ## cultivation

Propagation

Seed

Sow seeds in early spring into prepared seed trays, plug modules or a small container using a seed compost mixed in equal parts with perlite. Cover the seeds with perlite. Place in a warm position or in a propagator at 65°F (18°C). If no germination has occurred after 28 days, place the container outside for a further 21 days, then place back under cover, out of direct sunlight. Germination should then occur within the next 20 days. Once the seedlings are large enough, pot into a loam-based compost mixed in equal parts with composted fine bark. Once rooted, harden off, plant into a prepared site in the garden 12 in. apart.

Division

Divide established plants in the late fall when all the foliage has died back and the plant is dormant. Use the two forks back to back method. Replant immediately either into a prepared site in the garden, or alternatively, pot using a loam-based potting compost mixed in equal parts with composted fine bark. Container-raised plants can also be divided at this time of year.

Pests and Diseases

Echinacea, in general, is not prone to pests and diseases. In spring, young plants can be attacked by slugs and snails, so it is worth doing a couple of night patrols with a flashlight to remove any that you may find in the crown of the plant. In a damp, warm, late summer it can suffer from powdery mildew; if this happens cut off any affected parts, bin them and do not add to the compost.

Maintenance

Spring Sow seeds. Feed established plants lightly with well-rotted manure.
Summer Cut back stems as the blooms fade to encourage further flower production.
Fall Divide established plants.
Winter No need for protection from the cold, only from excessive wet.

Echinacea purpurea

Garden Cultivation

Echinacea grows wild on the fertile plains of North America, so, to keep it thriving in the garden, plant in a fertile loam soil which is free draining and in plenty of sun. It will adapt to most soils with the exception of excessive wet conditions and cold wet clay soils, which can cause the roots to rot. After flowering, cut back the plants, leaving 3 in. of growth above ground, collect the seeds and keep the flower heads for drying. Lightly mulch established plants with well-rotted manure in the spring. Spring growth and young echinacea plants are a snail delicacy, so it is worth checking around the plants daily in spring.

Harvesting

Pick the flowers and leaves during flowering before the cone is fully formed and the petals have started to fall back. When the petals have died back pick the seeds heads, dry well. If you wish to use the plant medicinally, dig up the roots of 4-year-old plants of *Echinacea angustifolia*, or *E. purpurea*, or *E. pallida* in the fall for drying and for making fresh tinctures.

 ## container growing

Echinacea adapts happily to being grown in containers. Use a loam-based potting compost mixed in equal parts with composted fine bark. Divide pot-bound plants in the fall, or replant in a pot one size up. Place in full sun for the growing season. Feed regularly with a liquid fertilizer following the manufacturer's instructions. In winter, if you live in a damp, wet, cold climate, place the container under the eaves of the house, or by a wall, to shelter it from the rain.

 ## medicinal

Echinacea has the ability to raise the body's resistance to infections by stimulating the immune system. It is reputedly very effective in preventing colds and flu or reducing their severity. A tincture made from the root is used to treat severe infections, and a decoction made from the root can be used as a gargle to treat sore throats and other throat infections. A decoction, or the juice extracted from the flowers, can be used externally to treat minor wounds, burns, boils and skin infections, including chilblains.

 ## other uses

The cone part of the flower head dries very well and looks most attractive in floral arrangements.

warning

If you are allergic to plants in the Asteraceae family, for example chrysanthemums, marigolds or daisies, then you could be allergic to echinacea.

People who are suffering from progressive systemic autoimmune disorders should not take this herb without full consultation.

Dried roots and flowers

Echium vulgare

VIPER'S BUGLOSS

Also known as Bugles, Wild borage, Snake flower, Blue devil, Blueweed, Viper's grass and Snakeflower. From the family Boraginaceae.

This plant originates from the Mediterranean region and is now widespread throughout the northern hemisphere, being found on light porous stones on semidry grassland, moorlands, and waste ground. It is regarded as a weed in some parts of America. To many farmers this will seem an understatement; they consider it a plague.

The common name, Viper's Bugloss, developed from the medieval Doctrine of Signatures, which ordained that a plant's use should be inferred from its appearance. It was noticed that the brown stem looked rather like a snake skin and that the seed is shaped like a viper's head. So, in their wisdom, they prescribed it for viper bites, which for once proved right; it had some success in the treatment of the spotted viper's bite.

 ## varieties

Echium vulgare
Viper's Bugloss
Hardy biennial. Ht. 2–4 ft. Bright blue/pink flowers in the second year. The leaves are mid-green and bristly. All zones.

 ## cultivation

Propagation
Seed
Viper's Bugloss is easily grown from seed. Start it off in a controlled way in spring by sowing the small seed into a prepared seed or plug module tray. Cover the seed with perlite. When the seedlings are large enough to handle, and after a period of hardening off, plant into a prepared site in the garden at 18 in. apart.

Pests and Diseases
It rarely suffers.

Maintenance
Spring First year, sow seeds; second year, clear around plants.
Summer Second year, pick off flowers as they die so that they cannot set seed.
Fall First year, leave well alone. Second year, dig up

plants and bin. Do not compost unless you want thousands of viper's bugloss plants all over your garden. *Winter* No need to protect first-year plant.

Garden Cultivation
This colorful plant is beautifully marked. Sow the seed in spring directly into the garden. It will grow in any soil and is great for growing in dry soils and on sea cliffs. With its long tap root, the plant will survive any drought but cannot easily be transplanted except when very young. The disadvantage is that it self-seeds and is therefore invasive.

Harvesting
Gather flowers in summer for fresh use.

 ## container growing

Because it is a rampant self-seeder, it is quite a good idea to grow it in containers. For the first year it bears only green prickly leaves and is very boring. However, the show put on in the second year is full compensation. Use a soil-based compost; no need to feed. Over-feeding will prohibit the flowering. Very tolerant of drought; nevertheless do water it regularly. Dies back in winter of first year—leave the container somewhere cool and water occasionally.

 ## culinary

The young leaves are similar to borage, but they have lot more spikes. It is said you can eat them when young, but I haven't tried this. The flowers look very attractive in salads. They can also be crystallized.

 ## medicinal

The fresh flowering tips can be chopped up for making poultices for treating whitlows and boils. Infuse lower leaves to produce a sweating in fevers or to relieve headaches.

Echium vulgare

Eruca vesicaria subsp. *sativa*
SALAD ROCKET

Also known as Rocquette. From the family Brassicaceae.

This native of the Mediterranean has only recently found its way back into the herb garden after an absence of a few hundred years. An annual salad plant with pungent tasting leaves, it is used a great deal in Southern France and Italy. It has been in continuous cultivation since the time of the Romans, who prized the flavor of its leaves and seeds. In England the Elizabethans were extremely partial to it. Some fascinating past uses suggest that it should be taken before a whipping to alleviate the pain, and used as protection against bites of the shrew mouse and other venomous beasts.

 container growing

Salad rocket is not really suitable for growing in containers, but it is possible. Sow in spring directly into a pot or a window box. Use a standard potting compost mixed in equal parts with composted fine bark. Water and pick regularly. Do not use liquid fertilizer, as this makes the leaves too lush and bereft of flavor.

 medicinal

At one time used medicinally in cough syrup.

 culinary

Add the leaves and flowers to all forms of salad. The younger leaves have a milder taste than the older ones, which have a definite peppery flavor. Leaves can also be added to sauces and to other vegetable dishes, either raw or steamed. This herb is one of many leaves included in the Provençal salad mixture called mesclun.

 varieties

Eruca vesicaria subsp. sativa
Salad Rocket
Half-hardy annual. Ht. 2–3 ft. The flowers are yellowish at first, then in the summer they become whiter with purple veins. The oval lanced-shaped leaves have a nutty flavor. All zones.

 cultivation

Propagation
Seed
This herb is better grown direct into the garden. In cool climates, sow in spring after the last frost, then sow in monthly successions to ensure a fresh supply of leaves. In warm climates, sow in the fall—this will ensure a supply of leaves in winter. Sow seeds in prepared rows in rich moist soil and a lightly shaded position. Thin the seedlings to 8 in. apart.

Pests and Diseases
Tiny round holes in the leaves is the flea beetle. Prevent this by covering the crop with a frost cloth from mid-spring until midsummer.

Maintenance
Spring Sow seeds.
Summer Pick like mad to prevent flowering.
Fall In mild climates sow seeds for winter salads.
Winter In cooler climates use a frost cloth for protection.

Garden Cultivation
In high summer or hot climates it will run to flower very quickly so choose a site that has some protection from the midday sun. If you have a light soil, mulch well prior to sowing to help the soil retain moisture.

Harvesting
The leaves can be harvested within 6–8 weeks of the spring and early fall sowings. The flowers can be harvested as soon as they appear. They have a wonderful nutty, sweet, peppery flavor.

Elettaria cardamomum

CARDAMOM

Also known as Ela, Ilaichi. From the family Zingiberaceae.

Cardamom is indigenous to southern India where it grows abundantly under the forest canopy. Until the 19th century, the world's supply of cardamom came mainly from the wild, in an area known as the Cardamom Hills in Western Ghat, India. The fruits have been traded in India for at least 1,000 years. It was known as the Queen of Spices, with black pepper being the King. Cardamom is the third most expensive spice after saffron and vanilla. It is traded internationally in the form of whole fruits, and to a lesser extent as seeds. Early Arabs enjoyed cardamom seeds in their coffee, a practice which continues today, and which explains why cardamoms are mentioned so often in Sir Richard Burton's translation of *The Arabian Nights*. In India it is common practice to offer cardamoms at the end of a meal, as a digestive and for freshening the breath.

 varieties

Elettaria cardamomum

Cardamom

Tropical, subtropical, evergreen perennial. Ht. 9 ft., spread indefinite. In summer the flowers grow on a single stem. They are creamy white, with deep purple lines over the lower lip. They are followed by pale green to fawn fruits, each having three chambers, containing several small aromatic seeds which start white and ripen to black. Aromatic, up to 2 ft. long, mid-green, lance-shaped leaves. The root is a thick branching rhizome. Zone 8.

 cultivation

Propagation

Seed

Outside the tropics it is very difficult to get fresh seed, which remains viable for only 7–10 days once harvested; therefore it is far easier to propagate by division. If you can get fresh seed, sow in the fall into prepared plug modules, using a seed compost. Place in a warm place or propagator at 75°F (24°C). Germination takes 14–21 days. Plants raised from seed take 3–5 years to flower.

Division

Divide established plants in late spring, early summer. Replant into a prepared site in a tropical garden or tropical greenhouse. Alternatively, if dividing a potted plant, replant using a loam-based potting compost mixed equally with composted fine bark. Plants in the tropics that have been divided take 3 years to flower; however, it rarely flowers outside the tropics, even when raised in a tropical house, due to the light levels.

Pests and Diseases

Red spider mite can be an occasional problem in older plants; regular misting with soft rain water and keeping the leaves well-washed will reduce this. If it gets out of hand use an insecticidal soap spray following the manufacturer's instructions.

If plants are too cold their leaves turn brown. If the leaves develop brown tips at any time (even if the plant is kept warm) it is a sign of overwatering. If the leaf develops creamy patches, this can be caused by too much sun and is a form of scorch.

Maintenance

Spring Divide established plants or pot plants.
Summer Spray leaves with rain water.
Fall Sow fresh seeds.
Winter Protect from cold weather.

Cardamom fruits and the smaller seeds contained within them

CARDAMOM

Garden Cultivation

When grown outdoors in the tropics, it is grown in the shade of the trees, in a deep fertile soil. It needs a minimum annual rainfall of 60 in., and a short dry season. It takes 3 years before the plant will flower and set seed.

In the northern hemisphere it is best grown as a potted plant indoors or in a heated greenhouse, even in hot summers, as it needs a minimum temperature of 64°F (18°C).

Harvesting

In tropical climates the fruit is harvested by hand from the third year onward. In cool climates pick fresh leaves for use as required.

 ## container growing

Cardamom can only be grown indoors in climates outside the tropics and subtropics. It will not flower, although you can use the leaves for flavoring. Grow your plant in loam-based potting compost mixed in equal parts with composted fine bark. Cardamoms can be fussy: they do not like draughts, sudden changes of temperature or direct sunlight. Grow them in a warm, steamy, shady place, like a warm bathroom and mist the plant daily with rainwater. Alternatively, stand the pot on a big saucer of pebbles which are kept moist, to encourage a humid atmosphere around the plant. In winter, keep the plant warm at a minimum of 20°C (68°F) and cut back on the watering, but do not allow the plant to dry out. Regularly liquid feed during the growing season with a general purpose foliage fertilizer following the manufacturer's instructions.

 ## medicinal

The medicinal properties of cardamom are found in the seeds, which have pain-relieving, anti-inflammatory, and antispasmodic properties that are often used to treat urine retention and stomach disorders. In Ayurvedic medicine it is often used to improve the flavor and quality of medicine and as an expectorant.

Seeds extracted from the pod, chewed after a meal, freshen the breath and aid digestion

 ## other uses

Cardamom oil made from the seeds is used in cosmetics, soaps, lotions and perfumes.

 ## culinary

In India and throughout South Asia the cardamom fruit is used not only in savory dishes, where it is an essential ingredient in garam masala, but also in sweets where it is often combined with rose water and thickened milk. The bright lime green pods are the best culinary variety and the true cardamom. There are brown pods that are confusingly also called cardamom, but these come from a plant called *Amomum subulatum*, and they are used in savory dishes, especially rice dishes.

The leaves don't smell the same as the seeds; they have a warm sweet aromatic scent and can be used to wrap around fish, rice or vegetables to add flavor during cooking. The long stalks are useful to tie the leaves together to make a neat parcel. When used with fish they keep it beautifully moist.

Garam Masala

There are many versions of Garam masala, some are spicy, some are hot; here is a fragrant version that is good with chicken and vegetables.

2 teaspoons cardamom seeds (removed from pods)
1 teaspoon cumin seeds
1 teaspoon whole black peppercorns
2 x 2 in. cinnamon sticks
1/2 teaspoon whole cloves
1/4 nutmeg seed, grated, or to taste

Heat a small frying pan and add each spice individually with the exception of the nutmeg. As each one starts to smell fragrant, remove it from the pan onto a plate and allow to cool . Put all the cooled spices into a pestle and mortar or an electirc blender, and grind to a fine powder. Add the finely grated nutmeg. Store in a glass jar with an airtight lid in a dark cupboard. Use within 4 weeks.

Eriocephalus africanus

SOUTH AFRICAN WILD ROSEMARY

Also known as Wild rosemary, Snowbush, Kapokbos. From the family Asteraceae.

This amazing drought-loving plant, which is well known in the Cape of South Africa, has a special place in my herb farm because, while the majority of my herbs are becoming dormant in winter, it goes into full flower, which lifts everyone's spirits during the short gray days of the winter months. These flowers are followed by the most attractive seedheads, which are covered in white tufts, hence its Afrikaans name Kapokbos, which is derived from Kapok, meaning "snow." I had been growing this herb for a number of years before realizing its full potential as a medicinal herb; for example it has been used for many hundreds of years by the Khoi people of southwestern Africa as a diuretic.

varieties

Eriocephalus africanus
South African Wild Rosemary
Half-hardy evergreen shrub. Ht. and spread 3 ft. Clusters of small white flowers with magenta centers from early to late winter, which are followed by seeds covered in masses of tiny white hairs that make them look fluffy. Small, needle-like, silver-haired, oval, slightly succulent, aromatic leaves which grow in tufts along the branch. Zone 9.

cultivation

Propagation
Seed
In spring sow fresh seeds into prepared plug modules, or small containers using a seed compost mixed in equal parts with perlite. Place in either a warm place or a propagator at 68°F (20°C), germination takes 10–15 days. Once large enough to handle, pot using a loam-based compost mixed with 25 percent river sand. In cool climates, winter young plants in a frost-free environment prior to planting in the following spring.

Cuttings
In late spring take softwood cuttings from the growing tips and insert into prepared plug modules, using a seed compost mixed in equal parts with perlite. In cool climates grow under protection for the first year prior to planting in the following spring.

Pests and Diseases
Very rarely suffers from pests or diseases. In cold climates excessive water in winter can cause the plant to rot.

Maintenance
Spring Prune after flowering in late spring to encourage new growth. Sow seeds. Take cuttings.
Summer Feed container-grown plants regularly.
Fall In cold climates protect from heavy fall rains.
Winter Protect from excessive wet and when temperatures fall consistently below 37°F (3°C) during the day.

Garden Cultivation
This amazingly drought-tolerant herb will adapt to most soils with the exception of heavy cold clay and marshy

Eriocephalus africanus **seedhead**

types of soil. The ideal situations are full sun and a well-drained soil. It makes an ideal coastal plant as it likes the sea spray and wind. In Mediterranean and other warm climates it can be grown as a hedge, or clipped into ball shapes. In situations where temperatures fall below 37°F (3°C) at night it is advisable to grow this herb in a container.

Harvesting
Pick the leaves to use fresh or to dry after flowering from spring until early fall. The twiggy branches are also used in some medicinal decoctions; pick these as and when required. Harvest the seeds when they start to drop.

 ## companion planting

Because this herb flowers in winter it is a most beneficial late nectar plant and therefore attracts beneficial insects to the garden, which increases pollination of late flowering plants.

 ## container growing

This wild rosemary makes a spectacular container plant as it cascades beautifully over the pot; another plus is that it does not mind a bit of neglect. Use a loam-based compost mixed with river sand, 75 percent loam, 25 percent sand. Repot every spring and give the plant a good hair cut after flowering. Water regularly throughout the summer and feed monthly with a general purpose liquid fertilizer from spring until first flowering in early fall.

 ## medicinal

Wild rosemary has traditionally been used as a medicine for many ailments like coughs and colds,

 ## culinary

The leaves can be used in a very similar way to rosemary *(Rosmarinus officinalis)*, especially with lamb dishes and vegetable stews as the flavor is fairly similar.

Special Lamb Stew
Serves 4–6

½ cup dried chick peas, soaked overnight,
   or use tinned
4 tablespoons light olive oil
1 large onion, finely chopped
11 lb. lean lamb, cubed
2 lemons, juice only
2 bay leaves
3 sprigs South African wild rosemary, roughly
   4 in. long
3 leeks, cleaned and chopped
1 cup spinach
¾ cup French flat-leaved parsley
1 fresh lime, sliced
Salt and black pepper

Strain the soaked chick peas, cook in fresh unsalted water for 15–20 minutes, drain, rinse under cold fresh water and set aside. Alternatively open can, drain, rinse under cold fresh water and set aside.
   Heat two tablespoons of olive oil in a large, heavy

flatulence and colic, and as a diuretic and a diaphoretic. It is said to have similar qualities to rosemary *(Rosmarinus officinalis)*. An infusion of the leaves can be relaxing in the bath, and also in a foot bath to stimulate the start of the menstrual period and to relieve swollen legs. An infusion of the leaves and twigs can be used to control dandruff and to stimulate hair growth.

 ## other uses

When dried it can be added to sachets and potpourri.

 ## warning

Do not take medicinally during pregnancy.

pan, slowly sauté the onion, add the lamb and brown on all sides, season with salt and pepper, pour over the lemon juice, add enough boiled hot water to just cover the meat. Add the bay leaves and South African wild rosemary. Cover and simmer for 30 minutes. Heat the remaining oil, sauté the leeks, spinach and parsley until just cooked. Add this to the meat together with the chick peas and sliced lime. Check that the liquid just covers the lamb, adding extra if required. Simmer all the ingredients for a further hour, checking from time to time that nothing is sticking to the bottom of the pan. Just before serving remove the remaining twigs of South African wild rosemary and find the limes, which can be used to decorate the serving plate. Serve with rice and either a green salad or green beans.

HORSETAIL

Equisetum arvense

Also known as Mare's tail, Shave grass, Bottle brush and Pewter wort. From the family Equisetaceae.

The Horsetail is a plant left over from prehistoric times. By the evidence of fossil remains, it has survived almost unchanged since the coal seams were laid. The Romans always used it to clean their pots and pans, not just to make them clean but also, thanks to the silica, to make them non-stick. The plant was used in the Middle Ages as an abrasive by cabinet makers and to clean pewter, brass and copper, and for scouring wooden containers and milk pans.

Equisetum arvense fertile shoots

 container growing

This is the only sane way to grow this herb. Choose a large tough container; trash cans are ideal. Fill it with a soil-based potting compost. If you wish to sink it into the garden make sure that the rim is at least 6 in. above the surface so that the rhizomes cannot penetrate or creep over the top.

Be sure to cut back in summer to prevent spread by the spores. No need to feed and it requires little watering. It can look attractive!

 culinary

It has been eaten as a substitute for asparagus, but I do not recommend it unless you are stuck on a desert island and there is no other food available.

 varieties

Equisetum arvense
Horsetail
Hardy perennial. Ht. 18 in. The plant does not flower. It grows on thin creeping rhizomes producing 8 in. long gray/brown fertile shoots with 4–6 sheaths in spring. The shoots die off and the spores are spread just like those of ferns. Zone 6.

 cultivation

Propagation
I am not sure that this is necessary because it is so invasive, but if you do require a supply of horsetail it may be of merit.

Cuttings
Take root cuttings in summer and place into prepared seed or plug module trays using a standard seed compost mixed in equal parts with fine composted bark. Plant into a prepared site the following spring.

Pests and Diseases
This herb is pest and disease free.

Maintenance
Spring Remove any fertile shoots to prevent the plant from spreading.
Summer Cut back plants as they begin to die back to prevent the spores spreading.
Fall Cut down to the ground.
Winter No need for protection; very hardy.

Garden Cultivation
If horsetail is to be introduced into the garden at all, and to be honest I do not recommend it, it is best to confine it to a strong container.

Harvesting
In summer, pick the green/brown shoots that look like miniature Christmas trees for drying.

 medicinal

This plant is a storehouse of minerals and vitamins, so herbalists recommend it in cases of amnesia and general debility. It also enriches the blood, hardens fingernails and revitalizes lifeless hair. Its astringent properties help to strengthen the walls of the veins, tightening up varicose veins and helping guard against fatty deposits in the arteries.

 other uses

The dried stems can be used to scour metal and polish pewter and fine woodwork. The whole plant yields a yellow ocher dye.

 warning

If you wish to take horsetail medicinally do not self-administer; consult a herbalist.

Ferula assa-foetida

ASAFOETIDA

Also known as Devil's dung, Food of the Gods and Hing. From the family Apiaceae.

This herb, indigenous to the Middle East, has for thousands of years been renowned for its gum resin which is extracted from its tuberous roots. Asafoetida gets its name from the Persian *aza*, "resin," and the Latin *foetidus*, "stinking," which is highlighted by one of its common names Devil's dung. Ironically it is also called Food of the Gods, because minute quantities of the sulphur-smelling resin can enhance the flavor of many foods.

 ## varieties

Ferula assa-foetida
Asafoetida
Perennial. Ht. 6 ft., spread 4½ ft. Flowers from the 4th year in early spring, with flat umbels of tiny yellow flowers, followed by small brown seeds. The flowering spikes can reach 12 ft. Large finely divided green/gray sulphuric, garlic-scented leaves. This plant often dies after flowering. Zone 7.

 ## cultivation

Propagation
Seed
Sow fresh seeds in late summer, into prepared plug modules or small pots using a seed compost mixed in equal parts with vermiculite. Once the seedlings are large enough, pot using a loam-based compost mixed in equal parts with river sand.

Pests and Diseases
Rarely suffers from pests or diseases. Container-raised plants can be attacked by aphids, however. Treat with an insecticidal soap spray following the manufacturer's instructions.

Maintenance
Spring Stake flowering spikes when grown on an exposed site.

Summer Sow seeds; harvest root from fourth year on.
Fall Mulch established plants with well-rotted manure.
Winter Protect from excessive wet.

Garden Cultivation
Plant in a warm, well-drained soil and a sunny position. Because of the height when in flower and because it dislikes being moved, position the plant with care. Protect it from prevailing winds, bearing in mind that it flowers in early spring.

Harvesting
Harvest the seed and resin in the summer from 4-year-old plants. Cut off the stems, and make successive slices through the roots. A smelly milky liquid will exude from the cuts. When dry it forms a resin which turns from creamy, grayish-white to reddish-brown as it is exposed to the air. One root, after successive slicing, can yield up to 2¼ lb. of resin.

 ## container growing

Only repot up one size up at a time; this plant does not like being over potted. Use a loam-based compost mixed in equal parts with river sand. Place the container in full sun and liquid feed regularly throughout the growing season following the manufacturer's instructions.

 ## medicinal

In Ayurvedic and Eastern herbal medicine asafoetida gum resin is used to treat bloating, wind, indigestion and constipation. It also helps lower blood pressure and thins the blood. Because of its foul taste and smell it is usually taken in pill form.

 ## other uses

A mixture of garlic and asafoetida apparently makes the ultimate insect repellent. I think it would also make the ultimate human repellent.

In Afghanistan it is said that asafoetida when rubbed over boots keeps snakes away.

 ## warning

Do not administer to very young children or babies.

 ## culinary

Asafoetida is used throughout southern India in the preparation of beans, peas and lentils, which are collectively known as *dal*. The best way to use asafoetida in the kitchen is to buy it already prepared in an airtight container. Add a minute pinch of resin to hot oil before adding the other ingredients; this calms the aroma and balances the other ingredients.

Filipendula
MEADOWSWEET

Also known as Bridewort, Meadow queen, Meadow-wort, and Queen of the Meadow. From the family Rosaceae.

Meadowsweet can be found growing wild in profusion near streams and rivers, in damp meadows, fens and marshlands, or wet woodlands to 3,300 ft. altitude. It is a native of Europe and Asia that has been successfully introduced into, and is naturalized in, North America.

The generic name, *Filipendula*, comes from *filum*, meaning "thread," and *pendulus*, meaning "hanging." This is said to describe the root tubers that hang, characteristically of the genus, on fibrous roots.

The common name, Meadowsweet, is said to be derived from the Anglo-Saxon word *medesweete*, which owes its origin to the fact that the plant was used to flavor mead, a drink made from fermented honey.

It has been known by many other names. In Chaucer's *The Knight's Tale* it is meadwort and was one of the ingredients in a drink called "save." It was also known as bridewort, because it was strewn in churches for festivals and weddings and made into bridal garlands. In Europe it took its name Queen of the Meadow from the way the herb can dominate a low-lying, damp meadow.

In the 16th century, when it was customary to strew floors with rushes and herbs (both to give warmth underfoot and to overcome smells and infections), it was a favorite of Queen Elizabeth I. She desired it above all other herbs in her chambers.

The sap contains a chemical of the same group as salicylic acid, an ingredient of aspirin. It was isolated for the first time in the 19th century by an Italian professor. When the drug company Bayer formulated acetylsalicylic acid, they called it aspirin after the old botanical name for Meadowsweet, *Spirea ulmaria*.

 ## varieties

Filipendula ulmaria
Meadowsweet
Hardy perennial. Ht. 2–4 ft., spread 2 ft. Clusters of creamy-white flowers in midsummer. Green leaf made up of up to 5 pairs of big leaflets separated by pairs of smaller leaflets. Zone 4.

Filipendula ulmaria 'Aurea'
Golden Meadowsweet
Hardy perennial. Ht. and spread 12 in. Clusters of creamy-white flowers in midsummer. Bright golden yellow, divided leaves in spring that turn a lime color in summer. Susceptible to sun scorch. Zone 4.

Filipendula ulmaria 'Variegata'
Variegated Meadowsweet
Hardy perennial. Ht. 18 in. and spread 12 in. Clusters of creamy-white flowers in midsummer. Divided leaf, dramatically variegated green and yellow in spring. Fades a bit as the season progresses. Zone 4.

Filipendula vulgaris
Dropwort
Hardy perennial. Ht. 2–3 ft., spread 18 in. Summertime clusters of white flowers (larger than meadowsweet). Fern-like green leaves. Zone 4.

cultivation

Propagation

Seed

Sow in prepared seed or plug module trays in the fall. Use a standard seed compost mixed in equal parts with composted fine bark. Cover lightly with compost (not perlite) and winter outside under glass. Check from time to time that the compost has not become dry as this will inhibit germination. Stratification is helpful but not essential (see page 264). Germination should take place in spring. When the seedlings are large enough to handle, plant 12 in. apart, into a prepared site.

Division

The golden and variegated forms are best propagated by division. This is easily done in the fall. Dig up established plant and tease the plantlets apart; they separate easily. Either replant in a prepared site, 12 in. apart, or, if it is one of the decorative varieties, pot using a loam-based potting compost

Pests and Diseases

Meadowsweet can be prone to powdery mildew; cut back and remove infected leaves.

Filipendula ulmaria

Maintenance

Spring Remove winter debris from around new growth.
Summer Cut back after flowering.
Fall Divide established plants, sow seed for wintering outside.
Winter No need for protection.

Garden Cultivation

Meadowsweet adapts well to the garden, but does prefer sun/semishade and a moisture-retentive soil. If your soil is free-draining, mix in plenty of well-rotted manure and/or leaf mold, and plant in semishade.

Harvesting

Gather young leaves for fresh or dry use before flowers appear. Pick flowers just as they open, use fresh or dry.

container growing

Golden and variegated meadowsweet look very attractive in containers, but use a loam-based compost to make sure moisture is retained. Position in partial shade to inhibit drying out and prevent sun scorch. The plant dies back in winter so leave it outside where the natural weathers can reach it. If you live in an extremely cold area, protect the container from damage by placing

Meadowsweet dye

in a site protected from continuous frost, but not warm. Liquid feed only twice during flowering.

other uses

A black dye can be obtained from the roots by using a copper mordant (see also page 289). Use dried leaves and flowers in potpourri.

medicinal

The whole plant is a traditional remedy for an acidic stomach. The fresh root is used in homeopathic preparations and is effective on its own in the treatment of diarrhea. The flowers, when made into a tea, are a comfort to flu victims.

culinary

A charming, local vet who made all kinds of vinegars and pickles gave me meadowsweet vinegar to try. Much to my amazement it was lovely, and combined well with oil to make a different salad dressing, great when used with a flower salad.

I am not a fan of meadowsweet flower fritters so mention them only in passing. The flowers do however make a very good wine, and add flavor to meads and beers. The flowers can also be added to stewed fruit and jams, introducing a subtle almond flavor.

Young leaves can be added to soups, but are not recommended for the faint-hearted!

Foeniculum vulgare

FENNEL

Also known as Large fennel, Sweet fennel and Wild fennel. From the family Apiaceae.

"So Gladiators fierce and rude,
Mingled it with their daily food,
And he who battled down subdued,
A wreath of Fennel wore."
Henry Wadsworth Longfellow (1807–1882)

Fennel grows wild in Europe and in most temperate countries and is naturalized in the western United States. The generic name, *Foeniculum*, derives from the Latin *foenum*, which means "hay," and refers to the foliar structure.

The ancient Greeks thought very highly of fennel and used it as a slimming aid and for treating more than 20 different illnesses. It was also much valued by the Romans in an age of banquets. They ate its leaf, root and seed in salads, and baked it in bread and cakes. Warriors took fennel to keep in good health, while Roman ladies ate it to prevent obesity. In Anglo-Saxon times it was used on fasting days presumably because, as the Greeks had already discovered, it calms pangs of hunger. More recently, in American Puritan communities, it became known as the Meeting Seeds, because seeds of fennel and dill were eaten to allay hunger during long church services.

In the Middle Ages, fennel was a favorite stewing herb, for not only is it fragrant and flavorsome, it also keeps insects at bay; it was used in the kitchen to protect and lend flavor to food that was often far from fresh, making it palatable. In the 16th century it was praised by Gerard as an aid to eyesight, and by Culpeper as treatment for poison by snakebite or mushrooms.

 varieties

Foeniculum vulgare
Fennel
Also known as garden fennel, common fennel, and green fennel. Hardy perennial. Ht. 4–7 ft., spread 18 in. Many small yellow flowers in large umbels in late summer. Soft green feathery foliage. Zone 5.

Foeniculum vulgare 'Purpureum'
Bronze Fennel
As *F. vulgare*. Very striking bronze feathery leaves. Zone 5.

Foeniculum vulgare var. dulce
Florence Fennel
Also known as Finocchio. Grown as an annual. Ht. 2½–3 ft. Clusters of small yellow flowers in late summer. Leaves feathery and green. The base develops to form a white bulbous sweet vegetable, with a crisp texture and a delicate aniseed flavor. All zones.

 cultivation

Propagation
Seeds
Sow all varieties early in spring in prepared pots or plug module trays, and cover with perlite. Bottom heat of 59–69°F (15–21°C) will speed germination. When large enough to handle, plant. Also sow in the fall for winter salads.

Roots
Division is only really successful if you have a light sandy soil, when roots will divide easily. This should be done in the fall.

Garden Cultivation
Fennel likes a sunny position in fertile, well-drained, loamy soil. Add an extra layer of sharp sand on a clay soil. Sow the seed after any frosts, thinning to 20 in. apart. Do not grow near dill or coriander as cross pollination will reduce seed production.
Fennel grown in a hot dry spot produces a sparse clump, 4–5 ft. high, with very thin, highly aromatic leaves. In a decent garden soil, fennel looks more like a dome of green or purple candyfloss. Fennel is an important food source for Swallowtail butterfly caterpillars.

 ## culinary

Fennel is an additional seasoning for fat meats like pork, and stuffings for poultry and lamb. It is as delicious as a salad or vegetable dressing.

Use seeds in sauces, fish dishes and bread; leaves finely chopped over salads and cooked vegetables, and in soups and stuffing for oily fish; and young stems to add an extra crunch to salads.

Cook the bulb of Florence fennel as a root vegetable or slice or grate raw into sandwiches or salads.

Fish with Fennel
Serves 4

Whole fish—trout, mackerel,
mullet (4 fish, approx. 1 lb. each)
1 cup of fresh sprigs of fennel
1 tablespoon cooking oil
Brandy

Clean the fish and fill with sprigs of chopped green fennel leaves. With a sharp knife score the fish on each side and brush with oil. Season lightly with salt and pepper. Arrange a bed of fennel sticks on the base of a greased oven-proof dish. Carefully place the fish on the sticks and cook in a hot oven (450°F/230°C) for 15 minutes.

To serve, transfer the fennel sticks and fish onto a flat fire-proof serving dish. Warm the brandy and pour over the fish and set alight. The fennel will burn and the whole dish becomes deliciously aromatic.

Finocchio Salad (with Florence Fennel)
Serves 2

2 medium-sized fennel bulbs
12 black olives
½ cup plain yogurt
1 small head of lettuce
Juice of 1 lemon
Chopped parsley

Trim the fennel bulbs and wash carefully. Cut into thin slices. Mix with yogurt, lemon juice and olives. Arrange the mixture decoratively on a bed of lettuce leaves. Garnish with lemon and chopped parsley.

Florence fennel is grown only from seed. Sow in shallow trenches during the early summer in a rich well-composted soil for the bulbous roots to reach maturity by the fall. Thin out to 8 in. apart.

During dry spells water well. When the root swelling is the size of a golf ball, blanch it by drawing some soil around it. After 2–3 weeks, when it is the size of a tennis ball, harvest.

Pests and Diseases
When the plants are very young, root rot may occur if overwatered. Greenfly may also occasionally infest the plant. They can be treated with insecticidal soap.

Maintenance
Spring Sow seed.
Summer Pick flowering heads to maintain leaf production.
Fall Sow seeds in trays and force with heat for use in winter salads.
Winter Cut back old growth, tidy up around plants. Fennel dies back into the ground in winter. No need to protect unless temperatures fall below 14°F (10°C).

Harvesting
Pick young stems and leaves as required. Freeze leaves or infuse in oil or vinegar.

Collect ripe seeds for sowing or to dry for culinary use. Dig up Florence fennel bulbs when sufficiently mature and as required.

 ## companion planting

Fennel attracts hoverflies so helps keep aphids at bay.

 ## container growing

The bronze variety looks especially attractive. Use a potting compost mixed in equal parts with composted fine bark. It may need staking when in flower. In the summer shelter from midday sun, water and feed regularly. Repot each year to maintain health.

 ## other uses

Seed and leaf can be used in facial steams and in baths for deep cleansing. A facial pack of fennel tea and honey is good for wrinkles. A yellow dye can be extracted.

 ## medicinal

To make fennel tea put a teaspoon of seeds in a tea cup, add boiling water, cover for 5 minutes, then strain and drink to aid digestion or prevent both heartburn or constipation. A teaspoon of this cooled tea is good for babies with colic. Steep a compress in the tea and place on the eyelid, to ease inflammation or watery eye, or let the solution cool and bathe the naked eye.

 ## warning

Taken in large doses, the essence can cause convulsions and disturb the nervous system.

Fragaria vesca

WILD STRAWBERRY

Also known as Mountain strawberry, Wood strawberry and Alpine strawberry. From the family Rosaceae.

These delightful plants are found mainly in forests, clearings and shady roadsides in the cool temperate climates of Europe, northern Asia, Australia and North America.

The name "strawberry" does not in fact originate from a traditional practice of placing straw beneath the berries to keep them clean. Rather, it dates back to the 10th century when the Anglo-Saxon word "straw" meant small particles of chaff, which in this case referred to the scattering of pips (achenes) over the surface of the fruit. *Fragaria* originates from *fraga*, the original old Latin name for *fragrans*, meaning "fragrant" referring to the scent of the fruit.

The fruit of this herb is dedicated to Venus and the Virgin Mary.

 varieties

There are many forms of this small strawberry, some with variegated leaves, some with white fruit; the two identified here are the originals.

Fragaria vesca
Wild Strawberry
Hardy perennial. Ht. 6–12 in., spread 7 in., more if you include the runners. The flowers have 4 or 5 white petals with a yellow center in spring to early summer. The leaf is composed of 3 brightish green leaflets with serrated edges. Zone 5.

Fragaria vesca 'Semperflorens'
Alpine Strawberry
Hardy perennial. Ht. 2–10 in., spread 6 in. The flowers have 4 or 5 white petals with a yellow center from spring to fall. The leaf is composed of 3 brightish green leaflets with serrated edges. True Alpine strawberries do not set down runners, so propagate by seed only. Zone 5.

 cultivation

Propagation
Seed
The seed of the strawberry is embedded all around the surface of the fruit. To collect it, leave the fruit in the summer sun until fully dry and shrivelled, then rub the seed off. Sow in late winter, early spring. Do not cover. A bottom heat of 60°F (15°C) is helpful. Germination will take place in a couple of weeks. Later in spring the seeds can be sown without heat, germination taking the same time. When the seedlings are large enough to handle, transplant to a prepared site in the garden at a distance of 12 in. apart.

Division
The daughter plants are produced on runners and easily propagated by division, each having its own small root system. These can be taken off and replanted where required during the growing season from spring to early fall.

Pests and Diseases
Obvious pests are slugs and birds, followed closely by children, and at flower shows by members of the public. With all of these there is not a lot you can do, apart from growing enough so that it does not matter. If grown in containers the plants can suffer from mildew. Remove the affected parts and make sure there is plenty of light and air.

Maintenance
Spring Divide runners.
Summer Feed with liquid fertilizer.
Fall Divide runners if they have become invasive.
Winter No need for protection. Sow seed.

Garden Cultivation
Wild strawberries prefer a good fertile soil that does not dry out in summer, and either full sun or shade. They grow well in woods and in the countryside and

WILD STRAWBERRY

make a great groundcover, the dainty white flowers standing out amongst bright green shiny leaves that, when dry have a fragrance of musk. The tiny, delicious summertime fruits are a terrific bonus and have a good flavor.

Feed regularly with a liquid fertilizer (one that is high in potash) as soon as the fruit begins, following the manufacturer's instructions. Wild strawberries are often regarded as a weed by tidy gardeners; if you cannot stand the idea of rampant strawberry plants, grow the Alpine variety.

Harvesting

Pick leaves as required. If needed for drying, pick before the fruit sets, and dry.

Pick fruits as they ripen to eat fresh. They can also be frozen.

 ## container growing

Being small plants, wild strawberries are wonderful grown in containers, window boxes, even those pots with holes in the side, and also hanging baskets, where the runners look most attractive trailing over the edge. Use a standard potting compost mixed in equal parts with composted fine bark. Water and feed with liquid fertilizer regularly, especially when the fruit begins to set.

 ## other uses

The strawberry is used extensively in the cosmetic industry in skin cream manufacture. Mash the fruit and extract juice to add to facepacks to whiten skin and lighten freckles.

Apply cut strawberries to the washed face to ease slight sunburn—makes a lovely picture. If you get bored you can always eat them.

 ## medicinal

The fruits of the wild strawberry (unlike those of the cultivated varieties) are excellent for treating anemia, bad nerves and stomach disorders. They are also an astringent, diuretic, tonic and laxative.

The leaves can be used to make a gargle and mouthwash for sore gums and mouth ulcers.

Strawberry leaf tea is said to be a good tonic for convalescence and is enjoyed by children.

 ## culinary

Eat the fruit fresh in fruit salads or on their own with cream, or use in cakes, pies and syrups and to flavor cordials. If you have enough you can also make jam. The leaves have a musky flavor and scent. A tea can be made from them, but it is better to combine them with other herbs.

 ## warning

Strawberries may produce an allergic response.

Galega officinalis

GOAT'S RUE

Also known as French lilac, Italian fitch and Professor-weed. From the family Papilionaceae.

This ancient herb, indigenous to central and southern Europe and western Asia, has been used for hundreds of years to treat plagues and infections. Historically it was also recommended for snake bites. The name *Galega* comes from the Greek *gala,* meaning "milk" because of its reputation for increasing lactation. The common name Goat's Rue originates from the leaves, which smell unpleasant when crushed.

varieties

Galega officinalis

Goat's Rue
Herbaceous perennial. Ht. 3–4½ ft., spread up to 3 ft. Attractive clusters of white or mauve flowers in summer, followed by long seed pods. Green, compound, divided, lance-shaped leaflets. Zone 3.

cultivation

Propagation

Seed
Sow the easy-to-handle seeds in the spring into prepared seed or plug module trays using a seed compost, and cover with perlite. Germination takes 10–20 days without extra heat. Once the seedlings are strong enough, either pot using a loam-based potting compost or alternatively in mid-spring, when the air and soil temperature has risen, plant at a distance of 30 in. apart.

Division
This is a good method of propagation for this herb as it prevents the plant from becoming too large and it encourages it to put on new growth. In the second or third year divide the root ball either by using two forks back to back or by digging up the whole plant and dividing. Once divided replant in a well-prepared site.

Pests and Diseases
Rarely suffers from pests. However it is prone to powdery mildew, especially when planted against a wall or fence.

Leaves of *Galega officinalis*

Maintenance
Spring Sow seeds, divide established plants.
Summer Cut back if growing too straggly; this will promote a second flowering.
Fall Collect seeds for drying.
Winter No need for protection.

Garden Cultivation
This fully hardy herb will grow in most soils. It prefers a deep soil that does not dry out in summer and allows the roots to become well established. This is important as they act as an anchor to stop it from being blown over in the summer when it is in full flower. If the plant becomes invasive or outgrows its position, cut it back hard; this will keep it under control and encourage flowering at a lower height, which can look most effective.

Harvesting
All the aerial parts of the plant are harvested in summer just before flowering, then dried for medicinal use.

container growing

I grow this herb in a container for exhibiting at flower shows, using a loam-based potting compost. However, for home display, I would not recommend it as it needs repotting at least three times in the growing season. Also, it grows very tall, requiring a large container, which makes it awkward to handle.

medicinal

Used medicinally to reduce the blood sugar levels and as a useful diuretic. It is also used to increase lactation in nursing mothers.

other uses

The leaves and stem are used as an animal food supplement to increase milk yield.

warning

Only to be used under professional supervision when treating diabetes.

Galium odoratum
SWEET WOODRUFF

Also known as New Mowed Hay, Rice flower, Ladies in the Hay, Kiss Me Quick, Master of the Wood, Woodward and Woodrowell. From the family Rubiaceae.

This is a native of Europe and has been introduced and cultivated in North America and Australia. It grows deep in the woods and in the countryside.

Records date back to the 14th century, when woodruff was used as a strewing herb, as bedstuffing and to perfume linen.

On May Day in Germany, it is added to Rhine wine to make a delicious drink called "Maibowle."

 ## varieties

Galium odoratum (Asperula odorata)
Sweet Woodruff
Hardy perennial. Ht. 6 in., spread 12 in. or more. White, star-shaped flowers from spring to early summer. The green leaves are neat and grow in a complete circle around the stem. The whole plant is aromatic. Zone 4.

 ## cultivation

Propagation
Seed
To ensure viability, only use fresh seed. Sow in early fall into prepared seed or plug module trays, and cover with compost. Water well. Seeds require a period of stratification (see page 264). Once the seedlings are large enough, either pot or plant out as soon as the young plants have been hardened off. Plant 4 in. apart.

Root Cuttings
The rootstock is very brittle and every little piece will grow. The best time to take cuttings is after flowering in the early summer. Lay small pieces of the root, 1–1½ in. long, evenly spaced, on the compost in a seed tray. Cover with a thin layer of compost, and water. Leave in a warm place, and the woodruff will begin to sprout again. When large enough to handle, split up and plant.

Pests and Diseases
This plant rarely suffers from pests and diseases.

Maintenance
Spring Take root cuttings after flowering.
Summer Dig up before the flowers have set, to check spreading.
Fall The plant dies back completely in the fall. Sow seeds.
Winter Fully hardy plant.

Garden Cultivation
Ideal for difficult places or underplanting in borders, it loves growing in the dry shade of trees right up to the trunk. Its rich green leaves make a dense and very decorative groundcover, its underground runners spreading rapidly in the right situation.

It prefers a rich alkaline soil with some moisture during the spring.

Harvesting
The true aroma (which is like new-mown hay) manifests when it is dried. Dry flowers and leaves together in early summer.

 ## container growing

Make sure the container is large enough, otherwise it will become root-bound very quickly. Use a soil-based compost mixed in equal parts with composted fine bark. Only feed with liquid fertilizer when the plant is flowering. Position the container in semishade and do not overwater.

 ## culinary

Add the flowers to salads. The main ingredients for a modern-day May Wine would be a bottle of Riesling, a glass of sherry, sugar, and strawberries, with a few sprigs of woodruff thrown in an hour before serving.

 ## medicinal

A tea made from the leaves is said to relieve stomach pain, act as a diuretic, and be beneficial for those prone to gall stones.

Sweet woodruff tea

 ## warning

Consumption of large quantities can produce symptoms of poisoning, including dizziness and vomiting.

Ginkgo biloba

GINKGO

Also known as Maidenhair tree and Bai guo. From the family Ginkgoaceae.

This beneficial herb is a living fossil, thought to be one of the oldest trees on the planet, dating back to when dinosaurs lived. Chinese monks are credited with keeping the tree in existence, as a sacred herb. The name *Ginkgo* is derived from the Japanese word *ginkyo*, meaning "silver apricot," referring to the fruit, and *biloba* translates as "two-lobed," which refers to the split in the middle of the fan-shaped leaf blades.

varieties

Ginkgo biloba
Ginkgo
Hardy deciduous tree. Ht. 120 ft. It is dioecious, meaning that it bears male catkins and female flowers on different trees in early summer. The female flowers are followed by small fruits. Fan-shaped green leaves are sometimes whole, but often have a single, central, vertical slit. Zone 4.

cultivation

Propagation
Seed
In the fall, prepare the seeds by removing the pith; wear gloves, as the pith can cause dermatitis, then wash in a mild detergent. Sow immediately, singly into small pots using a loam-based seed compost mixed in equal parts with horticultural grit. Cover with grit and place in a cold frame. Germination takes 4 months or longer. Grow on in a container for a minimum of 4 years before planting into the garden. You will only know the sex of your seed-raised plant when it flowers, which takes approximately 20 years.

Cuttings
Take cuttings from new growth in summer or semiripe growth in early fall. Place in a seed compost mixed in equal parts with horticultural grit. Keep frost-free until rooted. Grow as a container plant in exactly the same way as a seed-raised plant.

Pests and Diseases
Rarely suffers from pests or diseases.

Maintenance
Spring Repot or top dress container-raised plants.
Summer Take cuttings from new growth.
Fall Sow fresh seeds. Take cuttings.
Winter Fully hardy; no extra protection needed.

Garden Cultivation
Plant in full sun to partial shade in any fertile soil with the exception of heavy, cold, wet clay. To produce fruit (in warm climates only) a male and female tree need to be planted near each other.

Harvesting
In the fall pick the leaves for drying as they turn color from green to yellow. Also harvest the ripe, extremely fetid, small fruits from the female tree, and extract the kernel (nut) which is dried for medicinal use or used fresh in the kitchen.

container growing

Once the young plant is over 2 years old, use a loam-based potting compost mixed in equal parts with river sand. Water and liquid feed regularly throughout the growing season.

medicinal

Ginkgo is one of the bestselling Western herbal medicines and is taken to improve the memory. The dried leaves are used to improve circulation, ease tinnitus and in the treatment of asthma. Currently the leaves are being researched as a treatment for Alzheimer's disease.

warning

If taken in excess, it can cause a toxic reaction. Wear gloves when preparing fresh nuts. Children can be allergic to cooked nuts.

culinary

There is current debate regarding the toxicity of the fresh nut, as to whether it can be eaten raw or whether it needs to be cooked. I would err on the side of caution as most recipes say cooked, where it is used in soups, stir-fries and roasted. These nuts are available from Eastern supermarkets, where they are often called "White Nuts."

Glycyrrhiza glabra

LICORICE

**Also known as Liquorice, Sweet Licorice and Sweetwood.
From the family Papilionaceae.**

This plant, which is a native of the Mediterranean region, is commercially grown throughout the temperate zones of the world and extensively cultivated in Russia, Iran, Spain and India. It has been used medicinally for 3,000 years and was recorded on Assyrian tablets and Egyptian papyri. The Latin name *Glycyrrhiza* comes from *glykys*, meaning "sweet," and *rhiza*, meaning "root."

It was first introduced to England by Dominican friars in the 16th century and became an important crop. The whole of the huge cobbled courtyard of Pontefract Castle was covered by top soil simply to grow licorice. It is sad that Pontefract cakes are made from imported licorice today.

 ## varieties

Glycyrrhiza glabra
Licorice
Hardy perennial. Ht. 4 ft., spread 3 ft. Pea-like, purple/blue and white flowers borne in short spikes on erect stems in late summer. Large greenish leaves divided into oval leaflets. Zone 7.

 ## cultivation

Propagation
Seed
The seedlings often damp off. In cooler climates the seed tends not to be viable. Root division is a much easier method.

Division
Divide when the plant is dormant, making sure the root has one or more buds. Place into pots half filled with a loam-based potting compost. Cover with compost. Water well and leave in a warm place until shoots appear. Harden off, then plant in early spring or fall. If the latter, winter in a cold greenhouse or cold frame.

Maintenance
Spring Divide established plants.
Summer Do nothing.
Fall Divide established plants if necessary.
Winter In very cold winters protect first-year plants.

Garden Cultivation
Licorice needs a rich, deep, well-cultivated soil.
Plant pieces of the root, each with a bud, directly into a prepared site 6 in. deep and 3 ft. apart in early spring or in the fall during the dormant season, if the ground is workable and not frosty. Licorice does best in long, hot summers, but will need extra watering if your soil is very free draining.

Harvesting
Harvest roots for drying in early winter from established 3- or 4-year-old plants.

 ## container growing

Never displays as well as in the garden. Use a soil-based compost. Feed throughout the growing season and water until it dies back.

 ## culinary

Licorice is used as a flavoring in the making of Guinness and other beers.

 ## medicinal

The juice from the roots provides commercial licorice. It is used either to mask the unpleasant flavor of other medicines or to provide its own soothing action on troublesome coughs. The dried root, stripped of its bitter bark, is recommended as a remedy for colds, sore throats and bronchial congestion.
Licorice is a gentle laxative and lowers stomach acid levels, so relieving heartburn. It has a remarkable power to heal stomach ulcers because it spreads a protective gel over the stomach wall and in addition it eases spasms of the large intestine. It also increases the flow of bile and lowers blood cholesterol levels.

 ## warning

Large doses of licorice cause side effects, notably headaches, high blood pressure and water retention.

Licorice sticks

Helichrysum italicum
CURRY PLANT

From the family Asteraceae.

This plant is from southern Europe and has adapted well to damper, cooler climates. It is the sweet curry scent of its leaves that has caused its recent rise in popularity.

 varieties

Helichrysum italicum (H. angustifolium)
Curry Plant
Hardy evergreen perennial. Ht. 24 in., spread 3 ft. Clusters of tiny mustard-yellow flowers in summer. Narrow, aromatic, silver leaves. Highly scented. Planting distance for hedging 2 ft. Zone 8.

Helichrysum italicum 'Dartington'
Dartington Curry Plant
Hardy evergreen perennial. Ht. 18 in., spread 24 in. Compact plant with clusters of small yellow flowers in summer. Gray-green, highly scented, narrow leaves (half the size of *H. italicum*). Its compact upright habit makes this a good plant for hedges and edging in the garden. Planting distance for hedging 1 ft. Zone 8.

Helichrysum italicum 'Korma'
Korma Curry Plant
Hardy evergreen perennial. Ht. 24 in., spread 3 ft. Broad clusters of small bright yellow flowers, produced on upright white shoots. Narrow, aromatic, silver leaves. Planting distance for hedging 24 in. Zone 8.

 cultivation

Propagation
Seed
I have not known any *H. italicum* set good seed. For this reason I advise cuttings.

Cuttings
Take softwood cuttings in spring and semiripe ones in the fall. Use a seed compost mixed in equal parts with composted fine bark.

Pests and Diseases
Pests give this highly aromatic plant a wide berth, and it is usually free from disease.

Maintenance
Spring Trim established plants after frosts to maintain shape and promote new growth. Take

The silver leaves of *Helichrysum italicum* 'Korma'

softwood cuttings.
Summer Trim back after flowering, but not too hard.
Fall Take semiripe wood cuttings.
Winter If the temperature falls below 14°F (−10°C), protect from frost.

Garden Cultivation
The curry plant makes an attractive addition to the garden and it imparts a strong smell of curry even if untouched. It is one of the most silvery of shrubs and makes a striking visual feature all year round.

Plant in full sun in a well-drained soil. Do not cut the curry plant as hard back as cotton lavender, but it is worth giving a good hair cut after flowering to stop the larger ones flopping and to keep the shape of the smaller ones.

If it is an exceptionally wet winter, and you do not have a free-draining soil, lift some plants, and keep in a cold greenhouse, or cold frame.

Harvest
Pick leaves at any time for using fresh. Or before flowering for drying. Pick the flowers when fully open, in summer, for drying.

 container growing

All the curry plants grow happily in large containers (at least 8 in. in diameter). Use a soil-based compost mixed in equal parts with composted fine bark. Place in the sun to get the best effect, and do not overwater.

 culinary

There are not many recipes for the curry plant in cooking, and in truth the leaves smell stronger than they taste, but a small sprig stuffed into the cavity of a roasting chicken makes an interesting variation on tarragon.

Add sprigs to vegetables, rice dishes and pickles for a mild curry flavor. Remove before serving.

 other uses

The bright yellow button flowers can be used to add color to potpourri.

Hesperis matronalis
SWEET ROCKET

Also known as Damask violet and Dame's violet. From the family Brassicaceae.

This sweet-smelling herb is indigenous to Italy. It can now be found growing wild in much of the temperate world as a garden escapee. The old Greek name *Hesperis* was used by Theophrastus, the Greek botanist (370–285 BC). It is derived from *hesperos*, meaning "evening," which is when the flowers are at their most fragrant.

 varieties

Hesperis matronalis
Sweet Rocket
Hardy biennial; very occasionally perennial, sending out new shoots from the rootstock. Ht. 2–3 ft., spread 10 in. The four-petalled flowers are all sweetly scented and come in many colors—pink, purple, mauve and white—in the summer of the second year. The leaves are green and lance shaped. Zone 4.

There is a double-flowered form of this plant—*Hesperis matronalis* double-flowered. It can only be propagated by cuttings or division and needs a more sandy loam soil than sweet rocket.

 cultivation

Propagation
Seed
Sow the seed in the fall in prepared seed or plug trays, covering the seeds with perlite. Winter the young plants in a cold greenhouse for planting out in the spring at 18 in. apart. Propagated this way it may flower the first season as well as the second. Alternatively, sow seed in the garden in late spring.

Pests and Diseases
This herb is largely free from pests and diseases.

Maintenance
Spring Sow seed outdoors.
Summer In the second year deadhead flowers to prolong flowering.
Fall Sow seed under protection.
Winter No need to protect.

Garden Cultivation
It likes full sun or light shade and prefers a well-drained fertile soil. The seed can be sown directly into a prepared site in the garden in late spring, thinning to 12 in. apart, with a further thinning to 18 in. later on if need be.

Harvesting
Pick leaves when young for eating. Pick flowers as they open for using fresh or for drying.

 container growing

Sweet rocket is a tall plant. It looks attractive if three or four 1-year-old plants are potted together, positioned to make the most of the scent on a summer evening. Use a standard potting compost mixed in equal parts with composted fine bark and water well in summer months. No need to feed.

 culinary

Young leaves are eaten occasionally in salads. Use sparingly because they are very bitter. The flowers look attractive tossed in salads. They can also be used to decorate desserts.

 other uses

Add dried flowers to potpourri for pastel colors and sweet scent.

Hesperis matronalis

Helleborus niger
CHRISTMAS ROSE

Also known as Black Hellebore. From the family Ranunculaceae.

This ancient herb has had many stories attributed to its beauty and its medicinal properties. It is said to be one of Britain's oldest cultivated plants and it is thought to have been introduced by the Romans when they invaded those isles. There is an old legend, associated with the common name Christmas Rose, that it sprouted in the snow from the tears of a young shepherdess who had no gift to give Jesus, the new-born King. An angel, upon hearing her weeping, appeared and brushed away the snow to reveal the most beautiful flower, the Christmas Rose.

 ## varieties

 Helleborus niger
Christmas Rose
Evergreen perennial. Ht. and spread 12 in. Large, more outward facing flowers rounded and white sometimes fading to rose, white flowers with golden stamens from very early in the New Year until April. Leathery deep green divided basal leaves. Zone 4.

Helleborus foetidus
Stinking Hellebore
Evergreen perennial. Ht. and spread 18 in. Clusters of nodding cup-shaped pale green, red-margined flowers from very early in the New Year until April. Deeply divided dark green leaves. This variety is used in homeopathy in the treatment of headaches, psychic disorders, enteritis and spasms. Zone 5.

cultivation

Propagation
Seed
Sow fresh seed in late summer into prepared seed trays, plug modules or small pots using a loam-based seed compost mixed in equal parts with river sand. A word of warning about purchased seed: it must be fresh, old seed is nearly impossible to germinate. Cover with grit, and place the container outside for the winter as the seed needs frost to break its dormancy. Do not worry if the container becomes immersed in snow, as melting snow will aid germination. Germination will be erratic and may take a further season so do not throw away the sown seed after one winter.

Once it has germinated, grow on for one season in its container prior to planting in a well-prepared site in the garden. As this plant hates being transplanted, choose your site with care. Alternatively, as anyone who has grown this plant successfully in the garden will know, hellebores will happily self-seed. This is by far the easiest way to raise the plants from seed. When each seedling has at least one true leaf, carefully lift it and transplant into a prepared site that has moist, fertile soil in dappled shade. All seed-raised plants will take 3–5 years to flower.

Division
Hellebores hate their roots being disturbed, and are slow to re-establish after division. In early fall, choose

CHRISTMAS ROSE

Helleborus niger

a well-established plant and, with two forks back to back, very gently tease a clump away from the main plant. Carefully firm the soil in around the remaining clump and give the plant a feed with some well-rotted compost. As the original clump has had minimal disturbance it should flower in the early spring. Replant the divided section with the roots down, not spread out, into a well-prepared site that has had some new well-rotted compost dug in, and in partial dappled shade. It is unlikely to flower in the following spring but should do so the year after.

Pests and Diseases

Hellebores suffer from two diseases, black death and black spot. If you notice black streaking between the leaf veins, and seriously distorted stems and leaves, then this is most probably black death virus. Dig up the plants immediately to prevent it spreading and destroy, do not compost. Black spot fungus is identifiable by large, irregular brown or black spots on the leaves and stems which cause the leaf to die. Remove these leaves and burn or discard, again do not compost.

Hellebores can also suffer from root rot, a fungus that thrives on waterlogged soils. If you notice your plants are not thriving and you know you have very wet soil, then dig up the plants, and add some grit or bark to improve the drainage before replanting.

Maintenance

Spring Transplant self-sown seedlings into permanent positions.
Summer Sow fresh seed.
Fall Divide established plants.
Winter No need for protection, fully hardy.

Garden Cultivation

The Christmas Rose should be planted in a deep, fertile, well-draining but moisture-retaining soil, in partial dappled shade. Under deciduous trees is ideal. In the fall, it is well worth feeding the plants with well-rotted compost or leaf mold which will encourage it to flower profusely in the New Year.

Harvesting

The root is harvested in the fall, then dried for medicinal use.

companion planting

As this herb flowers so early it is very beneficial for early insects as an early nectar plant; it attracts beneficial predators, which makes it a good companion near the vegetable patch.

container growing

Because the Christmas Rose has a very long tap root, choose containers that are deep. Use a soil-based potting compost mixed with 25 percent sand, and place the container in partial shade. Feed weekly throughout the growing season with a liquid feed following the manufacturer's instructions. Repot one size up, or alternatively divide established plants in the fall once the plant is dormant. Remember that if you have divided the plant it is unlikely to flower in the following spring.

medicinal

Helleborus niger is a very poisonous plant that is toxic when taken in all but the smallest doses. This herb should not be self-administered and should only be taken under professional guidance. This herb contains properties similar to *Digitalis*, and was traditionally used as a heart stimulant and to treat dropsy, nervous disorders and hysteria. The best and safest way to take this herb is homeopathically, where it is used to treat headaches, psychic disorders, enteritis and spasms.

warning

Highly poisonous and toxic plant, not to be self-administered.

Helleborus niger

CHRISTMAS ROSE **123**

Humulus lupulus
HOPS

Also known as Hopbind and Hop vine. From the family Cannabaceae.

Native of the Northern temperate zones, cultivated commercially, especially in Northern Europe, North America and Chile.

Roman records from the first century AD describe hops as a popular garden plant and vegetable; young shoots were sold in markets to be eaten like asparagus. Hop gardens did not become widespread in Europe until the nineth century. In Britain the hop was a wild plant and used as a vegetable before it became one of the ingredients of beer. It was not until the 16th century that the word hop and the practice of flavoring and preserving beer with the strobiles or female flowers of *Humulus lupulus* were introduced into Britain by Flemish immigrants, and replaced traditional bitter herbs such as alehoof and alecost.

During the reign of Henry VIII, parliament was petitioned against the use of the hop, as it was said that it was a wicked weed that would spoil the taste of the drink, ale, and endanger the people. Needless to say the petition was thrown out. The use of hops revolutionized brewing since it enabled beer to be kept for longer.

Hops have also been used as medicine for at least as long as for brewing. The flowers are famous for their sedative effect and were either drunk as a tea or stuffed in a hop pillow to sleep on.

Humulus lupulus female flowers

 varieties

Humulus lupulus
Common Hop
Hardy perennial, a herbaceous climber. Ht. up to 20 ft. There are separate female and male plants. The male plant has yellowish flowers growing in branched clusters. They are without sepals and have five tepals and five stamen. The female plant has tiny greenish-yellow, scented flowers, hidden by big scales (see left). The scales become papery when the fruiting heads are ripe. These are the flowers that are harvested for beer. The mid-green leaves have three to five lobes with sharply toothed edges. The stems are hollow, and are covered with tiny hooked prickles. These enable the plant to cling to shrubs, trees, or anything else. It always entwines clockwise. Zone 3.

Humulus lupulus 'Aureus'
Golden Hop
Hardy perennial, a herbaceous climber. Ht. up to 20 ft. The main difference between this plant and the common hop is that the leaves and flowers are much more golden, which makes it very attractive in the garden and in dried flower arrangements. It has the same properties as the common hop. Zone 3.

 cultivation

Propagation
Seed
Beer is made from the unpollinated female flowers. If you grow from seed you will not know the gender for 2 to 3 years, which is the time it takes before good flowers are produced. Obtain seed from specialist seedsmen.

Sow in summer or the fall. The seed is on the medium to large side so sow sparingly; if using plug module trays, one per cell. Push the seed in and cover it with the compost. Then cover the tray with a sheet of glass or plastic wrap, and leave somewhere cool to germinate—a cold frame, a cold greenhouse, or a garage. Germination can be very erratic. If the seed is not fresh you may need to give the hot/cold treatment to break dormancy.

Warning: As the seed will be from wild hops these should not be grown in areas of commercial hop growing, because they might contaminate the crop.

Humulus lupulus **male flowers**

Cuttings
Softwood cuttings should be taken in spring or early summer from the female plant. Choose young shoots and take the cuttings in the morning as they will lose water very fast and wilt.

Division
In the spring, dig up and divide the root stems and suckers of established plants. Replant 3 ft. apart against support.

Pests and Diseases
The most common disease is hop wilt. If this occurs, dig up and burn. Do not plant hops in that area again. Leaf miner can sometimes be a problem. Remove infected leaves immediately. The golden variety sometimes suffers from sun scorch. If this occurs, prune to new growth, and change its position if possible the following season.

Maintenance
Spring Divide roots and separate rooted stems and suckers in spring. Repot container-grown plants. Check trellising. Take cuttings.
Summer Sow seed late in the season. Take cuttings.
Fall Cut back remaining growth into the ground. Give the plants a good feed of manure or compost. Bring containers into a cool place. Sow seed.
Winter No need for protection.

Garden Cultivation
For successful plants the site should be sunny and open, and the soil needs to be rich in humus and dug deeply. It is not generally necessary to tie the plants if good support is at hand. A word of warning: you must dominate the plant. It will definitely need thinning and encouraging to entwine where you want it to go rather than where it chooses. But remember that it dies back completely in winter. Cut the plant into the ground each fall and then give it a good feed of manure or compost.

Harvesting
Pick young fresh side shoots in spring. Gather young fresh leaves as required.
   Pick male flowers as required. Pick ripe female flowers in early fall. Dry and use within a few months, otherwise the flavor becomes unpleasant.

 ## container growing

Hops, especially the golden variety, can look very attractive in a large container with something to grow up. Use a soil-based compost mixed in equal parts with composted fine bark, and feed regularly with a liquid fertilizer from late spring to midsummer. Keep well-watered in the summer months and fairly dry in winter. It can be grown indoors in a position with good light such as a sunroom, but it seldom flowers. Provide some form of shade during sunny periods. During the winter months, make sure it has a rest by putting the pot in a cool place, keeping the compost on the dry side. Repot each year.

 ## other uses

The leaf can be used to make a brown dye. If you live close to a brewery it is worth asking for the spent hops each fall; they make either a great mulch or a layer in a compost heap.

 ## culinary

In early spring pick the young side shoots, steam them (or lightly boil), and eat like asparagus. The male flowers can be parboiled, cooled and tossed into salads. The young leaves can be quickly blanched to remove any bitterness and added to soups or salads.

 ## warning

Contact dermatitis can be caused by contact with the flower. Also, hops are not recommended in the treatment of depressive illnesses because of their sedative effect.

 ## medicinal

Hop tea made from the female flower only is recommended for nervous diarrhea, insomnia and restlessness. It also helps to stimulate appetite, dispel flatulence and relieve intestinal cramps. A cold tea taken an hour before meals is particularly good for digestion.
   It can be useful combined with fragrant valerian for coughs and nervous spasmodic conditions. Recent research into hops has shown that it contains a hormone that results in the beneficial effect of helping mothers improve their milk flow.
   To make a hop pillow, sprinkle hops with alcohol and fill a small bag or pillowcase with them (which all in all is bound to knock you out).

Hop pillow

Hyoscyamus niger

HENBANE

Also known as Devil's eye, Hen pen, Hen penny, Hog bean, Stinking Roger, Symphoniaca, Jusquiamus, Henbell, Belene, Hennyibone, Hennebane, Poisoned tobacco and Stinking nightshade. From the family Solanaceae.

This native of Europe has become widely distributed worldwide and is found growing wild and on roadsides in well-drained sandy or alkaline soils.

Two famous deaths are attributed to henbane. Hamlet's father was murdered by a distillation of henbane being poured in his ear, and in 1910 Dr. Crippen used hyoscine, which is extracted from the plant, to murder his wife. Every part of the plant is toxic.

Henbane has been considered to have aphrodisiac properties and is the main ingredient in some love potions and witches' brews. It was also placed by the hinges of outer doors to protect against sorcery.

 ## varieties

 ### Hyoscyamus niger
Henbane
Annual/biennial. Ht. up to 32 in., spread 12 in. Flowers bloom in summer, are yellow/brown or cream, funnel-shaped, and usually marked with purple veins. Leaves are hairy with large teeth, and the upper leaves have no stalks. The whole plant smells foul. All zones.

Hyoscyamus albus
White Henbane
Annual. Ht. 12 in., spread 12 in. Its summer flowers are pale yellow funnel-shaped and marked with violet veins. Leaves are identical to *H. niger*. All zones.

 ## cultivation

Propagation
Seed
Sow the fairly small seeds on the surface of pots or trays in spring, and cover with perlite. Germination takes 10–15 days. If you want henbane to behave like a biennial, sow in early fall, keeping the soil moist until germination (which can be erratic, but on average takes about 14–21 days). Winter the young plants in a cold frame or cold greenhouse. Plant the following spring at a distance of 12 in. apart.

Pests and Diseases
This plant is typically free from pests and diseases.

Maintenance
Spring Sow seed.
Summer Deadhead flowers to maintain plant (wear gloves).
Fall Sow seed for second-year flowers.
Winter Protect young plants.

Garden Cultivation
Choose the site for planting henbane with care, because it is poisonous. It will tolerate any growing situation but shows a preference for a well-drained sunny site. Sow seeds in late spring. When the seedlings are large enough to handle, thin to 12 in. apart. It can look striking in a mixed border.

Harvesting
Collect seed when the head turns brown and begins to open at the end.

 ## container growing

Inadvisable to grow such a poisonous plant this way.

 ## medicinal

This plant was used for a wide range of conditions that required sedation. The alkaloid hyoscine, which is derived from the green tops and leaves, is used as a hypnotic and brain sedative for the seasick, excitable and insane. It is also used externally in analgesic preparations to relieve rheumatism and arthritis. The syrup has a sedative effect in cases of Parkinson's disease.

warning

The whole plant is poisonous. Children have been poisoned by eating the seeds or seed pods. Use preparation and dosage only under strict medical direction.

126 THE COMPLETE HERB BOOK

Hypericum perforatum
ST. JOHN'S WORT

Also known as Warrior's wound, Amber, Touch and Heal, Grace of God and Herb of St. John. From the family Clusiaceae.

This magical herb is found in temperate zones of the world in open situations on semidry soils. Whoever treads on St. John's Wort after sunset will be swept up on the back of a magic horse that will charge-round the heavens until sunrise before depositing its exhausted rider on the ground.

Besides its magical attributes, *Hypericum* has medicinal properties and was universally known as the Grace of God. In England it cured mania, in Russia it gave protection against hydrophobia and the Brazilians knew it as an antidote to snake bite. St. John's Wort ("wort," incidentally, is Anglo-Saxon for "medicinal herb") has been used to raise ghosts and exorcise spirits. When crushed, the leaves release a balsamic odor similar to incense, which was said to be strong enough to drive away evil spirits. The red pigment from the crushed flowers was taken to signify the blood of St. John at his beheading, for the herb is in full flower on June 24, St. John's Day.

 ## varieties

Hypericum perforatum
St. John's Wort
Hardy perennial. Ht. 12–36 in., spread 12 in. Scented yellow flowers with black dots in summer. The small leaves are stalkless and covered with tiny perforations (hence *perforatum*), which are in fact translucent glands. This is the magical species. Zone 3.

 ## cultivation

Propagation
Seed
Sow very small seed in spring into prepared seed or plug module trays, and cover with perlite. Germination is usually in 10–20 days depending on the weather. When the seedlings are large enough to handle and after a period of hardening off, plant 12 in. apart.

Division
Divide established plants in the fall.

Pests and Diseases
Largely free from pests and diseases.

Maintenance
Spring Sow seeds.
Summer Cut back after flowering to stop self-seeding.
Fall Divide established clumps.
Winter No need for protection, fully hardy.

Garden Cultivation
Tolerates most soils, in sun or light shade, but it can be invasive in light soils.

Harvesting
Harvest leaves and flowers as required.

 ## container growing

Can be grown in containers, but it is a bit tall so you do need a large clump for it to look effective. Use a loam-based compost. Water in the summer months. Only feed with liquid fertilizer twice during the growing season, otherwise it produces more leaf than flower.

 ## other uses

The flowers release a yellow dye with alum, and a red dye with alcohol.

 ## warning

St. John's Wort has sometimes poisoned livestock. Its use also makes the skin sensitive to light.

 ## medicinal

Oil extracted by macerating the flowers in vegetable oil and applied externally eases neuralgia and the pain of sciatica, varicose veins, ulcers and sunburn. Only take internally under supervision.

St. John's Wort oil

HYSSOP

Hyssopus officinalis

"Purge me with Hyssop and I shall be clean."
Psalm 51, verse 7.

From the family Lamiaceae.

Hyssop is a native of the Mediterranean region, where it grows wild on old walls and dry banks. It is found as a garden escapee elsewhere in Europe and has been cultivated in gardens for about the last 600 years. It was one of the herbs taken to the New World by the colonists to use in tea, in herbal tobacco and as an antiseptic.

Hyssopus officinalis subsp. *aristatus*

There has been much debate about whether common hyssop is the one mentioned in the Bible. Some say it was oregano or savory. However, present thinking is that hyssop is flavor of the month, especially since it has been discovered that the mold that produces penicillin grows on its leaf. This may have acted as an antibiotic protection when lepers were bathed in hyssop.

The Persians used distilled hyssop water as a body lotion to give a fine color to their skin.

Hippocrates recommended hyssop for chest complaints, and today herbalists still prescribe it.

varieties

These are the common hyssops, readily available from nurseries and garden centers.

Hyssopus officinalis
Hyssop, Blue Hyssop
Hardy, semievergreen perennial. Ht. 32 in., spread 36 in. Blue flowers from summer to early fall. Small, narrow, lance-shaped leaves, aromatic and darkish green. Zone 3.

Hyssopus officinalis f. albus
White Hyssop
Hardy, semievergreen perennial. Ht. 32 in., spread 36 in. White flowers from summer to early fall. Small, narrow, lance-shaped leaves, aromatic, and darkish green in color. Zone 3.

Hyssopus officinalis subsp. aristatus
Rock Hyssop
Hardy, semi-evergreen, perennial. Ht. 12 in., spread 24 in. Dark blue flowers from summer to early fall. Small, narrow, lance-shaped leaves, aromatic and darkish green. Zone 3.

Hyssopus officinalis 'Roseus'
Pink Hyssop
Hardy, semievergreen, perennial. Ht. 32 in., spread 36 in. Pink flowers from summer to early fall. Small, narrow, lance-shaped leaves, aromatic and darkish green. Zone 3.

cultivation

Propagation
Seeds
In early spring, sow the small seeds in plug module or seed trays under protection, using a standard seed compost mixed in equal parts with composted fine bark. Cover with perlite. If very early in spring, a bottom heat of 60–70°F (15–21°C) would be beneficial. When the seedlings are large enough, pot or transplant into the garden 12 in. apart after a period of hardening off. All varieties can be grown from seed with the exception of rock hyssop, which can only be grown from cuttings. However, if you want a guaranteed pink or white hyssop, cuttings are a more reliable method.

Cuttings
In late spring or early summer, take softwood cuttings from the new lush growth and nonflowering stems.

Pests and Diseases
This genial plant rarely suffers from pests or diseases.

Maintenance
Spring Sow seeds. Trim mature plants. Trim hedges.
Summer Deadhead flowers to maintain supply, trim after flowering to maintain shape. Trim hedges.
Fall Cut back only in mild areas.
Winter Protect in cold, wet winters and temperatures that fall below 23°F (−5°C). Use a frost cloth, straw, bracken, etc.

Garden Cultivation
This attractive plant likes to be planted in conditions similar to rosemary and thyme, a well-drained soil in a sunny position. The seeds can be sown directly into

Hyssopus officinalis f. *albus*

the ground in very late spring or early summer, when the soil is warm. Thin to 12 in. apart if being grown as specimen plants. If for hedging, 7 in. As all parts of the plant are pleasantly aromatic and the flowers very attractive, plant it where it can be seen and brushed against. The flowers are also attractive to bees and butterflies. For these reasons hyssop makes a very good hedge or edging plant. Trim the top shoots to encourage bushy growth. In early spring, trim the plant into a tidy shape. To keep the plant flowering in summer, remove the dead heads. Cut back to 8 in. in the fall in mild areas, or trim back after flowering in cold areas. Keep formal hedges well clipped during the growing season.

Harvesting

Cut young leaves for drying in summer. The flowers should be picked during the summer too, when they are fully opened. The scent is generally improved with drying.

 ## companion planting

It is said that when grown near cabbages it lures away cabbage whiteflies. When planted near vines, it is reputed that the blue flowers of Hyssop attract the pollinating insects so helping to increase the yield.

 ## container growing

Hyssop is a lovely plant in containers. It is happy in plenty of sunshine and prefers a south-facing wall. It also likes dry conditions and its tough leaves are not affected by the fumes of city centers, making it ideal for window boxes. Equally, it is good on a patio as the scent is lovely on a hot summer's evening. Give it a liquid feed only during the flowering period. Cut back after flowering to maintain shape.

 ## medicinal

An infusion is used mainly for coughs, whooping cough, asthma and bronchitis, and upper respiratory congestion. It is also used for inflammation of the urinary tract. Externally it can be used for bruises and burns. It was once a country remedy for rheumatism.

 ## warning

Hyssop should not be used in cases of nervous irritability. Strong doses, particularly those of distilled essential oil, can cause muscular spasms. This oil should not be used in aromatherapy for highly strung patients, as it can cause epileptic symptoms. Do not use continuously for extended periods. No form of hyssop should be taken during pregnancy.

 ## culinary

The flowers are delicious tossed in a green salad. In small amounts, leaves aid digestion of fatty foods but as they are somewhat pungent use them sparingly. The herb has a slightly bitter, minty taste and is therefore good flavoring in salads or as an addition to game, meats and soups, stews and stuffings. A good idea is to add a teaspoon of chopped leaf to a Yorkshire pudding batter. Hyssop is sometimes used as one of the herbs in bouquet garni and for flavoring a concentrated purée of tomatoes preserved for the winter. It is used in continental sausages and also added to fruit pies, 1/4 teaspoon hyssop being sprinkled over the fruit before the top crust goes on.

When making a sugar syrup for fruit, add a sprig of hyssop as you boil the sugar and water; it adds a pleasant flavor, and the sprig can be removed before adding the fruit. When making cranberry pie, use the leaves as a lining for the dish.

Basque-Style Chicken
Serves 6

3 1/2 lb. chicken
4 sweet peppers (2 red, 2 green)
Hyssop olive oil
5 tablespoons dry white wine
4 medium tomatoes, peeled and roughly chopped
6 onions
4 cloves of garlic
1 bouquet garni with a sprig of hyssop
Salt and pepper

Deseed and slice the peppers into thin strips. Gently fry them in a small amount of oil until soft. Remove from pan and put to one side. Cut chicken into pieces and gently fry in the oil, turning all the time. Transfer to a casserole, and season with salt and pepper. Moisten with the wine, and leave over a gentle heat to finish cooking. Slice the onions and peel the garlic cloves, and soften without coloring, in the olive oil in the frying pan. Then add the tomatoes, peppers and bouquet garni, and season. When reduced almost to a cream, turn into the casserole over the chicken and keep on a low heat until ready to serve, about a further 20–30 minutes.

ELECAMPANE

Inula helenium

Also known as Allecampane, July campane, Elicompane, Dock, Sunflower, Wild sunflower, Yellow starwort, Elfdock, Elfwort, Horse elder, Horse heal and Scabwort. From the family Asteraceae.

Elecampane originates from Asia whence, through cultivation, it spread across Western Europe to North America and now grows wild from Nova Scotia to Ontario, North Carolina, and Missouri.

Sources for the derivation of the principal common name, Elecampane, and the botanical name, *Inula helenium*, are not altogether satisfactory, but I have found three possible explanations.

Helen of Troy was believed to be gathering the herb when she was abducted by Paris, hence *helenium*.

Down through the ages the herb was considered as good medicinally for horse or mule as for man; it was even sometimes called horselene. *Inula* could come from *hinnulus*, meaning "a young mule."

Finally, the Romans called the herb *Enula Campana* (Inula of the fields) from which Elecampane is a corruption.

According to the Roman writer Pliny, the Emperor Julius Augustus enjoyed elecampane so much he proclaimed, "Let no day pass without eating some of the roots candied to help the digestion and cause mirth." The Romans also used it as a candied sweetmeat, colored with cochineal. This idea persisted for centuries, and in the Middle Ages, apothecaries sold the candied root in flat pink sugary cakes, which were sucked to alleviate asthma and indigestion and to sweeten the breath. Tudor herbalists also candied them for the treatment of coughs, nasal congestion, bronchitis and chest ailments. Their use continued until the 1920s as a flavoring in sweets.

I have discovered an Anglo-Saxon ritual using elecampane—part medicinal, part magical. Prayers were sung of the *Helenium* and its roots dug up by the medicinal man, who had been careful not to speak to any disreputable creature—man, elf, goblin or fairy—he chanced to meet on the way to the ceremony. Afterward the elecampane root was laid under the altar for the night and eventually mixed with betony and lichen from a crucifix. The medicine was taken against elf sickness or elf disease.

There is an ancient custom in Scandinavia of putting a bunch of elecampane in the center of a nosegay of herbs to symbolize the sun and the head of Odin, the greatest of Norse gods.

ELECAMPANE

Inula helenium

 ## varieties

Inula helenium
Elecampane
Hardy perennial. Ht. 5–8 ft., spread 3 ft. Bright yellow, ragged, daisy-like flowers in summer. The leaves are large, oval-toothed, slightly downy underneath, and of a mid-green color. Dies back fully in winter. Zone 4.

Inula hookeri
Hardy perennial. Ht. 30 in., spread 18 in. Yellowish-green, ragged, daisy-like flowers slightly scented in summer. Lance-shaped hairy leaves, smaller than *I. magnifica*, and mid-green in color. Dies back fully in winter. Zone 4.

Inula magnifica
Hardy perennial. Ht. 6 ft., spread 3 ft. Large, ragged, daisy-like flowers. Lots of large, dark green lance-shaped rough leaves. May need staking in an exposed garden. This is often mistaken for *I. helenium*; the leaf color is the biggest difference, and on average *I. magnifica* grows much larger. Dies back fully in winter. Zone 4.

 ## cultivation

Propagation
Seed
The seed is similar to dandelion; when the plant has germinated you can see the seeds flying all over the garden, which should be all the warning you need. In spring sow on the surface of a pot or plug module

tray. Cover with perlite. Germination is 2–4 weeks, depending on the sowing season and seed viability. Prick out and plant 3–5 ft. apart when the seedlings are large enough to handle.

Root Division
If the plant grows too big for its position in the garden, divide in the fall when the plant has died back. As the roots are very strong, choose the point of division carefully. Alternatively remove the offshoots that grow around the parent plant; each has its own root system, so they can be planted immediately in a prepared site elsewhere in the garden. This can be done in the fall or spring.

Pests and Diseases
It rarely suffers from disease, although if the fall is excessively wet, as the leaves die back, they may suffer from a form of mildew. Simply cut back and destroy the leaves.

Maintenance
Spring Sow seed. Divide established plants.
Summer Remove flowerheads as soon as flowering finishes.
Fall Cut back growth to stop self-seeding and to prevent the plant becoming untidy. Remove offshoots for replanting. Divide large plants.
Winter The plant dies back so needs no protection.

Garden Cultivation
Plant in a moist, fertile soil, in full sun, sheltered from the wind (Elecampane grows tall and would otherwise need staking). It can look very striking at the back of a border against a stone wall, or in front of a screen of deciduous trees. In a very dry summer it may need watering.

Harvesting
Dig up second- or third-year roots in the fall; they can be used as a vegetable, or dried for use in medicine.
The flowers are good in fall flower arrangements and dry well upside down if you cut them just before the seeds turn brown.

 ## container growing

Elecampane grows too big for most containers and is easily blown over.

 ## culinary

Elecampane has a sharp, bitter flavor. Use dried pieces or cook as a root vegetable.

 ## other uses

Your cat may be interested to know that scientific research indicates that Elecampane has a sedative effect on mice.

 ## medicinal

The main use is for respiratory complaints, at one time specifically for tuberculosis. It is still employed in folk medicine as a favorite constituent of cough remedies, and has always been popular both as a medicine and as a condiment.

In America, elecampane oil is used for respiratory infections, intestinal catarrh, chronic diarrhea, chronic bronchitis and whooping cough.

A decoction of the root has long been used externally for scabies, herpes, acne and other skin diseases, hence its country name Scabwort.

Recent research shows that the lactines found in the roots are powerful agents against bacteria and fungi.

Elecampane oil

IRIS

From the family Iridaceae.

All those mentioned are native to the northern hemisphere and are cultivated in varying conditions, from dry light soil (orris—*Iris* "Florentina") to damp boggy soils (blue flag iris—*Iris versicolor*).

The Greek word *iris*, meaning "rainbow" and the name of the Greek goddess of the rainbow, was appended to describe the plant's variable colors. The iris is one of the oldest cultivated plants—it is depicted on the wall of an Egyptian temple dating from 1500 BC.

In this very large family, three stand out for their beneficial herbal qualities. Orris has a violet-scented root which has been powdered and used in perfumes since the times of the ancient Egyptians and Greeks. The Latin *Iris* "Florentina" depicts its association with Florence in the early Middle Ages. It is said to be the fleur-de-lys of French heraldry.

The blue flag iris is the common wetland plant, native to eastern North America and exported from there to Europe. Employed by the Native Americans and early settlers as a remedy for gastric complaints, it was included in the U.S. Pharmacopeia and is still believed in folk medicine to be a blood purifier of use in eruptive skin conditions. Sometimes the plant is known as liver lily because of its purifying effect.

Iris pseudacorus

The root of the yellow flag iris, a native of the British Isles, was powdered and used as an ingredient in Elizabethan snuff. It was taken to America and Australia by the earliest settlers.

 varieties

Iris 'Florentina'
Orris
Also known as florentine iris and orris root. Hardy perennial. Ht. 2–3 ft. Spread indefinite. Large white flowers tinged with pale lavender and with a yellow beard appearing in early to midsummer. Green, sword-shaped leaves. The rootstock is stout and rhizomatous with a violet scent. Grows well throughout Europe and North America, except in the warm, moist and humid Southern climates. Zone 4.

Iris germanica
Purple Iris
Also known as garden iris and flag iris. Hardy perennial. Ht. 2–3 ft., spread indefinite. The fragrant flowers are blue/violet, occasionally white, and form early to midsummer. Leaves are grayish-green and sword-shaped. The root is thickish rhizome. There are many cultivated varieties. It is grown commercially for the rhizomes and, like *Iris* 'Florentina,' is used in perfumery and pharmaceutical preparations. Zone 4.

Iris pseudacorus
Yellow Iris (Yellow Flag)
Perennial. Ht. 16 in.–5 ft., spread indefinite. Flowers are bright yellow with radiating brown veins and very slightly scented. They appear early to midsummer. The root is a thick rhizome from which many rootlets descend. Zone 4.

Iris versicolor
Blue Flag Iris
Also known as flag lily, fleur-de-lys, flower du luce, liver lily, poison flags, snake lily, water flag and wild iris. Hardy perennial. Ht. 12–39 in., spread indefinite. Flowers claret-purple-blue in summer. Large, sword-shaped, green leaves. Root large and rhizomatous. Zone 4.

IRIS

Iris 'Florentina'

 ## cultivation

Propagation

Seed
All the irises produce large seeds, which take some time to germinate and often benefit from a period of stratification. As the seeds are of a good size, sow directly into a 3 in. pot in the fall, using a standard seed compost mixed in equal parts with composted fine bark. Water well, and cover the pots with plastic wrap (to prevent mice from eating the seed). Put outside to get the weather. Check that the compost remains damp. If there is any danger of it drying out, stand the container in water. This is especially important for blue and yellow flag irises.

Division
Divide the rhizome roots in late spring or early fall. This suits all the varieties. Replant immediately in a prepared site. Leave a decent distance between plants; spread is indefinite.

Pests and Diseases
The only major pest is the iris sawfly, which is attracted to waterside irises. The darkish-gray larvae feed along the leaf-margins, removing large chunks. Pupation takes place in the soil beneath or near the host plants, and the adult sawflies mature during early to midsummer. Pick off the larvae when seen. This is an annual pest and there is not much be done to prevent it.

Maintenance
Spring Divide roots of mature plants.
Summer Collect the seeds as soon as ripe.
Fall Sow seeds and leave outside. Divide roots.
Winter Fully hardy; no need for protection.

Garden Cultivation
Orris and purple iris prefer a well-drained, rich soil and a sunny situation. When planting, make sure that part of the rhizome is exposed.

Yellow and blue flag irises are marsh-loving plants, ideal for those with a pond or ditch or piece of boggy ground. They grow happily in semishade but need full sun in order to produce the maximum bloom. In deep shade they will not flower at all but will spread quickly by stout underground rhizomes. A measure of control will be necessary.

Harvesting
The full violet fragrance of orris will not be apparent until the roots are 2 years old. Dig up these rhizomes in the fall and dry immediately.

Gather yellow flag flowers and roots for use as a dye, in early summer and fall respectively. Dig up blue flag roots in the fall and dry.

 ## container growing

These irises grow on strong rhizomes, so make sure that the container is strong enough, large enough, and shaped so that it will accommodate the plant happily and not blow over. For the bog lovers, use peat in the compost mix—75 percent peat mixed with 25 percent composted fine bark, but put lots of gravel and broken crocks in the bottom of the container to make up for loss of weight. For the dry gang, use a soil-based compost. Do not let either compost dry out. They become potbound very quickly, so split and repot every year.

 ## other uses

The violet-scented, powdered root of orris is used to add a fresh scent to linen, as a base for dry shampoo, and tooth powders, in face-packs, and as a fixative in potpourri.

Flowers of yellow flag make a good yellow dye, while the rhizomes yield a gray or black dye when used with an iron mordant.

 ## medicinal

Orris and yellow flag are rarely used medicinally nowadays. However, herbalists still use the blue flag as a blood purifier acting on the liver and gall bladder to increase the flow of bile, and as an effective cleanser of toxins. It is also said to relieve flatulence and heartburn, belching and nausea, and headaches associated with digestive problems.

 ## culinary

Apparently, if you roast the seed of the yellow flag iris, they make an excellent coffee substitute. Apart from this little gem, I cannot find any culinary uses for irises.

 ## warning

Always wash your hands well after handling this plant as it can cause uncontrollable vomiting and violent diarrhea. Large doses of the fresh root can cause nausea, vomiting and facial neuralgias.

Isatis tinctoria

WOAD

Also known as Dyers woad, Glastum. From the family Brassicaceae.

This ancient dye plant for cloth and wool has been used for thousands of years. It was the only source of blue dye available in Europe until the end of the 16th century, when indigo *(Indigofera tinctoria)* became available from India via the spice trade. There is a resurgence in interest in this herb not only because of recent films on Picts, Celts and Romans, but also due to current research into its medicinal properties.

 varieties

Isatis tinctoria
Woad

Hardy biennial. Ht. in first year 18 in., second year when in flower 4 ft., spread 18 in. Clusters of numerous, small bright yellow honey-scented flowers in the second summer, which are followed by pendulous black seeds. Lance-shaped, lightly toothed, blue/green leaves. The tap root in the second season can be 4½ ft. long. Zone 3.

 cultivation

Propagation
Seed

Sow fresh seeds in the fall into prepared plug modules or small pots using a seed compost mixed in equal parts with perlite. Place the container in a cold green house or cold frame. Germination takes 3–4 weeks. In the spring plant into a prepared site 12 in. apart. Alternatively sow in late spring, when the night time temperature does not fall below 48°F (9°C), direct into a well-prepared site. Once the seedlings have emerged, thin to 12 in. apart.

Pests and Diseases
Woad seedlings can be attacked by the flea beetle. To prevent this, in spring, cover with a fine frost cloth for the first season only.

Maintenance
Spring Protect new seedlings from flea beetle. Mulch second-year plants.
Summer Harvest seeds and roots of second-year plants.
Fall Sow fresh seeds.
Winter No need for protection; fully hardy.

Garden Cultivation
Plant in a sunny position in a well-drained, well-fed soil. Be aware that this herb has a very long tap root and hates being transplanted once the plant starts to become established. In late summer collect the seeds before they fall as it is renowned for self-seeding.

Harvesting
In late summer pick the leaves, either to dry for medicinal use, or to ferment and then dry for use as a dye. Dig up the roots of the second year's growth in late summer then dry for medicinal use. Harvest the seeds in late summer as they turn dark brown and before they drop.

 container growing

Being biennial, this herb looks very boring for the first year and when it goes to flower in the second it becomes very tall, which does not make it an ideal container plant.

 medicinal

In Chinese medicine the root of this herb is known as *ban lang gen*, and it is used to treat meningitis and mumps. However be aware that woad is very astringent and poisonous and should only be taken internally under supervision. In 2006 the *New Scientist* reported that Italian biochemists have discovered that woad contains more than 60 times the amount of glucobrassicin, a type of glucosinolate, in the leaves than are found in broccoli, which might help in the prevention of cancer.

 other uses

Traditional blue dye plant.

 warning

Astringent and poisonous when taken internally. It is classed as a noxious weed in Australia and the United States.

Woad dye

Jasminum officinale

JASMINE

Also known as Common jasmine, Yasmine, Chambeli, Jessamine and Mogra. From the family Oleaceae.

The scent of the jasmine flower wafting over the night air is very evocative. The jasmine flower symbolizes femininity. Traditionally Italian girls include jasmine in their bridal head dresses. There is a lovely story that the Duke of Tuscany in the 17th century introduced this herb from China, and one of his gardeners gave his betrothed a piece as a token of his love and was promptly dismissed for this misdemeanor. However his betrothed planted the cutting and their garden was soon festooned with jasmine, which was much sought after by the girls of the village for its aphrodisiac properties.

 ## varieties

Jasminum officinale
Jasmine/Jessamine
Hardy deciduous, occasionally semievergreen, climber. Ht. up to 30 ft., spread up to 9 ft. Small fragrant white flowers all summer, followed by black poisonous berries. Pinnate mid-green leaves with three to nine leaflets. Zone 8.

Jasminum grandiflorum
Royal Jasmine, Spanish Jasmine, Jati Tender evergreen climber. Ht. up to 15 ft. Clusters of highly scented white flowers with a pink tinge all summer. Pinnate dark green leaves with seven or nine leaflets. Zone 9.

 ## cultivation

Propagation
Seed
In the fall, extract the seeds from the berries, and sow into prepared pots or plug modules using a standard loam-based seed compost mixed in equal parts with coarse river sand. Cover with sand, and then place outside for the winter. The seeds need frost to break their dormancy. Germination takes 4–6 months, but it can be erratic, so be patient and do not discard the container.

Cuttings
Take cuttings from semiripe growth in summer into prepared plug modules or a small pot, using a seed compost mixed in equal parts with propagating bark. Place in a cold frame or cold greenhouse. Once rooted, pot into a loam-based potting compost, winter in a cold frame, plant in the following spring.

Pests and Diseases
Rarely suffers from pests or diseases.

Maintenance
Spring Prune established plants.
Summer Take cuttings from semiripe growth.
Fall Sow seeds.
Winter No need for protection, fully hardy.

Garden Cultivation
This sturdy climber, once established, will outgrow a trellis or need continual pruning if grown on a house, therefore is best grown over an arbor, porch, or a large old tree stump in a fertile soil and a sunny position. Prune in spring.

Harvesting
Pick flowers early in the morning, just as they open, for use as a flavoring, for infusions or for making oils.

 ## container growing

As this is a vigorous climber it is not ideally suited to container growing.

 ## medicinal

In Ayurvedic medicine, a juice pressed from the leaves is used to remove corns. The leaves are also used as a gargle for mouth ulcers. An infusion made from the flowers is used to cool inflamed and bloodshot eyes. The essential oil made from the flowers is considered an antidepressant and relaxant.

 ## other uses

The essential oil is used in perfumes and in several food flavorings.

 ## warning

Do not take jasmine essential oil internally. The berries are poisonous.

Jasminum officinale berries

Juniperus communis
JUNIPER

Juniperus communis 'Compressa'

From the family Cupressaceae.

Juniper is widely distributed throughout the world and grows either as a shrub or a small tree. It is a native of the Mediterranean region, but also grows in the Arctic, from Norway to the Soviet Union, in the North and West Himalayas and in North America. It is found in the countryside, open coniferous forests and mountain slopes.

This widely distributed plant was first used by the ancient Greek physicians and its use has continued right up to the modern day. It was believed to cure snake bites and protect against infectious diseases like the plague.

The English word "gin" is derived from an abbreviation of Holland's "geneva," as the spirit was first called. This in turn stems from the Dutch *jenever*, meaning juniper.

Juniperus communis 'Hibernica'
Irish Juniper
Hardy evergreen perennial tree. Ht. 9–15 ft., spread 12 in. Leaves small and bluish/silvery-green, sharply pointed and aromatic. Columnar in shape and with a hint of silver in certain lights. Very slow growing. Zone 2.

Juniperus communis 'Hornibrookii'
Juniper Hornibrookii
Hardy evergreen perennial tree. Ht. 20 in., spread 6 ft. Leaves small and darkish green, sharply pointed and aromatic. A big carpeting plant. Zone 2.

Juniperus communis 'Prostrata'
Prostrate Juniper
Hardy evergreen perennial tree. Ht. 8–12 in., spread 3–6 ft. Leaves small and bluish-green, sharply pointed and aromatic. A smaller carpeting plant. Zone 2.

Juniperus communis berries

 varieties

Juniper is a conifer, a group of trees and shrubs distinguished botanically from others by its production of seeds exposed or uncovered on the scales of the fruit. True to form, it is evergreen and has needlelike leaves.

There are many species and varieties available, *Juniperus communis*, being the main herbal variety. On the varieties detailed below, the flowers are all very similar: male flowers are very small catkins; female flowers are small, globose and berrylike, usually with 3–8 fleshy scales. Over a period of 3 years, these turn blue and then finally black as they ripen.

Juniperus communis
Juniper
Hardy evergreen perennial. Ht. 12 in.–24 ft., spread 3–12 ft. The size of the plant is very dependent on where it is growing. Leaves small and bright green, sharply pointed and aromatic. Zone 2.

Juniperus communis 'Compressa'
Juniper Compressa
Hardy evergreen perennial tree. Ht. 24 in., spread 6 in. The leaves are small and bluish-green, sharply pointed and aromatic. Very slow growing with an erect habit, ideal for rock gardens or containers. Zone 2.

 ## cultivation

Propagation

Seed

All the species can be propagated by seed. Sow seeds taken from ripe berries in a cold greenhouse, cold frame or cold sunroom in early fall. As junipers are extremely slow growing, it is best to grow the seedlings in a controlled environment for 1 or 2 years before planting in a permanent position in the garden. Start in seed or plug module trays; then, when the seedlings are large enough, pot into small pots using a soil-based seed compost. This method is the easiest but to be sure of the plant's gender and leaf color, taking cuttings is more reliable.

Cuttings

It is quite easy to raise juniper from semihardwood cuttings taken from fresh current growth in either spring or fall.

Pests and Diseases

Various rusts attack juniper. If you see swellings on the branches with rusty, gelatinous extrusions, cut the branches out and burn them.

Honey fungus attacks many conifers. If this occurs, dig up the plant, making sure you have all the roots, burn it, and plant no further trees in that space.

Maintenance

Spring Plant 2-year-old plants. Remove any leaders growing incorrectly in late spring/early summer.
Summer Take semihardwood cuttings. Harvest berries

and store in a dry place.
Fall Sow seeds. Take cuttings.
Winter Winter young plants in cold frames, or provide added protection.

Garden Cultivation

Juniper likes an exposed, sunny site. It will tolerate an alkaline or neutral soil. Both male and female plants are necessary for berry production. The berries, which only grow on the female bush, can be found in various stages of ripeness on the same plant. Their flavor is stronger when grown in warm climates.

To maintain the shape of the juniper, trim with pruning shears to ensure that there is no more than one leader, the strongest and straightest. Remember, when trimming, that most conifers will not make new growth when cut back into old wood, or into branches that have turned brown.

Harvesting

Harvest the berries when ripe in late summer. Dry them spread out on a tray, as you would leaves.

 ## container growing

Juniper is slow growing and can look most attractive in pots. Use a soil-based compost, starting off with a suitable-sized pot, only repotting once a year if necessary. If the root ball looks happy, do not disturb it. Do not overwater. As the plant is hardy and evergreen, the container will need more protection than the plant during the winter months. Feed during the summer months only with a liquid fertilizer as per the manufacturer's guidelines.

 ## medicinal

Juniper is used in the treatment of cystitis, rheumatism and gout. Steamed inhalations of the berries are an excellent treatment for coughs, colds and congestion.

⚠ warning

Juniper berries should not be taken during pregnancy or by people with kidney problems. Internal use of the volatile oil must only ever be prescribed by professionals.

 ## culinary

Crushed berries are an excellent addition to marinades, sauerkraut and stuffing for guinea fowl and other game birds. Although no longer generally considered as a spice, it is still an important flavoring for certain meats, liqueurs, and especially gin.

Pork Chops Marinated with Juniper
Serves 4

Marinade
2 tablespoons olive oil
6 juniper berries, crushed
2 cloves of garlic, crushed
Salt and pepper

Mix the oil, juniper berries, garlic and seasoning together in a bowl.

4 pork chops
2 tablespoons plain flour
1 1/8 cups dry cider

Lay the pork chops in the base of a shallow dish and cover them with the marinade, turning the chops over once to make sure they are covered. Leave for a minimum of 3 hours, or if possible overnight. Remove the chops from the marinade, and reserve it. Heat a large frying pan and add the reserved marinade. When hot, add the pork chops and cook over a moderate heat for about 20 minutes, turning the chops regularly. When all traces of pink have gone from the meat, remove from the heat, and put the chops on a plate. Return the pan to the heat and stir the flour into the remaining juices. Add the cider and bring to the boil. Return the chops to the sauce in the pan. Heat slowly, and serve with mashed potato and broccoli.

Laurus nobilis
BAY

From the family
Lauraceae.

Bay is an evergreen tree
native to southern Europe,
and now found
throughout the world.

That this ancient plant
was much respected in
Roman times is reflected
in the root of its family
name, Lauraceae, the
Latin *laurus*, meaning
"praise," and in its main
species epithet, *Laurus
nobilis*, the Latin *nobilis*
meaning "famous,"
"renowned." A bay wreath
became a mark of
excellence for poets and
athletes, a symbol of
wisdom and glory. The
word laureate means
"crowned with laurels" (synonym for bay), hence Poet Laureate, of
course, and the French *baccalauréat*.

The bay tree was sacred even earlier—to Apollo, Greek god of prophecy,
poetry and healing. His priestesses ate bay leaves before expounding his
oracles at Delphi. As large doses of bay induce the effect of a narcotic,
this may explain their trances. His temple had its roof made entirely of
bay leaves, ostensibly to protect against disease, witchcraft and
lightning. Apollo's son Asclepius, the Greek god of Medicine, also had
bay dedicated to him as it was considered a powerful antiseptic and
guard against disease, in particular the plague.

In the 17th century, Culpeper wrote that "neither witch nor devil,
thunder nor lightening, will hurt a man in the place where a bay-tree is."
He also wrote that "the berries are very effectual against the poison of
venomous creatures, and the stings of wasps and bees."

 varieties

Laurus azorica (Laurus canariensis)
Canary Island Bay
Perennial evergreen tree. Ht. to 20 ft. Reddish-brown
branches, a color that sometimes extends to the
leaves. Zone 9.

Laurus nobilis
Bay
Also known as sweet bay, sweet laurel, laurel, Indian
bay, Grecian laurel. Perennial evergreen tree. Ht. up to
26 ft., spread 12 ft. Small, pale yellow, waxy flowers in
spring. Green oval berries turning black in the fall. The
leaves may be added to stock, soups and stews and are
among the main ingredients of bouquet garni. *L. nobilis*
is the only bay used for culinary purposes. Zone 8.

Laurus nobilis f. *angustifolia*
Willow Leaf Bay
Perennial evergreen tree. Ht. up to 23 ft. Narrow-
leafed variety, said to be hardier than *L. nobilis*. This is
not strictly true. Zone 8.

Laurus nobilis 'Aurea'
Golden Bay
Perennial evergreen tree. Ht. up to 18 ft. Small, pale
yellow, waxy flowers in spring. Green berries turning
black in the fall. Golden leaves can look sickly in damp,
cooler countries. Needs good protection in winter
especially from wind scorch and frosts. Trim in the
fall/spring to maintain the golden leaves. Zone 9.

Umbellularia californica
Californian Laurel
Perenial evergreen tree. Ht. up to 60 ft. Pale yellow
flowers in late spring. Very pungent/aromatic leaves.
Can cause headaches and nausea when the leaves
are crushed. NOT culinary. Zone 8.

 cultivation

Propagation
Seed
Bay sets seed in its black berries, but rarely in cooler
climates. Sow fresh seed in spring on the surface of
either a seed or plug tray or directly into pots. Use a
standard seed compost mixed in equal parts with
composted fine bark. Keep warm: 68°F (21°C).

Laurus nobilis

Germination is erratic, may take place within 10–20 days, in 6 months, or even longer. Make sure the compost is not too wet or it will rot the seeds.

Cuttings
Not a plant for the faint hearted. When I started propagating over 30 years ago, I thought my bay cuttings were doing really well, but a year later not one had properly struck, and three-quarters of them had turned black and died. A heated propagator is a great help and high humidity is essential. Use either a misting unit or cover the cutting in plastic wrap and maintain the compost or perlite at a steady moisture. Cuttings are taken in late summer/early fall 4 in. long.

Division
If offshoots are sent out by the parent plant, dig them up or they will destroy the shape of the tree. Occasionally roots come with them and these can then be potted in a standard seed compost mixed in equal parts with composted fine bark. Place a plastic bag over the pot to maintain humidity. Leave somewhere warm and check from time to time to see if new shoots are starting. When they do, remove the bag. Do not plant for at least a year.

Layering
In spring. A good way of propagating a difficult plant.

Pests and Diseases

Bay is susceptible to sooty mound, caused by the scale insect which sticks both to the undersides of leaves and to the stems, sucking the sap. Get rid of them by hand or use a liquid insecticidal soap. Bay sucker distorts the leaf so as soon as you see it, cut back the branch to clean growth.

Maintenance

Spring Sow seeds. Cut back standard and garden bay trees to maintain shape and to promote new growth. Cut back golden bay trees to maintain color. Check for pests and eradicate at first signs. Give container-grown plants a good liquid feed.
Summer Check that young plants are not drying out too much. In very hot weather, and especially in a city, spray-clean container-grown plants with water. Propagate by taking stem cuttings or layering in late summer.
Fall Take cuttings of mature plants. Protect container-grown and young garden plants. Cover garden plants in straw or bracken, if in a sufficiently sheltered position, or use a frost blanket.

Winter In severe winters the leaves will turn brown, but don't despair. Come the spring, it may shoot new growth from the base. To encourage this, cut the plant nearly down to the base.

Garden Cultivation

Bay is shallow rooted and therefore more prone to frost damage. Also, leaves are easily scorched in very cold weather or in strong, cold winds. Protection is thus essential, especially for bay trees under 2 years old. When planting, position the plant in full sun, protected from the wind, and in a rich well-drained soil at least 3 ft. away from other plants to start with, allowing more space as the tree matures. Mulch in the spring to retain moisture throughout the summer.

Harvesting

Being evergreen, leaves can be taken all year round. It is fashionable now to preserve bay leaves in vinegars.

 ## culinary

Fresh leaves are stronger in flavor than dried ones. Use in soups, stews and stocks.

Add leaves to poached fish, like salmon.
Put on the coals of a barbecue.
Put fresh leaves in jars of rice to flavor the rice.
Boil in milk to flavor custards and rice pudding.

Bouquet Garni

I quote from my grandmother's cookbook, *Food for Pleasure*, published in 1950: "A bouquet garni is a bunch of herbs constantly required in cooking." The essential herbs in a bouquet garni are bay leaf, parsley and thyme.

Berries are cultivated for use in laurel oil and laurel butter. The latter is a vital ingredient of laurin ointment, which is used in veterinary medicine.

 ## container growing

Bay makes a good container plant. Young plants benefit from being kept in a container and indoors for the winter in cooler climates. The kitchen windowsill is ideal. Do not water too much, and let the compost dry out in the winter months.

Large standard bays or pyramids look very effective in half barrels or containers of a similar size. They will need extra protection from frosts and wind, so if the temperature drops below 25°F (−5°C) bring the plants in.

To produce a standard bay tree, start with a young containerized plant with a straight growing stem. As it begins to grow, remove the lower side shoots below where you want the ball to begin. Allow the tree to grow to 8 in. higher than desired, then clip back the growing tip. Cut the remaining side shoots to about three leaves. When the side shoots have grown a further four or five leaves, trim again to two or three leaves. Repeat until you have a leafy ball shape. Once established, prune with pruning shears in late spring and late summer to maintain it.

 ## other uses

Place in flour to deter weevils. Add an infusion to a bath to relieve aching limbs.

 ## medicinal

Infuse the leaves to aid digestion and increase appetite.

Lavandula

LAVENDER

From the family Lamiaceae.

Native of the Mediterranean region, Canary Isles and India. Now cultivated in different regions of the world, growing in well-draining soil and warm, sunny climates.

Long before the world made deodorants and bath salts, the Romans used lavender in their bath water; the word is derived from the Latin *lava*, "to wash." It was the Romans who introduced this plant to Britain and from then on monks cultivated it in their monastic gardens. Little more was recorded until Tudor times when people noted its fragrance and a peculiar power to ease stiff joints and relieve tiredness. It was brought in quantities from herb farms to the London Herb Market at Bucklesbury. "Who will buy my lavender?" became perhaps the most famous of all London street cries.

It was used as a strewing herb for its insect-repellent properties and for masking household and street smells. It was also carried in nosegays to ward off the plague and pestilence. In France in the 17th century, huge fields of lavender were grown for the perfume trade. This has continued to the present day.

Lavandula stoechas subsp. *stoechas* f. *rosea* 'Kew Red'

 varieties

This is another big genus of plants that are eminently worth collecting. I include here a few of my favorites.

Lavandula angustifolia L. spica, L. officinalis
Common/English Lavender
Hardy evergreen perennial. Ht. 32 in., spread 3 ft. Mauve/purple flowers on a long spike in summer. Long, narrow, pale greenish-gray, aromatic leaves. One of the most popular and well known of the lavenders. Zone 5.

Lavandula angustifolia 'Alba'
White Lavender
Hardy evergreen perennial. Ht. 28 in., spread 32 in. White flowers on a long spike in summer. Long, narrow, pale greenish-gray, aromatic leaves. Zone 5.

Lavandula angustifolia 'Bowles' Early'
Lavender Bowles
Hardy evergreen perennial. Ht. and spread 24 in. Light blue flowers on a medium-size spike in summer. Medium-length, narrow gray/greenish, aromatic leaves. Zone 5.

Lavandula angustifolia 'Folgate'
Lavender Folgate
Hardy evergreen perennial. Ht. and spread 18 in. Purple flowers on a medium spike in summer. Leaves as above. Zone 5.

Lavandula angustifolia 'Hidcote'
Lavender Hidcote
Hardy evergreen perennial. Ht. and spread 18 in. Dark blue flowers on a medium spike in summer. Fairly short, narrow, aromatic, gray/greenish leaves. One of the most popular lavenders. Often used in hedging, planted at a distance of 12–16 in. Zone 5.

Lavandula x intermedia 'Old English'

Lavandula angustifolia 'Munstead'

Lavandula angustifolia **'Loddon Pink'**
Lavender Loddon Pink
Hardy evergreen perennial. Ht. and spread 18 in. Pale pink flowers on a medium-length spike in summer. Fairly short, narrow, gray/greenish, aromatic leaves. Good compact habit. 'Loddon Blue' is the same size, same height, with pale blue flowers. Zone 5.

Lavandula angustifolia **'Munstead'**
Lavender Munstead
Hardy evergreen perennial. Ht. and spread 18 in. Purple/blue flowers on a fairly short spike in summer. Medium length, greenish/gray, narrow, aromatic leaves. This is now a common lavender and used often in hedging, planted at a distance of 12–16 in. Zone 5.

Lavandula angustifolia **'Nana Alba'**
Dwarf White Lavender
Hardy evergreen perennial. Ht. and spread 12 in. White flowers in summer. Green/gray narrow short leaves. This is the shortest growing lavender and is ideal for hedges. Zone 5.

Lavandula angustifolia **'Rosea'**
Lavender Pink/Rosea
Hardy evergreen perennial. Ht. and spread 18 in. Pink flowers in summer. Medium length greenish/gray, narrow, aromatic leaves. Zone 5.

Lavandula angustifolia **'Twickel Purple'**
Lavender Twickel Purple
Hardy evergreen perennial. Ht. and spread 20 in. Pale purple flowers on fairly short spike. Medium length, greenish/gray, narrow, aromatic leaves. Compact. Zone 5.

Lavandula dentata
Fringed Lavender

Sometimes called French lavender. Half-hardy evergreen perennial. Ht. and spread 24 in. Pale blue/mauve flowers from summer to early fall. Highly aromatic, serrated, pale green, narrow leaves. This plant is a native of southern Spain and the Mediterranean region and so needs protecting in cold damp winters. It is ideal to bring inside into a cool room in early fall as a flowering potted plant. Zone 10.

Lavandula x *intermedia* **Dutch Group** *(L. vera)*
Lavender Vera
Hardy evergreen perennial. Ht. and spread 18 in. Purple flowers in summer on fairly long spikes. Long greenish/gray, narrow, aromatic leaves. Zone 5.

Lavandula x *intermedia* **'Old English'**
Old English Lavender
Hardy evergreen perennial. Ht. and spread 24 in. Light lavender-blue flowers on long spikes. Long, narrow, silver/gray/green, aromatic leaves. Zone 5.

Lavandula x *intermedia* **'Pale Pretender'** *(L. 'Grappenhall')*
Lavender Pale Pretender
Hardy evergreen perennial. Ht. and spread 3 ft. Large pale mauve flowers on long spikes in summer. The flowers are much more open than those of other species. Long greenish/gray, narrow, aromatic leaves. Zone 5.

Lavandula x *intermedia* **'Seal'**
Lavender Seal
Hardy evergreen perennial. Ht. 36 in., spread 24 in. Long flower stems, mid-purple. Long, narrow, silver/gray/green aromatic leaves. Zone 5.

Lavandula angustifolia 'Twickel Purple'

Lavandula pendunculata subsp. *pedunculata*

Lavandula lanata
Woolly Lavender
Hardy evergreen perennial. Ht. 20 in., spread 18 in. Deep purple flowers on short spikes. Short, soft, narrow, silver/gray aromatic foliage. Zone 6.

Lavandula pedunculata subsp. *pedunculata*
Lavender Pedunculata
Sometimes known as Papillon. Half-hardy evergreen perennial. Ht. and spread 24 in. The attractive purple bracts have an extra mauve center tuft, which looks like two rabbit ears. The aromatic leaves are long, very narrow and gray. Protect in winter. Zone 8.

Lavandula stoechas
French Lavender
Sometimes called Spanish lavender. Hardy evergreen perennial. Ht. 20 in., spread 24 in. Attractive purple bracts in summer. Short, narrow, gray/green, aromatic leaves. Zones 7–9.

Lavandula stoechas subsp. *stoechas* f. *leucantha*
White French Lavender
As *L. stoechas* except white bracts in summer. Zone 7–9.

Lavandula stoechas subsp. *stoechas* f. *rosea* 'Kew Red'
Lavender Kew Red
Half-hardy evergreen perennial. Ht. and spread 16 in. Deep crimson flowers and pale pink "ears." Short, narrow, gray/green aromatic leaves. Prefers an acidic soil. Zones 7–9.

Lavandula viridis
Green Lavender, Lemon Lavender
Half-hardy evergreen perennial. Ht. and spread 3 ft. This unusual plant has green bracts with a cream center tuft. The leaves are green, narrow, and highly aromatic. Protect in winter. Zone 9.

Lavenders—Small
Grow to 18–20 in.:
L. angustifolia 'Folgate', *L. angustifolia* 'Hidcote', *L. angustifolia* 'Loddon Pink', *L. angustifolia* 'Munstead', *L. angustifolia* 'Nana Alba', *L. angustifolia* 'Twickel Purple'

Lavenders—Medium
Grow to 3 ft.:
L. angustifolia 'Bowles' Early', *L. x intermedia* 'Old English'

Lavandula viridis

Lavenders—Large
28 in. and above:
L. angustifolia 'Alba', *L. x intermedia* 'Seal'.

Half-hardy Lavenders
L. dentata (20 in.), *L. lanata* (20 in.), *L. stoechas* (20 in.), *L. stoechas* subsp. *stoechas* f. *leucantha* (20 in.), *L. pedunculata* subsp. *pedunculata* (24 in.), *L. viridis* (20 in.).

 ## cultivation

Propagation
Seed
Lavender can be grown from seed but it tends not to be true to species, with the exception of *L. stoechas*.

Seed should be sown fresh in the fall on the surface of a seed or plug tray and covered with perlite. It germinates fairly readily with a bottom heat of 40–50°F (4–10°C). Winter the seedlings in a cold greenhouse or cold sunroom with plenty of ventilation. In the spring, prick out and pot using a standard seed compost mixed in equal parts with composted fine bark. Let the young plant establish a good-size root ball before planting out in a prepared site in the early summer. For other species you will find cuttings much more reliable.

Cuttings
Take softwood cuttings from nonflowering stems in spring. Root in a standard seed compost mixed in equal parts with composted fine bark. Take semi-hardwood cuttings in summer or early fall from the strong new growth. Once the cuttings have rooted well, it is better to pot them and winter the young lavenders in a cold greenhouse or sunroom rather than plant them in the first winter. In the spring, plant them in well-drained, fertile soil, at a distance of 18–24 in. apart or 12 in. apart for an average hedge.

Layering
This is easily done in the fall. Most hardy lavenders respond well to this form of propagation.

Pests and Diseases
The chief and most damaging pest of lavender is the rosemary beetle. The beetle and its larvae feed on the leaves from fall until spring. As soon as you see this small shiny beetle, place some newspaper under-

Lavandula angustifolia 'Loddon Pink'

neath the plant, then tap or shake the branches, which will knock the beetles and larvae on to the paper, making them easy to destroy.

The flowers in wet seasons may be attacked by gray mold (*Botrytis*). This can occur all too readily after a wet winter. Cut back the infected parts as far as possible, again remembering not to cut into the old wood if you want it to shoot again.

There is another fungus (*Phoma lavandulae*) that attacks the stems and branches, causing wilting and death of the affected branches. If this occurs dig up the plant immediately and destroy, keeping it well away from any other lavender bushes.

Maintenance
Spring Give a spring hair cut.
Summer Trim after flowering. Take cuttings.
Fall Sow seed. Cut back in early fall, never into the old wood. Protect all the half-hardy lavenders. Bring containers inside before frosts start.
Winter Check seedlings for disease. Keep watering to a minimum.

Lavender herb jelly

Garden Cultivation

Lavender is one of the most popular plants in today's herb garden and is particularly useful in borders, edges, as internal hedges, and on top of dry walls. All the species require an open sunny position and a well-drained, fertile soil. But lavender will adapt to semishade as long as the soil conditions are met, otherwise it will die in winter. If you have very cold winter temperatures, it is worth growing lavenders in containers to move inside in winter.

The way to maintain a lavender bush is to trim to shape every year in the spring, remembering not to cut into the old wood as this will not reshoot. After flowering, trim back to the leaves. In the early fall trim again, making sure this is well before the first fall frosts, otherwise the new growth will be too soft and be damaged. By trimming this way, you will keep the bush neat and encourage it to make new growth, so stopping it becoming woody.

If you have inherited a straggly mature plant then give it a good cut back in the fall, followed by a second cut in the spring and then adopt the above routine. If the plant is aged, I would advise that you propagate some of the fall cuts, so preserving the plant if all else fails.

Harvesting

Gather the flowers just as they open, and dry on open trays or by hanging in small bunches. Pick the leaves any time for use fresh, or before flowering if drying.

 ## container growing

If you have low winter temperatures, lavender cannot be treated as a hardy evergreen. Treated as a container plant, however, it can be protected in winter and enjoyed just as well in the summer. Choose containers to set off the lavender; they all suit terracotta. Use a soil-based compost mixed in equal parts with composted fine bark. The ideal position is sun, but all lavenders will cope with partial shade, though the aroma can be impaired.

Feed regularly through the flowering season with liquid fertilizer, following the manufacturer's instructions. Allow the compost to dry out in winter (not totally, but nearly), and slowly reintroduce watering in spring.

 ## medicinal

Throughout history, lavender has been used medicinally to soothe, sedate and suppress. Nowadays it is the essential oil that is in great demand for its many beneficial effects.

The oil was traditionally inhaled to prevent vertigo and fainting. It is an excellent remedy for burns and stings, and its strong antibacterial action helps to heal cuts. The oil also kills diphtheria and typhoid bacilli as well as streptococcus and pneumococcus.

Add 6 drops of oil to bath water to calm irritable children and help them sleep. Place 1 drop on the temple for a headache relief. Blend for use as a massage oil in aromatherapy for throat infections, skin sores, inflammation, rheumatic aches, anxiety, insomnia and depression. The best oil is made from distillation, and may be bought from many stores.

 ## other uses

Rub fresh flowers onto skin or pin a sprig on clothes to discourage flies. Use flowers in potpourri, herb pillows, and linen sachets, where they make a good moth repellent.

Left: Lavender sachets make good presents and can be used as moth repellents

culinary

Lavender has not been used much in cooking, but as there are many more adventurous cooks around, I am sure it will be used increasingly in the future. Use the flowers to flavor a herb jelly or a vinegar. Equally the flowers can be crystallized.

Lavender Cookies

1/2 cup butter
1/4 cup superfine sugar
3/4 cup self-raising flour
2 tablespoons fresh chopped lavender leaves
1 teaspoon lavender flowers removed from spike

Cream the sugar and butter together until light. Add the flour and lavender leaves to the butter mixture. Knead well until it forms a dough. Gently roll out on a lightly floured board. Scatter the flowers over the rolled dough and lightly press in with the rolling pin. Cut into small rounds with cutter. Place cookies on a greased baking sheet. Bake in a hot oven 450°F/230°C for 10–12 minutes until golden and firm. Remove at once and cool on a wire rack.

Levisticum officinale

LOVAGE

Also known as Love parsley, Sea parsley, Lavose, Liveche, Smallage and European lovage. From the family Apiaceae.

This native of the Mediterranean can now be found naturalized throughout the temperate regions of the world, including Australia, North America and Scandinavia.

Lovage was used by the ancient Greeks, who chewed the seed to aid digestion and relieve flatulence. Knowledge of it was handed down to Benedictine monks by the Romans, who prescribed the seeds for the same complaints. In Europe a decoction of lovage was reputedly a good aphrodisiac that no witch worthy of the name could be without. The name is likely to have come from the Latin *ligusticum*, after Liguria in Italy, where the herb grew profusely.

Because lovage leaves have a deodorizing and antiseptic effect on the skin, they were laid in the shoes of travelers in the Middle Ages to revive their weary feet, like latter-day odor eaters.

Pests and Diseases

Leaf miners are sometimes a problem. Watch out for the first tunnels, pick off the affected leaves and destroy them, otherwise broad, dry patches will develop and the leaves will start to wither away. To control heavy infestations, cut the plant down to the ground, burning the affected shoots. Feed the plant and it will shoot with new growth. The young growth is just what is needed for cooking.

Maintenance

Spring Divide established plants. Sow seeds.
Summer Clip established plants to encourage the growth of new shoots.
Fall Dry seeds. Divide roots.
Winter No need for protection.

Garden Cultivation

Lovage prefers a rich, moist but well-drained soil. Prior to first planting, dig over the ground deeply and manure well. The site can be either in full sun or partial shade. Seeds are best sown in the garden in the fall. When the seedlings are large enough, thin to 2 ft. apart. It is important that lovage has a period of dormancy so that it can complete the growth cycle.

Lovage is a tall plant, so position it carefully. It will reach its full size in 3–5 years. To keep the leaves young and producing new shoots, cut around the edges of the clumps.

Harvesting

After the plant has flowered, the leaves tend to have more of a bitter taste, so harvest in early summer. I personally believe that lovage does not dry that well and it is best to freeze it (see page 285 and use the parsley technique).

Harvest seed heads when the seeds start to turn brown. Pick them on a dry day, tie a paper bag over their heads, and hang upside down in a dry, airy place. Use, like celery seed, for winter soups. Dig the root for drying in the fall of the second or third season.

 ## varieties

Levisticum officinale

Lovage
Hardy perennial. Ht. up to 6 ft., spread 3 ft. or more. Tiny, pale, greenish-yellow flowers in summer clusters. Leaves darkish green, deeply divided, and large toothed. Zone 3.

A close relation, **Ligusticum scoticum**, shorter with white clusters of flowers, is sometimes called lovage. It can be used in the same culinary way, but lacks its strong flavor and the growth.

 ## cultivation

Propagation

Seed
Sow under protection in spring into prepared plug or seed trays and cover with perlite; a bottom heat of 60°F (15°C) is helpful. When the seedlings are large enough to handle and after a period of hardening off, transplant into a prepared site in the garden about 2 ft. apart.

Division
The roots of an established plant can be divided in the spring or fall. Make sure that each division has some new buds showing.

 ## container growing

Lovage is fine grown outside in a large container. To keep it looking good, keep it well-clipped. I do not advise letting it run to flower unless you can support it. Remember at flowering stage, even in a pot, it can be in excess of 5 ft. tall.

medicinal

Lovage is a remedy for digestive difficulties, inflammation of gastric mucus membranes and flatulence. I know of a recipe—a teaspoon of lovage seed steeped in a glass of brandy, strained and sweetened with sugar. It is taken to settle an upset stomach!

Infuse either seed, leaf or root and take to reduce water retention. Lovage assists in the removal of waste products, acts as a deodorizer, and aids rheumatism.

Its deodorizing and antiseptic properties enable certain skin problems to respond to a decoction added to bath water. This is made with an ⅛–¼ cup of rootstock in 2 cups water. Add to your bath.

 ## warning

As lovage is very good at reducing water retention, people who are pregnant or who have kidney problems should not take this herb medicinally.

Lovage, brandy and sugar settles an upset stomach

Lovage soup

 ## culinary

Lovage is an essential member of any culinary herb collection. The flavor is reminiscent of celery. It adds a meaty flavor to foods and is used in soups, stews and stocks. Also add fresh young leaves to salads, and rub on chicken, and round salad bowls.

Crush seeds in bread and pastries, sprinkle on salads, rice and mashed potato.

If using the rootstock as a vegetable in casseroles, remove the bitter-tasting skin.

Lovage Soup
Serves 4

2 tablespoons butter
2 medium onions, finely chopped
2 cups potatoes, peeled and diced
4 tablespoons finely chopped lovage leaves
3½ cups chicken or vegetable stock
1 cup milk or cream
Grated nutmeg
Salt and pepper

Melt the butter in a heavy pan and gently sauté the onions and diced potatoes for 5 minutes until soft. Add the chopped lovage leaves and cook for 1 minute. Pour in the stock, bring to the boil, season with salt and pepper, cover and simmer gently until the potatoes are soft (about 15 minutes). Purée the soup through a sieve or liquidizer and return to a clean pan. Blend in the milk or cream, sprinkle on a pinch of nutmeg and heat through. Do not boil OR

IT WILL CURDLE. Adjust seasoning. This soup is delicious hot or cold. Serve garnished with chopped lovage leaves.

Lovage and Carrot
Serves 2

2 teaspoons chopped lovage leaves
3 carrots, grated
1 apple, grated
⅔ cup plain yogurt
2 tablespoons mayonnaise
1 teaspoon salt (if needed)
Lettuce leaves
1 onion sliced into rings
Chives

Toss together the grated carrots, apple, lovage, mayonnaise and yogurt. Arrange the lettuce leaves on a serving dish and fill with the lovage mixture. Decorate with a few raw onions rings, chives and tiny lovage leaves.

Lovage as a Vegetable
Treat lovage as you would spinach. Use the young growth of the plant stalks and leaves. Strip the leaves from the stalks, wash, and cut the stalks up into segments. Bring a pan of water to the boil add the lovage, bring the water back to the boil, cover, and simmer for about 5–7 minutes until tender. Strain the water. Make a white sauce using butter, flour, milk, salt, pepper and grated nutmeg. Add the lovage. Serve and wait for the comments!

Lonicera
HONEYSUCKLE

Also known as Woodbine, Beerbind, Bindweed, Evening pride, Fairy trumpets, Honeybind, Irish vine, Trumpet flowers, Sweet suckle, and Woodbind. From the family Caprifoliaceae.

*"Come into the garden, Maud,
I am here at the gate alone;
And the woodbine spices are
wafted abroad,
And the musk of the rose is blown."*
Alfred Lord Tennyson (1809–1892)

Honeysuckle grows all over northern Europe, including Britain, and can also be found wild in North Africa, Western Asia and North America.

Honeysuckle, *Lonicera*, receives its common name from the old habit of sucking the sweet honey-tasting nectar from the flowers. Generically it is said to have been named after the 16th-century German physician, Lonicer.

Honeysuckle was among the plants that averted the evil powers abroad on May Day and took care of milk, butter and the cows in the Scottish Highlands and elsewhere. Traditionally it was thought that if honeysuckle was brought into the house, a wedding would follow, and that if the flowers were placed in a girl's bedroom, she would have dreams of love.

Honeysuckle's rich fragrance has inspired many poets, including Shakespeare, who called it woodbine after its notorious habit of climbing up trees and hedges and totally binding them up.

*"Where oxlips and the nodding violet grows
quite over-canopied with luscious woodbine . . ."*
A Midsummer Night's Dream

The plant appeared in John Gerard's 16th-century *Herbal*; he wrote that "the flowers steeped in oil and set in the sun are good to anoint the body that is benummed and grown very cold."

 varieties

There are many fragrant climbing varieties of this lovely plant. I have only mentioned those with a direct herbal input.

Lonicera x americana (Miller)
American Honeysuckle
Deciduous perennial. Ht. up to 23 ft. Strongly fragrant yellow flowers starting in a pink bud turning yellow and finishing with orangish-pink throughout the summer. The berries are red, and the leaves are green and oval, the upper ones being united and saucer-like. Zone 6.

Lonicera caprifolium
Deciduous perennial. Ht. up to 20 ft. The buds of the fragrant flowers are initially pink on opening; they then change to a pale white/pink/yellow as they age and finally turn deeper yellow. Green oval leaves and red berries, which were once fed to chickens. The Latin species name, *caprifolium*, means goats' leaf, reflecting the belief that honeysuckle leaves were a favorite food of goats. This variety and *Lonicera periclymenum* can be found growing wild. Zone 5.

Lonicera etrusca
Etruscan Honeysuckle
Semievergreen perennial. Ht. up to 12 ft. Fragrant, pale, creamy yellow flowers which turn deeper yellow to red in the fall and are followed by red berries. Leaves oval, mid-green, with a bluish underside. This is the least hardy of those mentioned here, and should be grown on a sunny wall, and protected in winter where temperatures fall below 23°F (−3°C). Zone 7.

Lonicera japonica
Japanese Honeysuckle
Semievergreen perennial. Ht. up to 33 ft. Fragrant, pale, creamy white flowers turning yellow as the season progresses, followed by black berries. The leaves are oval and mid-green in color. In the garden it is apt to build up an enormous tangle of shoots and best allowed to clamber over tree stumps or a low roof or walls. Attempts to train it tidily are a lost cause. Still used in Chinese medicine today. Zone 5.

Lonicera periclymenum
Deciduous perennial. This is the taller of the two common European honeysuckles, and reaches a

height of 23 ft. It may live for 50 years. Fragrant yellow flowers appear mid-summer to mid-fall, followed by red berries. Leaves are oval and dark green with a bluish underside. Zone 5.

cultivation

Propagation

Seed

Sow seed in the fall thinly on the surface of a prepared seed or plug tray. Cover with glass and winter outside. Keep an eye on the compost moisture and only water if necessary. Germination may take a long time, it has been known to take 2 seasons, so be patient. A more reliable alternative method is by cuttings.

Cuttings

Take from nonflowering, semihardwood shoots in summer and root in a standard seed compost mixed in equal parts with composted fine bark. Alternatively, take hardwood cuttings in late fall, leaving them in a cold frame or cold greenhouse for the winter.

Layering

In late spring or fall honeysuckle is easy to layer. Do not disturb until the following season when it can be severed from its parent.

Pests and Diseases

Grown in too sunny or warm a place, it can become infested with greenfly, blackfly, caterpillars and red spider mites. Use an insecticidal soap, and spray the pests according to the manufacturer's instructions. To prevent powdery mildew, avoid dryness around the root.

Lonicera caprifolium

Maintenance

Spring Prune established plants.
Summer Cut back flowering stems after flowering. Take semihardwood cuttings.
Fall Layer established plants. Lightly prune if necessary.
Winter Protect certain species in cold winters.

Garden Cultivation

This extremely tolerant, traditional herb garden plant will flourish vigorously in the most unpromising sites. Honeysuckle leaves are among the first to appear, sometimes mid-winter, the flowers appearing in very early summer and deepening in color after being pollinated by the insects that feed on their nectar. Good as cover for an unattractive wall or to provide a rich summer evening fragrance in an arbor.

Plant in the fall or spring in any fertile, well-drained soil, in sun or semishade. The best situation puts its feet in the shade and its head in the sunshine. A position against a shady wall is ideal, or on the shady side of a support such as a tree stump, pole or pergola. Prune in early spring, if need be. Prune flowering wood on climbers after flowering.

Harvesting

Pick and dry the flowers for potpourri just as they open. This is the best time for scent although they are at their palest in color.

Pick the flowers for use in salads as required. Again the best flavor is before the nectar has been collected, which is when the flower is at its palest.

container growing

This is not a plant that springs to mind as a good potted plant, certainly not indoors. But with patience, it makes a lovely mop head standard if carefully staked and trained; use an evergreen variety like *Lonicera japonica*. The compost should be a soil-based one. Water and feed regularly throughout the summer and in winter keep in a cold frame or greenhouse and water only occasionally.

warning

The berries are poisonous. Large doses cause vomiting.

Honeysuckle tea

culinary

Add flowers to salads.

medicinal

An infusion of the heavy perfumed flowers can be taken as a substitute for tea. It is also useful for treating coughs, chest congestion and asthma. As a lotion it is good for skin infections.

Recent research has proved that this plant has an outstanding curative action in cases of colitis.

other uses

Flowers are strongly scented for potpourri, herb pillows and perfumery. An essential oil was once extracted from the plant to make a very sweet perfume but the yield was extremely low.

Malva
MALLOW

Also known as High Mallow, Country Mallow, Billy buttons, Pancake plant and Cheese flower. From the family Malvaceae.

Native to Europe, Western Asia and North America, it can be found growing in hedgebanks, field edges, and on road sides and wastelands in sunny situations.

The ancient Latin name given to this herb by Pliny was *malacho*, which was probably derived from *malachi*, the Greek word meaning "to

soften," after the mallow's softening and healing properties. Young mallow shoots were eaten as vegetables, and it was found on vegetable lists in Roman times. It was used in the Middle Ages for its calming effect as an antidote to aphrodisiacs and love-potions. The shape of its seed rather than its flowers suggested the folk name.

 ## varieties

Malva sylvestris
Common Mallow
Biennial. Ht. 18–36 in., spread 24 in. Flower, dark pink or violet form, early summer to fall. Mid-green leaves, rounded at the base, ivy shaped at stem. Zone 4.

Malva moschata
Musk Mallow
Perennial. Ht. 12–32 in., spread 24 in. Rose/pink flowers, late summer to early fall. Mid-green leaves—kidney-shaped at base, deeply divided at stem—emit musky aroma in warm weather or when pressed. Zone 4.

Malva rotundifolia
Dwarf Mallow
Also known as cheese plant, low mallow and blue mallow. Annual. Ht. 6–12 in., a creeper. Purplish-pink, trumpet-shaped flowers from early summer to mid-fall. Leaves rounded, slightly lobed and greenish. North American native. All zones.

 ## cultivation

Propagation
Seed
Sow in prepared seed or plug trays in the fall. Cover lightly with compost (not perlite). Winter outside, covered with glass. Germination is erratic but should take place in the spring. Plant seedlings when large enough to handle, 24 in. apart.

Cuttings
Take cuttings from firm basal shoots in late spring or summer. When hardened off the following spring, plant 24 in. apart into a prepared site.

Pests and Diseases
Mallows can catch hollyhock rust. There is also a fungus that produces leaf spots and a serious black canker on the stems. If this occurs dig up the plants and destroy them. This is a seed-borne fungus and may be carried into the soil, so change planting site each season.

Maintenance
Spring Take softwood cuttings from young shoots.

Sow seeds in the garden.
Summer Trim after flowering. Take cuttings.
Fall Sow seed under protection.
Winter Hardy enough.

Garden Cultivation
Mallows are very tolerant of site, but prefer a well-drained and fertile soil (if too damp they may well need staking in summer), and a sunny position (though semishade will do). Sow where it is to flower from late summer to spring. Press gently into the soil, 24 in. apart, and cover with a light compost. Cut back stems after flowering, not only to promote new growth, but also to keep under control and encourage a second flowering. Cut down the stems in the fall.

Harvesting
Harvest young leaves for fresh use as required throughout the spring. For use in potpourri, gather for drying in the summer after first flowering.

 ## container growing

Malva moschata is the variety to grow in a large container. It can look very dramatic and smells lovely on a warm evening. Water well in the growing season, but feed only twice. Maintain as for garden cultivation.

 ## medicinal

Marshmallow (*Althaea officinalis*) is used in preference to the mallows (*Malva* subsp.) in herbal medicine. However, a decoction can be used in a compress, or in bath preparations, for skin rashes, boils and ulcers, and in gargles and mouth washes.

 ## culinary

Young tender tips of the common mallow may be used in salads or steamed as a vegetable. Young leaves of the musk mallow can be boiled as a vegetable.
   Young leaves of the dwarf mallow can be eaten raw in salads or cooked as a spinach.

Mandragora
MANDRAKE

Mandragora autumnalis

Mandrake root

Also known as Devil's apples, Satan's apples. From the family Solanaceae.

Mandrake is indigenous to the Mediterranean. It is steeped in myth and magic. Historically it is recorded that in 200 BC the Carthaginians created a bait for the Romans who were invading their city, made from wine spiked with mandrake juice. This rendered the Romans insensible and the city was saved. It has been used in witchcraft to make barren women fertile and it is also mentioned in the Bible, Genesis 30, where Rachel, the second wife of Jacob becomes fertile after her sister found mandrake growing in a field.

Maintenance

Spring Sow seeds and cuttings of *Mandragora autumnalis*.
Summer Check watering.
Fall Sow seeds and take cuttings of *Mandragora officinarum*.
Winter Protect from excessive wet.

Garden Cultivation

Plant in a well-drained, deep, fertile soil in partial shade. Because mandrake has a very long tap root, up to 4 ft., it dislikes being transplanted, so choose your site carefully. In summer the plant will become dormant if the soil dries out

Harvesting

Dig up the roots in the fall or spring when the plant is dormant for medicinal use.

 ## varieties

 ### *Mandragora officinarum*
Mandrake, Satan's Apple
Hardy herbaceous, perennial. Ht. 2 in., spread 12 in. Small bell-shaped, very pale blue flowers in spring, followed by aromatic round, yellow, toxic fruits in late summer. Large, up to 12 in. long, oblong rough green leaves. Zone 6.

Mandragora autumnalis
Hardy herbaceous, perennial. Ht. 2 in. and spread 12 in. Small-bell shaped pale blue/violet flowers in the fall, followed in the third year by aromatic round, yellow, toxic fruits in late summer. Large, oblong, hairy dark green leaves. Zone 6.

 ## cultivation

Propagation
Seed
Sow the fresh seeds *M. officinarum* in the fall and *M. autumnalis* in spring, into prepared plug modules, using a soil-based seed compost mixed in equal parts with coarse river sand. Cover with coarse sand and place in a cold frame. Germination can take anything from 4 months to 2 years. Once the seedling is large enough to handle, pot and grow for 2 years prior to planting in the garden.

Cuttings
In the early spring (fall for *M. autumnalis*) when you can see the new shoots appearing, clear around the plant to expose the crown and the top of the roots. Choose a side with new shoot appearing and, using a sharp knife, slice the root including a new shoot. Place the cutting into a small pot filled with a soil-based potting compost mixed in equal parts with coarse river sand. Place the container in a warm position until rooted. Grow for 2 years prior to planting into a prepared site.

Pests and Diseases
Slugs can decimate a plant overnight. So check regularly at night and remove any that are found.

 ## container growing

Mandrake's long tap root makes it not particularly suitable for growing in containers. It is possible, but the plant will be smaller and rarely set fruit. Use a soil-based potting compost that has been mixed in equal parts with coarse river sand.

 ## medicinal

Both the species mentioned have the same medicinal properties. Today, mandrake is rarely used in herbal medicine. However tinctures made from the root are still widely used in homeopathy as a treatment for asthma and coughs.

warning

The whole plant, including the root, is toxic. Only take under professional supervision. Not to be taken in any form during pregnancy.

Marrubium vulgare

WHITE HOREHOUND

Also known as Horehound and Maribeum. From the family Lamiaceae.

Common throughout Europe and America, the plant grows wild everywhere from coastal to mountainous areas.

The botanical name comes from the Hebrew *marrob*, which translates as "bitter juice." The common name is derived from the old English *har hune*, meaning "a downy plant."

 varieties

Marrubium vulgare
White Horehound
Hardy perennial. Ht. 18 in., spread 12 in. Small clusters of white flowers from the second year in midsummer. The leaves are green and wrinkled with an underside of a silver woolly texture. There is also a variegated version. Zone 4.

 cultivation

Propagation
Seed
The fairly small seed should be sown in early spring in a seed or plug tray, using a standard seed compost mixed in equal parts with composted fine bark. Germination takes 2–3 weeks. Prick out into pots or transplant to the garden after a good period of hardening off.

Cuttings
Softwood cuttings taken from the new growth in summer usually root within 3–4 weeks. Use a standard seed compost mixed in equal parts with composted fine bark. Winter under protection in a cold frame or cold greenhouse.

Division
Established clumps benefit from division in the spring.

Pests and Diseases
If it is very wet and cold in winter, the plant can rot.

Maintenance
Spring Divide established clumps. Prune new growth to maintain shape. Sow seed.
Summer Trim after flowering to stop the plant flopping and prevent self-seeding. Take cuttings.
Fall Divide only if it has dangerously transgressed its limits.
Winter Protect only if season excessively wet.

Garden Cultivation
White horehound grows best in well-drained, dryish soil, biased to alkaline, sunny and protected from high winds. Seed can be sown direct into a prepared garden in late spring, once the soil has started to warm up. Thin the seedlings to 12 in. apart.

Harvesting
The leaves and flowering tops are gathered in the spring, just as the plants come into flower, when the essential oil is at its richest. Use fresh or dried.

 container growing

Horehound can be grown in a large container situated in a sunny position. Use a compost that drains well and do not overwater. Only feed after flowering, otherwise it produces lush growth that is too soft.

 other uses

Traditionally an infusion of the leaf was used as a spray for cankerworm in trees. Also the infusion was mixed with milk and put in a dish as a fly killer.

 medicinal

White horehound is still extensively used in cough medicine, and for calming a nervous heart; its property, marrubiin, in small amounts, normalizes an irregular heart beat. The plant has also been used to reduce fevers and treat malaria.

A Traditional Cold Cure
Finely chop 9 small horehound leaves. Mix 1 tablespoon of honey and eat slowly to ease a sore throat or cough. Repeat several times if necessary.

Traditional Cough Sweets

¹/₂ cup fresh white horehound leaves
¹/₂ teaspoon of crushed aniseed
3 crushed cardamom seeds
1¹/₂ cups white sugar
1¹/₂ cups moist brown sugar

Put the horehound, aniseed and cardamom into 2 cups of water and simmer for 20 minutes. Strain through a filter. Over a low heat, dissolve the sugars in the liquid; boil over a medium heat until the syrup hardens when drops are put into cold water. Pour into an oiled tray. Score when partially cooled. Break up and store in wax paper.

Mentha pulegium
PENNYROYAL

Also known as European pennyroyal and Pudding grass. From the family Lamiaceae.

Pulegium is derived from the Latin *pulex*, meaning "flea" because both the fresh plant and the smoke from the burning leaves were used to exterminate the insect. Long ago, the wise women of the village used pennyroyal to induce abortion. It has since been medicinally used to facilitate menstruation. In the 17th century the herbalist John Gerard called it pudding grass. He claimed it would purify corrupt water on sea voyages.

Mentha pulegium 'Upright'

 varieties

Mentha pulegium
Pennyroyal
Also known as Cunningham mint and creeping pennyroyal. Semievergreen hardy perennial. Ht. 6 in., spread indefinite. Clusters of mauve flowers in summer. Bright green, oval, highly peppermint scented leaves. Zone 6.

Mentha pulegium 'Upright'
Pennyroyal Upright
Semievergreen hardy perennial. Ht. 12 in., spread indefinite. Clusters of mauve flowers in summer. Bright green, oval, highly peppermint scented leaves. Zone 6.

The American pennyroyal or rock pennyroyal *(Hedeoma pulegioides)* has a similar aroma and usage as the European species.

 cultivation

Propagation
Seed
Sow the very fine seed in late spring, using the cardboard technique (see page 265), into prepared plug module trays using a standard seed compost. Cover with perlite. Place under protection at 64°F (18°C); germination takes 10–20 days. Leave in the modules to become well established before planting out in early summer 12 in. apart.

Cuttings
This plant roots where it touches the ground. In spring dig up a plant, divide it into small sections including some root, and put into prepared plug modules or small pots using a standard seed compost mixed in equal parts with composted fine bark.

Division
Established or invasive plants can be divided in spring and early fall.

Pests and Diseases
Pennyroyal likes a well-drained soil; when grown in damp conditions it can suffer from mildew. Remove infected plants. If grown in a container cut back on the watering.

Maintenance
Spring Sow seed, divide established plants.
Summer Cut back after flowering.
Fall Divide established plants. Dig up a plant as insurance against a wet winter and winter in a cold frame or greenhouse.
Winter This mint hates wet winters, it will stand temperatures below 18°F (−8°C) only in a well-drained soil.

Garden Cultivation
Plant in a well-drained fertile soil in a sunny position. This may seem a contradiction, but it does like to be watered well in summer.

Harvesting
Pick leaves as required to use fresh. Pick either side of flowering for freezing. Not worth drying.

 container growing

Both species can be happily grown in containers. Use a soil-based compost mixed in equal parts with composted fine bark.

 culinary

This mint has a very strong peppermint flavor so use sparingly. It is a good substitute for peppermint in water ice.

 medicinal

A hot infusion from the leaves of this plant is an old-fashioned remedy for colds and head colds. The essential oil from this plant is highly toxic and should only be used by professionals. If incorrectly self administered it can cause irreversible kidney damage.

 other uses

The fresh leaves rubbed onto bare skin is an excellent insect and mosquito repellent. Equally if you have been bitten by a horsefly or mosquito and rub the fresh leaves onto the bite it alleviates the itching.

 warning

Not to be medicinally used in pregnancy or if suffering from kidney disease. May cause contact dermatitis.

Melissa officinalis
LEMON BALM

Also known as Balm, Melissa, Balm mint, Bee balm, Blue balm, Cure all, Dropsy plant, Garden balm and Sweet balm. From the family Lamiaceae.

This plant is a native of the Mediterranean region and Central Europe. It is now naturalized in North America and as a garden escapee in Britain.

This ancient herb was dedicated to the goddess Diana, and used medicinally by the Greeks some 2,000 years ago. The generic name, *Melissa*, comes from the Greek word for bee and the Greek belief that if you put sprigs of balm in an empty hive it would attract a swarm; equally, if planted near bees in residence in a hive they would never go away. This belief was still prevalent in medieval times when sugar was highly priced and honey a luxury.

In the Middle Ages lemon balm was used to soothe tension, to dress wounds, as a cure for toothache, mad dog bites, skin eruptions, crooked necks, and sickness during pregnancy. It was even said to prevent baldness, and ladies made linen or silk amulets filled with lemon balm as a lucky love charm. It has been acclaimed the world over for promoting long life. Prince Llewellyn of Glamorgan drank melissa tea, so he claimed, every day of the 108 years of his life. Wild claims apart, as a tonic for melancholy it has been praised by herbal writers for centuries and is still used today in aromatherapy to counter depression.

Melissa officinalis 'Aurea'

 ## varieties

Melissa officinalis
Lemon Balm
Hardy perennial. Ht. 30 in., spread 18 in. or more. Clusters of small, pale yellow/white flowers in summer. The green leaves are oval toothed, slightly wrinkled, and highly aromatic when crushed. Zone 5.

Melissa officinalis 'All Gold'
Golden Lemon Balm
Half-hardy perennial. Ht. 24 in., spread 12 in. or more. Clusters of small, pale yellow/white flowers in summer. The leaves are all yellow, oval in shape, toothed, slightly wrinkled and aromatic with a lemon scent when crushed. The leaves are prone to scorching in high summer. More tender than the other varieties. Zone 6.

Melissa officinalis 'Aurea'
Variegated Lemon Balm
Hardy perennial. Ht. 24 in., spread 12 in. or more. Clusters of small, pale yellow/white flowers in summer. The green/gold variegated leaves are oval toothed, slightly wrinkled and aromatic with a lemon scent when crushed. This variety is as hardy as common lemon balm. The one problem is that in high season it reverts to green. To maintain variegation keep cutting back; this in turn will promote new growth, which should be variegated. Zone 6.

 ## cultivation

Propagation
Seed
Common lemon balm can be grown from seed. The seed is small but manageable, and it is better to start

it off under protection. Sow in prepared seed or plug trays in early spring, using a standard seed compost mixed in equal parts with composted fine bark, and cover with perlite. Germination takes between 10 and 14 days. The seeds dislike being wet, so after the initial watering, try not to water again until germination starts. When seedlings are large enough to handle, prick out and plant in the garden, 18 in. apart.

Cuttings

The variegated and golden lemon balm can only be propagated by cuttings or division. Take softwood cuttings from the new growth in late spring/early summer. As the cutting material will be very soft, take extra care when collecting it.

Division

The rootstock is easy to divide (fall or spring). Replant directly into the garden in a prepared site.

Pests and Diseases

The only problem likely to affect lemon balm is a form of fungus similar to mint rust; cut the plant back to the ground and dispose of all the infected leaves, including any that may have accidentally fallen on the ground.

Maintenance

Spring Sow seeds. Divide established plants. Take cuttings.
Summer Take cuttings. Keep trimming established plants. Cut back after flowering to reduce self-seeding.
Fall Divide established plants, or any that may have encroached on other plant areas.
Winter Protect plants if the temperature falls below 23°F (−5°C). The plant dies back, leaving but a small presence on the surface of the soil. Protect with a bark or straw mulch or a frost cloth.

Garden Cultivation

Lemon balm will grow in almost any soil and in any position. It does prefer a fairly rich, moist soil in a sunny position with some midday shade. Keep all plants trimmed around the edges to restrict growth and encourage fresh shoots. In the right soil conditions this can be a very invasive plant. Unlike horseradish, the established roots are not difficult to uproot if things get out of hand.

Harvesting

Pick leaves throughout the summer for fresh use. For drying, pick just before the flowers begin to open when flavor is best; handle gently to avoid bruising. The aroma is rapidly lost, together with much of its therapeutic value, when dried or stored.

 ## container growing

If you live in an area that suffers from very cold winters, the gold form would benefit from being grown in containers. This method suits those with a small garden who do not want a takeover bid from lemon balm. Use a soil-based compost mixed in equal parts with composted fine bark. Only feed with liquid fertilizer in the summer, otherwise the growth will become too lush and soft, and aroma and color will diminish. Water normally throughout the growing season. Allow the container to become very dry (but not totally) in winter, and keep the pots in a cool, protected environment.

 ## medicinal

Lemon balm tea is said to relieve headaches and tension and to restore the memory. It is also good after meals to ease the digestion, flatulence and colic. Use fresh or frozen leaves in infusions because the volatile oil tends to disappear during the drying process.

The isolated oil used in aromatherapy is recommended for nervousness, depression, insomnia and nervous headaches. It also helps eczema sufferers.

 ## other uses

This is a most useful plant to keep bees happy. The flower may look boring to you but it is sheer heaven to them. So plant lemon balm around beehives or orchards to attract pollinating bees.

 ## culinary

Lemon balm is one of those herbs that smells delicious but tastes like boiled cabbage water when cooked.

Add fresh leaves to vinegar.

Add leaves to wine cups, teas and beers, or use chopped with fish and mushroom dishes. Mix freshly chopped with soft cheeses.

It has frequently been incorporated in proprietary cordials for liqueurs and its popularity in France led to its name "Tea de France."

It is used as a flavoring for certain cheeses in parts of Switzerland.

Lemon balm with cream cheese

Mentha
MINT

From the family Lamiaceae.

The *Mentha* family is a native of Europe that has naturalized in many parts of the world, including North America, Australia and Japan.

Mint has been cultivated for its medicinal properties since ancient times and has been found in Egyptian tombs dating back to 1000 BC. The Japanese have been growing it to obtain menthol for at least 2,000 years. In the Bible the Pharisees collected tithes in mint, dill and cumin. Charlemagne, who was very keen on herbs, ordered people to grow it. The Romans brought it with them as they marched through Europe and into Britain, from where it found its way to America with the settlers.

Its name was first used in Greek mythology. There are two different stories, the first that the nymph Minthe was being chatted up by Hades, god of the Underworld. His queen Sephony became jealous and turned her into the plant, mint. The second that Minthe was a nymph beloved by Pluto, who transformed her into the scented herb after his jealous wife took umbrage.

Mentha x piperita f. *citrata*

 varieties

The mint genus is large and well known. I have chosen a few to illustrate the diversity of the species.

Mentha aquatica
Water Mint
Hardy perennial. Ht. 6–24 in., spread indefinite. Pretty purple/lilac flowers borne all summer. Leaves soft, slightly downy, mid-green in color. The scent can vary from a musty mint to a strong peppermint. This should be planted in water or very wet marshy soil. It can be found growing wild around ponds and streams. Zone 5.

Mentha arvensis var. *piperascens*
Japanese Peppermint
Hardy perennial. Ht. 2–3 ft., spread 24 in. and more. Loose purplish whorls of flowers in summer. Leaves, downy, oblong, sharply toothed and green/gray; they provide an oil (90 percent menthol), said to be inferior to the oil produced by *M. x piperita*. This species is known as English mint in Japan. Zone 5.

Mentha x gracilis (Mentha x gentilis)
Ginger Mint
Also known as Scotch mint. Hardy perennial. Ht. 18 in., spread 24 in. The stem has whorls of small, two-lipped, mauve flowers in summer. The leaf is variegated, gold/green with serrated edges. The flavor is a delicate, warm mint that combines well in salads and tomato dishes. Zone 5.

Mentha longifolia Buddleia Mint Group

Mentha longifolia Buddleia Mint Group
Buddleia Mint

Hardy perennial. Ht. 32 in., spread indefinite. Long purple/mauve flowers that look very like buddleia (hence its name). Long gray/green leaves with a musty minty scent. Very good plant for garden borders. Zone 6.

Mentha longifolia subsp. schimperi
Desert Mint, Eastern Mint

Hardy perennial. Ht. 24–32 in., spread indefinite. Long pale mauve flowers in summer. Long narrow gray/green leaves with a highly pepperminted scent and flavor used to make tea. Plant in free-draining soil. Zone 6.

Mentha x piperita
Peppermint, White Peppermint

Also known as mentha d'Angleterre, mentha Anglais, pfefferminze and Englisheminze. Hardy perennial. Ht. 12–24 in., spread indefinite. Pale purple flowers in summer. Pointed leaves, darkish green with a reddish tinge, serrated edges. Very peppermint scented. This is the main medicinal herb of the genus. There are two species worth looking out for—M x piperita black peppermint, with leaves much darker, nearly brown, and M x piperita 'Black Mitcham' with dark brown, tinged with reddish-brown leaves. Zone 5.

Mentha x piperita f. citrata
Eau de Cologne Mint

Also known as orange mint and bergamot mint.

Mentha spicata var. *crispa*

Hardy perennial. Ht. 24–32 in., spread indefinite. Purple/mauve flowers in summer. Purple tinged, roundish, dark green leaves. A delicious scent that has been described as lemon, orange, bergamot, lavender, as well as eau de cologne. This plant is a vigorous grower. Use in fruit dishes with discretion. Best use is in the bath. Zone 5.

Mentha x piperita f. citrata 'Chocolate'
Chocolate Peppermint

Hardy perennial. Ht. 16–24 in., spread indefinite. Pale purple flowers in summer. Pointed dark green/brown leaves with serrated edges. Very peppermint scented with deep chocolate undertones. Great in desserts. Zone 5.

Mentha x piperita f. citrata 'Lemon'
Lemon Mint

Hardy perennial. Ht. 18–24 in., spread indefinite. Purple whorl of flowers in summer. Green serrated leaf, refreshing minty lemon scent. Good as a mint sauce, or with fruit dishes. Zone 5.

Mentha requienii
Corsican Mint

Also known as rock mint. Hardy semievergreen perennial. Ground cover, spread indefinite. Tiny purple flowers throughout the summer. Tiny bright green leaves, which, when crushed, smell strongly of peppermint. Suits a rock garden or paved path, grows naturally in cracks of rocks. Needs shade and moist soil. Zone 8.

Mentha spicata
Spearmint

Also known as garden mint and common mint. Hardy perennial. Ht.18–24 in., spread indefinite. Purple/mauve flowers in summer. Green pointed leaves with serrated edges. The most widely grown of all mints. Good for mint sauce, mint jelly, mint julep. Zone 5.

Mentha spicata var. crispa
Curly Mint

Hardy perennial. Ht. 18–24 in., spread indefinite. Light mauve flowers in spring. When I first saw this mint I thought it had a bad attack of aphids, but it has grown on me! The leaf is bright green and crinkled, its serrated edge slightly frilly. Flavor very similar to spearmint, so good in most culinary dishes. Zone 5.

Mentha longifolia subsp. *schimperi*

Mentha spicata var. crispa 'Moroccan'
Moroccan Mint

Hardy perennial. Ht. 18–24 in., spread indefinite. White flowers in summer. Bright green leaves with a texture and excellent mint scent. This is the one I use for all the basic mint uses in the kitchen. A clean mint flavor and scent, lovely when served with yogurt and cucumber. Zone 5.

Mentha suaveolens
Apple Mint

Hardy perennial. Ht. 2–3 ft., spread indefinite. Mauve flowers in summer. Roundish hairy leaves. Tall vigorous grower. Gets its name from its scent, which is a combination of mint and apples. More subtle than some mints, so good in cooking. Zone 5.

Mentha suaveolens 'Variegata'
Pineapple Mint

Hardy perennial. Ht. 18–24 in., spread indefinite. Seldom produces flowers, all the energy going into producing very pretty cream and green, slightly hairy leaves that look good in the garden. Not a rampant mint. Grows well in hanging baskets. Zone 6.

Mentha suaveolens 'Variegata'

Mentha x piperita f. *citrata* 'Chocolate'

Mentha x villosa var. *alopecuroides*
Bowles' mint
Bowles Mint
Hardy perennial. Ht. 2–3 ft., spread indefinite. Mauve flowers, round, slightly hairy green leaves, vigorous grower. Sometimes incorrectly called apple mint. Has acquired reputation as the "connoisseur's culinary mint." Not sure I agree, but mint tastes do vary. Zone 5.

Pycnanthemum pilosum
Mountain Mint
Hardy perennial. Ht. 3 ft., spread 2 ft. Knot-like white/pink flowers, small and pretty in summer. Leaves long, thin, pointed, and gray/green with a good mint scent and flavor. Not a *Mentha*, so therefore not a true mint, and does not spread. Looks very attractive in a border, and is also appealing to butterflies. Any soil will support it provided it is not too rich. Zone 5.

cultivation

Propagation
Seed
The seed on the market is not worthwhile—leaf flavor is inferior and quite often it does not run true to species.

Cuttings
Root cuttings of mint are very easy. Simply dig up a piece of root. Cut it where you can see a little growing node (each piece will produce a plant) and place the cuttings either into a plug or seed tray. Push them into the compost (a standard seed compost mixed in equal parts with composted fine bark). Water and leave. This can be done any time during the growing season. If taken in spring, in about 2 weeks you should see new shoots emerging through the compost.

Division
Dig up plants every few years and divide, or they will produce root runners all over the place. Each bit of root will grow, so take care.

Corsican mint does not set root runners. Dig up a section in spring and divide by easing the plant apart and replanting.

Pests and Diseases
Mint rust appears as little rusty spots on the leaves. Remove them immediately, otherwise the rust will wash off into the soil and the spores spread to other plants. One sure way to be rid of it is to burn the affected patch. This effectively sterilizes the ground.

Another method, which I found in an old gardening book, is to dig up the roots in winter when the plants are dormant, and clean off the soil under a tap. Heat some water to a temperature of 105°–111°F (40–44°C) and pour into a bowl. Place the roots in the water for 10 minutes. Remove the runners and wash at once in cold water. Replant in the garden well away from the original site.

Maintenance
Spring Dig up root if cuttings are required. Split established plants if need be.
Summer Give plants a hair cut to promote new growth. Control the spread of unruly plants.
Fall Dig up roots for forcing. Bring in containers.
Winter Sterilize the roots if rust is evident during the growing season.

Garden Cultivation
Mint is one of those plants that will walk all over the plot if not severely controlled. Also, mint readily hybridizes itself, varying according to environmental factors.

If choosing a plant in a nursery or garden center, rub the leaf first to check the scent. Select a planting site in sun or shade but away from other mints. Planted side by side they seem to lose their individual scent and flavor.

To inhibit spread, sink a large bottomless container (bucket or custom-made frame) in a well-drained and fairly rich soil to a depth of at least 12 in., leaving a small ridge above soil level. Plant the mint in the center.

Harvesting
Pick the leaves for fresh use throughout the growing season. Pick leaves for drying or freezing before the mint flowers.

companion planting

Spearmint or peppermint planted near roses may deter aphids. Buddleia mint will attract hoverflies, which are predators of greenfly.

container growing

Mint is good in containers. Make sure the container is large enough, use a soil-based compost mixed in equal parts with composted fine bark, and do not let the compost dry out. Feed regularly throughout the growing season with a liquid fertilizer. Place the container in semishade.

Forcing
One good reason for growing mint in containers is to prolong the season. This is called forcing. In early fall dig up some root. Fill a container, or wooden box lined with plastic, with compost. Lay the root down its length and cover lightly with compost. Water and place in a light, warm greenhouse or warm sunroom (even the kitchen windowsill will do). Keep an eye on it, and fresh shoots should sprout within a couple of weeks. This is great for fresh mint sauce out of season.

culinary

For many years French foodies have made fun of the British custom of eating mint sauce with lamb. Mint has not been used very much in traditional cooking. But slowly, even in France, this herb is gaining favor. Mint is good in vinegars and jellies. Peppermint makes a great tea. And there are many, many uses for mint in cooking with fish, meat, yogurt, fruit, and so on. Here is a recipe for chocoholics like me:

Chocolate Mint Mousse
Serves 2

½ cup plain dark chocolate
2 eggs, separated
1 teaspoon instant coffee
1 teaspoon fresh chopped mint, either Moroccan, spearmint or curly
Whipped cream for decoration
4 whole mint leaves

Melt the chocolate either in a microwave, or in a double boiler. When smooth and liquid, remove from heat. Beat egg yolks and add to the chocolate while hot (this will cook the yolks slightly). Add coffee and chopped mint.

Leave the mixture to cool for about 15 minutes. Beat the egg whites (not too stiff) and fold them into the cooling chocolate mixture. Spoon into containers. When you are ready to serve put a blob of whipped cream in the middle and garnish with whole leaves.

Fresh mint tea

 ## other uses

Pick a bunch of eau de cologne mint, tie it up with string, and hang it under the hot water tap when you are drawing a bath. You will scent not only your bath, but the whole house. It is very uplifting (unless you too have a young son, who for some reason thinks it is "gross").

 ## medicinal

Peppermint is aromatic, calmative, antiseptic, antispasmodic, anti-inflammatory, antibacterial, antiparasitic, and is also a stimulant. It can be used in a number of ways for a variety of complaints including gastrointestinal disorders where antispasmodic, antiflatulent and appetite-promoting stimulation is required. It is particularly useful for nervous headaches, and as a way to increase concentration. Externally, peppermint oil can be used in a massage to relieve muscular pain.

 ## warning

The oil may cause an allergic reaction. Avoid prolonged intake of inhalants from the oil, which must never be used by babies.

Monarda
BERGAMOT

Monarda citriodora

Also known as Oswego tea, Bee balm, Blue balm, High balm, Low balm, Mountain balm and Mountain mint. From the family Lamiaceae.

This beautiful plant with its flamboyant flower is a native of North America and is now grown horticulturally in many countries throughout the world.

The species name *Monarda* honors the Spanish medicinal botanist Dr. Nicholas Monardes of Seville who, in 1569, wrote a herbal on the flora of the United States. The common name, bergamot, is said to have come from the scent of the crushed leaf which resembles the small, bitter Italian Bergamot orange *(Citrus bergamia)*, from which oil is produced that is used in aromatherapy, perfumes and cosmetics.

The wild or purple bergamot *(Monarda fistulosa)* grows around the Oswego River district near Lake Ontario in the United States. The Native Americans in this region used it for colds and bronchial complaints as it contains the powerful antiseptic, thymol. They also made tea from it, hence Oswego tea, which was drunk in many American households, replacing Indian tea, following the Boston Tea Party of 1773.

Monarda didyma

Monarda citriodora
Lemon bergamot; Wild Bee Balm
Hardy annual. Ht. 24 in., spread 18 in. Beautiful mauve surrounded by pale mauve bracts. Intense lemon-scented leaves. Zone 5.

Monarda 'Croftway Pink'
Bergamot Croftway Pink
Hardy perennial. Ht. 3 ft., spread 18 in. Soft pink flowers throughout summer. Aromatic green leaves. Zone 4.

Monarda didyma
Bergamot (Bee Balm Red)
Hardy perennial. Ht. 2½ ft., spread 18 in. Fantastic red flowers throughout summer. Aromatic, mid-green foliage. Zone 4.

Monarda 'Schneewittchen'
Bergamot Snow Maiden
Hardy perennial. Ht. 2½ ft., spread 18 in. Very attractive white flowers throughout summer. Aromatic, mid-green, pointed leaves. Zone 6.

 varieties

There are too many species and cultivars of bergamot to mention here, so I have included a short selection:

Monarda 'Beauty of Cobham'
Bergamot Beauty of Cobham
Hardy perennial. Ht. 30 in., spread 18 in. Attractive dense two-lipped pale pink flowers throughout summer. Toothed mid-green aromatic leaves. Zone 4.

Monarda 'Blaustrumpf'
Bergamot Blue Stocking
Hardy perennial. Ht. 32 in., spread 18 in. Attractive purple flowers throughout summer. Aromatic, green, pointed foliage. Zone 4.

Monarda 'Cambridge Scarlet'
Bergamot Cambridge Scarlet
Hardy perennial. Ht. 3 ft., spread 18 in. Striking rich red flowers all summer. Aromatic mid-green leaves. Zone 4.

Monarda 'Cambridge Scarlet'

 ## cultivation

Propagation

Seed

Only species will grow true from seed. Cultivars (i.e., named varieties) will not.

Sow the very small seed indoors in the spring on the surface of either seed or plug trays, or on individual pots, using a standard seed compost mixed in equal parts with composted fine bark. Cover with perlite. Germination is better with added warmth: 65°F (21°C). Thin or transplant the strongest seedlings when large enough to handle. Harden off. Plant in the garden at a distance of 18 in. apart.

Cuttings

Take first shoots in early summer, as soon as they are 3–4 in. long.

Division

Divide in early spring. Either grow on in pots, or replant in the garden, making sure the site is well prepared with well-rotted compost. Planting distance from other plants 18 in.

Pests and Diseases

Bergamot is prone to powdery mildew. At the first sign, remove leaves. If it gets out of hand, cut the plant back to ground level. Select and plant mildew resistant varieties.

Young plants are tasty tidbits for slugs!

Maintenance

Spring Sow seeds of species. Divide roots. Dig up 3-year-old plants, divide and replant.
Summer Take cuttings of cultivars and species, when you need them.
Fall Cut back to the ground, and give a good feed with manure or compost.
Winter All perennial bergamots die right back in winter. In hard winters protect with a mulch.

Garden Cultivation

Bergamot is a highly decorative plant with long-lasting, distinctively fragrant flowers that are very attractive to bees, hence the country name bee balm. All grow well in moist, nutrient-rich soil, preferably in a semishady spot; deciduous woodland is ideal. However, they will tolerate full sun provided the soil retains moisture. Like many other perennials, bergamot should be dug up and divided every 3 years, and the dead center discarded.

Harvesting

Pick leaves as desired for use fresh in the kitchen. For drying, harvest before the flower opens.

Cut flowers for drying as soon as they are fully opened. They will then dry beautifully and retain their color.

It is only worth collecting seed if you have species plants situated well apart in the garden. If near one another, cross-pollination will make the seed variable, which is great provided you don't mind unpredictably mixed colors. Collect the flower heads when they turn brown.

 ## container growing

Bergamot is too tall for a window box, but it can look very attractive growing in a large pot, say 14–18 in. across, as long as the soil can be kept moist and the plant be given some afternoon shade.

 ## other uses

Because the dried bergamot flowers keep their fragrance and color so well, they are an important ingredient in potpourri.

The oil is sometimes used in perfumes, but should not be confused with the similarly smelling bergamot orange.

 ## medicinal

Excellent herb tea to relieve nausea, flatulence, menstrual pain and vomiting.

Aromatherapists have found bergamot oil good for depression, as well as helping the body to fight infections.

 ## culinary

Pick the small flower petals separately and scatter over a green salad at the last moment. Put fresh leaf into China tea for an Earl Grey flavor, and into wine cups and lemonade. The chopped leaves can be added sparingly to salads and stuffings, and can also be used to flavor jams and jellies.

Pork Fillets with Bergamot Sauce

Serves 2

2 large pork fillets
1/3 cup butter
2 shallots, very finely chopped
1/4 cup flour
4 tablespoons dry white wine
3 1/2 tablespoons chopped bergamot leaves
Salt, black pepper
1 tablespoon heavy whipping cream

Preheat the oven to 400°F/200°C.

Wash the fillets of pork. Pat dry, season and smear with half the butter. Roast in a shallow greased pan for 25 minutes. Allow to rest for 5 minutes before slicing. Arrange slices in a warmed serving dish.

Prepare this sauce while the fillets are in the oven. Sweat the shallots in half the butter until soft. Stir in the flour and cook for about a minute, stirring all the time. Whisk in the stock. Simmer until it thickens, stirring occasionally. Then slowly add the wine and 3 tablespoons of the chopped bergamot. Simmer for several minutes then season to taste. Remove from heat, stir in the cream, pour over arranged pork slices, garnish with remaining chopped bergamot.

Serve with mashed potato and fresh green vegetables such as broccoli.

Murraya koenigii

CURRY TREE

Also known as Indian bay, Nim leaves, Kahdi patta and Karapincha. From the family Rutaceae.

The curry leaf trees are indigenous to India, and they have naturalized in forests and wasteland throughout the subcontinent, except in the higher parts of the Himalayas. Curry leaves are closely associated with South India where the word "curry" originates from the Tamil *kari* for spiced sauces. The use of curry leaves as a flavoring for vegetables is described in early Tamil literature dating back to the first century AD. These leaves are absolutely necessary for the authentic flavor of Southern Indian and Sri Lankan cuisine. Please do not confuse this herb with *Helichrysum italicum* (see page 120), which is known in Europe as the curry plant.

 varieties

Murraya koenigii
Curry Leaf, Kahdi Patta
Tropical, subtropical, evergreen shrub or small tree. Ht. 14–18 ft., spread up to 15 ft. Clusters of small creamy white sweetly scented, star-shaped flowers from late summer, followed by small black edible fruit, the seed of which is poisonous if digested. Oval, soft, glossy, pinnate aromatic leaves, each leaf divided into 11–21 leaflets. The bark is dark brown, nearly black, and the wood is grayish/white, hard and close grained. Zone 10.

 cultivation

Propagation
Seed
Sow fresh ripe seed in the fall into prepared plug module trays using a seed compost mixed in equal parts with perlite. Cover the seeds with perlite, put in a warm place or propagator at 68°F (20°C). Germination is erratic, approximately 2–4 months.

Cuttings
Take semiripe stem cuttings in late spring or early summer. Place the cuttings into prepared plug module trays using a standard seed compost mixed in equal parts with perlite. If you do not have a covered propagator, either cover the cuttings in white plastic or place in a white plastic bag and put in a warm place. Check the bag regularly and do not allow the compost to dry out; equally do not overwater. The cuttings should root in about 1 month. Once rooted, remove the bag or covering, grow on until fully rooted, then put into a small pot, using a soil-based potting compost mixed in equal parts with horticultural grit.

Division
Plants grown outside in the garden often set suckers. In summer, using a spade, these can be removed gently, including some root. Put into a pot that fits the size of root using a soil-based potting compost mixed in equal parts with horticultural grit. Replant in the garden after two seasons.

Pests and Diseases
Being an aromatic plant, it is usually unaffected by pests When grown as a potted plant it can be attacked by scale insects. Rub them off by hand, or use an insecticidal soap spray following the manufacturer's instructions.

Maintenance
Spring Take cuttings. Increase the watering of pot-raised plants.
Summer Feed container-raised plants weekly. Take cuttings. Remove suckers.
Fall Sow fresh seeds.
Winter In areas outside the tropics, cut back on watering, protect from frost.

Garden Cultivation
Only in the tropics or subtropics can this herb be grown in the garden. Plant in a fertile, light soil in partial shade. Young plants need to be watered daily for the first 3 years. In dry hot climates protect from the midday sun. This tropical plant will need protection when the night temperatures fall below 55°F (13°C).

Harvesting
Pick the fresh leaves for using in cooking and medicine as required. The leaves freeze well.

 container growing

In cool climates this herb makes an ideal container

plant. It prefers to be pot bound, so do not over pot. Use a soil-based potting compost mixed in equal parts with horticultural grit. Place the container in partial shade. Water daily and feed weekly throughout the growing season. As the plants grow, keep trimming them regularly to maintain a supply of young leaves for cooking. Water very sparingly during the winter months and do not feed. Reintroduce water and feed as soon as the light levels and temperatures increase in the spring and move the plants to a warm light place (around 64–68°F/18–20°C).

 ## medicinal

Curry leaves have been used in both Ayurvedic and Hindu medicine for many cures. A paste is made from the leaves to cure skin rashes and bites. Fresh leaves eaten raw are reputedly a good cure for dysentery, or when drunk as an infusion are said to stop vomiting. The traditional use of the curry leaf to treat diabetes has attracted a great deal of interest. Recent medicinal research has found special compounds that could be used to make an effective new medicine for treatment of diabetes.

 ## other uses

The twigs from the branches make a good toothbrush. This is a very popular method for cleaning the teeth as it is said that it helps to strengthen the gums and the teeth. The hard wood is used to make agricultural tools.

 ## warning

Seed is poisonous if ingested.

Murraya koenigii

 ## culinary

Curry leaves are usually used fresh but can be found dried or in powder form. In some recipes the leaves are oven-dried, toasted immediately before use or quickly fried in butter or oil; this scented oil is then poured on top of many dishes to add richness and flavor. Equally, the leaves can be dropped into hot oil before adding the main ingredient. Since South Indian cuisine is dominantly vegetarian, curry leaves seldom appear in nonvegetarian food; the main applications are thin lentil or vegetable curries and stuffings for samosas. Because of their soft texture, they are not always removed before serving.

Personally, I love the flavor of the leaves and have adapted many dishes to include them. This is a winter family favorite.

Curried Parsnip Soup
Serves 6

1½ lb. parsnips, peeled, chopped into
   small pieces.
¼ cup butter
1 tablespoon light olive oil
2 medium onions, chopped
2 cloves of garlic, chopped
4 cups vegetable stock
1 teaspoon ground ginger
8 curry leaves plus 6 leaves for garnish
1 teaspoon turmeric

Heat a nonstick frying pan and quickly fry 4 of the curry leaves; remove as soon as you can smell the wonderful aroma. Crush the leaves up. Return the frying pan to the heat, add the butter and oil. Once the butter has melted add the onions and cook gently until they become translucent. Add the ginger, dried curry leaves, fresh curry leaves and turmeric, stir, then add the parsnips. Toss them so they are covered in the wonderful spices and then transfer all this to a saucepan with the stock. Stir, bring to a very gentle simmer, cook for about 1 hour stirring from time to time. Remove from the heat, purée, then return to the saucepan, gently warm, do not boil. Serve in soup bowls garnished with a curry leaf.

Myrrhis odorata

SWEET CICELY

Also known as Anise, Myrrh, Roman plant, Sweet bracken, Sweet fern and Switch. From the family Apiaceae.

Sweet Cicely was once cultivated as a pot shrub in Europe and is a native of this region and other temperate countries.

The Greeks called sweet Cicely *seselis* or *seseli*. It is logical to suppose that "Cicely" was derived from them, "sweet" coming from its flavor.

In the 16th century John Gerard recommended the boiled roots as a pick-me-up for people who were "dull." According to Culpeper, the roots were thought to prevent infection by the plague. In South Wales, Sweet Cicely is quite often seen growing in graveyards, planted around the headstones to commemorate a loved one.

In some areas, sweet bracken (Cicely) was not only used in desserts but also for rubbing upon oak panels to make the wood shine and smell good.

Myrrhis odorata

 varieties

Myrrhis odorata
Sweet Cicely
Hardy perennial. Ht. 2–3 ft., spread 2 ft. or more. The small white flowers appear in umbels from spring to early summer. The seeds are long, first green, turning black on ripening. The leaves are fern-like, very divided, and smell of aniseed when crushed. Zone 4.

The following plant is called Sweet Cicely in North America. It is unrelated to the European one, but used in a similar way:

Osmorhiza longistylis
Also known as anise root, Sweet Anise and sweet chervil. Perennial. Ht. 18–36 in. Inconspicuous white flowers appear in loose compound umbels in summer. The leaves are oval to oblong and grow in groups of three. The whole plant has an aniseed odor. Its roots used to be nibbled by children for their anise licorice flavor. Zone 4.

cultivation

Propagation

Seed

Sow the seed when ripe in early fall. Use prepared plug or seed trays and, as the seed is so large, sow only one per plug and cover with compost. Then cover the trays with glass and leave outside for the whole winter.

The seed requires several months of cold winter temperatures to germinate. Keep a check on the compost, making sure it does not dry out. When germination starts, bring the trays into a cold greenhouse. A spring sowing can be successful provided the seed is first put in a plastic bag mixed with a small amount of damp sharp sand, refrigerated for 4 weeks, and then sown as normal in prepared seed or plug trays. When the seedlings are large enough to handle, which is not long after germination, and after the frosts are over, transplant to a prepared site in the garden, 2 ft. apart.

Root Cuttings

The tap root may be lifted in spring or fall, cut into sections each with a bud, and replanted either in prepared plug trays or direct into a prepared site in the garden at a depth of 2 in.

Division

Divide the plant in the fall when the top growth dies down.

Pests and Diseases

Sweet Cicely is, in the majority of cases, free from pests and diseases.

Maintenance

Spring Take root cuttings.
Summer Cut back after flowering, to produce new leaves and to stop self-seeding.
Fall Sow seeds. Divide established plants. Take root cuttings.
Winter No need for protection.

Garden Cultivation

It is one of the first garden herbs to emerge after winter and is almost the last to die down, and is therefore a most useful plant.

If you have a light well-drained poor soil you may find that Sweet Cicely spreads all around the garden, and when you try to dig out established plants the tap root is very long; even a tiny bit remaining will produce another plant. On the soil at my farm, which is heavy clay, it is a lovely, well-behaved plant, however, remaining just where it was planted in a totally controlled fashion.

The situation it likes best is a well-draining soil, rich in humus, and light shade. If the seed is not wanted for propagation or winter flavoring, the whole plant should be cut down immediately after flowering. A new batch of leaves will soon develop.

Sweet Cicely is not suitable for growing in humid areas because it needs a good dormant period before winter to produce its root and lush foliage.

Harvesting

Pick young leaves at any time for fresh use.

Collect unripe seeds when green; ripe seeds when dark brown.

The foliage and seed do not dry or freeze, but the ripe seed stores well in a dry container.

Dig up roots for drying in the fall when the plant has died back.

 ## container growing

As this herb has a very long tap root it does not grow happily in a container. But it can be done. Choose a container that will give the root plenty of room to grow, and use a soil-based compost mixed in equal parts with composted fine bark. Place it in a semi-shady place and keep it well watered throughout the growing season.

 ## medicinal

This herb is now rarely used medicinally. The boiled root is said to be a tonic for both the teenager and the elderly alike.

Sweet cicely wine

 ## culinary

The root can be cooked as a vegetable and served with butter or a white sauce, or allow to cool and chop up for use in salads. Alternatively, it can be eaten raw, or peeled and grated, and served in a French salad dressing. It is difficult to describe the flavor—think of parsnip, add a hint of aniseed. The root makes a very good wine.

Toss unripe seeds, which have a sweet flavor and a nutty texture, into fruit salads. Chop them into ice cream. Use ripe seeds whole for flavoring cooked dishes such as apple pie, otherwise use them crushed.

The leaf flavor is sweet aniseed. Chop finely and stir in salads, dressings and omelettes. Add to soups, stews and to boiling water when cooking cabbage.

Add to cream for a sweeter, less fatty taste. It is a valuable sweetener, especially for diabetics, but also for the many people who are trying to reduce their sugar intake.

When cooking tart fruit, such as rhubarb, plums, gooseberries, or blackcurrants, add 4–6 teaspoons of chopped Sweet Cicely leaf. Or, as I do sometimes, mix a handful of large fresh leaves with some lemon balm and add to the boiling water in which the fruit is to be stewed. It gives a delightful flavor and helps to save almost half the sugar needed.

Myrtis communis
MYRTLE

From the family Myrtaceae.

Myrtle comes from a fragrant genus that is widely distributed in warm, temperate and tropical regions of the world.

Myrtle is a direct descendant of the Greek *myrtos*, the "herb of love." It has been dedicated to Venus and was planted all round her temples. The story goes that Venus transformed one of her priestesses called Myrrh into myrtle in order to protect her from an over-eager suitor. Also, Venus herself wore a wreath of myrtle when she was given the golden apple by Paris in recognition of her beauty. When she arose out of the sea she was carrying a sprig of myrtle, and to this day it grows very well by the sea, flourishing in the salt air.

Subsequently it was considered an aphrodisiac, and brides carried it in their bouquets or wore wreaths of it at weddings to symbolize love and constancy.

 varieties

Myrtus communis
Myrtle
Half-hardy evergreen perennial. Ht. and spread 6–10 ft. Fragrant white flowers from spring to midsummer, each with a dense cluster of golden stamens, followed by dark, purple-black fruits. The leaves are oval, glossy, dark green and aromatic. Zone 8.

Myrtus communis 'Variegata'
Variegated Myrtle
Half-hardy evergreen perennial. Ht. and spread 3–6 ft. Fragrant white flowers from spring to midsummer, each with a hint of pink, and a dense cluster of golden stamens, followed by dark, purple-black fruits. Leaves are oval and dark green with silver variegation, and a pink tinge in the fall. Zone 9.

Myrtus communis subsp. *tarentina*
Tarentina Myrtle
Half-hardy evergreen perennial. Ht. and spread 3–6 ft. Fragrant white flowers from spring to midsummer, each with a dense cluster of golden stamens, followed by dark, purple-black fruits. Leaves are small and oval, dark green and aromatic. This myrtle is a good hedge in mild areas. Plant 24 in. apart. Zone 9.

Myrtus communis 'Variegata'

Myrtus communis berries

Myrtus communis flower buds

Myrtus communis subsp. *tarentina* 'Microphylla Variegata'

Variegated Tarentina Myrtle
Half-hardy evergreen perennial. Ht. 3 ft., spread 24 in. Fragrant white flowers from spring to midsummer, each with a hint of pink and a dense cluster of golden stamens, followed by dark, purple-black fruits. Leaves are small, oval, and dark green with silver variegation, and a pink tinge in the fall. Zone 9.

I have included the following two because they have only relatively recently been reclassified as *Luma* and are worth looking out for.

Luma chequen (*Myrtus chequen*)

Half-hardy evergreen perennial. Ht. and spread 30 ft. Fragrant white flowers from spring to midsummer, each with a dense cluster of golden stamens; followed by dark purple-black fruits. The leaves are more oblong with a point at the end: glossy dark green and aromatic. Zone 9.

Luma apiculata 'Glanleam Gold' (*Myrtus* 'Glanleam Gold')

Half-hardy evergreen perennial. Ht. and spread 30 ft. Fragrant white flowers from midsummer to mid-fall,

each with a hint of pink and a dense cluster of golden stamens, followed by red fruits, which darken to deep purple as they ripen. Leaves oval, bright green, edged with creamy yellow. Zone 9.

cultivation

Propagation
Cuttings
Take softwood cuttings in spring, semihardwood cuttings in summer. As these are tender plants, it is as well to grow them in pots for the first 2 years at least. If you live in an area where the winter temperatures fall continuously below 32°F (0°C)—for variegated varieties 41°F (5°C)—it would be better to leave them in their pots for the winter. Use a standard seed compost mixed in equal parts with composted fine bark.

Pests and Diseases
In the majority of cases, myrtles are free from pests and diseases, but they can be susceptible to root rot from overwatering.

Maintenance
Spring Trim back growth to regain shape. Take softwood cuttings.
Summer Take semihardwood cuttings.
Fall Protect from early frosts.
Winter Protect in the winter if you live in a frost area.

Garden Cultivation
This lovely, tender, aromatic shrub will grow in fertile well-drained soil in full sun. Where your winters are borderline, plant against a warm, sheltered wall to restrict the amount of water it receives from rain, and protect it from the winds.
If a frost is forecast, cover the plant lightly with a frost cloth.
Trim back growth (where possible) to maintain shape in mid-spring after the frosts have finished.

Harvesting
Pick leaves for sweetness and scent when myrtle is in flower; they can be used dried or fresh.
Preserve the leaves in bottles of oil or vinegar for use in cooking.
Pick flowers for drying just as they open.

container growing

This plant, when young, is well suited to containers. Use a soil-based compost mixed in equal parts with composted fine bark. As an evergreen plant, it looks attractive all year round. Place in a cold sunroom away from any heat source. Water in the summer months, and allow the compost to nearly dry out in winter. Watch the watering at all times; if ever in doubt give it less rather than more. Feed with a liquid fertilizer during the flowering period.

culinary

Leaves can be added to pork for the final 10 minutes of roasting, or to lamb when barbecuing. They have a spicy flavor. After drying, the berries can be ground and used like juniper as a spice for game and venison.

medicinal

The leaves have astringent and antiseptic properties. Rarely used medicinally, but a leaf decoction may be applied externally to bruises and hemorrhoids. Recent research has revealed a substance in myrtle that has an antibiotic action.

other uses

Every part of the shrub is highly aromatic and can be used dried in potpourri.

Myrtle leaves in potpourri

Nepeta

CATNIP

Also known as Catnep, Catmint, Catrup, Catswart and Field Balm. From the family Lamiaceae.

The species name may have derived from the Roman town Nepeti, where it was said to grow in profusion.

The Elizabethan herbalist, Gerard, recorded the source of its common name: "They do call it herba cataria and herba catti because cats are very much delighted herewith for the smell of it is so pleasant unto them, that they rub themselves upon it and wallow or tumble in it and also feed on the branches and leaves very greedily."

This herb has long been cultivated both for its medicinal and seasoning properties, and in the hippie era of the late 1960s and 1970s for its mildly hallucinogenic quality when smoked.

Nepeta x faassenii 'Alba'

Nepeta cataria

 varieties

Nepeta cataria*, *Nepeta x faassenii and all ***Nepeta racemosa*** are all called catnip, which can be confusing. However the first is the true herb with the medicinal and culinary properties and, just to be more confusing, is known also as dog mint! Zones 4–8.

Nepeta camphorata
Camphor Catmint
Hardy perennial. Ht. and spread 24–30 in. Very different from ordinary catnip and very fragrant. Tiny white blooms all summer. Small, silvery gray, aromatic foliage. Prefers a poor, well-drained, dryish soil, not too rich in nutrients, and full sun. However, it will adapt to most soils except wet and heavy. Zone 8.

Nepeta cataria
Dog Mint, Nep-in-a-Hedge
Hardy perennial. Ht. 3 ft., spread 24 in. White to pale pink flowers from early summer to early fall. Pungent aromatic leaves. This plant is the true herb. In the 17th century it was used in the treatment of barren women. Zone 4.

Nepeta x faassenii 'Alba'
Hardy perennial. Ht. and spread 18 in. Loose spikes of white flowers from early summer to early fall. Small grayish/green aromatic leaves form a bushy clump. Zone 4.

Nepeta racemosa 'Walker's Low'
Hardy perennial. Ht. and spread 32 in. Spikes of lavender blue/purple flowers from late spring to fall. Small, mildly fragrant, grayish leaves. Marvelous edging plant for tumbling out over raised beds or softening hard edges of stone flags. Combines especially well with old-fashioned roses. Zone 4.

 cultivation

Propagation
Seed
Sow its small seed in spring or late summer, either where the plant is going to flower or onto the surface of pots, plug or seed trays. Cover with perlite. Gentle bottom heat can be of assistance. Germination takes 10–20 days, depending on the time of year (faster in late summer). Seed is viable for 5 years. When large enough to handle, thin the seedlings to 12 in. The seed of *N. camphorata* should be sown in the fall to late winter. It will usually flower the following season.

Cuttings
Take softwood cuttings from new growth in late spring through to midsummer. Do not choose flowering stems.

Division
A good method of propagation, particularly if a plant is becoming invasive. Divide established plants in spring. But beware of cats! The smell of a bruised root is irresistible. Cats have been known to destroy a specimen replanted after division. If there are cats around, protect the newly divided plant.

Nepeta racemosa 'Walker's Low'

Pests and Diseases

These plants are aromatic and not prone to pests. However, in cold wet winters, they tend to rot.

Maintenance

Spring Sow seeds. Take cuttings. Divide established plants.

Summer Sow seeds until late in the season. Cut back hard after flowering to encourage a second flush. Take cuttings.

Fall Cut back after flowering to maintain shape and produce new growth. If your winters tend to be wet and cold, pot and over-winter this herb in a cold frame.

Winter Sow seeds of *Nepeta camphorata*.

Garden Cultivation

The main problem with catnip is the love cats have for it. If you have ever seen a cat spaced-out after feeding and rolling on it, then you will understand why cat lovers love catnip, and why cat haters who grow it get cross with cat neighbors. The reason why cats are enticed is the smell; it reminds them of the hormonal scent of cats of the opposite sex. Bearing all this in mind, make your choice of planting site carefully.

Nepeta make very attractive border or edging subjects. They like a well-drained soil, sun, or light shade. The one thing they dislike is a wet winter; they may well rot.

Planting distance depends on species, but on average plant 20 in. apart. When the main flowering is over, catmint should be cut back hard to encourage a second crop and to keep a neat and compact shape.

Harvesting

Whether you pick to use fresh or to dry, gather leaves and flowering tops when young.

 ## companion planting

Planting *Nepeta cataria* close to vegetables is said to deter flea beetle.

 ## container growing

N. x *faassenii* and all *N. racemosa* look stunning in large terracotta pots. The gray/green of the leaves and the blue/purple of the flowers complement the terracotta, and their sprawling habit in flower completes the picture. Use a soil-based compost mixed in equal parts with composted fine bark. Note that both varieties tend to grow soft and leggy indoors.

Nepeta racemosa 'Walker's Low'

 ## culinary

Use freshly picked young shoots in salads or rub on meat to release their mintish flavor. Catnip was drunk in a tea before China tea was introduced into the West. It makes an interesting cup!

 ## other uses

Dried leaves stuffed into toy mice will keep kittens and cats amused for hours. The scent of catnip is said to repel rats, so put bunches in hen and duck houses to discourage them. The flowers of *Nepeta* x *faassenii*, and *Nepeta racemosa* are suitable for formal displays.

 ## medicinal

Nepeta cataria is now very rarely used for medicinal purposes. In Europe it is sometimes used in a hot infusion to promote sweating. It is said to be excellent for colds and flu. It soothes the nervous system and helps one to sleep. It also helps to calm upset stomachs and counters colic, flatulence and diarrhea. An infusion can be applied externally to soothe scalp irritations, and the leaves and flowering tops can be mashed for a poultice to be applied to external bruises.

Ocimum basilicum
BASIL

Also known as Common basil, St. Joseph wort, and Sweet basil. From the family Lamiaceae.

Basil is native to India, the Middle East and some Pacific Islands. It has been cultivated in the Mediterranean for thousands of years, but the herb only came to Western Europe in the 16th century with the spice traders, and to America and Australia with the early European settlers.

Ocimum basilicum var. purpurascens

This plant is steeped in history and intriguing lore. Its common name is believed to be an abbreviation of *Basilikon phuton*, Greek for "kingly herb," and it was said to have grown around Christ's tomb after the resurrection. Some Greek Orthodox churches use it to prepare their holy water, and put pots of basil below their altars. However, there is some question as to its sanctity—both Greeks and Romans believed that people should curse as they sow basil to ensure germination. There was even some doubt about whether it was poisonous or not, and in Western Europe it has been thought both to belong to the Devil and to be a remedy against witches. In Elizabethan times sweet basil was used as a snuff for colds and to clear the brain and deal with headaches, and in the 17th century Culpeper wrote of basil's uncompromising if unpredictable appeal—"It either makes enemies or gains lovers but there is no in-between."

 ## varieties

Ocimum basilicum
Sweet Basil
Annual. Ht. 18 in. A strong scent. Green, medium-sized leaves. White flowers. Without doubt the most popular basil. Use sweet basil in pasta sauces and salads, especially with tomato. Combines very well with garlic. Do not let it flower if using for cooking. All zones.

Ocimum basilicum 'Cinnamon'
Cinnamon Basil
Annual. Ht. 18 in. Leaves olive/brown/green with a hint of purple, highly cinnamon-scented when rubbed. Flowers pale pink. Comes from Mexico and is used in spicy dishes and salad dressings. All zones.

Ocimum basilicum 'Green Ruffles'
Green Ruffles Basil
Annual. Ht. 12 in. Light green leaves, crinkly and larger than sweet basil. Spicy, aniseed flavor, good in salad dishes and with stir-fry vegetables. But it is not, to my mind, an attractive variety. In fact the first time I grew it I thought its crinkly leaves had a bad attack of greenfly. Grow in pots and protect from frost. All zones.

Ocimum basilicum 'Horapha' ('Thai')
Thai Basil, Horapha Basil (Rau Que)
Annual. Ht. 15 in. Leaf olive/purplish. Stems red. Flowers with pink bracts. Aniseed in scent and flavor. A special culinary basil from Thailand. Use the leaves as a vegetable in curries and spicy dishes. All zones.

Ocimum basilicum 'Napolitano'
Lettuce-leaved Basil
Annual. Ht. 18 in. Leaves very large, crinkled, and with a distinctive flavor, especially good for pasta sauce.

Ocimum tenuiflorum

BASIL

Ocimum basilicum 'Cinnamon'

Originates in Naples region of Italy and needs a hot summer in cooler countries to be of any merit. All zones.

Ocimum basilicum var. purpurascens
Purple Basil, Dark Opal Basil
Annual. Ht. 12 in. Strongly scented purple leaves. Pink flowers. Very attractive plant with a perfumed scent and flavor that is especially good with rice dishes. The dark purple variety that was developed in 1962 at the University of Connecticut represents something of a

breakthrough in herb cultivation, not least because, almost exclusively, herbs have escaped the attentions of the hybridizers. The variety was awarded the All American Medal by the seedsmen. All zones.

Ocimum basilicum var. purpurascens 'Purple Ruffles'
Purple Ruffles Basil
Annual. Ht. 12 in. Very similar to purple basil, though the flavor is not as strong and the leaf is larger with a feathery edge. Flowers are pink. It can be grown in pots in a sunny position outside, but frankly it is a pain to grow because it damps off so easily. All zones.

Ocimum x citriodorum
Lemon Basil (Kemangie)
Annual. Ht. 12 in. Light, bright, yellowish-green leaves, more pointed than other varieties, with a slight serrated edge. Flowers pale, whitish. Lemon basil comes from Indonesia, is tender in cooler climates, and susceptible to damping off. Difficult to maintain but well worth the effort. Both flowers and leaves have a lemon scent and flavor that enhance many dishes. All zones.

Ocimum basilicum 'Horapha'

Ocimum minimum
Bush Basil
Annual. Ht. 12 in. Small green leaves, half the size of sweet basil. Flowers small, scented and whitish. Spread from Chile throughout South America, where, in some countries, it is believed to belong to the Goddess Erzulie and is carried as a powerful protector against robbery and by women to keep a lover's eye from roving. Excellent in pots on the windowsill. Delicious whole in green salads and with ricotta cheese. All zones.

Ocimum minimum 'Greek Mini'
Greek Basil (Fine-leaved Miniature)
Annual. Ht. 9 in. This basil has the smallest leaves, tiny replicas of the bush basil leaves but, despite their size, they have a good flavor. As its name suggests, it originates from Greece. It is one of the easiest basils to look after—especially good in a pot. Use leaves un-chopped in all salads and in tomato sauces. All zones.

Ocimum tenuiflorum (Ocimum sanctum)
Sacred Basil, Kha Prao, Tulsi
Annual. Ht. 12 in. A small basil with olive/purple leaves with serrated edges. Stems deep purple. Flowers mauve/pink. The whole plant has a marvelously rich scent. Originally from Thailand, where it is grown around Buddhist temples. Can be used in Thai cooking with stir-fry, hot peppers, chicken, pork or beef. The Indian-related form is considered kingly or holy by the Hindus, sacred to the gods Krishna and Vishnu. It was the herb upon which to swear oaths in courts of law. It was also used throughout the Indian subcontinent as a disinfectant against malaria. All zones.

Mixed basils growing around a tree on the Sinai Peninsula

cultivation

Propagation

Seed

All basils can be grown from seed. Sow direct into pots or plug trays in early spring and germinate with warmth. Avoid using seed trays because basil has a long tap root and dislikes being transplanted. Plugs also help minimize damping off, to which all basil plants are prone (see below).

Water well at midday in dry weather even when transplanted into pots or containers: basil hates going to bed wet. This minimizes the chances of damping off and will prevent root rot, a hazard when air temperature is still dropping at night.

Plant seedlings when large enough to handle and the danger of frost has passed. The soil needs to be rich and well drained, and the situation warm and sheltered, preferably with sun at midday. However, prolific growth will only be obtained usually in the greenhouse or in large pots on a sunny patio. I suggest that you plant basil in between tomato plants for the following reasons:

1. Being a good companion plant, it is said to repel flying insects, so may help to keep the tomatoes pest-free.
2. You will remember to use fresh basil with tomatoes.
3. You will remember to water it.
4. The situation will be warm and whenever you pick tomatoes you will tend to pick basil, which will encourage bushy growth and prevent it flowering, which in turn will stop the stems becoming woody and the flavor of its leaves bitter.

Ocimum basilicum

Pests and Diseases

Greenfly and whitefly may be a problem with pot-grown plants. Wash off with liquid insecticidal soap.

Seedlings are highly susceptible to damping off, a fungal disease encouraged by overcrowding in overly wet conditions in seed trays or pots. It can be prevented by sowing the seed thinly and widely and guarding against an over-humid atmosphere.

Maintenance

Spring Sow seeds in early spring with warmth and watch out for damping off; plant around the end of the season. Alternatively, sow directly into the ground after any frosts.

Summer Keep pinching off young plants to promote new leaf growth and to prevent flowering. Harvest the leaves.

Fall Collect seeds of plants allowed to flower. Before first frosts, bring pots into the house and place on the windowsill. Dig up old plants and dig over the area ready for new plantings.

Garden Cultivation

This is only a problem in areas susceptible to frost and where you can't provide for its great need for warmth and nourishment. In such areas, plant after the frosts have finished; choose a well-drained, rich soil in a warm, sunny corner, protected from the wind.

Harvesting

Pick leaves when they are young and always from the top to encourage new growth. If freezing to store, paint both sides of each leaf with olive oil to stop it sticking to the next leaf and to seal in its flavor. If drying, do it as fast as you can. Basil leaves are some of the more difficult to dry successfully and I do not recommend it. The most successful course, postharvest, is to infuse the leaves in olive oil or vinegar. As well as being very useful in your own kitchen, both the oil and the vinegar make great Christmas presents (see also page 286).

Gather flowering tops as they open during the summer and early autumn. Add them fresh to salads, or dry to potpourri.

 container growing

Basil is happy on a kitchen windowsill and in pots on the patio, and purple basil makes a good centerpiece in a hanging basket. In Europe basil is placed in pots outside houses to repel flies. Use a standard potting

Ocimum minimum 'Greek'

compost mixed in equal parts with composted fine bark.

Water containers before midday but do not overwater. If that is not possible, water earlier in the day rather than later and again do not overwater.

 medicinal

Once prescribed as a sedative against gastric spasms and as an expectorant and laxative, basil is rarely used in herbal medicines today. However, leaves added to food are an aid to digestion and if you put a few drops of basil's essential oil on a sleeve and inhale, it can allay mental fatigue. For those that need a zing it can be used to make a very refreshing bath vinegar, which also acts as an antiseptic.

 other uses

Keep it in a pot in the kitchen to act as a fly repellent, or crush a leaf and rub it on your skin, where the juice repels mosquitoes.

Basil oil

 culinary

Basil has a unique flavor, so newcomers should use with discretion otherwise it will dominate other flavors. It is one of the few herbs to increase its flavor when cooked. For best results add at the very end of cooking.

Hints and Ideas

1. Tear the leaves, rather than chop. Sprinkle over green salads or sliced tomatoes.

2. Basil combines very well with garlic. Tear into French salad dressing.

3. When cooking pasta or rice, heat some olive oil in a saucepan, remove it from the heat, add some torn purple basil leaves, toss the pasta or rice in the basil and oil, and serve. Use lemon basil to accompany a fish dish—it has a sharp lemon/spicy flavor when cooked.

4. Add to a cold rice or pasta salad.

5. Mix low fat cream cheese with any of the basils and use in baked potatoes.

6. Basil does not combine well with strong meats such as goat or vension. However, aniseed basil is very good with stir-fried pork.

7. Sprinkle on fried or grilled tomatoes while they are still hot as a garnish.

8. Very good with French bread and can be used instead of herb butter in the traditional hot herb loaf. The tiny leaves of Greek basil are best for this because you can keep them whole.

9. Sprinkle on top of pizzas.

10. Basil makes an interesting stuffing for chicken. Use sweet basil combined with crushed garlic, breadcrumbs, lemon peel, beaten egg, and chopped nuts.

Pesto Sauce
One of the best-known recipes for basil, here is a simple version for 4 people.

1 tablespoon pine nuts
4 tablespoons chopped basil leaves
2 cloves garlic
1/3 cup Parmesan cheese
6 tablespoons sunflower oil or olive oil (not virgin)

Blend the pine nuts, basil and chopped garlic until smooth. Add the oil slowly and continue to blend the mixture until you have a thick paste. Season with salt to taste. Stir the sauce into the cooked and drained pasta and sprinkle with Parmesan cheese.

Pesto sauce will keep in a sealed container in the fridge for at least a week. It can also be frozen but it is important, as with all herbal mixtures, to wrap the container with at least two thicknesses of plastic wrap to prevent the aroma escaping.

Oenothera
EVENING PRIMROSE

Also known as Common evening primrose, Evening star, Fever plant, Field primrose, King's cure-all, Night willowherb, Scabish, Scurvish, Tree primrose, Primrose, Moths moonflower and Primrose tree. From the family Onagraceae.

A native of North America, evening primrose was introduced to Europe in 1614 when botanists brought it from Virginia as a botanical curiosity. In North America it is sometimes regarded as a weed, but usually it is seen as a pretty garden plant.

The generic name, *Oenothera*, comes from the Greek *oinos*, meaning "wine" and *thera*, "hunt." According to ancient herbals the plant was said to dispel the ill effects of wine, but both plant and seed have been used for other reasons—culinary and medicinal—by Native Americans for hundreds of years. The Flambeau Ojibwe tribe were the first to realize its medicinal properties. They used to soak the whole plant in warm water to make a poultice to heal bruises and overcome skin problems. Traditionally, too, it was used to treat asthma, and its medicinal potential is under research. Oil of evening primrose is currently attracting considerable attention worldwide as a treatment for nervous disorders, in particular multiple sclerosis. There may well be a time in the very near future when the pharmaceutical industry will require fields of this beautiful plant to be grown on a commercial scale.

The common name comes from the transformation of its bedraggled daytime appearance into a fragrant, phosphorescent, pale yellow beauty with the opening of its flowers in the early evening. All this show is for one night only, however. Towards the end of summer the flowers tend to stay open all day long. (It is called evening star because the petals emit phosphorescent light at night.) Many strains of the plant came to Britain as stowaways in soil used as ballast in cargo ships.

Oenothera fruticosa subsp. *glauca*

 ## varieties

Oenothera biennis
Evening Primrose
Hardy biennial. Ht. 3–4 ft., spread 3 ft. Large evening scented yellow flowers for most of the summer. Long green oval or lance-shaped leaves. This is the medicinal herb, and the true herb. Zone 4.

Oenothera fruticosa subsp. *glauca*
Perennial. Ht. 20 in., spread 18 in. Small clusters of trumpet-shaped golden flowers, buds and flowers, often tinged with red. Lance-shaped mid green leaves. The flowers are edible. Zone 4.

Oenothera macrocarpa
Hardy perennial. Ht. 9–12 in., spread 16 in. or more. Large yellow bell-shaped flowers, sometimes spotted with red, open at sundown throughout the summer. The small to medium green leaves are of a narrow oblong shape. Zone 4.

 ## cultivation

Propagation
Seeds
Sow in early spring on the surface of pots or plug trays, or in late spring direct into a prepared site in the garden. Seed is very fine so be careful not to sow it too thick. Use the cardboard method (see page 265). When the weather has warmed up sufficiently, plant out at a distance of 12 in. apart. Often the act of transplanting *O. biennis* will encourage the plant to flower during the first year. This variety is a prolific self-seeder. So once it has been introduced into the garden, it will stay there.

EVENING PRIMROSE

Pests and Diseases

This plant rarely suffers from pests or diseases.

Maintenance

Spring Sow seed.
Summer Deadhead plants to cut down on self-seeding.
Fall Dig up old roots of second-year growth of the biennials.
Winter No need to protect.

Garden Cultivation

Choose a well-drained soil in a dry, sunny corner for the best results. It is an extremely tolerant plant, happy in most situations, and I have known the seedlings of *O. biennis* to appear in a stone wall, so be forewarned.

Harvesting

Use leaves fresh as required. Best before flowering.

Pick the flowers when in bud or when just open. Use fresh. Picked flowers will always close and are no good for flower arrangements.

Collect the seeds as the heads begin to open at the end. Store in jar for sowing in the spring. Dig up roots and use fresh as a vegetable or to dry.

 container growing

The lower-growing varieties are very good when grown in window boxes and tubs. Tall varieties need support from other plants or stakes. None are suitable for growing indoors.

 culinary

It is a pot herb—roots, stems, leaves, and even flower buds may be eaten. The roots can be boiled—they taste like sweet parsnips, or alternatively pickled and tossed in a salad.

 other uses

Leaf and stem can be infused to make an astringent facial steam. Add to hand cream as a softening agent.

Evening Primrose soap

 medicinal

Soon this plant will take its place in the hall of herbal fame. It can have startling effects on the treatment of premenstrual tension. In 1981 at St. Thomas's Hospital, London, 65 women with PMS were treated. 61 percent experienced complete relief and 23 percent partial relief. One symptom, breast engorgement, was especially improved—72 percent of women reported feeling better. In November 1982, an edition of the prestigious medical journal *The Lancet* published the results of a double-blind crossover study on 99 patients with ectopic eczema, which showed that when high doses of evening primrose oil were taken, about 43 percent of the patients experienced improvement of their eczema. Studies of the effect of the oil on hyperactive children also indicate that this form of treatment is beneficial.

True to the root of its generic name, the oil does appear to be effective in counteracting alcohol poisoning and preventing hangovers. It can help withdrawal from alcohol, easing depression. It helps dry eyes and brittle nails and, when combined with zinc, the oil may be used to treat acne.

But it is the claim that it benefits sufferers of multiple sclerosis that has brought controversy. It has been recommended for MS sufferers by Professor Field, who directed MS research for the U.K. Medical Research Council.

Claims go further. It is said to be effective in guarding against arterial disease; the effective ingredient, gami-linolelic acid (GLA), is a powerful anticoagulant.

It is also said to aid weight-loss; a New York hospital discovered that people more than 10 percent above their ideal body weight lost weight when taking the oil. It is thought that this occurs because the GLA in evening primrose oil stimulates brown fat tissue

In perhaps the most remarkable study of all, completed in Glasgow Royal Infirmary in 1987, it helped to relieve the symptoms of 60 percent of patients suffering from rheumatoid arthritis. Those taking fish oil, in addition to evening primrose oil, fared even better.

The scientific explanation for these extraordinary results is that GLA is a precursor of a hormone-like substance called PGEl, which has a wide range of beneficial effects on the body. Production of this substance in some people may be blocked.

GLA has also been found in oil extracted from blackcurrant seed and borage seed, both of which are now a commercial source of this substance.

Oenothera biennis

Olea europaea

OLIVE TREE

Also known as Olive. From the family Oleaceae.

The olive tree, the branch of which has been the symbol of peace for many centuries, is steeped in the history and culture of the Mediterranean. The Greeks and Romans valued the oil, and the winners of the Olympic Games were initially crowned with the leaves. It is said that there is one tree on Crete that is over 2,000 years old, and it is also said that there are some trees in the garden of Gethsemane that date back to the time of Jesus. Today, throughout the Mediterranean, it is an important part of the everyday diet, an essential crop and a lucrative export.

 varieties

Olea europaea
Olive Tree
Evergreen tree. Height up to 30 ft. Numerous clusters of small creamy white fragrant flowers are borne in early summer, followed by green fruits which ripen to black. Oval green/gray, leathery leaves with silvery undersides. Zone 9.

There are literally thousands of olive cultivars; many are self sterile, which is why they are planted in pairs or in alternate rows. Some European cultivars are:
'Arbequina,' a small brown olive from the region of Catalonia, Spain.
'Kalamata,' a large black olive named after the city of Kalamata in Greece.
'Picholine,' a long medium green olive from France.

 cultivation

Propagation
Seed
In early fall sow fresh seed, which has been scarified by putting a nick in the rounded end, into prepared plug module trays, using a seed compost mixed in equal parts with river sand. Cover with river sand and place under protection at 70°F (21°C) for 3–4 weeks, then lower the temperature to 60°F (15°C). Germination takes 1–12 months, and can be longer, so do not give up.

Cuttings
In summer take cuttings from healthy new growth and place them in prepared plug module trays using a seed compost mixed in equal parts with river sand. Do not allow the cuttings to dry out. They will take 4–8 weeks to root. Grow all young plants for 2 years before planting out, or grow for 4 years in cool climates.

Alternatively, the suckers around the roots of mature trees can be removed. If this is done carefully, they will have a few roots. Pot them using a loam-based potting compost mixed in equal parts with composted fine bark. Place the cuttings in a warm position until they are rooted, and grow for 2 years before planting them. It is worth noting that olives grown using the sucker method will not produce a prolific crop.

Pests and Diseases

Rarely suffers from pests or diseases, however when grown as a container plant olive trees can be attacked by scale insects. Either rub them off by hand, or use an insecticidal soap spray following the manufacturer's instructions.

Maintenance

Spring Cut back to maintain shape.
Summer Take cuttings from new growth.
Fall Sow fresh seeds.
Winter Protect from excessive wet in cold climates.

Garden Cultivation

Plant in a well-drained soil in full sun. It is the wet combined with cold that kills quicker than the cold. In spring cut the plant back as hard as you like, it will shoot from old wood. To produce a good crop of olives, do not allow the plant to dry out in summer. Feed established plants every fall with well-rotted manure or compost.

Harvesting

For medicinal use, pick leaves to use fresh as required. The olive fruit is harvested in the fall to early winter; the time will vary according to cultivar and climate. Place large sheets under the tree, then either shake the boughs or whole tree or bang the branches with a rake.

 ## container growing

Olive trees look very attractive as container plants. They like being pot bound so be mean when you pot them. Use a loam-based potting compost. Water and liquid feed regularly throughout the growing season.

 ## medicinal

Medicinally the leaves can be infused and used as an antiseptic wash for cuts and grazes or made into a tea

Olea europaea in Tuscany

to lower the blood pressure and relieve nervous tension. Virgin olive oil, i.e., olive oil that has not been refined or industrially treated, is medicinally the best form of olive oil. It is high in vitamins, especially vitamin E, and has a compound called oleuropein which is a useful antioxidant, protecting against damage from free radicals. Virgin olive oil is also good for circulatory diseases and helps improve digestion, especially if one suffers from indigestion. Olive oil is one of the safest laxatives.

 ## culinary

Fresh olives picked straight from the tree are unpalatable; they need to be processed before they become edible. There are nearly as many processing methods as there are cultivars. A good basic method for home use was given to me by a wonderful Spaniard as we traveled to see the Alhambra in Granada.

Home Processing of Fresh Olives

Fresh olives
Cooking salt, or coarse sea salt
Fresh cold water
Large plastic or china container for washing and soaking
Olive oil
Storage jars

First choose your olives carefully, removing any stalks and any olives that are damaged. Wash them in fresh water then place on a cutting board. My guide informed me that in his home they bruised the fruit with a rolling pin; alternatively you can prick them with a fork, or slit them with a knife. This process allows the water and salt to penetrate the fruit, drawing out the bitter flavors, and also allows the salt to preserve the fruit more effectively.

Put the olives into a large clean plastic or china container, add one cup of coarse or cooking salt to 20 cups of water. Make sure that there is enough water to cover the olives. Place a plate over the olives to keep them submerged. The next day pour off the saline solution and replace with fresh water and fresh salt. Repeat this process daily for the next 12 days for green olives or 10 days for black olives. After 10 or 12

days, test the olives to see if the bitterness has gone by eating a small bit. When you are happy, the olives are ready for the final salting. On the final day pour off and measure the last lot of water so you know the volume of brine required. Measure the equivalent amount of fresh water, place this in a large pan, add one cup of salt per 10 cups of water, bring this salt water to the boil, then allow it to cool. Place the olives in a clean, sterile bottle, pour over the warm brine until the olives are completely submerged, but leave at least ¾ in. from the top.

Then this is the best part: top up the bottles with olive oil. This will stop the air getting to the fruit. Seal the jars with lids. Placed in a cupboard, these olives will keep for a year until the following year's harvest is ready.

When you wish to eat the olives, pour off the saline solution, wash the olives under cold fresh water, wash out the jar and refill with fresh water, add the olives and place in the refrigerator. If they taste too salty, repeat this process for a few days, always replacing the olives back into the refrigerator. Serve with fresh basil, lemon juice, and some crushed garlic.

OREGANO & MARJORAM

Also known as Wild marjoram, Mountain mint, Winter marjoram, Winter sweet, Marjolaine and Origan. From the family Lamiaceae.

For the most part these are natives of the Mediterranean region. They have adapted to many countries, however, and a native form can now be found in many regions of the world, even if under different common names. For example, *Origanum vulgare* growing wild in Britain is called wild marjoram (the scent of the leaf is aromatic but not strong, the flowers are pale pink); while in Mediterranean countries wild *Origanum vulgare* is known as oregano (the leaf is green, slightly hairy and very aromatic, the flowers are similar to those found growing wild in Britain).

Oregano is derived from the Greek *oros*, meaning "mountain," and *ganos*, meaning "joy" and "beauty." It therefore translates literally as "joy of the mountain." In Greece it is woven into the crown worn by bridal couples.

According to Greek mythology, the King of Cyprus had a servant called Amarakos, who dropped a jar of perfume and fainted in terror. As his punishment the gods changed him into oregano, after which, if it was found growing on a burial tomb, all was believed well with the dead. Venus was the first to grow the herb in her garden.

Origanum 'Rosenkuppel'

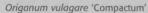

Origanum vulagare 'Compactum'

Aristotle reported that tortoises, after swallowing a snake, would immediately eat oregano to prevent death, which gave rise to the belief that it was an antidote to poison.

The Greeks and Romans used it not only as scent after taking a bath and as a massage oil, but also as a disinfectant and preservative. More than likely they were responsible for the spread of this plant across Europe, where it became known as marjoram. The New Englanders took it to North America, where there arose a further confusion of nomenclature. Until the 1940s, common marjoram was called wild marjoram in America, but is now known as oregano. In certain parts of Mexico and the southern states of America, oregano is, confusingly, the colloquial name for a totally unrelated plant that has a similar flavor.

Sweet marjoram, which originates from North Africa, was introduced into Europe in the 16th century and was incorporated in nosegays to ward off the plague and other pestilence.

Origanum vulgare 'Aureum Crispum'

varieties

Origanum amanum
Hardy perennial. Ht. and spread 6–8 in. Open, funnel-shaped, pale pink or white flowers borne above small heart-shaped, aromatic, pale green leaves. Makes a good alpine house plant. Dislikes a damp atmosphere. Zone 9.

Origanum x applii
Winter Marjoram
Half-hardy perennial. Ht. 9 in., spread 12 in. Small pink flowers. Very small aromatic leaves which, in the right conditions, are available all year round. Good to grow in a container. Zone 10.

Origanum dictamnus
Ditany of Crete
Hardy perennial. Ht. 5–6 in., spread 16 in. Prostrate habit, purplish pink flowers that appear in hop-like clusters in summer. The leaves are white and woolly and grow on arching stems. Pretty little plant, quite unlike the other origanums in appearance. Tea made from the leaves is considered a panacea in Crete. Zone 8.

Origanum 'Kent Beauty'
Hardy perennial. Ht. 6–8 in., spread 12 in. Whorls of tubular pale pink flowers with darker bracts appear in summer on short spikes. Round, oval and aromatic leaves on trailing stems, which give the plant its prostrate habit and make it suitable for a wall or ledge. Decorative more than culinary. Zone 8.

Origanum 'Kent Beauty'

Origanum laevigatum
Hardy perennial. Ht. 9–12 in., spread 8 in. Summer profusion of tiny, tubular, cerise/pink/mauve flowers, surrounded by red/purple bracts. Aromatic, dark green leaves, which form a mat in winter. Decorative more than culinary. Zone 8.

Origanum majorana
Sweet Marjoram
Also known as Knotted Marjoram or Knot Marjoram. Half-hardy perennial. Grown as an annual in cool climates. Ht. and spread 12 in. Tiny white flowers in a knot. Round pale green leaves, highly aromatic. This is the best variety for flavor. Use in culinary recipes that state marjoram. The leaf is also good for drying, retaining a lot of its scent and flavor. Zone 10.

Origanum onites
Pot Marjoram
Hardy perennial. Ht. and spread 18 in. Pink/purple flowers in summer. Green aromatic leaves that form a mat in winter. Good grower with a nice flavor. Difficult to obtain the true seed; grows easily from cuttings, however. Zone 8.

Origanum 'Rosenkuppel'
Hardy perennial. Ht. 24 in. Clusters of small dark pink flowers in summer. Dark green, oval, slightly hairy leaves. Can be used in cooking, but has an inferior flavor to *Origanum onites*. Zone 5.

Origanum rotundifolium
Hardy perennial. Ht. 9–12 in., spread 12 in. Prostrate habit. The pale pink, pendant, funnel-shaped flowers appear in summer in whorls surrounded by yellow/green bracts. Leaves are small, round, mid-green, and aromatic. Decorative more than culinary. Zone 8.

Origanum vulgare
Oregano
Also known as Wild Marjoram
Hardy perennial. Ht. and spread 18 in. Clusters of tiny tubular mauve flowers in summer. Dark green, aromatic, slightly hairy leaves, which form a mat in winter. When grown in its native Mediterranean, it has a very pungent flavor, which bears little resemblance to that obtained in the cooler countries. When cultivated in the garden it becomes similar to pot marjoram. Zone 4.

Origanum vulgare 'Aureum'
Golden Marjoram
Hardy perennial. Ht. and spread 18 in. Clusters of tiny tubular mauve/pink flowers in summer. Golden, aromatic, slightly hairy leaves, which form a mat in winter. The leaves have a warm, aromatic flavor when used in cooking; combines well with vegetables. Zone 5.

Origanum vulgare 'Aureum Crispum'
Golden Curly Marjoram
Hardy perennial. Ht. and spread 18 in. Clusters of tiny tubular mauve/pink/white flowers in summer. Leaves small, golden, crinkled, aromatic and slightly hairy, which form a mat in winter. The leaves have a slightly milder savory flavor (sweeter and spicy) that combines well with vegetable dishes. Zone 5.

Origanum vulgare 'Compactum'
Compact Marjoram
Hardy perennial. Ht. 6 in., spread 12 in. Lovely large pink flowers. Smallish green aromatic leaves, which form a mat in winter, have a deliciously warm flavor and combine well with lots of culinary dishes. Zone 5.

Origanum vulgare 'Gold Tip'
Gold Tipped Marjoram
Also known as Gold Splash
Hardy perennial. Ht. and spread 12 in. Small pink flowers in summer. The aromatic leaves are green and yellow variegated. Choose the garden site carefully: shade prevents the variegation. The leaves have a mild savory flavor. Zone 5.

Origanum vulgare subsp. hirtum 'Greek'
Greek Oregano
Hardy perennial. Ht. and spread 18 in. Clusters of tiny tubular white flowers in summer. Gray/green hairy leaves, which are very aromatic and excellent to cook with. Zone 5.

Origanum vulgare 'Nanum'
Dwarf Marjoram
Hardy perennial. Ht. 4 in., spread 6 in. White/pink flowers in summer. Tiny green aromatic leaves. It is a lovely, compact, neat little bush, great in containers and at the front of a herb garden. Good in culinary dishes. Zone 5.

Origanum onites

cultivation

Propagation

Seed

The following can be grown from seed: *O. vulgare, O. majorana, O. vulgare* subsp. *hirtum* 'Greek'. The seed is very fine, so sow in spring into prepared seed or plug trays. Use the cardboard trick (see page 265). Leave uncovered and give a bottom heat of 60°F (15°C). Germination can be erratic or 100 per cent successful. Watering is critical when the seedlings are young; keep the compost on the dry side. As the seed is so fine, thin before pricking out to allow the plants to grow. When large enough, either pot, using a standard seed compost mixed in equal parts with composted fine bark, or if the soil is warm enough and you have grown them in plugs, plant into the prepared garden.

Cuttings

Apart from the three species mentioned above, the remainder can only be propagated successfully by cuttings or division. Softwood cuttings can be taken from the new growing tips of all the named varieties in spring. Use a standard seed compost mixed in equal parts with composted fine bark.

Division

A number of varieties form a mat during the winter. These lend themselves to division. In spring, or after flowering, dig up a whole clump and pull sections gently away. Each will come away with its own root system. Replant as wanted.

Pests and Diseases

Apart from occasional frost damage, marjorams and oreganos, being aromatic, are mostly pest free.

Maintenance

Spring Sow seeds. Divide established plants. Take softwood cuttings.

Summer Trim after flowering to stop plants becoming straggly. Divide established plants in late summer.

Fall Before they die down for winter, cut back the year's growth to within 2½ in. of the soil.

Winter Protect pot-grown plants and tender varieties.

Garden Cultivation

O. majorana and *O. x applii* need a sunny garden site and a well-drained, dry, preferably alkaline/limy, soil. Otherwise plant them in containers. All the rest are hardy and adaptable, and will tolerate most soils as long as they are not waterlogged in winter. Plant gold varieties in some shade to prevent the leaves from scorching. For the majority, a good planting distance is 10 in., closer if being used as an edging plant.

Harvesting

Leaves

Pick leaves whenever available for use fresh. They can be dried or frozen, or be used to make oil or vinegar.

Flowers

The flowers can be dried just as they open for dried flower arrangements.

container growing

The oreganos look great in containers. Use a soil-based compost mixed in equal parts with composted fine bark. Make sure that they are not overwatered and that the gold and variegated forms get some shade at midday. Cut back after flowering and give them a liquid fertilizer feed.

medicinal

This plant is one of the best antiseptics owing to its high thymol content.

Marjoram tea helps ease bad colds, has a tranquillizing effect on nerves, and helps settle upset stomachs. It also helps to prevent sea sickness.

For temporary relief of toothache, chew the leaf or rub a drop of essential oil on the gums. A few drops of essential oil on the pillow will help you sleep.

other uses

Make an infusion and add to the bath water to aid relaxation.

culinary

Marjoram and oregano aid the digestion, and act as an antiseptic and as a preservative.

They are among the main ingredients of bouquet garni, and combine well with pizza, meat and tomato dishes, vegetables and milk-based desserts.

Red Mullet with Tomatoes and Oregano

Serves 4–6

4–6 red mullet, cleaned

3 tablespoons olive oil

1 medium onion, sliced

1 clove garlic, chopped

2¼ cups tomatoes, peeled and chopped

1 green or red pepper, seeded and diced

1 teaspoon sugar

1 teaspoon chopped fresh oregano or

  ½ teaspoon dried oregano

Freshly milled salt and pepper

Oil for baking or shallow frying

Rinse the fish in cold water and drain on kitchen paper. Heat the olive oil in a pan and cook the onion and garlic slowly until golden brown; add the tomatoes, pepper, sugar and oregano, and a little salt and pepper. Bring to the boil, then simmer for 20 minutes until thickened.

Bake or fry the fish. Brush them with oil, place in an oiled ovenproof dish and cook at a moderately hot temperature, 375°F/190°C for 7–8 minutes. Serve with the sauce.

Papaver
POPPY

From the family Papaveraceae.

The poppy is widely spread across the temperate zones of the world. For thousands of years corn and poppies and civilizations have gone together. The Romans looked on the poppy as sacred to their corn goddess, Ceres, who taught men to sow and reap. The ancient Egyptians used poppy seed in their baking for its aromatic flavor.

The field poppy grew on Flanders fields after the battles of World War I and became the symbol of Remembrance Day.

Papaver rhoeas

 varieties

Papaver commutatum
Ladybird Poppy
Hardy annual. Ht. 12–36 in., spread 18 in. Red flowers in summer, each with black blotch in center. Leaf oblong and deeply toothed. Native of Asia Minor. All zones.

Papaver rhoeas
Field Poppy
Also known as common poppy, corn poppy, blind eyes, blind man, red dolly, red huntsmen, poppet, old woman's petticoat, thunderbolt, and wartflower. Hardy annual. Ht. 8–24 in., spread 18 in. Brilliant scarlet flower with black basal blotch from summer to early fall. The mid-green leaf has 3 lobes and is irregularly toothed. All zones.

Papaver somniferum
Opium Poppy
Hardy annual. Ht. 12–36 in., spread 18 in. Large pale lilac, white, purple or variegated flowers in summer. The leaf is long with toothed margins and bluish in color. There is a double-flowered variety, *P. somniferum* var. *paeoniiflorum*. All zones.

Meconopsis cambrica
Welsh Poppy
Hardy perennial. Ht. 12–24 in. Yellow flowers in summer. Green leaves are divided into many leaflets. It differs from *Papaver* in that seeds are released through slits in the seed heads, not through pepper-pot heads. Zone 6.

 cultivation

Propagation
Seed
Sow the very fine seed in the fall onto the surface of prepared seed or plug trays, using a standard seed compost mixed in equal parts with composted fine bark. Cover with glass and leave outside for winter stratification. In spring, when seedlings are large enough, plant out into the garden in groups.

Pests and Diseases
Largely pest and disease free.

Maintenance
Spring Plant in garden.
Summer Deadhead flowers to prolong flowering and prevent self-seeding.
Fall Sow seed. Dig up old plants.
Winter No need to protect.

Garden Cultivation
Poppies all prefer a sunny site and a well-drained fertile soil. Sow in the fall in a prepared site; press seed into the soil but do not cover. Thin to 8–12 in. apart. Remove the heads after flowering to prevent self-seeding.

Harvesting
The ripe seeds can be collected from both field and opium poppies, the seed of which is not narcotic. It must be ripe, otherwise it will go moldy in storage.

 container growing

Use a standard potting compost mixed in equal parts with composted fine bark. Place in full sun out of the wind, and water well in the summer. Avoid feeding as this will produce lots of soft growth and few flowers.

 medicinal

The unripe seed capsules of the opium poppy are used for the extraction of morphine and the manufacture of codeine.

 other uses

The oil extracted from the seed of the opium poppy is used not only as a salad oil, and for cooking, but also for burning in lamps, and in the manufacture of varnish, paint and soap.

 warning

All parts of the opium poppy, except the ripe seeds, are dangerous and should be used only by trained medical staff.

 culinary

Sprinkle the ripe seeds on bread, cakes and biscuits for a pleasant nutty flavor. Add to curry powder for texture, flavor, and as a thickener.

Pelargonium
SCENTED GERANIUMS

From the family Geraniaceae.

These form a group of marvelously aromatic herbs that should be used more. Originally native to South Africa, they are now widespread throughout many temperate countries, where they should be grown as tender perennials.

The generic name, *Pelargonium*, is said to be derived from *pelargos*, "a stork." With a bit of imagination one can understand how this came about: the seed pods bear a resemblance to a stork's bill.

Nearly all the species of scented geranium (the name is a botanical misnomer) came from the Cape of South Africa to England in the mid-17th century. The aromatic foliage found popular assent among Victorians, who used them as houseplants to scent the room. In the early 19th century the French perfumery industry recognized its commercial potential. Oil of geranium is now not only an ingredient of certain perfumes for men, but also an essential oil in aromatherapy.

 ## varieties

There are many different scented geraniums. I am mentioning a few typical of the species that I have a soft spot for. They are very collectable plants. All are tender.

Pelargonium 'Attar of Roses'
Half-hardy evergreen perennial. Ht. 12–24 in., spread 12 in. Small pink flowers in summer. Three-lobed, mid-green leaves that smell of roses.

Pelargonium 'Atomic Snowflake'
Half-hardy evergreen perennial. Ht. 12–24 in., spread 12 in. Small pink flowers in summer. Intensely lemon-scented, roundish leaves with silver gray/green variegation.

Pelargonium capitatum
Half-hardy evergreen perennial. Ht. 12–24 in., spread 12 in. Small mauve flowers in summer, irregular three-lobed green leaves, rose scented. This is now mainly used to produce geranium oil for the perfume industry.

Pelargonium 'Chocolate Peppermint'
Half-hardy evergreen perennial. Ht. 12–24 in., spread 3 ft. Small white/pink flowers in summer. Large, rounded, shallowly lobed leaves, velvety green with brown marking and a strong scent of chocolate peppermints! This is a fast grower so pinch out growing tips to keep shape.

Pelargonium 'Clorinda'
Half-hardy evergreen perennial. Ht. and spread 3 ft. Large pink attractive flowers in summer. Large rounded leaves, mid-green and eucalyptus-scented.

Pelargonium crispum
Half-hardy evergreen perennial. Ht. and spread 12–24 in. Small pink flowers in summer. Small three-lobed leaves, green, crispy crinkled and lemon scented. Neat habit.

Pelargonium crispum 'Peach Cream'
Half-hardy evergreen perennial. Ht. and spread 12–24 in. Small pink flowers in summer. Small three-lobed leaves, green with cream and yellow variegation, crispy crinkled and peach-scented.

Pelargonium 'Lemon fancy'

Pelargonium 'Atomic Snowflake'

Pelargonium crispum 'Variegatum'

Half-hardy evergreen perennial. Ht. and spread 12–24 in. Small pink flowers in summer. Small three-lobed leaves, green with cream variegation, crispy crinkled, and lemon scented.

Pelargonium denticulatum

Half-hardy evergreen perennial. Ht. and spread 3 ft. Small pinky-mauve flowers in summer. Deeply cut palmate leaves, green with a lemon scent.

Pelargonium denticulatum 'Filicifolium'

Half-hardy evergreen perennial. Ht. and spread 3 ft. Small pink flowers in summer. Very finely indented green leaves with a fine brown line running through, slightly sticky and not particularly aromatic, if anything a scent of balsam. Prone to whitefly.

Pelargonium Fragrans Group

Half-hardy evergreen perennial. Ht. and spread 12 in. Small white flowers in summer. Grayish green leaves, rounded with shallow lobes, and a strong scent of nutmeg/pine.

Pelargonium 'Fragrans Variegatum' Fragrans Group

Half-hardy evergreen perennial. Ht. and spread 12 in. Small white flowers in summer. Grayish green leaves with cream variegation, rounded with shallow lobes and a strong scent of nutmeg/pine.

Pelargonium graveolens

Rose Geranium
Half-hardy evergreen perennial. Ht. 24 in.–3 ft. Spread up to 3 ft. Small pink flowers in summer. Fairly deeply cut green leaves with a rose/peppermint scent. One of the more hardy of this species, with good growth.

Pelargonium 'Lady Plymouth'

Half-hardy evergreen perennial. Ht. and spread 12–24 in. Small pink flowers in summer. Fairly deeply cut grayish green leaves with cream variegation and a rose/peppermint scent.

Pelargonium 'Lemon Fancy'

Half-hardy evergreen perennial. Ht. 12–24 in., spread 12–18 in. Smallish pink flowers in summer. Small roundish green leaves with shallow lobes and an intense lemon scent.

Pelargonium 'Lilian Pottinger'

Half-hardy evergreen perennial. Ht. 12–24 in., spread 3 ft. Small whitish flowers in summer. Leaves brightish green, rounded, shallowly lobed with serrated edges. Soft to touch. Mild spicy apple scent.

Pelargonium 'Mabel Grey'

Half-hardy evergreen perennial. Ht. 18–24 in., spread 12–18 in. Mauve flowers with deeper veining in summer. If I have a favorite scented geranium, this is it: the leaves are diamond-shaped, roughly textured, mid-green and oily when rubbed and very strongly lemon-scented.

Pelargonium odoratissimum

Half-hardy evergreen perennial. Ht. 12–24 in., spread 3 ft. Small white flowers in summer. Green, rounded, shallowly lobed leaves, fairly bright green in color and soft to touch, with an apple scent. Trailing habit, looks good in large containers.

Pelargonium 'Chocolate Peppermint'

Mixed *Pelargonium*

Pelargonium 'Prince of Orange'

Half-hardy evergreen perennial. Ht. and spread 12–24 in. Pretty pink/white flowers in summer. Green, slightly crinkled, slightly lobed leaves, with a refreshing orange scent. Prone to rust.

Pelargonium quercifolium

Oak-Leafed Pelargonium
Half-hardy evergreen perennial. Ht. and spread up to 3 ft. Pretty pink/purple flowers in summer. Leaves oak-shaped, dark green with brown variegation, and slightly sticky. A different, spicy scent.

Pelargonium 'Rober's Lemon Rose'

Half-hardy evergreen perennial. Ht. and spread up to 3 ft. Pink flowers in summer. Leaves grayish-green—oddly shaped, lobed and cut—with a rose scent. A fast grower, so pinch the growing tips regularly to maintain shape.

Pelargonium 'Royal Oak'

Half-hardy evergreen perennial. Ht. 15 in., spread 12 in. Small pink/purple flowers in summer. Oak-shaped, dark green leaves with brown variegation, slightly sticky with spicy scent. Very similar to *P. quercifolium*, but with a more compact habit.

Pelargonium tomentosum

Half-hardy evergreen perennial. Ht. 12–24 in., spread 3 ft. Small white flowers in summer. Large rounded leaves, shallow lobed, velvet gray-green in color with a strong peppermint scent. Fast grower, so pinch off growing tips regularly to maintain shape. Protect from full sun.

Pelargonium odoratissimum

 cultivation

Propagation

Seed
Although I have known scented geraniums to have been grown from seed, I do not recommend this method. Cuttings are much more reliable for the majority. However, if you want to try, sow in spring in a standard seed compost mixed in equal parts with composted fine bark at a temperature no lower than 59°F (15°C).

Cuttings
All scented geraniums can be propagated by softwood cuttings, which generally take very easily in the summer. Take a cutting about 4–6 in. long and strip the leaves from the lower part with a sharp knife. At all costs do not tear the leaves off as this will cause a hole in the stem and the cutting will be susceptible to disease, such as blackleg. This is a major caveat for varieties such as *Pelargonium crispum* 'Variegatum.' Use a sharp knife and slice the leaf off, insert the cutting into a tray containing equal parts seed compost and composted bark. Water and put the tray away from direct sunlight. Keep an eye on the compost, making sure it does not thoroughly dry out, but only water if absolutely necessary. The cuttings should root

in 2 to 3 weeks. Put into separate pots containing a standard potting compost mixed in equal parts with composted fine bark. Place in a cool greenhouse or cool conservatory for the winter, keeping the compost dry and watering only very occasionally. In the spring repot into larger pots and water sparingly. When they start to produce flower buds give them a liquid feed. In early summer pinch off the top growing points to encourage bushy growth.

Pests and Diseases
Unfortunately pelargoniums suffer from a few diseases.

1. Cuttings can be destroyed by blackleg disease. The cutting turns black and falls over. The main cause of this is too much water. So keep the cuttings as dry as possible after the initial watering.

2. Gray mold (*Botrytis*) is also caused by the plants being too wet and the air too moist. Remove damaged leaves carefully so as not to spread the disease, and burn. Allow the plants to dry out, and increase ventilation and spacing between plants.

3. Leaf gall appears as a mass of small proliferated shoots at the base of a cutting or plant. Destroy the plant, otherwise it could affect other plants.

4. Geraniums, like mint and comfrey, are prone to rust, especially on *P.* 'Prince of Orange.' Destroy the affected plants, or it will spread to others.

5 Whitefly. Be vigilant. If you catch it early enough, you will be able to control it by spraying with a liquid insecticidal soap. Follow manufacturer's instructions.

Maintenance
Spring Sow seed. Trim, slowly introduce watering, and start feeding. Repot if necessary.
Summer Feed regularly. Trim to maintain shape. Take cuttings.
Fall Trim back plants. Bring in for the winter to protect from frost.
Winter Allow the plants to rest. Keep watering to a minimum.

Garden Cultivation
Scented pelargoniums are so varied that they can look very effective grown in groups in the garden. Plant as soon as there is no danger of frost. Choose a warm site with well-drained soil. A good method is to sink the repotted, overwintered geraniums into the soil. This makes sure the initial compost is correct, and makes it easier to dig up the pot and bring inside before the first frost.

Harvesting
Pick leaves during the growing season, for fresh use or for drying. Collect seeds before the seed pod ripens and ripen in paper bags. If allowed to ripen on the plant, the pods will burst, scattering the seeds everywhere.

Pelargonium quercifolium

SCENTED GERANIUMS

Geranium oil

 ## container growing

Scented pelargoniums make marvelous potted plants. They grow well, look good, and smell lovely. Pot as in "Propagation" using a standard potting compost mixed in equal parts with composted fine bark. Place so that you can rub the leaves as you walk past.

 ## other uses

In aromatherapy, geranium oil is relaxing but use it in small quantities. Dilute 2 drops in 2 teaspoons of soy oil for a good massage, or to relieve premenstrual tension, dermatitis, eczema, herpes or dry skin.

 ## warning

None of the crispums should be used in cooking as it is believed that they can upset the stomach.

 ## culinary

Before artificial food flavorings were produced, the Victorians used scented pelargonium leaves in the bottom of cake pans to flavor their cakes. Why not follow suit? When you grease and line the bottom of a 8 in. cake pan, arrange approximately 20 leaves of either *P.* 'Lemon Fancy,' *P.* 'Mabel Grey,' or *P. graveolens*. Fill the tin with a cake mix of your choice and cook as normal. Remove the leaves with the parchment paper when the cake has cooled. Scented pelargonium leaves add distinctive flavor to many dishes although, like bay leaves, they are hardly ever eaten, being removed after the cooking process. The main varieties used are *P. graveolens*, *P. odoratissimum*, *P.* 'Lemon Fancy' and *P.* 'Attar of Roses.'

Geranium Leaf Sorbet

12 scented Pelargonium graveolens leaves
6 tablespoons superfine sugar
1 cup water
Juice of 1 large lemon
1 egg white, beaten
4 leaves for decoration

Wash the leaves and shake them dry. Put the sugar and water in a saucepan and boil until the sugar has dissolved, stirring occasionally. Remove the pan

from the heat. Put the 12 leaves in the pan with the sugar and water, cover and leave for 20 minutes. Taste. If you want a stronger flavor bring the liquid to the boil again, add some fresh leaves and leave for a further 10 minutes. When you have the right flavor, strain the syrup into a rigid container, add the lemon juice and leave to cool. Place in the freezer until semifrozen (approximately 45 minutes)—it must be firm, not mushy—and fold in the beaten egg white. Put back into freezer for a further 45 minutes. Scoop into individual glass bowls, and decorate with a geranium leaf.

Rose Geranium Punch

4 cups of apple juice
4 limes
1 cup sugar
6 leaves of Pelargonium graveolens
6 drops of green vegetable coloring (optional)

Boil the apple juice and sugar and geranium leaves for 5 minutes. Strain the liquid. Cool and add coloring if required. Thinly slice and crush limes, add to the liquid. Pour onto ice in glasses and garnish with geranium leaves.

Rose Geranium Butter

Butter pounded with the leaves makes a delicious filling for cakes and cookies. It can also be spread on bread and topped with apple jelly.

Perilla frutescens
SHISO

Also known as Beefsteak plant, Chinese basil, Wild sesame, Rattle snake weed, Egoma and Zi su. From the family Lamiaceae.

The common name "beefsteak plant" is in reference to the large purple shiso leaves looking like a slice of raw beef. This name originated in the United States, where it has become a naturalized wild plant in many southern and eastern states. Shiso has been used in Chinese medicine for thousands of years to treat morning sickness. Until recently, however, the culinary uses of this Far Eastern herb were relatively unknown in Western countries. Even in the early 1980s purple shiso was being used in the UK only as a spectacular spot bedding plant rather than in the kitchen. It has now become a chef's designer herb, often served in baby leaf form, which intensifies its unique flavors.

Perilla frutescens var. purpurascens

varieties

Perilla frutescens var. *frutescens*
Zi su, Egoma
Hardy annual. Ht. up to 4$\frac{1}{2}$ ft., spread 24 in. Mauve flowers in summer. Large aromatic, green with a hint of brown, leaves that have a deep purple underside. This is an important culinary and medicinal herb from Korea. Warmer zones.

Perilla frutescens var. *crispa*
Green Shiso, Aojiso and Perilla
Hardy annual. Ht. up to 4 ft., spread 24 in. Pink flowers during summer. Aromatic, anise-flavored, deeply cut bright green leaf that has crinkled edges. Warmer zones.

Perilla frutescens var. *purpurascens*
Purple Shiso, Beefsteak Plant
Hardy annual. Ht. up to 4 ft., spread 24 in. Pink flowers in summer. Deeply cut, aromatic, dark purple leaf with crinkled bronzed edges. There can be considerable variation in seed-raised plants; the flowers can be red and the leaves smoother. Warmer zones.

cultivation

Propagation
Seed
In spring sow seeds into prepared seed trays, module plugs or small pots using a seed compost mixed in equal parts with perlite, and place under protection at 68°F (20°C). Germination takes 1–2 weeks. Do not over-water once germinated as seedlings are prone to damping off, especially when the nights are cold. Once large enough to handle, pot using a potting compost mixed in equal parts with composted fine bark. Grow until seedlings are large enough to plant into a prepared site 12 in. apart. Alternatively sow into prepared open ground in late spring, when the air temperature does not go below 45°F (8°C) at night. Germination takes 14–20 days.

Pests and Diseases
Beware of caterpillars especially in late summer. Pick them off by hand as soon as they appear.

Maintenance
Spring Sow seeds.

Perilla frutescens var. *frutescens*

Summer Keep pinching off the growing tips to maintain shape and to produce a bushy plant.
Fall Harvest leaves, then seeds.
Winter Clean the seed for next year's sowing.

Garden Cultivation

Plant in a fertile, well-drained soil on a site that has been prepared with well-rotted compost or leaf mold in the previous fall. Plant in the late spring, in sun or partial shade. In arid climates, regular irrigation will be necessary.

Harvesting

Pick leaves to use fresh as required throughout the growing season. Pick flowering tops in late summer. Harvest the seeds in late fall.

 ## container growing

This herb looks lovely growing in containers, especially the purple-leaved varieties. Plant in a potting compost mixed in equal parts with composted fine bark. Place the container in a sunny position. Water regularly and liquid feed weekly through the summer, following the manufacturer's instructions.

 ## medicinal

Shiso has been used for centuries in Oriental medicine. It is a pungent, aromatic, warming herb. An infusion of the plant is useful in the treatment of asthma, colds, coughs and lung afflictions, constipation, food poisoning and allergic reactions, especially from seafood. An infusion made from the stems of this herb is a traditional Chinese remedy to alleviate morning sickness; however this should only be taken under the guidance of a Chinese doctor or fully trained herbalist.

 ## other uses

When walking or hiking in the country, rub the leaves directly on your skin and clothes and on to your dog to repel ticks. Before using, rub a bit on the back of your hand to see if you are allergic to it.

 ## warning

Do not take medicinally during pregnancy. Can cause contact dermatitis. Do not plant where horses or cattle can eat this plant as it can cause respiratory failure.

 ## culinary

This herb is one of the few aromatic plants to have established itself in Japanese cuisine, although it is a relatively newcomer to the European kitchen. It is sometimes confused with basil *(Ocimum)*, however the flavor is very different being, in my opinion, a mixture of cumin, mint and nutmeg with a hint of plums for the purple variety and anise for the green variety. Purple shiso is used as a dye for pickling fruit and vegetables, as a side dish with rice in the form of a dried powder, as an ingredient in cake mixes and as flavoring in beverages. The flower heads are used as a condiment with sushi. Green leaf shiso, the variety most commonly seen in Japanese markets, is used as a vegetable. The leaves are used as a wrapping for rice cake, in salads and tempura. The seeds from this variety are used as a condiment and with pickles. The essential oil extracted from the leaf and flowering parts contains a substance used in confectionery that is many times sweeter than sugar.

Shiso, Mooli and Kiwi Fruit Salad

1 mooli (This is a Japanese white radish which has a crunchy texture and a mild peppery flavor and can be found in large supermarkets, or in Asian or Caribbean grocery stores.)
Lemon juice

3 kiwi fruits, peeled and sliced
A good handful (approx 24 tips) of young purple shiso new growing tips, 6 tips put aside and the remainder finely chopped
3 tablespoons light olive oil
1 tablespoon white wine vinegar or rice vinegar
Salt and black pepper

Peel and slice the mooli thinly, sprinkling the slices with lemon juice to prevent discoloration. Make the dressing with the oil and vinegar, season to taste. Arrange the sliced kiwi fruit and the mooli on a plate. Scatter over the chopped shiso, then drizzle the dressing over the salad, and decorate with the remaining purple shiso tips.

Persicaria odorata
VIETNAMESE CORIANDER

Also known as Rau Ram, Laksa plant and Vietnamese mint. From the family Polygonaceae.

Vietnamese coriander is indigenous throughout the tropics and subtropics of South and Eastern Asia, where it is used in the kitchen and as a herbal remedy. It is a member of the knotweed family of plants that are notoriously invasive and more often than not considered as weeds. It should not be confused with a native wild flower found in Northwest Europe called *Persicaria bistorta*, common bistort, which has pink flowers and leaves that smell of vegetables when crushed, as opposed to the warm fragrant spicy scent of the tropical Vietnamese coriander leaves.

 varieties

Persicaria odorata
Vietnamese Coriander
Tropical evergreen perennial. Ht. 18 in., spread indefinite. Attractive small creamy white flowers in summer until late fall, rarely produced under cultivation and in cold climates. Highly aromatic leaves when crushed, narrow pointed, with a brown/maroon V-shaped marking near the base. Zone 9.

Persicaria bistorta
Common Bistort
Hardy perennial. Ht. 8 in.–3 ft., spread indefinite. Dense clusters of small pink flowers in summer until early fall. Hairless triangular mid-green leaves.
   Medicinally the root of this species is used to staunch blood flow and contract tissues. It is one of the most astringent of all medicinal plants. Zone 4.

 cultivation

Propagation
Cuttings
Cuttings can be taken from spring until late summer. Take the cutting just below the stem joint, place in prepared module plug trays or a small pot filled with a standard seed compost. Put in a sheltered warm position, bottom heat is not required; it will root within 10 days in mid-spring. Alternatively, as this plant will root anywhere that the stem touches the ground, it is possible to take a stem cutting with some roots attached. Grow in exactly the same way as taking a standard cutting. Once the cuttings are fully rooted, in warm climates plant into the garden into a prepared site; in cool and cold climates pot and grow on as a container plant.

Division
Garden and container-grown plants will need dividing to keep the plant healthy and productive and also to stop it either invading the garden or outgrowing the pot. With both situations you can be as vigorous as you like, either replanting divisions into a prepared site in the garden or repotting into a loam-based potting compost.

Pests and Diseases
This highly aromatic plant rarely suffers from any pests or diseases.

Persicaria odorata flower

VIETNAMESE CORIANDER

Maintenance

Spring Reintroduce regular watering. Take cuttings.
Summer Cut back to produce new growth.
Fall Protect from frosts.
Winter In cool and cold climates cut back on watering.

Garden Cultivation

As this herb is a tropical plant it will need protection when temperatures fall below 45°F (7°C) at night. It can be grown outside in summer, planted in a rich fertile soil, in partial shade, but it will need lifting well before the winter before the first hint of frost. Be warned in warm climates: if you introduce this plant to your garden it will be more invasive than mint.

Harvesting

Pick the leaves to use fresh as required throughout the growing season.

 container growing

Vietnamese coriander grows very happily in containers; use a loam-based potting compost. Place the container in a warm greenhouse, sunroom or on a windowsill. Protect from the midday sun as this will and can scorch the leaves, which will then taste bitter. To maintain good-quality leaves, either divide the plant annually or repot one size up. Water and liquid feed regularly from spring until the fall. Outside the tropics it is wise to reduce the watering and stop feeding in the winter months.

 medicinal

Throughout the Far East, Vietnamese coriander is used to treat indigestion, flatulence and stomach aches. It is also reputedly eaten by Buddhist monks to suppress sexual urges.

 other uses

Currently in Australia there is interesting research into the essential oil of Vietnamese coriander, called Kesom oil, for use in food flavoring.

 culinary

In some countries this herb goes under the name Vietnamese mint, which is a misnomer in all aspects as it is certainly not a member of the mint family (Lamiaceae), nor does it in any way have a mint flavor. The first time I ate the leaves of this herb I was totally taken by surprise. To begin with the taste is mild with a hint of lime and spice, then as the flavor developed it became hot and peppery. This herb is never cooked, it is used as a fresh leaf condiment, always added at the end of cooking. In Asia it is usually eaten raw as a salad or herb accompaniment. It combines well with meat, vegetables and fruit. It is important in Vietnamese cooking being used copiously with noodle soups (pho) where large heaps of the leaves are dipped into the soup using chopsticks. Personally I like it scattered over stir-fried vegetables, which then gives the dish an extra zing.

Stir-fried Vegetables
Serves 4

½ oz. dried Chinese mushrooms, soaked in warm water for 20 minutes.
½ cup white cabbage, washed and finely sliced
½ cup carrots, peeled and sliced into thin strips
½ cup cucumber, cut into thin strips
½ cup bamboo shoots.
4 tablespoons chicken or vegetable stock
4 tablespoons sesame seed oil
2 tablespoons soy sauce
Salt and pepper to taste
1 pinch sugar
10 Vietnamese coriander leaves, finely chopped.

Drain the Chinese mushrooms and cut into small pieces. Heat the oil in a large frying pan or wok, add the cabbage, stir-fry for 2 minutes. Add the mushrooms, carrots, cucumber and bamboo shoots, stir-fry for a further 2 minutes. Add the stock, soy sauce, and pinch of sugar, salt and pepper to taste. Stir-fry for 2 minutes to heat through, add the chopped Vietnamese coriander leaves and serve with rice or noodles.

Petroselinum
PARSLEY

Also known as Common parsley, Garden parsley and Rock parsley. From the family Apiaceae.

Best-known of all garnishing herbs in the West. Native to central and southern Europe, in particular the Mediterranean region, now widely cultivated in several varieties throughout the world.

The Greeks had mixed feelings about this herb. It was associated with Archemorus, the Herald of Death, so they decorated their tombs with it. Hercules was said to have chosen parsley for his garlands, so they would weave it into crowns for victors at the Isthmian Games. But they did not eat it themselves, preferring to feed it to their horses. However, the Romans consumed parsley in quantity and made garlands for banquet guests to discourage intoxication and to counter strong odors.

It was believed that only a witch or a pregnant woman could grow it, and that a fine harvest was ensured only if the seeds were planted on Good Friday. It was also said that if parsley was transplanted, then misfortune would descend upon the household.

 ## varieties

Petroselinum crispum
Parsley
Hardy biennial. Ht. 12–16 in. Small creamy white flowers in flat umbels in summer. The leaf is brightish green and has curly toothed edges and a mild taste. It is mainly used as a garnish. Zone 6.

Petroselinum crispum French
French Parsley
Also known as Broad-Leafed Parsley. Hardy biennial. Ht. 18–24 in. Small creamy white flowers in flat umbels in summer. Flat dark green leaves with a stronger flavor than *P. crispum*. This is the one I recommend for culinary use. Zone 6.

Petroselinum crispum var. tuberosum
Hamburg Parsley
Also known as Turnip-Rooted Parsley. Perennial, grown as an annual. Root length up to 6 in. Leaf green and very similar to French parsley. This variety, probably first developed in Holland, was introduced into England in the early 18th century, but it was only popular for 100 years. The plant is still frequently found in vegetable markets in France and Germany, where it is sold as a root vegetable. Zone 6.

Warning: In the wild there is a plant called fool's parsley (*Aethusa cynapium*), which both looks and smells to the novice like French parsley. Do not be tempted to eat it as it is extremely poisonous.

 ## cultivation

Propagation
Seed
In cool climates, to ensure a succession of plants, sow seedlings under cover only in plug trays or pots. Avoid seed trays because it hates being transferred. Cover with perlite. If you have a heated propagator, a temperature of 65°F (18°C) will speed up germination. It takes 4–6 weeks without bottom heat and 2–3 weeks with. When the seedlings are large enough and the air and soil temperature have started to rise (about mid-spring), plant out 6 in. apart in a prepared garden bed. Alternatively, in late spring sow into a prepared site in the garden, in drills 12–18 in. apart and about 1¼ in. deep. Germination is very slow.

Parsley seed tea

Keep the soil moist at all times, otherwise the seed will not germinate. As soon as the seedlings are large enough, thin to 3 in. and then 6 in. apart.

Pests and Diseases

Slugs love young parsley plants. There is a fungus that may attack the leaves. It produces first brown then white spots. Where this occurs the whole stock should be destroyed. Get some fresh seed.

Maintenance

Spring Sow seed.
Summer Sow seed. Cut flower heads as they appear on second-year plants.
Fall Protect plants for winter crop.
Winter Protect plants for winter picking.

Garden Cultivation

Parsley is a hungry plant, it likes a good deep soil, not too light and not acid. Always feed the chosen site well in the previous fall with well-rotted manure.

If you wish to harvest parsley all year round, prepare two different sites. For summer supplies, a western or eastern border is ideal because the plant needs moisture and prefers a little shade. For winter supplies, a more sheltered spot will be needed in a sunny place.

The seeds should be sown thinly, in drills. If at any time the leaves turn a bit yellow, cut back to encourage new growth and feed with a liquid fertilizer. At the first sign of flower heads appearing, remove them if you wish to continue harvesting the leaves. Remember to water well during hot weather. In the second year parsley runs to seed very quickly. Dig it up as soon as the following year's crop is ready for picking, and remove it from the garden.

Hamburg or turnip parsley differs only in the respect that it is a root not a leaf crop. When the seedlings are large enough, thin to 8 in. apart. Water well all summer. The root tends to grow more at this time of year, and unlike a lot of root crops the largest roots taste the best. Lift in late fall, early winter. They are frost resistant. Foliage provides a food source for the Black Swallowtail Butterfly.

Harvesting

Pick leaves during first year for fresh use or for freezing (by far the best method of preserving parsley).

Dig up roots of Hamburg parsley in the fall of the first year and store in peat or sand.

container growing

Parsley is an ideal herb for containers, it even likes living inside on the kitchen windowsill, as long as it is watered, fed, and cut. Use a standard potting compost mixed in equal parts with composted fine bark. Curly parsley can look very ornamental as an edging to a large pot of nasturtiums. It can also be grown in hanging baskets, (keep well watered), window boxes (give it some shade in high summer), and containers. That brings me to the parsley pot, the one with six holes around the side. Do not use it. As I have already said, parsley likes moisture, and these containers dry out too fast as the holes in the side are small and make it very difficult to water; also, parsley has too big a tap root to be happy.

medicinal

All parsleys are a rich source of vitamins, including vitamin C. They are also high in iron and other minerals and contain the antiseptic chlorophyll.

It is a strong diuretic suitable for treating urinary infections as well as fluid retention. It also increases mothers' milk and tones the uterine muscle.

Parsley is a well-known breath freshener, being the traditional antidote for the pungent smell of garlic. Chew raw, to promote a healthy skin.

Use in poultices as an antiseptic dressing for sprains, wounds and insect bites.

other uses

A tea made from crushed seeds kills head lice vermin. Pour it over the head after washing and rinsing, wrap your head in a towel for 30 minutes and then allow to dry naturally. Equally, the seeds or leaves steeped in water can be used as a hair rinse.

warning

Avoid medicinal use during pregnancy. There is an oil produced from parsley, but it should be used only under medical supervision.

culinary

Parsley is a widely used culinary herb, valued for its taste as well as its rich nutritional content. Cooking with parsley enhances the flavor of other foods and herbs. In bland food, the best flavor is obtained by adding it just before the end of cooking.

As so many recipes include parsley, here are some basic herb mixtures.

Fines Herbes

You will see this mentioned in a number of recipes and it is a classic for omelettes.

1 sprig parsley, chopped
1 sprig chervil, chopped
Some chives cut with scissors
1–2 leaves French tarragon

Chop up all the herbs finely and add to egg dishes.

Fish Bouquet Garni

2 sprigs parsley
1 sprig French tarragon
1 sprig fennel (small)
2 leaves lemon balm

Tie the herbs together in a bundle and add to the cooking liquid.

Boil Hamburg parsley as a root vegetable or grate raw into salads. Use in soup mixes; the flavor resembles both celery and parsley.

Phlomis fruticosa

JERUSALEM SAGE

From the family Lamiaceae.

Originates from the Mediterranean region but is now cultivated widely as an ornamental garden plant.

The generic name, *Phlomis*, was used by Dioscorides, a Greek physician in the first century whose *Materia Medica* was the standard reference on the medical application of plants for over 1,500 years.

Winter Protect outside plants if the winter temperature is persistently below 23°F (−5°C).

Garden Cultivation
Jerusalem sage is an attractive plant, making a fine mound of gray-furred leaves, proof against all but the most severe winter. A prolific summer flowerer, happy in a dry, well-drained, sunny spot. Cut back each year after flowering (late summer) and you will be able to control and maintain its soft gray dome all year round. Do not trim in the fall as any frost will damage and in some cases kill the plant.

Harvesting
Pick leaves for drying before plant flowers.

 ## varieties

Phlomis fruticosa
Jerusalem Sage
Hardy evergreen perennial. Ht. and spread 4 ft. Whorls of hooded yellow flowers in summer. Gray/green oblongish leaves, slightly wrinkled. Zone 8.

Phlomis italica
Narrow-Leaved Jerusalem Sage
Hardy evergreen perennial. Ht. 36 in., spread 30 in. Whorls of lilac/pink flowers in midsummer, borne at the ends of shoots amid narrow, woolly, gray/green leaves. Zone 8

Phlomis italica

 ## cultivation

Propagation
Seeds
Sow the medium-sized seed in the fall into either seed or plug trays and cover with a thin layer of compost. Winter in a cold greenhouse or cold frame. Does not need stratification nor heat, just cool temperature. Germination is erratic. When the seedlings are large enough to handle, prick out into pots using a potting compost mixed in equal parts with composted fine bark. Plant the young plants into the garden when there is no threat of frosts.

Cuttings
Take softwood cuttings in summer from nonflowering shoots; they root easily.

Division
If an established plant has taken over its neighbor's spot, dig up and divide it in the spring; replant into a prepared site.

Pests and Diseases
This plant is mostly free from pests and diseases.

Maintenance
Spring Divide established plants if need be.
Summer Cut back after flowering to maintain shape.
Fall Sow seeds.

 ## container growing

Jerusalem sage is happy in a large container using a soil-based compost mixed in equal parts with composted fine bark. Be mean on the feeding and watering as it is a drought-loving plant. Trim back especially after flowering to restrict its rampant growth. Protect during the winter in a cool greenhouse or conservatory. Keep watering to the absolute minimum.

 ## other uses

The slightly aromatic leaves are attractive in a potpourri.

 ## culinary

Although not listed amongst culinary herbs, the leaves are pleasantly aromatic. In Greece the leaves are collected from the hillside and, once dried and bundled together with other related species, are hung up for sale. The dried leaves can be used in stews and casseroles.

Phytolacca americana

POKE WEED

Phytolacca americana

Also known as Poke root, Red ink plant, Virginia poke weed, Pigeon berry, Coccum, Poke, Indian poke, American poke and Cancer root. From the family Phytolaccaceae.

This herbaceous plant is a native to the warmer regions of North America, Africa and Asia. It has been introduced elsewhere, particularly in the Mediterranean region.

Its generic name is derived from two Greek words: *phyton*, meaning "plant" and *lac*, meaning "lake," referring to the purple/blue dye that flows from some of the phytolaccas when crushed.

The herb was introduced to European settlers by the Native Americans, who knew it as pocan or coccum, and used it as an emetic. It acquired a reputation as a remedy for internal cancers and was called cancer root.

Summer Cut off the flowers if you do not want berries.
Fall Sow seeds. Divide established plants.
Winter Dies back into the ground; no protection needed.

Garden Cultivation
Plant poke weed in sun or shade in a moist, fertile soil, sheltered from the wind. This plant can look marvelous in a garden, especially in the fall.

Harvesting
It can be used as a pot herb, the young shoots being picked in the spring. But because it is easy to confuse the identity of species, and toxicity varies among them, only do this if you really know what you are doing. So it is better to err on the side of caution and pick some nice fresh sorrel or red orach instead.

 ## container growing

It is a tall plant, and when in berry is sufficiently heavy to unbalance even a large pot. Keep the poisonous berries out of reach of children.

If you choose to try it, use a soil-based compost mixed in equal parts with composted fine bark and water well during the summer months.

 ## medicinal

Herbalists prescribe it for the treatment of chronic rheumatism, arthritis, tonsillitis, swollen glands, mumps and mastitis. An extract from the roots can destroy snails. This discovery is being explored in Africa as a possible means to control the disease bilharzia, which is carried by water snails.

 ## warning

POISONOUS. When handling either seeds, roots or the mature plant, gloves should be worn. It is toxic and dangerous. It should be used only by professionally trained herbalists.

 ## varieties

☠ *Phytolacca americana (P. decandra)*
Poke Weed
Hardy perennial. Ht. and spread 4–5 ft. Shallow, cup-shaped flowers, sometimes pink, flushed white and green, borne in terminal racemes in summer. They are followed by round fleshy blackish-purple berries with poisonous seeds that hang down when ripe. Oval to lance-shaped mid-green leaves, tinged purple in the fall. There is a variegated form with green and white leaves. Zone 3.

☠ *Phytolacca polyandra (P. calvigera)*
Hardy perennial. Ht. and spread 4 ft. Clusters of shallow, cup-shaped, pink flowers in summer, followed by rounded blackish berries with poisonous seeds. Has brilliant crimson stems, oval to lance-shaped, mid-green leaves that turn yellow in summer through fall. This plant is a native of China. Zone 6.

 ## cultivation

Propagation
Seed
Wearing gloves, sow the seeds fresh in the fall or spring in prepared seed or plug trays. Cover with perlite. If sown in the fall, winter the young plants in a cold greenhouse or cold frame. In the spring, after a period of hardening off, plant them in a prepared site in the garden, 3 ft. apart.

Division
Both species have large root systems that can be divided (wearing gloves) either in the fall or spring.

Pests and Diseases
Largely free from pests and diseases.

Maintenance
Spring Sow seeds. Divide established plants.

JACOB'S LADDER
Polemonium caeruleum

Polemonium reptans

Also known as Blue jacket, Charity, Jacob's walking stick, Ladder to heaven, Greek valerian. From the family Polemoniaceae.

This herb is steeped in history. It was known to the ancient Greeks as *Polemonium* and they administered a decoction made from the root mixed with wine in cases of dysentery, toothache and against the bites of poisonous animals. As late as the 19th century it was known as Valeranae Graecae or Greek Valerian and was being used in some European pharmacies. It was predominantly used as an antisyphilitic agent and in the treatment of rabies. To confuse things, the American Shakers called it "Abscess" and used it for pleurisy and fevers.

 ## varieties

Polemonium caeruleum
Jacob's Ladder
Hardy perennial. Ht. and spread 18–24 in. Clusters of attractive cup-shaped lavender blue flowers in summer. The mid-green leaves are finely divided into small lance shapes. Zone 3.

Polemonium reptans
Also known as false Jacob's ladder or American Greek valerian. Hardy perennial. Ht. 8–18 in. and spread 12 in. Clusters of attractive cup-shaped blue flowers in summer. The silver/green leaves are finely divided into small lance shapes. Native of Eastern North America. The root of this species is bitter in flavor and is employed as an astringent and as an antidote against snake bites. Zone 3.

 ## cultivation

Propagation
Seed
For flowering early the following spring, sow the fairly small seeds in the fall into a prepared seed or plug module tray using a standard seed compost. Winter the seedlings in a cool/cold, but frost-free greenhouse. Prick out in spring, when the threat of frosts has passed, then plant directly into the garden after hardening off, at a distance of 12 in. apart.

Division
Divide established plants in the spring. Dig the whole plant up and ease it in half using two forks back to back. Replant in a prepared site in the garden.

Pests and Diseases
These plants rarely suffer from pests or diseases.

Maintenance
Spring Sow seeds if not previously done, divide established plants if needed.
Summer Deadhead flowers and, after flowering, cut back to prevent self-seeding.
Fall Sow seeds under protection.
Winter Established plants are hardy and should not need protection.

Garden Cultivation
Jacob's ladder prefers a rich, moisture-retentive soil, with added lime in a sunny position. However it is a most tolerant plant and will adapt to most soils with the exception of those that are very dry.

Harvesting
Cut the flowers just as they open for drying. Dry either in small bunches or individual sprays.

 ## container growing

This herb looks most attractive grown in a container. Use a loam-based potting compost and place the container in semishade to help prevent the compost from drying out. Feed regularly only when the plant is flowering, using a liquid fertilizer and following the manufacturer's instructions.

 ## medicinal

This herb is rarely used in modern herbal medicine.

 ## other uses

The dried flowers do not smell, but do look attractive in potpourri.
When the roots are combined with olive oil, it makes a black dye.

Polemonium caeruleum

Polygonatum
SOLOMON'S SEAL

Also known as David's harp, Lady's lockets, Lily of the mountain, Drop berry, Seal root or Sealwort. From the family Convallariaceae.

This plant's generic name *Polygonatum* is derived from *Poly,* meaning "many" and *gonu,* meaning "knee joint," which may refer to the many-jointed rhizome.

King Solomon, wiser than all men, gave his approval to the use of the roots (which are said to resemble cut sections of Hebrew characters) as a poultice for wounds, and to help heal broken limbs.

Pests and Diseases
If you notice clean-cut holes in the leaves it is likely to be the sawfly caterpillar. This will not irrreversibly damage the plant, but it can look devastated. Pick the larvae off or treat with soft insecticidal soap, although this is unlikely to completely eradicate the caterpillars.

Maintenance
Spring When the soil is damp, divide established plants.
Summer Make sure the soil does not dry out, and water if necessary.
Fall Sow fresh seeds, divide established plants.
Winter Protect with a layer of mulch if the winter has a prolonged frost below 14°F (−10°C)

Garden Cultivation
Plant in a cool shady position in fertile well-drained soil. Dig the soil over before planting with some well-rotted leaf mold, and each winter top dress with extra leaf mold. This plant looks much better planted in large drifts than as single plants.

Harvesting
In the fall, after the foliage has died back, dig up and dry the roots for medicinal use from a well-established 3-year-old plant.

 ## container growing

Solomon's seal can be successfully grown in a container. Use a soil-based potting compost and top dress in the fall with well-rotted leaf mould. Position the container in semishade and water regularly throughout the summer months.

 ## medicinal

The powdered roots and rhizomes make a good poultice for bruises, inflammation and wounds and a good skin wash for rashes and blemishes.

 ## other uses

The plant has for centuries been employed as a cosmetic to clear freckles and as a skin tonic.

 ## warning

All parts of the plant are poisonous and should be taken internally only under the supervision of a qualified medicinal or herbal practitioner. Large doses can be harmful.

 ## varieties

☠ *Polygonatum* x *hybridum*
Solomon's Seal
Hardy perennial. Ht. 12–32 in., spread 12 in. White waxy flowers tipped with green hang from arching stems in spring to summer and are followed by blue/black berries. Oval to lance-shaped, mid-green leaves. Zone 4.

☠ *Polygonatum odoratum*
(*Polygonatum officinale*)
Angular Solomon's Seal
Hardy perennial. Ht. 24 in., spread 12 in. Produces pairs of fragrant tubular bell-shaped, green-tipped white flowers in spring, which are followed by blue/black berries. Oval to lance-shaped mid-green leaves. Zone 4.

 ## cultivation

Propagation
Seed
In the fall, sow fresh seeds into prepared seed or plug module trays using a standard seed compost mixed in equal parts with fine composted bark. Cover with compost then with glass and leave outside for the winter. Remove the glass as soon as germination starts in early spring. Once the seedlings are large enough to handle, plant into a well-prepared site, and water regularly throughout the first season.

Division
This is a far more reliable method of propagation. Divide established plants in spring or fall. Replant into a prepared site in the garden.

Portulaca oleracea

PURSLANE

Also known as Kulfa and Baqli. From the family Portulacaceae.

This yummy culinary and medicinal herb can be found growing wild throughout Europe and India. Historically this plant has been grown for medicinal use for over 2,000 years, being used as an antidote for wasp stings and snake bites. Recently reading Matthew Biggs's *Complete Book of Vegetables*, I discovered that its name in Malawi translates as "buttocks of the wife of a chief," obviously referring to its succulent round leaves and juicy stems!! The mind boggles.

 ## varieties

Portulaca oleracea
Purslane
Hardy annual. Ht. and spread 18 in. Small, yellow, stalkless 4–6-petalled flowers in summer, which open in the sun and close in the shade. Thick fleshy spoon-shaped, mid-green leaves. Warmer zones.

Portulaca oleracea var. *aurea*
Golden Purslane
Hardy annual. Ht. 10 in., spread 7 in. Small, yellow, stalkless 4–6-petalled flowers in summer, which open in the sun and close in the shade. Large golden, round, disc-shaped succulent leaves. This variety is ideal for container growing because of its compact habit. Warmer zones.

 ## cultivation

Propagation
Seed
In spring sow the small seeds into prepared module plug trays using a standard seed compost. Cover with perlite, place under protection at 68°F (20°C).

Germination takes 1–2 weeks. Alternatively, when the night temperature does not fall below 50°F (10°C), sow into a prepared site and subsequently thin the seedlings to 6 in. apart.

Pests and Diseases
Seedlings are prone to damping off in the garden, when the night temperatures fall below 50°F (10°C). Beware: slugs love this herb, so check plants regularly and remove any found.

Maintenance
Spring Sow seeds.
Summer Water regularly. Nip out flowering tip to encourage new growth.
Fall Liquid feed to prolong season.
Winter Order the seeds for next year.

Garden Cultivation
Plant in a sunny position in a moisture-retentive, light soil, which was not fed in the previous fall. It is more attractive and more productive if grown in thick rows or clumps in the garden rather than as an isolated plant. I have seen golden purslane used as an edging plant to great effect in a formal vegetable garden.

Harvesting
Pick the leaves and flower buds for use fresh throughout the growing season. Always pick from the top, not the sides, to encourage new growth. Purslane does not dry or freeze well; preserve by extracting the juice or pickling in vinegar.

 ## container growing

Golden purslane looks very pretty and is easy to look after. Use a loam-based compost mixed with 25 percent sharp grit for extra drainage. Place the container in partial shade. Water regularly and liquid feed monthly to maintain succulent leaf production.

 ## culinary

The leaves of purslane have the flavor and texture of fresh mangetout. The stems and flower buds add a delightful crunch to a mixed salad. In the Middle East it is an ingredient of a traditional salad called Fattoush.

 ## medicinal

Recent research has shown that purslane is a rich source of omega-3 fatty acids, which are thought to be important in preventing heart attacks and strengthening the immune system. The fresh juice is soothing when applied to insect bites and burns and it takes away the irritating itch in eczema.

 ## warning

Should not be taken medicinally when pregnant or by those who suffer from digestive problems.

Portulaca oleracea var. *aurea* **showing seeds**

Primula veris

COWSLIP

Also known as St. Peter's keys, Palsywort, Coweslop, Fair bells and Keys of Heaven. From the family Primulaceae.

This traditional herb is a native of Northern and Central Europe. Also known as Marsh Marigold in the United States. A legend of northern Europe is that St. Peter let his keys to Heaven drop when he learned that a duplicate set had been made. Where they fell the cowslip grew, hence the common name Keys of Heaven.

Dried cowslips

Garden Cultivation

Plant cowslips in semishade or sun, in a moist but well-drained soil. They look better grown in clumps and drifts rather than singularly.

Harvesting

I am sure I do not need to remind you, please do not dig up wild plants. This is prohibited in many countries. Pick leaves and flowers as required to use fresh. Dig up the roots of cultivated cowslips for drying in the fall.

 varieties

Primula veris

Cowslip

Hardy perennial. Ht. and spread 6–8 in. Tight clusters of fragrant, tubular, yellow flowers produced on stout stems in spring. Oval mid-green leaves. Zone 5.

Cowslips are often mistaken for oxlip *(P. elatior)*, which is a hybrid of the cowslip and the primrose *(P. vulgaris)*. Oxlips have large pale yellow flowers in a one-sided cluster.

 cultivation

Propagation

Seed

Sow fresh seed in the fall onto the surface of prepared plug module trays or small pots, using a standard seed compost. Cover with perlite or a piece of glass. Place in a cold frame or cold greenhouse. Germination takes 4–6 weeks. If covered with glass, remove immediately when you see the seeds break. Winter the young plants in the cold frame or cold greenhouse before planting in the following spring. If you sow old seed in winter you will need to stratify the seed (the cold

treatment; see page 264) to enable the seed to germinate.

Division

All *Primula* divide easily and this is by far the easiest method of propagation. Divide established plants in early fall either using two hand forks back to back or by digging up a clump, dividing by hand and replanting into a prepared site 6 in. apart.

Ensure plants bought come from a cultivated source and are not dug from the wild.

Pests and Diseases

The scourge of all *Primula* plants, when grown in containers, is the vine weevil. To eradicate in pots, water with nematodes, following the manufacturer's instructions, in spring and fall when the soil temperature does not fall below 40°F (5°C).

Maintenance

Spring Clear winter debris from around plants.
Summer Deadhead if you do not require seeds.
Fall Collect fresh seeds and sow. Divide established plants.
Winter No need for protection.

 container growing

Cowslips adapt happily to being grown in containers outside. Use a loam-based compost. Protect the container from the midday sun.

 culinary

Use young leaves and flowers in salads; the leaves can also be added to meat stuffings. The flowers can be used to make wine.

 medicinal

A tea made from the flowers is a simple remedy for insomnia and nervous tension. Cowslip syrup was a country remedy for palsy, hence the common name palsywort. The roots have a high saponin content and are used to treat whooping cough and bronchitis.

 warning

Primula veris is renowned for causing contact dermatitis.

Primula vulgaris
PRIMROSE

Also known as Early rose, Easter rose, First rose and May flower. From the family Primulaceae.

This herald of spring is a native of Europe. The name Primrose originates from the Latin *prima*, meaning "first" and *rosa*, meaning "rose."

In the Middle Ages, concoctions were made from primroses which were used as a remedy for gout and rheumatism.

Due to the encouragement of sympathetic farming practices, it is possible to see this once-endangered wildflower in the countryside. However it is still illegal to pick or dig this flower in the wild.

Primrose tisane

 varieties

Primula vulgaris
Primrose

Hardy perennial. Ht. and spread 6 in. The fresh yellow, sweetly scented flowers with darker yellow centers are borne singly on hairy stems in early spring. Mid-green, wrinkled, oval leaves. Zone 5.

 cultivation

Propagation
Seed

Sow fresh seed, while it is still green and before it becomes dry and turns brown, in late summer onto the surface of prepared plug module trays or small pots, using a standard seed compost. Cover with perlite or a piece of glass. Place in a cold frame or cold greenhouse. Germination takes 4–6 weeks. If covered with glass, remove when you see the seeds break. Winter the young plants in the cold frame or cold greenhouse before planting out in the following spring. If you sow dry brown seeds in winter you will need to stratify the seed (the cold treatment, see page 264). Be patient, it can take 2 years to germinate.

Division

All *Primula* divide easily, and this is by far the easiest method of propagation. Divide established plants in early fall either using two hand forks back to back or by digging up a clump, dividing by hand and replanting into a prepared site 6 in. apart.

Pests and Diseases
The scourge of all *Primula* plants, when grown in containers, is the vine weevil. To eradicate in pots, water with nematodes, following the manufacturer's instructions, in spring and fall when the soil temperature does not fall below 40°F (5°C).

Maintenance
Spring Plant out fall-germinated plants.
Summer Sow fresh seed.
Fall Divide established plants.
Winter No need for protection.

Garden Cultivation
Plant primroses in semishade, under a deciduous tree or near hedges, in a moist but well-drained soil. They look better grown in clumps and drifts rather than singly. When growing primroses in a wild garden, delay cutting the grass until midsummer, which is after the plants have self-seeded.

Harvesting
In spring pick young leaves and flowers to use fresh. In summer collect seed for immediate sowing.

 container growing

Primroses adapt happily to being grown in containers outside and are a great pick-me-up as they flower early in spring. Use a loam-based compost. Position the container in semishade.

 culinary

The flowers are lovely in green salads, and they can be crystallized to decorate puddings and cakes. The young leaves make an interesting vegetable when steamed and tossed in butter.

 medicinal

Medicinally this herb is rarely used today. However, if nothing else is available, a tisane made from the leaves and flowers can be used as a mild sedative.

 warning

Primulas are renowned for causing contact dermatitis.

Prostanthera

PROSTANTHERA

Also known as Mint Bush. From the family Lamiaceae.

These highly attractive aromatic shrubs are natives of Australia.

I have fallen in love with these most generous of flowers. When I was exhibiting one in flower at the Chelsea Flower Show, some member of the public fell in love with it in equal measure and tried to liberate it from my display!

I can find no historical references other than in the RHS *Dictionary of Gardening*, which states that the generic name, *Prostanthera*, comes from *prostithemi*, "to append," and *anthera*, meaning "anther," the pollen-bearing part of the stamen. This therefore alludes to the appendages usually borne by the anthers.

Prostanthera ovalifolia

Pests and Diseases
Over-watering young plants causes root rot—a killer.

Maintenance
Spring Take cuttings.
Summer Cut back after flowering only if necessary.
Fall Protect from frosts.
Winter Protect from hard frosts and excessive water.

Garden Cultivation
In cool climates with persistent frosts they are better grown in a container. However if your climate is mild, plant in the spring in a warm corner, in a lime-free, well-draining soil at a distance of 24–36 in. apart. Rain combined with frost is the killer in winter. If you want to make a low hedge out of *Prostanthera cuneata* then plant specimens 18 in. apart.

Harvesting
Pick leaves in the summer after flowering for drying and inclusion in potpourri.

 ## container growing

This is a real crowd puller when in flower, and even when not, makes a most attractive aromatic plant. Use a soil-based compost mixed with 25 percent composted fine bark and 25 percent peat. Keep young plants on the dry side, but water freely in the growing season.

 ## medicinal

I am sure that a plant such as *P. cuneata* that gives off as much scent, and has obviously so much oil in the leaf, will one day have some use.

Prostanthera lasianthos

 ## varieties

Prostanthera cuneata
Evergreen half-hardy perennial. Ht. and spread 24–36 in. Very attractive white flowers with purple spots that look rather like little orchids; late spring, early summer. Round, dark green, slightly leathery and shiny, mint-scented leaves. Can withstand a minimum temperature of 28°F (−2°C). Zone 9.

Prostanthera lasianthos
Victorian Christmas bush.
Evergreen large shrub. Ht. 3–18 ft. Profuse sprays of white pale lilac flowers. Long, narrow toothed menthol-scented green leaves.
Zone 9.

Prostanthera ovalifolia
Evergreen tender perennial. Reaches a height and spread of 4 ft. in its native country. Attractive purple flowers on short leafy racemes throughout spring and summer. Dark green aromatic leaves. Can only withstand a minimum temperature of 41°F (5°C). Zone 9.

Prostanthera rotundifolia 'Rosea'
Evergreen half-hardy perennial. A small tree up to 9 ft. tall in its native country; in cooler climates it's a lot smaller. Pretty mauve/purple flowers in spring that last a long time. The dark green leaves (not as dark as *P. cuneata*) are round and mint-scented. Withstands a minimum temperature of 32°F (0°C). Zone 9.

 ## cultivation

Propagation
Cuttings
Take cuttings in spring or late summer. Use a standard seed compost mixed in equal parts with composted fine bark. When the cuttings are well rooted, in 8–12 weeks, pot again using the same mix and keep in containers for the first year.

Prunella vulgaris

SELF HEAL

Also known as Carpenter's herb, Sticklewort, Touch and heal, All heal, Woundwort, Hercules' woundwort, Blue curls, Brownwort and Hock heal. From the family Lamiaceae.

This herb is found growing wild throughout all the temperate regions of the northern hemisphere, including Europe, Asia and North America. It is found on moist, loamy, well-drained soils, in grassland, pastures and open woodland, especially in sunny situations. Now introduced into China and Australia.

In strict 16th-century adherence to the Doctrine of Signatures, whereby it was believed that every plant bore an outward sign of its value to mankind, people noted that the upper lip of the flower was shaped like a hook, and as billhooks and sickles were a main cause of wounds in their agrarian society, they decided that the purpose of the herb was to heal wounds (hence Self Heal). They also saw the shape of the throat in the flower, which was why it was introduced to treat diseases of the throat such as quinsy and diphtheria, a propensity with a precedent in ancient Greece, where physicians used it to cure sore throats and tonsillitis.

 varieties

Prunella vulgaris
Self Heal
Hardy perennial. Ht. 2–12 in., spread 6–12 in. Clusters of blue/purple flowers all summer. Oval leaves of a bright green. Zone 4.
   There is a much rarer white-flowered species, *Prunella laciniata*, which has very deeply cut leaves.

 cultivation

Propagation
Seed
Sow the small seeds into prepared seed or plug trays in either spring or fall and cover with perlite; no extra heat is required. If a fall sowing, winter the young plants in a cold frame. In spring, when the plants are large enough, plant at a distance of 6–8 in. apart.

Division
This plant grows runners that have their own small root systems and is, therefore, easy to divide. Dig up in the spring or fall, and split and replant either in the garden or amongst grass.

Garden Cultivation
This plant, which is easy to establish, makes a colorful ground cover with attractive flowers. It is happy in full sun to semishade and will grow in most soils, including those that are rather acid, though it does best if the soil is fertile. It can be grown in a lawn, and while the mower keeps its spread and height in check, it will still flower and be much visited by bees and butterflies.

Pests and Diseases
In most cases it is free from pests and diseases.

Maintenance
Spring Sow seed. Divide established plants.
Summer Cut back after flowering to curtail self-seeding.
Fall Divide established plants. Sow seeds.
Winter No need for protection, fully hardy.

Harvesting
Harvest for medicinal use only. Dry both the leaves and flowers.

 container growing

Self heal can be grown in containers using a soil-based compost. However, as it looks a bit insipid on its own, it is better combined with plants like heartsease, poppies and cowslips.
   Water well during the growing season, but only feed with liquid fertilizer twice otherwise it will produce too lush a growth.

 medicinal

Used in herbal medicines as a gargle for sore throats and inflammation of the mouth. A decoction is used to wash cuts and to soothe burns and bruises.

Prunella vulgaris

Pulmonaria
LUNGWORT

Also known as Jerusalem cowslip, Adam and Eve, Lady Mary's tears, Spotted bugloss, and Spotted comfrey. From the family Boraginaceae.

Lungwort is a native plant of Europe and northern parts of the United States. The markings on the leaves were attributed to the Virgin Mary's milk or her tears; however the generic name *Pulmonaria*, comes from *pulmo*, meaning "lung." The Doctrine of Signatures, which held that each plant must be associated either by appearance, smell or habit, with the disease which it was said to heal, thought that the leaves resembled a diseased lung, and so used it to treat various lung disorders with some success.

 varieties

Pulmonaria angustifolia
Semievergreen hardy perennial. Ht. 9 in., spread 8–12 in. Pink flowers that turn bright blue in spring. Lance-shaped mid-green leaves with no markings. Zone 3.

Pulmonaria longifolia
Hardy perennial. Ht. 12 in., spread 18 in. Pink flowers that turn purplish-blue in spring. Lanced-shaped, slightly hairy, dark green leaves with white spots. Zone 4.

Pulmonaria officinalis
Lungwort
Semi-evergreen hardy perennial. Ht. 12 in., spread 24 in. Pink flowers that turn blue in spring. Oval leaves with blotchy white/cream markings on a mid-green, slightly hairy surface. Zone 6.

Note The American native Virginian cowslip, *Mertensia virginica*, is sometimes known as smooth lungwort. It belongs to the same Boraginaceae family, but does not have the same medicinal properties.

 cultivation

Propagation
Seed
This plant rarely produces viable seed. However it has been known to self-seed erratically around the garden.

Division
This is by far the easiest way to propagate this herb. Divide established plants either after flowering in late spring or alternatively in early fall, using the two forks back to back technique.

Pests and Diseases
In long, dry, hot summers this herb can be prone to powdery mildew. Cut back and burn infected growth, and then water the plant well.

Maintenance
Spring Dig up and replant seedlings.
Summer Water well especially if the ground is drying out.
Fall Divide established plants.
Winter No need for protection; fully hardy.

Garden Cultivation
Lungwort prefers to be planted in semishade and in a moist but free-draining soil, which has been well fed with leaf mold or well-rotted compost the season prior to planting. The leaf mold is particularly important if you live in a drought area or if your soil is prone to becoming excessively dry in summer.

Harvesting
For medicinal use, pick the leaves after flowering for drying.

 container growing

Lungwort can be grown successfully in a container as long as it has enough room for the creeping rhizomes to spread. Use a loam-based potting compost in a frost hardy container. Winter the plants outside; if brought in they become prone to mildew.

 medicinal

Lungwort is a soothing expectorant. The silica contained in the leaves was traditionally used to restore the elasticity of the lungs. Externally the leaves have been used for healing all kinds of wounds.

 warning

Like many in the Boraginaceae family, lungwort has leaves that can cause contact dermatitis.

Lungwort potpourri

Rheum palmatum

CHINESE RHUBARB

Also known as Da Huang. From the family Polygonaceae.

To many people rhubarb may seem a very Western fruit; it is in fact a vegetable and an important medicinal herb, native to China and Tibet where it has been used for over 2,000 years to treat many digestive problems. It was first mentioned in the Shen Nong *Canon of Herbs* which was written in the Han dynasty (206 BC–AD 23).

 ## varieties

 ### *Rheum palmatum*
Chinese Rhubarb
Herbaceous perennial. Ht. up to 6 ft. in flower, spread 24–30 in. Panicles of deep red flowers in summer followed by three-winged fruit. Large, up to 3 ft., palmate, lobed mid-green leaves. Nearly round green stems are NOT edible. Zone 5.

cultivation

Propagation
Division
The easiest method of propagation is by root division. To start, buy a plant from a reputable nursery. Once you have an established plant, over 3 years old, it can then be divided as necessary. Do this when the plant is dormant, in late fall. Lift the crown, then with a sharp knife or spade, divide the crown into 4 in. sections including as much root as possible and a new bud with each section. Pot immediately into a soil-based potting compost with the bud tip just below the surface of the compost. Leave the container in a cold frame or cold greenhouse until early spring, then plant into a previously prepared site at a distance of 30 in. apart.

Pests and Diseases
Rhubarb can suffer from crown rot, which causes the rotting of the stalks and leaves. If you see infected plants, dig up and burn and do not replant in that position again.

Maintenance
Spring Plant out divided plants.
Summer Remove flower heads once they form seeds to prevent self-seeding.
Fall Divide established plants. Feed plants with well-rotted manure.
Winter No need for protection, fully hardy.

Garden Cultivation
Plant in a sunny position, in a deep fertile soil that has been fed with well-rotted manure in the previous fall. If you are growing this herb for use medicinally it will need to stay in position for at least 6 years, so choose your site with care.

Harvesting
In the fall, lift 6-year-old rhizomes for medicinal use. Either dry or create tinctures.

 ## container growing

Rhubarb is not ideally suited for growing in containers because of its long root system.

 ## culinary

Chinese rhubarb is not a culinary herb.

 ## medicinal

The rhizomes are used to improve digestion, for liver and gall bladder complaints and as a laxative. It can be made into a mouthwash for mouth ulcers but it tastes revolting! In homeopathy it is used to treat teething children.

 ## other uses

Traditionally an infusion of the leaves was used as an effective spray to control aphids and to check black spots on roses. As this infusion is poisonous when used in the kitchen garden, the gardeners would not harvest the treated vegetables for a minimum of 7 days.

 ## warning

The leaves are very toxic; on no account eat them. Do not take as a medicine during pregnancy or when breastfeeding.

Ground Chinese rhubarb root

Ricinus communis

CASTOR OIL PLANT

Also known as Palma-Christi, Eranda and Rendi. From the family Euphorbiaceae.

The castor oil plant is one of the first medicinal plants known to man. Its seeds have been found in Egyptian tombs and it is mentioned in papyrus scrolls written in 1500 BC. The Greek historian Herodotus noted its use as a lamp oil, a purpose for which it is still employed in the temples of Southern India. The lampblack produced by the combination of castor oil with wicks dipped in herbal preparations, has provided the universal eye cosmetic of India known as kohl. In the 18th century this herb became popular in Europe as a laxative.

Pests and Diseases
This herb rarely suffers from disease and is not affected by pests; because the leaves have insecticidal properties, it actually repels insects.

Maintenance
Spring Sow seeds.
Summer Stake flowering heads in exposed sites.
Fall Harvest seeds.
Winter When grown as an annual, feed soil where the plant was grown.

Garden Cultivation
This frost-tender fast-growing evergreen shrub is often grown just for its attractive foliage in the garden. Plant in a sheltered position in full sun, in a rich fertile soil. It may need support in exposed areas.

Harvesting
The seed capsules can be gathered throughout the year when nearly ripe and then put out in the sun to dry and mature before the oil is extracted.

 ## companion planting

It is reputedly a good mole repellent.

 ## medicinal

The oil extracted from the seeds is well known for its strong laxative properties. It is also used as a massage oil in India where it is used on tender joints.

 ## other uses

The oil extracted from the seeds is used in numerous ways: in the manufacture of high-grade lubricants, as a fabric coating, as a leather preservative and in the manufacturing of inks, dyes and fibers.

 ## warning

Do not eat the seeds: they are extremely poisonous. Do not take castor oil during pregnancy. Wear gloves when handling this plant, because it can cause an allergic reaction.

 ## varieties

☠ *Ricinus communis*
Castor oil plant
Half-hardy evergreen shrub, grown as an annual in cool climates. Ht. up to 12 ft. The separate male and female flowers are borne together in dense upright branching heads. The male flowers have yellow stamens and the green petal-less female flowers have beard-like red stigmas, which are followed by fruits each containing three seeds. The seeds are poisonous. The large palmate leaves when young are often red, turning green as they mature. Warmer zones.

 ## cultivation

Propagation
Seed
Sow the large, fresh seeds, in early spring individually into prepared pots or module plug trays using a standard seed compost mixed in equal parts with perlite. As the seeds are large, push them into the compost and cover with perlite. Place under protection at 70°F (21°C); germination takes 14–21 days. Once large enough to handle, pot using a standard loam-based compost. Plant into a prepared site in the garden once the nighttime temperature does not drop below 50°F (10°C). When grown in cool climates it will die with the first frosts. Wearing gloves, clear the plant from the ground, dig the site over and feed with well-rotted manure.

ROSEMARY

Rosmarinus officinalis

Rosmarinus officinalis 'Majorca Pink'

From the family Lamiaceae.

Rosemary is a shrub that originated in the Mediterranean area and is now widely cultivated throughout the temperate regions. The ancient Latin name means sea-dew. This may come from its habit of growing close to the sea and the dew-like appearance of its blossom at a distance. It is steeped in myth, magic and folk medicinal use. One of my favorite stories about rosemary comes from Spain. It relates that originally the blue flowers were white. When the Holy family fled into Egypt, the Virgin Mary had to hide from some soldiers, so she spread her cloak over a rosemary bush and knelt behind it. When the soldiers had gone by she stood up and removed her cloak and the blossoms turned blue in her honor. Also connected to the Christian faith is the story that rosemary will grow for 33 years, the length of Christ's life, and then die.

In Elizabethan days, the wedding couple wore or carried a sprig of rosemary as a sign of fidelity. Also bunches of rosemary were tied with colored ribbon tipped with gold and given to guests at weddings to symbolize love and faithfulness.

Rosemary was burnt in sick chambers to freshen and purify the air. Branches were strewn in courts of law as a protection from jail fever. During the plague, people used to wear it in neck pouches to sniff as they traveled, and in Victorian times it was carried in the hollow handles of walking sticks for the same reasons.

 varieties

Rosmarinus officinalis
Rosemary
Evergreen hardy perennial. Ht. and spread 3 ft. Pale blue flowers in early spring to early summer and then sometimes in early fall. Needle-shaped dark green leaves are highly aromatic. Zone 8.

Rosmarinus officinalis var. *albiflorus*
Rosemary White
Evergreen hardy perennial. Ht. and spread 32 in. White flowers in early spring to early summer and then sometimes in early fall. Needle-shaped dark green leaves are highly aromatic. Zone 8.

Rosmarinus officinalis var. *angustissimus* 'Benenden Blue'
Rosemary Benenden Blue
Evergreen hardy perennial. Ht. and spread 32 in. Dark blue flowers in early spring to early summer and then sometimes again in early fall. Leaves are fine needles and fairly dense on the stem, good aroma. Zone 8.

Rosmarinus officinalis 'Blue Lagoon'

Rosmarinus officinalis 'Aureus'
Rosemary Golden

Evergreen hardy perennial. Ht. 32 in., spread 24 in. It hardly ever flowers, but if it does they are pale blue. The thin needle leaves are green splashed with gold. If you did not know better you would think the plant was suffering from a virus. It still looks very attractive. Zone 8.

Rosmarinus officinalis 'Blue Lagoon'
Rosemary Blue Lagoon

Evergreen hardy perennial. Ht. 16 in., spread 32 in. Striking small dark blue flowers in spring. Short dark green needle-shaped aromatic leaves. Arching semi-prostate habit. Zone 8.

Rosmarinus officinalis 'Boule'
Rosemary Boule

Evergreen hardy perennial. Ht. 12 in., spread 32 in. Small mid-blue flowers in spring. Short, dark green needle-shaped aromatic leaves with a white underside. Prostate hanging habit. Ideal for walls and containers. Zone 8.

Rosmarinus officinalis 'Fota Blue'
Rosemary Fota Blue

Evergreen hardy perennial. Ht. and spread 32 in. Very attractive dark blue flowers in early spring to early summer and then sometimes again in early fall. Very well-spaced narrow, needle-like dark green leaves; the plant has a fairly prostrate habit. Zone 8.

Rosmarinus officinalis 'Sissinghurst Blue'

Rosmarinus officinalis 'Majorca Pink'
Rosemary Majorcan Pink

Evergreen half-hardy perennial. Ht. and spread 32 in. Pink flowers in early spring to early summer and then sometimes again in early fall. The needle-shaped dark green leaves are highly aromatic. This is a slightly prostrate form of rosemary. Zone 8.

Rosmarinus officinalis 'Miss Jessopp's Upright'
Rosemary Miss Jessopp's Upright

Evergreen hardy perennial. Ht. and spread 6 ft. Very pale blue flowers in early spring to early summer and then sometimes again in early fall. This rosemary has a very upright habit, making it ideal for hedges (see page 204). The leaves are dark green needles spaced closely together, making the plant very bushy. Zone 8.

Rosmarinus officinalis 'Primley Blue'
Rosemary Primley Blue

(Not Frimley, which it has been incorrectly called for a few years.)
Evergreen hardy perennial. Ht. and spread 32 in. Blue flowers in early spring to early summer and then sometimes again in early fall. The needle-shaped dark green leaves are highly aromatic. This is a good hardy bushy variety. Zone 8.

Rosmarinus officinalis 'Roseus'

Rosmarinus officinalis Prostratus Group
Rosemary Prostrate

Evergreen hardy perennial. Ht. 12 in., spread 3 ft. Light blue flowers in early spring to early summer and then sometimes again in early fall. The needle-shaped dark green leaves are highly aromatic. This is a great plant for trailing on a wall or slope. Zone 8.

Rosmarinus officinalis 'Roseus'
Rosemary Pink

Evergreen half-hardy perennial. Ht. and spread 32 in. Pink flowers in early spring to early summer and then sometimes again in early fall. The needle-shaped dark green leaves are highly aromatic. Zone 8.

Rosmarinus officinalis 'Severn Sea'
Rosemary Severn Sea

Evergreen half-hardy perennial. Ht. and spread 32 in. Mid-blue flowers in early spring to early summer and sometimes again in early fall. Highly aromatic needle-shaped dark green leaves. The whole plant has a slightly prostrate habit with arching branches. Zone 8.

Rosmarinus officinalis 'Sissinghurst Blue'
Rosemary Sissinghurst

Evergreen hardy perennial. Ht. 4½ ft., spread 3 ft. Light blue flowers in early spring to early summer and then sometimes again in early fall. The plant has an upright habit and grows very bushy. The needle-shaped dark green leaves are highly aromatic. Zone 8.

cultivation

Propagation

Seed

Rosmarinus officinalis can, with care, be grown from seed. It needs a bottom heat of 80–90°F (27–32°C) to be successful. Sow in the spring in prepared seed or plug trays, using a standard seed compost mixed in equal parts with composted fine bark, and cover with perlite. Having got it to germinate, be careful not to over-water the seedlings as they are prone to damping off. Harden off the young plant slowly in summer and pot. Keep it in a pot for the first winter, and plant out the following spring into the required position at a distance of 24–36 in. apart.

Cuttings

As cultivated varieties do not come free from seed, this is a more reliable method of propagation as it ensures that you achieve the variety you require.

Softwood: Take these in spring off the new growth. Cut lengths of about 6 in. Use a standard seed compost mixed in equal parts with composted fine bark.

Semihardwood: Take these in summer from the non-flowering shoots, using the same compost as for softwood cuttings.

Rosmarinus officinalis 'Foto Blue'

Rosmarinus officinalis Prostratus Group

Layering

Layer established branches in summer.

Pests and Diseases

Rosemary beetle and its larvae feed on the leaves from fall until spring. Place some newspaper underneath the plant, then tap or shake the branches, which will knock the beetles and larvae on to the paper, making them easy to destroy.

Maintenance

Spring Trim after flowering. Sow seeds of *Rosmarinus officinalis*. Take softwood cuttings.
Summer Feed container plants. Take semihardwood cuttings. Layer plants.
Fall Protect young tender plants.
Winter Put a mulch, or straw, or a frost cloth around all plants.

Garden Cultivation

Rosemary requires a well-drained soil in a sheltered sunny position. It is frost hardy but in cold areas it prefers to grow against a warm, sunny wall. If the plant is young it is worth giving some added protection in winter. If trimming is necessary, cut back only when the frosts are over; if possible leave it until after the spring flowering. Sometimes rosemary looks a bit scorched after frosts, in which case it is worth cutting the damaged plants to healthy wood in spring. Straggly old plants may also be cut back hard at the same time. Never cut back plants in the fall or if there is any chance of frost, as the plant will be damaged or even killed. On average, despite the story about rosemary growing for 33 years, it is best to replace bushes every 5 to 6 years.

Harvesting

As rosemary is evergreen, you can pick fresh leaves all year round as long as you are not greedy. If you need large quantities, then harvest in summer and either dry the leaves or make an oil or vinegar.

Hedges

Rosemary certainly makes an effective hedge; it looks pretty in flower, smells marvelous and is evergreen. In fact it has everything going for it if you have the right soil conditions which, more importantly than ever, must be well drained and carry a bias toward lime. The best varieties for hedges are 'Primley Blue' and 'Miss Jessopp's Upright'. Both are upright, hardy and bushy. 'Primley Blue' has a darker blue flower and I think is slightly prettier. Planting distance 18 in. apart. Again, if you need eventually to trim the hedge, do it after the spring flowering.

 ## companion planting

If planted near carrots it is reputed to repel carrot fly. It is also said to be generally beneficial to sage.

 ## container growing

Rosemary does well in pots and this is the preferred way to grow it in cold districts. The prostrate and less hardy varieties look very attractive and benefit from the extra protection offered by a container. Use a soil-based compost mixed in equal parts with composted fine bark, and make sure the compost is well drained. Do not overwater, and feed only after flowering.

Rosmarinus officinalis 'Boule'

Rosemary infusion

other uses

Put rosemary twigs on the barbecue; they give off a delicious aroma. If you have a wood-burning stove, a few twigs thrown onto it makes the whole house smell lovely.

Rosemary is used in many herbal shampoos and the plant has a long reputation as a hair tonic. Use an infusion in the final rinse of a hair wash, especially if you have dark hair, as it will make it shine. (Use chamomile for fair hair.)

medicinal

Like many other essential oils, rosemary oil has anti-bacterial and anti-fungal properties, and it helps poor circulation if rubbed into the affected joints.

The oil may be used externally as an insect repellent. It also makes an excellent remedy for headaches if applied directly to the head.

Rosemary tea makes a good mouthwash for halitosis and is also a good antiseptic gargle. Drunk in small amounts it reduces flatulence and stimulates the smooth muscle of the digestive tract and gall bladder and increases the flow of bile. Put a teaspoon of chopped leaves into a cup and pour on boiling water; cover and leave it to stand for 5 minutes.

An antiseptic solution of rosemary can be added to the bath to promote heathy skin. Boil a handful in 2 cups of water for 10 minutes.

warning

The oil should not be used internally. Also, extremely large doses of the leaf are toxic, possibly causing abortion, convulsions and, very rarely, death.

culinary

This is one of the most useful of culinary herbs, combining well with meat, especially lamb, casseroles, tomato sauces, baked fish, rice, salads, egg dishes, apples, summer wine cups, cordials, vinegars and oils.

Vegetarian Goulash
Serves 4

2 tablespoons rosemary olive oil
2 medium onions, sliced
2 teaspoons wholemeal flour
1 tablespoon paprika
1¼ cups hot water mixed with 1 teaspoon tomato purée
1¾ cups Italian tomatoes
2 sprigs rosemary, 4 in. long
1 cup cauliflower sprigs
1 cup new carrots, washed and cut into chunks
1 cup new potatoes, washed and cut into halves
½ green pepper, deseeded and chopped
⅔ cup sour cream or Greek yogurt
Salt and freshly milled black pepper

Heat the rosemary oil in a flame-proof casserole, fry the onion until soft, then stir in three quarters of the paprika. Cook for 2 minutes. Stir in the water, tomatoes and sprigs of rosemary. Bring to the boil stirring all the time. Add all the vegetables and the seasonings. Cover and bake in the preheated oven (375°F/190°C) for 30–40 minutes. Remove from the oven, carefully take out the rosemary sprigs and stir in the sour cream or yogurt, plus the remaining paprika. Serve with fresh pasta and/or garlic bread.

Rumex
SORREL

Rumex acetosa seed

Also known as Bread and cheese, Sour leaves, Tom thumbs, Thousand fingers and Sour sauce. From the family Polygonaceae.

Sorrel is a native plant of Europe, Asia and North America. It has naturalized in many countries throughout the world on rich, damp, loamy, acid soils. The generic name, *Rumex*, comes from the Latin *rumo*, "I suck." Apparently, Roman soldiers sucked the leaves to relieve thirst, and their doctors used them as a diuretic.

The name sorrel comes from the old French word *surelle*, meaning "sour." The Tudors considered the herb to be one of the best English vegetables; Henry VIII held it in great esteem. In Lapland, sorrel juice has been used instead of rennet to curdle milk.

Rumex scutatus

For an early crop start off under protection in early spring. Sow into prepared seed or plug trays, using a standard seed compost mixed in equal parts with composted fine bark, and covering the seeds with perlite. Germination is fairly quick, 10–20 days without extra heat. When the seedlings are large enough and the soil has started to warm up, plant 12 in. apart.

Division
Sorrel is easy to divide and it is a good idea to divide broad-leaf sorrel every other year to keep the leaves succulent. Fall is the best time to do this, replanting in a prepared site.

Pests and Diseases
Wood pigeons, slugs and occasionally leaf miners attack sorrel, but should cause no problems with established plants. Remove the affected leaves, and put out traps for the slugs.

Maintenance
Spring Sow seed, under protection, in early spring and outdoors from mid-spring.
Summer Cut off flowers to maintain leaf production and prevent self-seeding. In a hot summer, water regularly to keep the leaves succulent.
Fall Divide established plants.
Winter Fully hardy.

Garden Cultivation
This perennial herb likes a rich acid soil that retains moisture in full sun to partial shade. Sow the seeds in late spring into a prepared site. When germinated, thin

varieties

Rumex acetosa
Sorrel
Also known as broad-leafed sorrel, common sorrel, garden sorrel, meadow sorrel, and confusingly (see below), French sorrel. Hardy perennial. Ht. 24–48 in., spread 12 in. The flowers are small, dull and inconspicuous; color greenish, turning reddish-brown as the fruit ripens. The mid-green leaves are lance-shaped with two basal lobes pointing backward. Zone 3.

Rumex acetosella
Sheep's Sorrel
Hardy perennial. Ht. 6–12 in., spread indefinite (can be very invasive). The flowers are small, dull and inconspicuous; color greenish, turning brown as the fruit ripens. The mid-green leaves are shaped like a

barbed spear. It grows wild on open land and in grassy places, but is rarely found on limy soil. Zone 3.

Rumex scutatus
Buckler-Leaf Sorrel
Also known as French sorrel. Hardy perennial. Ht. 6–18 in., spread 24 in. The flowers are small, dull and inconspicuous; color greenish, turning brown as the fruit ripens. The mid-green leaves are shaped like squat shields. Zone 3.
Rumex scutatus 'Silver Sheild' is a variegated form of *Rumex scutatus*.

cultivation

Propagation
Seed

seedlings out to a distance of 3 in. and finally to a distance of 12 in. apart. Can be grown under cloches to provide leaf throughout the year. The plant tends to run to seed quickly so, to keep the leaves fresh and succulent, remove flowerheads as they appear.

In really warm summers or generally warm climates, sorrel leaves tend to become bitter as the season progresses. A mulch will keep the soil cooler and, once the season cools down, the flavor will improve. Grow buckler-leaf sorrel with its smaller leaf, as it is less susceptible.

If sorrel is causing a problem in your garden simply add a few applications of lime to eradicate it.

Harvesting

Pick young leaves throughout the growing season for fresh use and for freezing. Sorrel does not dry well.

 ## container growing

The buckler variety makes a good low-growing potted plant. Use a soil-based compost mixed in equal parts with composted fine bark, and make sure the container has room for the plant to spread. It is a very useful culinary herb, so for those with a small garden or who live on a limy soil, this makes an ideal container plant. Remember to keep cutting off flowers to keep leaves tender. Water well in the growing season, and feed with liquid fertilizer, especially if you are picking a lot.

 ## medicinal

Sorrel is considered to have blood cleansing and blood improving qualities in a similar way to spinach, which improves the hemoglobin content of the blood. It also contains vitamin C. A leaf may be used in a poultice to treat certain skin complaints, including acne.

 ## other uses

Sorrel is a good dye plant; with an alum mordant it makes a yellow or green dye (see also pages 288–289). Use juice of the leaf to remove rust, mold and ink stains from linen, wicker and silver.

 ## warning

Care has to be taken that sorrel is not used in too great a quantity or too frequently. Its oxalic acid content may be damaging to health if taken in excess. Very large doses are poisonous, causing severe kidney damage.

The herb should not be used medicinally by those predisposed to rheumatism, arthritis, gout, kidney stones or gastric hyperacidity.

The leaf may cause dermatitis.

Rumex scutatus 'Silver Shield'

Sorrel and lettuce soup

 ## culinary

This is an excellent herb with which to experiment. Use sparingly in soups, omelettes, fish sauces, and with poultry and pork. It is useful for tenderizing meat. Wrap it around steaks or add pounded leaf to a marinade.

Eat leaves raw in salads, especially the buckler-leaf sorrel, but reduce the vinegar or lemon in any accompanying dressing to compensate for the increased acidity.

Cook like spinach, changing the cooking water once to reduce acidity.

A Green Sauce

Wash a handful each of sorrel and lettuce leaves and a handful of watercress. Cook in a little water with a whole peeled onion until tender. Remove onion and discard. Allow the (mushy) leaves to cool then add 1 tablespoon of olive oil, 1 tablespoon of wine vinegar, pepper and salt. Stir until creamy. Serve with fish or cold poultry.

Sorrel and Lettuce Soup

Serves 4

½ cup sorrel
½ cup lettuce
½ cup potatoes, peeled and sliced
¼ cup French parsley
¼ cup butter
2 cups chicken stock
4 tablespoons cream

Wash the sorrel, lettuce and French parsley, pat dry and roughly chop. Heat the butter in a heavy pan and add the sorrel, lettuceand parsley. Stew very gently for about 5 minutes, and then add the potato. Mix all together, pour over the heated stock, and simmer covered for 25 minutes. Put in a food processor, or, if you are a purist, through a coarse food mill. Return to the pan and heat gently (do not boil). Swirl in some cream just before serving.

Ruta graveolens
RUE

Also known as Herb of grace and Herbygrass. From the family Rutaceae.

Rue is a native of Southern Europe, especially the Mediterranean region, and is found growing in poor, free-draining soil. It has established itself in North America and Australia in similar conditions. It has also adapted to cooler climates and is now naturalized in Northern Europe. Rue was known as herb of grace, perhaps because it was regarded as a protector against the Devil, witchcraft and magic.

It was also used as an antidote against every kind of poison from toadstools to snake bites. The Romans brought it across northern Europe to Britain, where it did not gain favor until the Middle Ages, when it was one of the herbs carried in nosegays by the rich as protection from evil and the plague. Also, like rosemary, it was placed near the judge before prisoners were brought out, as protection from the pestilence-ridden jails and jail fever.

It was famous for preserving eyesight and was said to promote second sight, perhaps acting on the third eye. Both Leonardo da Vinci and Michelangelo are supposed to have said that their inner vision had been enhanced by this herb.

Ruta graveolens

 varieties

Ruta graveolens
Rue
Hardy evergreen perennial. Ht. and spread 24 in. Yellow waxy flowers with four or five petals in summer. Small rounded lobed leaves of a greeny blue color. Zone 5.

Ruta graveolens 'Jackman's Blue'
Rue Jackman's Blue
Hardy evergreen perennial. Ht. and spread 24 in. Yellow waxy flowers with four or five petals in summer. Small rounded lobed leaves of a distinctive blue color. Zone 5.

Ruta graveolens 'Variegata'
Variegated Rue
Hardy evergreen perennial. Ht. and spread 24 in. Yellow waxy flowers with four or five petals in summer. Small rounded lobed leaves with a most distinctive cream/white variegation, which is partic-ularly marked in spring, fading in the summer unless the plant is kept well clipped. I have known people mistake the variegation for flowers and try to smell them, which shows how attractive this plant is. Smelling it at close quarters is not, however, a good idea as this plant, like other rues, can cause the skin to blister. Zone 5.

Ruta graveolens 'Jackman's Blue'

 cultivation

Propagation

Seed

In spring sow the fine seed using the cardboard trick (see page 265) in prepared plug or seed trays. Use a standard seed compost mixed in equal parts with composted fine bark, and cover with perlite. You may find that a bottom heat of 68°F (20°C) is helpful. Germination can be an all or nothing affair, depending on the source of the seed. Young seedlings are prone to damping off, so watch the watering, and just keep the compost damp, not wet.

Unlike many variegated plants, the variegated rue will be variegated from seed. When the seedlings are large enough, plant into a prepared site in the garden at a distance of 18 in.

Cuttings

Take cuttings of new shoots in spring or early summer. 'Jackman's Blue' can only be propagated from cuttings. Use a standard seed compost mixed in equal parts with composted fine bark for the cuttings; again, do not overwater.

Pests and Diseases

Rue is prone to whitefly followed by black sooty mold. Treat the whitefly with a liquid insecticidal soap as soon as the pest appears, following manufacturer's instructions. This should then also control the sooty mould.

Ruta graveolens 'Variegata'

Maintenance

Spring Cut back plants to regain shape. Sow seed. Take softwood cuttings.

Summer Cut back after flowering to maintain shape.

Fall The variegated rue is slightly more tender than the other two varieties, so protect when frosts go below 23°F (−5°C).

Winter Rue is hardy and requires protection only in extreme conditions.

Garden Cultivation

All the rues prefer a sunny site with a well-drained poor soil. They are best positioned away from paths or at the back of beds where people won't brush against them accidentally, especially children, whose skin is more sensitive than adults. In the spring, and after flowering in the summer (not fall), cut back all the plants to maintain shape, and the variegated form to maintain variegations. Foliage provides food for the Black Swallowtail Butterfly.

Harvesting

Pick leaves for use fresh. No need to preserve.

 container growing

Rue can be grown in containers; use a soil-based compost mixed in equal parts with composted fine bark. Position the container carefully so as not to accidentally brush the leaves. Although it is drought tolerant, in containers it prefers to be watered regularly in summer. Allow to dry in winter, watering only once a month. Feed plants in the spring with liquid fertilizer following the manufacturer's instructions.

 warning

Handling the plant can cause allergic reactions or phytol-photodermatitis. If you have ever seen a rue burn, it really is quite serious, so do heed this warning.

To minimize this risk do not take cuttings off the plants either when they are wet after rain or when in full sun, as this is when the plant is at its most dangerous. Wait until the plant has dried out or the sun has gone in; alternatively wear gloves.

Must only be used by medical personnel and not at all by pregnant women, as it is abortive. Large doses are toxic, sometimes precipitating mental confusion, and the oil is capable of causing death.

 culinary

I seriously cannot believe that people enjoy eating this herb; it tastes incredibly bitter. It can be added finely chopped with discretion to egg, fish or cheese dishes.

 medicinal

This ancient medicinal herb is used in the treatment of strained eyes, and headaches caused by eye strain. It is also useful for nervous headaches and heart palpitations, for treating high blood pressure and helping to harden the bones and teeth. The anti-spasmodic action of its oil and the alkaloids explains its use in the treatment of nervous digestion and colic. The tea also expels worms.

Salvia
SAGE

From the family Lamiaceae.

"How can a man grow old who has sage in his garden?" Ancient Proverb

This large family of over 750 species is widely distributed throughout the world. It consists of annuals, biennials and perennials, herbs, sub-shrubs and shrubs of various habits. It is an important horticultural group. I have concentrated on the medicinal, culinary and a special aromatic species.

The name *Salvia* is derived from the Latin *salveo*, meaning "I save" or "I heal," because some species have been highly regarded medicinally.

Salvia lavandulifolia

The Greeks used it to heal ulcers, consumption and snake bites. The Romans considered it a sacred herb to be gathered with ceremony. A special knife was used, not made of iron because sage reacts with iron salts. The sage gatherer had to wear clean clothes, have clean feet and make a sacrifice of food before the ceremony could begin. Sage was held to be good for the brain, the senses and memory. It also made a good gargle and mouthwash and was used as a toothpaste.

There are many stories about why the Chinese valued it so highly, and in the 17th century Dutch merchants found that the Chinese would trade three chests of China tea for one of sage leaves.

 varieties

I have only chosen a very few species to illustrate; they are the main ones used in cooking and medicine—with two exceptions, with which I begin.

Salvia argentea
Silver Sage
Hardy biennial. Ht. up to 4 ft. in second season. Pale pinkish-white flowers in second season. Splendid large silvery gray leaves covered in long silvery white hairs. Protect from excessive rainwater. Zone 4.

Salvia elegans 'Scarlet Pineapple' (S. rutilans)
Pineapple Sage
Half-hardy perennial. Ht. 36 in., spread 24 in. Striking red flowers, mid- to late summer. The leaves are green with a slight red tinge to the edges and have a glorious pineapple scent. This sage is subtropical and must be protected from frost. In temperate climates it is basically a house plant and if kept on a sunny windowsill can be used throughout the year. It can only be grown from cuttings. This is an odd sage to cook with; it does not taste as good as it smells. It is fairly good with apricots as a stuffing for pork, otherwise my culinary experiments with it have not met with great success. Zone 8.

Salvia lavandulifolia
Narrowed-Leaved Sage
Also known as Spanish Sage. Hardy evergreen perennial. Ht. and spread 18 in. Attractive blue flowers in summer. The leaves are green and textured, small, thin, and oval in shape and highly aromatic. This is an excellent sage to cook with, very pungent. It also makes a good tea. Can only be grown from cuttings. Zone 5.

Salvia officinalis
Sage
Also known as common sage, garden sage, broad-leaved sage, and sawge. Hardy evergreen perennial. Ht. and spread 24 in. Mauve/blue flowers in summer. The leaves are green and textured, thin and oval in shape and highly aromatic. This is the best-known sage for culinary use. Can be easily grown from seed. There is also a white flowering sage *Salvia officinalis* 'Albiflora,' which is quite rare. Zone 5.

Salvia officinalis broad-leaved

Salvia officinalis 'Purpurascens'

Salvia officinalis broad-leaved

Broad-Leaved Sage

Hardy evergreen perennial. Ht. and spread 24 in. Very rarely flowers in cool climates; if it does, flowers are blue/mauve in color. The leaves are green and textured, larger than the ordinary sage, with an oval shape and highly aromatic. Good for cooking. Can only be grown from cuttings. Zone 6.

Salvia officinalis 'Purpurascens'

Purple/Red Sage

Hardy evergreen perennial. Ht. and spread 28 in. Mauve/blue flowers in summer. The leaves are purple and textured, a thin oval shape and aromatic. If you clip it in the spring, it develops new leaves and looks really good but flowers only a small amount. If you do not clip it and allow it to flower it goes woody. If you then cut it back it does not produce new growth until the spring, so can look a bit bare. So what to do? There is also a variegated form of this purple sage *Salvia officinalis* 'Purpurascens Variegata.' Both of these can only be grown from cuttings. Zone 8.

Salvia officinalis 'Tricolor'

Tricolor Sage

Half-hardy evergreen perennial. Ht. and spread 16 in. Attractive blue flowers in summer. The leaves are green with pink, white and purple variegation, with a texture. They are small, thin, and oval in shape and highly aromatic. It has a mild flavor, so can be used in cooking. Can only be grown from cuttings. Zone 8.

Salvia viridis var. comata

Painted Sage, Red-topped Sage

Hardy annual. Ht. 18 in. Striking red, blue, purple-pink bracts and tiny bi-colored flowers in summer. Green, oval rough-textured leaves. Zone 4.

Salvia officinalis 'Tricolor'

🌸 cultivation

Propagation

Seed

Common and painted sage can be grown successfully in the spring from seed sown into prepared seed or plug trays, using a standard seed compost mixed in equal parts with composted fine bark and covered with perlite. The seeds are a good size. If starting off under protection in early spring, warmth is of benefit—temperatures of 60–70°F (15–21°C). Germination takes 2–3 weeks. Pot or plant when the frosts are over at a distance of 18–24 in. apart.

Cuttings

This is a good method for all variegated species and

Salvia viridis var. *comata*

the ones that do not set seed in cooler climates. Use a standard seed compost mixed in equal parts with composted fine bark. Take softwood cuttings in late spring or early summer from the strong new growth. All forms take easily from cuttings; rooting is about 4 weeks in summer.

Layering

If you have a well-established sage, or if it is becoming woody, layer established branches in spring or fall.

Pests and Diseases

Sage grown in the garden does not suffer over much from pests and disease. Sage grown in containers, especially pineapple sage, is prone to red spider mite and leaf hopper. When you see these pests, treat with a liquid insecticidal soap as per the instructions.

Maintenance

Spring Sow seeds. Trim if needed, and then take softwood cuttings.

Summer Trim back after flowering.

Fall Protect all half-hardy sages, and first-year plants.

Winter Protect plants if they are needed for fresh leaves.

Salvia viridis var. *comata*

Salvia argentea

Garden Cultivation

Sage, although predominately a Mediterranean plant, is sufficiently hardy to withstand any ordinary winter without protection, as long as the soil is well drained and not acid, and the site is as warm and dry as possible. The flavor of the leaf can vary according to how rich, damp, etc., the soil is. If wishing to sow seed outside, wait until there is no threat of frost and sow direct into prepared ground, spacing the seeds 9 in. apart. After germination thin to 18 in. apart. For the first winter, cover the young plants with a frost cloth or a mulch.

To keep the plants bushy, prune in the spring to encourage young shoots for strong flavor, and also after flowering in late summer. Mature plants can be pruned hard in the spring after some cuttings have been taken as insurance. Never prune in the fall as this can kill the plant. As sage is prone to becoming woody, replace the plant every 4–5 years.

Harvesting

Since sage is an evergreen plant, the leaves can be used fresh any time of the year. In Mediterranean-type climates, including the southern United States, the leaves can be harvested during the winter months. In cold climates this is also possible if you cover a chosen bush with a frost cloth as this will keep the leaves in better condition. They dry well, but care should be taken to keep their green color. Because this herb is frequently seen in its dried condition people assume it is easy to dry. But beware, although other herbs may lose some of their aroma or qualities if badly dried or handled, sage seems to pick up a musty scent and a flavor really horrible to taste—better to grow it in your garden to use fresh.

 ## companion planting

Sage planted with cabbages is said to repel cabbage white butterflies. Planted next to vines it is reputed to be beneficial.

 ## container growing

All sages grow happily in containers. Pineapple sage is an obvious one as it is tender, but a better reason is that if it is at hand one will rub the leaves and smell that marvelous pineapple scent. Use a soil-based compost mixed in equal parts with composted fine bark for all varieties, feed after flowering, and do not overwater.

 ## other uses

The dried leaves, especially those of pineapple sage, are good added to potpourri.

Sage tea

 ## medicinal

For centuries, sage has been esteemed for its healing powers. It is a first-rate remedy as a hot infusion for colds. Sage tea combined with a little cider vinegar makes a gargle that is excellent for sore throats, laryngitis and tonsillitis. It is also beneficial for infected gums and mouth ulcers.

The essential oil is obtained by steamed distillation of the fresh or partially dried flower stems and leaves. It is used in herbal medicine but more widely in toilet waters, perfumes and soap, and to flavor wine, vermouth and liqueurs.

 ## warning

Extended or excessive use of sage can cause symptoms of poisoning. Although the herb seems safe and common, if you drink the tea for more than a week or two at a time, its strong antiseptic properties can cause potentially toxic effects.

Salvia officinalis 'Purpurascens'

culinary

This powerful healing plant is also a strong culinary herb, although it has been misused and misjudged in the culinary world. Used with discretion it adds a lovely flavor, aids digestion of fatty food, and being an antiseptic it kills off any bugs in the meat as it cooks. It has long been used with sausages because of its preservative qualities. It also makes a delicious herb jelly, or oil or vinegar. But I like using small amounts fresh. The original form of the following recipe comes from a vegetarian friend of mine. I fell in love with it and have subsequently adapted it to include some other herbs.

Hazelnut and Mushroom Roast
Serves 4

A little sage oil
²/₃ cup long grain brown rice
1¹/₄ cups boiling water
1 teaspoon salt
1 large onion, peeled and chopped
¹/₂ cup mushrooms, wiped and chopped
2 medium carrots, pared and roughly grated
¹/₂ teaspoon coriander seed
1 tablespoon soy sauce
¹/₂ cup wholewheat breadcrumbs
³/₄ cup ground hazelnuts
1 teaspoon chopped sage leaves
1 teaspoon chopped lovage leaves
Sunflower seeds for decoration
A 2 lb. loaf pan, lined with greaseproof paper

Preheat the oven (180°C/350°F).

Heat 2 teaspoons of sage oil in a small saucepan, toss the rice in it to give it a coating of oil, add boiling water straight from the kettle and the teaspoon of salt. Stir, and let the rice cook slowly for roughly 40 minutes or until the liquid is absorbed.

While the rice is cooking, heat 1 tablespoon of sage oil in a medium sized frying-pan, add the onions, mushrooms, carrots, the ground coriander seed and soy sauce. Mix them together and let them cook for about 10 minutes.

Combine the cooked brown rice, breadcrumbs, hazelnuts, sage and lovage; mix with the vegetables and place the complete mixture in the prepared loaf pan. Scatter the sunflower seeds on top and bake in the oven for 45 minutes. Leave to cool slightly in the pan. Slice and serve with a home-made tomato sauce and a green salad.

Sambucus
ELDER

Also known as Boun-tree, Boon-tree, Dogtree, Judas tree, Scores, Score tree, God's stinking tree, Black elder, Blackberried, European elder, Ellhorne and German elder. From the family Caprifoliaceae.

Elder grows worldwide throughout temperate climates. Its common name is probably derived from the Anglo-Saxon *Ellaern* or *Aeld*, which means "fire" or "kindle," because the hollow stems were once used for getting fires going. The generic name, *Sambucus*, dates from ancient Greek times and may originally have referred to *sambuke*, a kind of harp made of elderwood. Pipes were made from its branches too, possibly the original Pan pipes. People thought that if you put it on the fire you would see the Devil. They believed it unlucky to make cradle rockers out of it, that the spirit of the tree might harm the child. Again, farmers were unwilling to use an elder switch to drive cattle and one folktale had it that elder would only grow where blood had been shed. Planting it outside the back door was a sure way of protecting against evil and black magic, and for keeping witches out of the house, which would never be struck by lightning. It was thought that Christ's cross was made of elderwood.

Sambucus nigra

Black berries in early fall. Its green leaves are oblong, lance-shaped, and toothed around the edges. Dwarf elder grows in small clusters in Europe and in the Eastern and Central United States. Zone 5.

Warning: All parts of *S. ebulus* are slightly poisonous and children should be warned not to eat the bitter berries. It has a much stronger action than its close relative, common *S. nigra*. Large doses cause vertigo, vomiting and diarrhea, the latter, denoted colloquially as 'the Danes,' being the origin of Danewort. Nowadays *S. ebulus* is rarely used and should be taken internally only under strict medical supervision.

Sambucus nigra
Common Elder
Also known as European elder, black elder, bore tree. Deciduous hardy perennial. Ht. 20–23 ft., spread 15 ft. Spreading branches bear flat heads of small, star-shaped, creamy-white flowers in late spring and early summer, followed in early fall by drooping purplish-black juicy berries. The leaves of *Sambucus nigra* are purgative and should not be taken internally; decoctions have an insecticidal effect. Zone 5.

Sambucus nigra 'Aurea'
Golden Elder
Deciduous shrub. Ht. and spread 20 ft. Flattened heads of fragrant, star-shaped, creamy-white flowers from early to mid-summer. Black fruits in early fall. Golden yellow, oval, sharply toothed leaves usually in groups of five. Zone 5.

☠ *Sambucus racemosa*
Red Elder
Deciduous hardy perennial. Ht. and spread 10–13 ft. Brown bark and pale brown pith. Flowers arranged in dense terminal panicles of yellowish cream. *Racemosa* refers to the flower clusters. The fruits are also distinct in being red in drooping clusters. It rarely fruits freely.

Red berried elder is native to central and southern Europe. It has naturalized in Scotland, the northern United States and Canada. The fully ripe fruits are used medicinally. Bitter tasting, they may be used fresh or dried, and are high in vitamin C, essential oil, sugar and pectins. Fruits are a laxative and the leaves are a diuretic. This is the most edible and tasty of the elders. Zone 3.

Warning: The seeds inside the berries of *S. racemosa* are poisonous before being cooked.

 varieties

☠ *Sambucus canadensis*
American Elder
Also known as black elder, common elder, Rob elder, sweet elder. Deciduous hardy perennial. Ht. 5–12 ft. Numerous small white flowers in flat cymes throughout summer. Berries are dark purple in early fall; its leaves long, sharply toothed and bright green. Zone 3.

Warning: All parts of the fresh *S. canadensis* can poison. Children have even been poisoned by chewing or sucking the bark. Once cooked, however, flowers and berries are safe. Some Native American tribes use a tea made from the root-bark for headaches, mucous congestion, and to promote labor in childbirth.

☠ *Sambucus canadensis* 'Aurea'
Deciduous hardy perennial. Ht. and spread 12 ft. Creamy white flowers in summer, red fruits in early fall. Large golden yellow leaves. Zone 3.

☠ *Sambucus ebulus*
Dwarf Elder
Also known as blood Elder, danewort, wild elder, walewort. Deciduous hardy perennial. Ht. 2–4 ft., spread 3 ft. White flowers with pink tips in summer.

Elderflower sorbet

 cultivation

Propagation

Seed
Sow ripe berries ¾ in. deep in a pot outdoors using a soil-based seed compost. Plant seedlings in semi-shade in the garden when large enough to handle.

Cuttings
Take semihardwood cuttings in summer from the new growth. Use a seed compost mixed in equal parts with composted fine bark, and winter these cuttings in a cold frame or cold greenhouse. When rooted, either pot or plant into a prepared site 12 in. apart.
Take hardwood cuttings of bare shoots in the fall and replant in the garden 12 in. apart. The following fall lift and replant.

Pests and Diseases
Rarely suffers from pests or diseases apart from black-fly, which can be treated with insecticidal soap.

Maintenance
Spring Prune back golden and variegated elders.
Summer Take semiripe cuttings.
Fall Take hardwood cuttings. Prune back hard.
Winter Established plants do not need protection.

Garden Cultivation
Elder tolerates most soils and *S. nigra* is very good for limy/alkaline sites. They all prefer a sunny position.
Elder grows very rapidly indeed and self-sows freely to produce new shoots 4 ft. long in one season. It is short-lived. It is important to dominate elder otherwise it will dominate your garden. Cut back in late fall,

unless it is gold or variegated, when it should be pruned in early spring before growth begins.

Harvesting
Handle flower heads carefully to prevent bruising, spread out to dry with heads down on a fine net without touching one another. Pick the fruits in the fall, as they ripen, when they become shiny and violet.

 container growing

Golden varieties of elder can look good in containers, as long as the containers are large enough and positioned to give the plants some shade, to stop the leaves scorching. Use a soil-based compost. Keep well-watered, feed with a liquid fertilizer.

 other uses

Elderflower water whitens and softens the skin, removes freckles. The fruits make a lavender or violet dye when combined with alum.
The flowers and berries of *Sambucus nigra* are used in industry for cosmetics. The wood from the adult plant is highly prized by craftsmen.

 medicinal

Elderflowers reduce bronchial and upper respiratory congestion and are used in the treatment of hay fever. Externally a cold infusion of the flowers may be used as an eye wash for conjunctivitis and as a compress for chilblains. A gargle made from elderflower infusion or

 culinary

Only common elder is used for culinary purposes, and its berries should not be eaten raw, nor fresh juice used. Be sure to cook very slightly first.

Elderflower Cordial
Pick flowers on a dry sunny day, as the yeast is mainly in the pollen.

14 cups of water
3 cups sugar
Juice and thinly peeled rind of 1 lemon
2 tablespoons of cider or wine vinegar
12 elderflower heads

Bring the water to the boil and pour into a sterilized container. Add the sugar, stirring until dissolved. When cool add the lemon juice and the rind, vinegar and elderflowers. Cover with several layers of muslin and leave for 24 hours. Filter through muslin into strong glass bottles. This drink is ready after 2 weeks. Serve chilled.

elderflower vinegar alleviates tonsillitis and sore throats. Elderflowers have a mild laxative action and in Europe have a reputation for treating rheumatism and gout. The berries are a mild laxative and sweat inducing. 'Elderberry Rob' is traditionally made by simmering the berries and thickening with sugar as a winter cordial for coughs and colds.

Elderberry Conserve (for neuralgia and migraine)

2¼ cups elderberries
2¼ cups sugar

Boil the elderberries with the least quantity of water to produce a pulp. Pass through a sieve and simmer the juice gently to remove most of the water. Add the sugar and stir constantly until the consistency of a conserve is produced. Pour into a suitable container. Take two tablespoons as required.

 warning

Use parts of plants from this genus with care; many are poisonous. See warnings under relevant species.

Sambucus nigra

Sanguisorba minor

SALAD BURNET

Also known as Drumsticks, Old man's pepper and Poor man's pepper. From the family Rosaceae.

This herb is a native of Europe and Asia. It has been introduced and naturalized in many places elsewhere in the world, especially Britain and the United States. Popular for both its medicinal and culinary properties, it was taken to New England in the Pilgrim Fathers' plant collection and called pimpernel. It is found in dry, free-draining soil in grassland and on the edges of woodland. The name *Sanguisorba* comes from *sanguis*, meaning "blood," and *sorbere*, meaning "to soak up." It is an ancient herb, which has been grown in Britain since the 16th century. Traditionally it was used to staunch wounds. In Tudor times salad burnet was planted along borders of garden paths so the scent would rise up when trodden on.

Sanguisorba minor flower heads

 cultivation

Propagation

Seed
Sow the small flattish seed in spring or fall into prepared seed or plug trays and cover the seeds with perlite; no need for extra heat. If sown in the fall, winter the seedlings under protection and plant in spring in a prepared site, 12 in. apart. If spring sown, allow to harden off and plant in the same way. When used as an edging plant it needs to be planted at 8 in. intervals.

Division
It divides very easily. Dig up an established plant in the early fall, cut back any excessive leaves, divide the plant and replant in a prepared site in the garden.

Pests and Diseases
This herb is, in the main, free from pests and diseases.

Maintenance
Spring Sow seeds.
Summer Keep cutting to stop it flowering, if being used for culinary purposes.
Fall Sow seeds if necessary. Divide well-established plants.
Winter No protection needed, fully hardy.

 varieties

Sanguisorba minor
Salad Burnet
Evergreen hardy perennial. Ht. 8–24 in., spread 12 in. Produces small spikes of dark crimson flowers in summer. Its soft mid-green leaves are divided into oval leaflets. Zone 4.

Sanguisorba officinalis
Great Burnet
Also known as drumsticks, maidens hairs, red knobs, and redheads. Perennial. Ht. up to 4 ft., spread 2 ft. Produces small spikes of dark crimson flowers in summer. Its mid-green leaves are divided into oval leaflets. This wild plant is becoming increasingly rare due to modern farming practices. Zone 4.

Garden Cultivation

This is a most attractive, soft-leaf evergreen and is very useful in both kitchen and garden. That it is evergreen is a particular plus for the herb garden, where it looks most effective as an edging plant. It also looks good in a wildflower garden, where it grows as happily as in its original grassland habitat.

With no special requirements, it prefers limy/alkaline soil, but it will tolerate any well-drained soil in sun or light shade. It is deep rooting and very drought resistant.

The art with this plant is to keep cutting, which stops it flowering and encourages lots of new growth.

Harvesting

Pick young tender leaves when required. Not necessary to dry leaves (which in any case do not dry well), as fresh leaves can be harvested all year round.

 ## container growing

Salad burnet will grow in containers, and will provide an excellent source of soft evergreen leaves throughout winter for those with no garden. Use a soil-based compost. Water regularly, but not too frequently; feed with liquid fertilizer in the spring only. Do not overfeed, otherwise the leaf will soften and lose its cool cucumber flavor, becoming more like a spinach. For regular use, the plant should not be allowed to flower. Cut back constantly to about 6 in. to ensure a continuing supply of tender new leaves.

 ## medicinal

Chewing the leaf assists digestion. An infusion of the whole plant is used for treating hemorrhoids and diarrhea.

Infusion of salad burnet

 ## culinary

The leaves of salad burnet have a nutty flavor and a slight taste of cucumber. The young leaves are refreshing in salads and can be used generously—they certainly enhance winter salads. Tender young leaves can also be added to soups, cold drinks, cream cheeses, or used (like parsley) as a garnish or to flavor casseroles—add at the beginning of cooking. The leaves also make an interesting herbal vinegar.

Salad burnet combines with other herbs, especially rosemary and tarragon. Serve in a sauce with white fish.

Salad Burnet Herb Butter

This butter is lovely with grilled fish, either cooked under the grill or on the barbecue, and adds a cucumber flavor.

1/3 cup butter
1 1/2 tablespoons chopped salad burnet
1 tablespoon chopped garden mint (spearmint)
Salt and black pepper
Lemon juice

Mix the chopped herb leaves together. Melt the butter in a saucepan, add the herbs and simmer on a very low heat for 10 minutes. Season the sauce to taste with salt and pepper, and a squeeze (no more) of lemon. Pour over grilled fish (plaice or sole).

 ## other uses

Because of its high tannin content, the root of great burnet can be used in the tanning of leather.

 ## warning

Great burnet should never be taken in large doses.

Santolina
COTTON LAVENDER

Also known as Santolina and French lavender. From the family Asteraceae.

Cotton lavender is a native of Southern France and the Northern Mediterranean area, where it grows wild on calcareous ground. It is widely cultivated, adapting to the full spectrum of European and Australian climates and to warm-to-hot regions of North America, surviving even an Eastern Canadian winter on well-drained soil.

The Greeks knew cotton lavender as *abrotonon* and the Romans as *habrotanum,* both names referring to the tree-like shape of the flying branches. It was used medicinally for many centuries by the Arabs. It was valued in medieval England as an insect and moth repellent and vermifuge.

The plant was probably brought into Britain in the 16th century by French Huguenot gardeners, who were skilled in creating the knot garden so popular among the Elizabethans. Cotton lavender was used largely in low clipped hedges, and as edging for the geometrical beds.

Santolina chamaecyparissus 'Small-Ness'

 varieties

Despite its common name, this is not a member of the *Lavandula* family, but is a member of the daisy family.

Santolina chamaecyparissus
Cotton Lavender
Hardy evergreen shrub. Ht. 2½ ft., spread 3 ft. Yellow button flowers from midsummer to early fall, silver coral-like aromatic foliage. Zone 7.

Santolina chamaecyparissus 'Lemon Queen'
Cotton Lavender Lemon Queen
As 'Edward Bowles,' but feathery, deep-cut gray foliage. Zone 7.

Santolina chamaecyparissus 'Small-Ness'
Hardy evergreen shrub. Ht. and spread 18 in. Aromatic, deeply cut blue/green foliage. Very neat, tight habit.

Santolina pinnata subsp. neapolitana 'Edward Bowles'
Cotton Lavender Edward Bowles
Hardy evergreen shrub. Ht. 2½ ft., spread 3 ft. Cream button flowers in summer. Feathery, deep-cut, gray/green foliage. Zone 7.

Santolina rosmarinifolia subsp. rosmarinifolia 'Primrose Gem'
Cotton Lavender Primrose Gem
Hardy evergreen shrub. Ht. 24 in., spread 3 ft. Pale yellow button flowers in summer. Finely cut green leaves. Zone 6.

Santolina rosmarinifolia subsp. rosmarinifolia
Cotton Lavender, Holy Flax, Virens
As 'Primrose Gem.' Bright yellow button flowers in summer. Finely cut, bright green leaves. Zone 6.

Santolina rosmarinifolia subsp. *rosmarinifolia* 'Primrose Gem'

COTTON LAVENDER

cultivation

Propagation

Seed
Seed is not worth the effort as germination is poor.

Cuttings
Take 2–3 in. soft stem cuttings in spring before flowering, or take semiripe stem cuttings from mid-summer to fall. Use a standard seed compost mixed in equal parts with composted fine bark. They root easily without the use of any rooting compound.

Pests and Diseases
Compost or soil that is too rich will attract aphids.

Maintenance
Spring Cut straggly old plants hard back. Take cuttings from new growth.
Summer I cannot stress enough that after flowering the plants should be cut back or the bushes will open up and lose their attractive shape.
Fall Take semiripe cuttings, protect them from frost in a cold frame or greenhouse.
Winter Protect in only the severest of winters.

Santolina pinnata subsp. *neapolitana*

Garden Cultivation
This elegant aromatic evergreen is ideal for the herb garden as a hedging or specimen plant in its own right. Plant in full sun, preferably in sandy soil. If the soil is too rich the growth will become soft and start to lose color. This is particularly noticeable with the silver varieties.

Planting distance for an individual plant 18–24 in., for hedging 12–15 in. Hedges need regular clipping to shape in spring and summer. Do not cut back in the fall in frosty climates, as this can easily kill the plants. If temperatures drop below 5°F (−15°C) protect with a frost cloth or a layer of straw, spruce or bracken.

Harvesting
Pick leaves and dry any time before flowering. Pick small bunches of flower stems for drying in late summer. They can be dried easily by hanging the bunches upside down in a dry, airy place.

container growing

Cotton lavender cannot be grown indoors; however as a patio plant, a single plant clipped to shape in a large terracotta pot can look very striking. Use a soil-based compost mixed in equal parts with composted fine bark. Place pot in full sun. Do not overfeed with liquid fertilizer or growth will be too soft.

culinary

Cotton lavender (*S. chamaecyparissus*) makes an interesting addition to shortbread biscuits instead of rosemary. Interesting being the operative word.

medicinal

Although not used much nowadays, it can be applied to surface wounds, hastening the healing process by encouraging scar formation. Finely ground leaves ease the pain of insect stings and bites.

other uses

Lay in drawers, under carpets and in closets to deter moths and other insects, or make a herbal moth bag.

Herbal moth bag, using cotton lavender

Santolina pinnata subsp. *neapolitana* 'Edward Bowles'

Herbal Moth Bag

A handful of wormwood
A handful of spearmint
A handful of cotton lavender
A handful of rosemary
1 tablespoon of crushed coriander

Dry and crumble the ingredients, mix together and put in a muslin or cotton bag.

Saponaria officinalis

SOAPWORT

Also known as Bouncing Bet, Bruisewort, Farewell summer, Fuller's herb, Joe run by the street, Hedge pink, Dog's clove, Old maid's pink and Soaproot. From the family Caryophyllaceae.

Soapwort, widespread on poor soils in Europe, Asia and North America, was used by medieval Arab physicians for various skin complaints. Fullers used soapwort for soaping cloth before it went on the stamps at the mill, and sheep were washed with a mixture of the leaves, roots and water before being shorn.

 varieties

Saponaria officinalis
Soapwort
Hardy perennial. Ht. 12–36 in., spread 24 in. or more. Compact cluster of small pretty pink or white flowers in summer to early fall. The leaf is smooth, oval, pointed and mid-green in color. Zone 3.

Saponaria officinalis 'Rubra Plena'
Double-Flowered Soapwort
Hardy perennial. Ht. 36 in., spread 12 in. Clusters of red, ragged, double flowers in summer. The leaves are mid-green and oval in shape. Zone 3.

Saponaria ocymoides
Tumbling Ted
Hardy perennial. Ht. 1–3 in., spread 16 in. or more. Profusion of tiny, flat, pale pink/crimson flowers in summer. Sprawling mats of hairy oval leaves. Zone 4.

 cultivation

Propagation
Seed
Only soapwort and tumbling Ted can be grown from seed. Sow in the fall into prepared seed or plug trays and cover with compost. Place glass over container and leave out over winter. Usually germinates in spring, but can be erratic. When large enough, plant 24 in. apart.

Cuttings
Softwood cuttings of the nonflowering shoots can be taken from late spring to early summer.

Division
The creeping rootstock is easy to divide in the fall.

Garden Cultivation
Plant it in a sunny spot in a well-drained poor soil; in rich soil it can become very invasive. Do not plant near ponds because the creeping rhizomes excrete a poison.

Pests and Diseases
Soapwort is largely free from pests and disease.

Maintenance
Spring Take cuttings.
Summer Cut back after flowering to encourage a second flowering and to prevent self-seeding.
Fall Divide established plants. Sow seed.
Winter Fully hardy.

Harvesting
Pick the leaves when required. Dig up the roots in the fall and dry for medicinal use.

 container growing

S. ocymoides is the best variety for container growing. Use a soil-based compost. Water well during the growing season, but only feed twice. In winter keep in a cold greenhouse with minimum watering.

 medicinal

It has been used not only for treating skin conditions such as eczema, cold sores, boils, and acne, but also for gout and rheumatism. It is probably effective due to the anti-inflammatory properties of its saponins.

 warning

This herb should only be prescribed by a qualified herbalist because of the high saponin content, which makes it mildly poisonous.

 other uses

The gentle power of the saponins in soapwort makes the following shampoo ideal for upholstery and delicate fibers.

Soapwort Shampoo

1 tablespoon dried soapwort root or two large handfuls of whole fresh stems
3 cups water

Crush the root with a rolling pin or roughly chop the fresh stems. If using dried soapwort, prepare by soaking first overnight. Put the soapwort into an enamel pan with water and bring to the boil, cover and simmer for 20 minutes, stirring occasionally. Allow to stand until cool and strain through a fine sieve.

Soapwort shampoo

Scutellaria
SKULLCAP

Also known as Helmet flower, Mad dog weed, Blue skullcap and Blue pimpernel. From the family Lamiaceae.

The various varieties of skullcap are natives of different countries. They are found in the United States, Britain, India, and one grows in the rain forests of the Amazon.

The name *Scutellaria* is derived from *scutella,* meaning "a small shield," which is exactly how the seed looks.

Scutellaria lateriflora

The Native North American Indians used *Scutellaria lateriflora* as a treatment for rabies. In Europe it was used for epilepsy.

 ## varieties

Scutellaria galericulata
Skullcap
Hardy perennial. Ht. 6–20 in., spread 12 in. and more. Small purple/blue flowers with a longer spreading lower lip in summer. Leaves bright green and lance-shaped with shallow round teeth. This plant is a native of Europe. Zone 5.

Scutellaria minor
Lesser Skullcap
As *S. galericulata* except Ht. 8–12 in., spread 12 in. and more. Small purple/pink flowers. Leaves lance-shaped with four rounded teeth. Found on wet land. Zone 5.

Scutellaria lateriflora
Virginian Skullcap
As *S. galericulata* except Ht. 12–24inch, spread 12inch and more. Leaves oval and lance-shaped with shallow, round teeth. Native of America. Zone 5.

 ## cultivation

Propagation
Seed
Sow the small seeds in the fall into prepared seed or plug trays and cover the seeds with compost. Leave the tray outside under glass. If germination is rapid, winter the young seedlings in a cold greenhouse. If there is no germination within 10–20 days leave well alone. The seed may need a period of stratification. In the spring, when the plants are large enough, plant out into a prepared site in the garden 12 in. apart.

Scutellaria galericulata

Root Cuttings
Take cuttings from the rhizomous root. In spring, dig up an established clump carefully, for any little bits of root left behind will form another plant. Ensure each cutting has a growing node; place in a seed tray and cover with compost. Put into a cold greenhouse to root.

Division
Established plants can be divided in the spring.

Pests and Diseases
Skullcap is normally free from pests and disease.

Maintenance
Spring Divide established plants. Take root cuttings.
Summer Cut back to restrain.
Fall Sow seeds.
Winter No need for protection, fully hardy.

Garden Cultivation
Tolerates most soils but prefers a well-drained, moisture-retentive soil in sun or semishade. Make sure this plant gets adequate water.

Harvesting
Dry flowers and leaves for medicinal use only.

 ## container growing

It can be grown in containers but ensure its large root system has room to spread. Use a soil-based compost. Feed only rarely with liquid fertilizer or it will produce too lush a growth and inhibit flowering. Leave outside in winter in a sheltered spot, allowing the plant to die back.

 ## medicinal

S. lateriflora is the best medicinal species; the two European species are a little less strong. It is used in the treatment of anxiety, nervousness, depression, insomnia and headaches. The whole plant is effective as a soothing antispasmodic tonic and a remedy for hysteria. Its bitter taste also strengthens and stimulates the digestion.

⚠ warning

Should only be dispensed by a trained herbalist.

Satureja
SAVORY

From the family Lamiaceae.

Savory is a native of southern Europe and North Africa, especially around the Mediterranean. It grows in well-drained soils and has adapted worldwide to similar climatic conditions. Savory has been employed in food flavoring for over 2,000 years. Romans added it to sauces and vinegars, which they used liberally as flavoring. The Ancient Egyptians on the other hand used it in love potions. The Romans also included it in their wagon train to northern Europe, where it became an invaluable disinfectant strewing herb. It was used to relieve tired eyes, for ringing in the ears, indigestion, wasp and bee stings, and for other shocks to the system.

Satureja spicigera

varieties

Satureja hortensis
Summer Savory
Also known as bean herb. Half-hardy annual. Ht. 8–12 in., spread 6 in. Small white/mauve flowers in summer. Aromatic leaves, oblong, pointed, and green. A favorite on the Continent and in America, where it is known as the bean herb. It has become widely used in bean dishes as it helps prevent flatulence. All zones.

Satureja coerulea
Purple-Flowered Savory
Semi-evergreen hardy perennial. Ht. 12 in., spread 8 in. Small purple flowers in summer. The leaves are darkish green, linear and very aromatic. Zone 6.

Satureja montana
Winter Savory
Also known as mountain savory. Semievergreen hardy perennial. Ht. 12 in., spread 8 in. Small white/pink flowers in summer. The leaves are dark green, linear and very aromatic. Zone 5.

Satureja spicigera
Creeping Savory
Perennial. Ht. 3 in., spread 12 in. Masses of small white flowers in summer. The leaves are lime greenish and linear. This is a most attractive plant and is often mistaken for thyme or even heather. Zone 5.

cultivation

Propagation
Seed
Only summer and winter savory can be grown from seed, which is tiny, so it is best to sow into prepared seed trays under protection in the early spring, using the cardboard method (see page 265). The seeds should not be covered as they need light to germinate. Germination takes about 10–15 days—no need to use bottom heat. When the seedlings are large enough, and after a period of hardening off (making quite sure that the frosts have finished), they can be planted into a prepared site in the garden, 6 in. apart.

Cuttings
Creeping, purple-flowered and winter savory can all be grown from softwood cuttings in spring, using a standard seed compost mixed in equal parts with composted fine bark. When these have rooted they should be planted out—12 in. apart for creeping savory, 6 in. apart for the others.

Division
Creeping savory can be divided, as each section has its own root system similar to creeping thymes. Dig up an established plant in the spring after the frosts have finished and divide into as many segments as you require. Minimum size is only dependent on each having a root system and how long you are prepared to wait for new plants to become established. Replant in a prepared site.

Pests and Diseases
Being an aromatic plant, savory is, in the main, free from pests and diseases.

Maintenance
Spring Sow seed. Take softwood cuttings. Divide established plants.
Summer Keep picking and do not allow summer savory to flower, if you want to maintain its flavor.
Fall Protect from prolonged frosts.
Winter Protect.

Garden Cultivation
All the savories featured here like full sun and a poor, well-drained soil. Plant summer savory in the garden in a warm, sheltered spot and keep picking the leaves to

SAVORY

Satureja montana

stop it getting leggy. Do not feed with liquid fertilizer, otherwise the plant will keel over.

S. montana can make a good edging plant and is very pretty in the summer, although it can look a bit sparse in the winter months. Again, trim it from time to time to maintain shape and promote new growth. Creeping savory does not like cold wet winters, or for that matter clay soil, so in this nursery I grow it in a pot (see below). If, however, you wish to grow it in your garden, plant it in a sunny rockery or a well-drained, sheltered corner.

Harvesting

For fresh use, pick leaves as required. For drying, pick those of summer savory before it flowers. They dry easily.

 container growing

All savories can be grown in containers, and if your garden suffers from prolonged cold wet winters it may be the only way you can grow this delightful plant successfully. Use a soil-based compost mixed in equal parts with composted fine bark. Pick the plants continuously to maintain shape, especially the summer

savory, which can get straggly. If you are picking the plants a lot they may benefit from a feed of liquid fertilizer, but keep this to a minimum as they get over-eager when fed. Summer savory, being an annual, dies in winter; creeping savory dies back; the winter savory is a partial evergreen. So, the latter two will need protection in winter. Place them in a cool greenhouse or conservatory. If the container cannot be moved, wrap it up in paper or a frost cloth. Keep watering to the absolute minimum.

 culinary

The two savories that are used in cooking are winter and summer savory. The other varieties are edible but their flavor is inferior. Summer and winter savory combine well with vegetables, legumes and rich meats. These herbs both stimulate the appetite and aid digestion. The flavor is hot and peppery, and so the leaves should be added sparingly in salads.

Summer savory can replace both salt and pepper and is a great help to those on a salt-free diet. It is a pungent herb and until one is familiar with its strength it should be used carefully. Summer savory also makes a good vinegar and oil. The oil is used commercially as a flavoring, as is the leaf, which is an important constituent of salami.

The flavor of winter savory is both coarser and stronger; its advantage is that it provides fresh leaves into early winter.

 medicinal

Summer savory is the plant credited with medicinal virtues and is said to alleviate the pain of bee stings if rubbed on the affected spot. Infuse as a tea to stimulate appetite and to ease indigestion and flatulence. It is also considered a stimulant and was once in demand as an aphrodisiac. Winter savory is also used medicinally but is inferior.

Beans with Garlic and Savory

Serves 3–4

1 cup dried haricot beans
1 Spanish onion
1 carrot, scrubbed and roughly sliced
1 stick celery
1 clove garlic
3 tablespoons olive oil
1 tablespoon white wine vinegar
2 tablespoons chopped summer savory
2 tablespoons chopped French parsley

Soak the beans in cold water overnight or for at least 3–4 hours. Drain them and put them in a saucepan with plenty of water. Bring to the boil slowly. Add half the peeled onion, the carrot and celery, and cook until tender. As soon as the beans are soft, drain and discard the vegetables. Mix the oil, vinegar and crushed garlic. While the beans are still hot, stir in the remaining half onion (thinly sliced), the chopped herbs, and pour over the oil and vinegar dressing. Serve soon after cooling. Do not chill.

Sempervivum
HOUSELEEK

Also known as Bullocks eye, Hen and chickens, Jupiter's eye, Jupiter's beard, Live for ever, Thunder plant, Aaron's rod, Healing leaf, Mallow rock and Welcome-husband-though-never-so-late. From the family Crassulaceae.

Originally from the mountainous areas of central and southern Europe, now found growing in many different areas of the world, including North America.

The generic name *Sempervivum* comes from the Latin *semper vivo* meaning "to live for ever." The specific epithet, *tectorum*, means "of the roofs," there being records dating back 2,000 years of houseleeks growing on the tiles of houses. The plant was said to have been given to humankind by Zeus or Jupiter to protect houses from lightning and fire. Because of this the Romans planted courtyards with urns of houseleek, and Charlemagne ordered a plant to be grown on every roof. This belief continued throughout history and in medieval times the houseleek was thought to protect thatched roofs from fire from the sky and witchcraft. In the Middle Ages the plant was often called Erewort and employed against deafness. When the settlers packed their bags for America they took houseleek with them.

Sempervivum 'Commander Hay'

Sempervivum tectorum with offsets

 varieties

This genus of hardy succulents had 25 species 40 years ago. Now, due to reclassification, it has over 500 different varieties. As far as I am aware only houseleek has medicinal properties.

Sempervivum tectorum
Houseleek
Hardy evergreen perennial. Ht. 4–6 in. (when in flower) otherwise it is 2 in., spread 8 in. Flowers are star-shaped and pink in summer. The leaves, gray/green in color, are oval, pointed and succulent. Zone 4.

Some other *Sempervivum* worth collecting:

Sempervivum arachnoideum
Cobweb Houseleek
Hardy evergreen perennial. Ht. 4–5 in., when in flower, otherwise it is 2 in., spread 4 in. Flowers are star-shaped and pink in summer. The leaves, gray/green in color, are oval, pointed and succulent. The tips of the leaves are covered in a web of white hairs. Zone 5.

Sempervivum 'Commander Hay'
Hardy evergreen perennial. Ht. 4–6 in., when in flower, otherwise it is 2 in., spread 8 in. Flowers star-shaped, pink in summer. The leaves are deep maroon in color, oval, pointed and succulent. Zone 4.

Sempervivum montanum

Hardy evergreen perennial. Ht. 3–6 in., when in flower, otherwise 2 in., spread 4 in. Flowers star-shaped and deep red in summer. Leaves gray/green in color, oval, pointed and succulent. Zone 5.

cultivation

Propagation

Seed

Most species hybridize readily, so seed cannot be depended upon to reproduce the species true to type. When you buy seed it often says, "mixture of several species and varieties" on the packet. It can be good fun to sow these as long as you do not mind what you get; it is even more fun trying to name them as they develop.

The seed is very small, so start off in a seed or plug tray in spring. Sow on the surface. Do not cover except with a sheet of glass. No need for bottom heat. Use a standard seed compost mixed in equal parts with composted fine bark.

Offsets

All the houseleeks produce offsets that cluster around the base of the parent plant. In spring gently remove them and you will notice each has its own root system. Either put straight into a pot, using a standard seed compost mixed in equal parts with composted fine bark, or plant where required. Plant 9 in. apart.

Pests and Diseases

Vine weevil, the scourge of the garden, is very destructive to a number of plants and one of these is houseleek. You will know they have been when you see rosettes lying on their sides with no roots. See page 291 for methods of destroying the pests.

Maintenance

Spring Sow seeds. Pot up or replant offsets.
Summer Collect seeds if they are required from flowering plants.
Fall Remove offsets if the plant is becoming too invasive, and pot up for following season's display.
Winter No need for protection.

Garden Cultivation

Basically the soil should be well-drained and thin, as houseleeks prefer very little to no soil. They will grow anywhere, on weathered rocks and screes and of course rock gardens. Another good place to plant them is between paving stones, or in between other creeping plants like thymes. They can take many years to flower, and when they do they die, but by then there will be many offsets to follow.

Harvesting

Pick leaves to use fresh as required. There is no good way of preserving them.

Sempervivum mixed in flower

Juice from a houseleek soothes burns and insect bites

container growing

If the Romans could do it, so can we. Houseleeks do look good in containers and shallow stone troughs. The compost must be poor and very well drained. Use a soil-based compost mixed with 50 percent horticultural grit and 25 percent composted fine bark. No need to feed, and do not overwater.

medicinal

The leaves are an astringent and when broken in half can be applied to burns, insect bites and other skin problems. Press the juice from the leaf onto the infected part. My son, when he goes on hikes or is building dens, always has some in his pockets for when he gets stung by nettles as houseleeks are more soothing than dock when applied.

To soften skin around corns, bind one leaf for a few hours, soak foot in water in attempt to remove corn. Repeat as necessary.

Infuse as a tea for septic throats, bronchitis and mouth ailments. It is also said that chewing a few leaves can ease toothache.

culinary

The leaves can be added to salad dishes. I think it would be polite to say that it is an acquired taste.

GOLDENROD

Solidago

Solidago 'Goldenmosa'

Also known as Woundwort, Aaron's rod, Cast the spear and Farewell summer. From the family Asteraceae.

This plant is widely distributed throughout Europe including the British Isles, and North America. It is common from the plains to the hills, but especially where the ground is rich in silica.

Its generic name, *Solidago,* is derived from the Latin word *solido,* which means "to join" or "make whole," a reference to the healing properties attributed to Goldenrod.

The plant, originally called Heathen Wound Herb in Britain, was first imported from the Middle East, where it was used by the Saracens, and it was some time before it was cultivated here. In Tudor times it was available in London but at a price, its expense due to the fact that it was still available only as an import. Gerard wrote, "For in my remembrance, I have known the dry herb which comes from beyond the sea, sold in Bucklesbury in London for half a crown an ounce," and went on to say that when it was found growing wild in Hampstead wood, no one would pay half a crown for a hundred weight of it, a fact which the herbalist felt bore out the old English proverb, "Far fetch and dear, bought is best for ladies."

From Culpeper, around the same time, we know that Goldenrod was used to fasten loose teeth and as a remedy for kidney stones (which it still is).

 varieties

Solidago odora
Sweet Goldenrod
Also known as aniseed-scented goldenrod, blue mountain tea, common goldenrod and woundweed. Perennial. Ht. 2–4 ft., spread 2 ft. Golden-yellow flowers on a single stem from midsummer to fall. The green leaf is linear and lance-shaped. Zone 6.

Solidago nemoralis
Grey Goldenrod
Also known as dyer's weed, field goldenrod and yellow goldenrod. Perennial. Ht. 2–3 ft., spread 2 ft. Yellow flowers on large terminals on one side of the panicle. Leaves grayish-green or olive-green. Zone 3.

Solidago 'Goldenmosa'

Solidago virgaurea
Goldenrod
Also known as European goldenrod. Perennial. Ht. 12–24 in., spread 24 in. Small yellow flowers from summer to fall. The green leaves are lance-shaped. Zone 3.

Solidago 'Goldenmosa'
Golden Mimosa
Perennial. Ht. 3 ft., spread 2 ft. Sprays of mimosa-like yellow flowers from summer to fall. Lance-shaped green leaves. Attractive border plant. Has no herbal use. Zone 4.

226 THE COMPLETE HERB BOOK

cultivation

Propagation

Seeds

Sow in plug or seed trays in spring. As seed is fine, sow on the surface of a standard seed compost mixed in equal parts with composted fine bark, and cover with perlite. Germination within 14–21 days without bottom heat. Prick out, harden off, and plant into prepared site in the garden at a distance of 18 in. Remember, the plant will spread.

Division

Divide established plants in spring or fall. Dig up the plant, split into required size, half, third, etc., and replant in a prepared site in the garden.

Pests and Diseases

This plant rarely suffers from pests or diseases.

Maintenance

Spring Sow seeds.
Summer Enjoy the flowers. If you have rich soil, the plants may become very tall and need support in exposed sites.
Fall Divide mature plants.
Winter No need for protection.

Garden Cultivation

It is an attractive plant and has been taken into cultivation as a useful late-flowering ornamental. It is ideal for the herbaceous border, as it spreads rapidly to form clumps.

In late summer, sprays of bright yellow flowers crowd its branching stems amongst sharply pointed hoary leaves. When planting in the garden, it prefers open conditions and soils that are not too rich and are well drained. It tolerates sites in sun, semishade and shade, and, being a wild plant, it can be naturalized in poor grassland.

Sow seed thinly in spring or fall in the chosen flowering position, having prepared the site, and cover lightly with soil. When the seedlings are large enough, thin to 12 in. apart. (The plant will spread and you may have to do a second thinning.) If sown in the fall, the young plants may, in very cold temperatures, need added protection. Use a mulch that they can grow through the following spring, or which can be removed.

Solidago virgaurea

Harvesting

Collect the flowering tops and leaves in summer. Dry for medicinal use.

Goldenrod in potpourri

container growing

Goldenrod can be grown in containers, but being a tall plant, it looks much more attractive in a garden border. Use a soil-based compost mixed in equal parts with composted fine bark, and in the summer only give it liquid fertilizer and water regularly.

In winter, as the plant dies back, move the container into a cool and airy place that is completely protected from frost, but not warm. Keep the compost on the dry side.

medicinal

Goldenrod is used in cases of urinary and kidney infections and stones, and inflammation of the mucus membranes. It also helps to ease backache caused by renal conditions because of its cleansing, eliminative action. It is used to treat arthritis.

A cold compress is helpful on fresh wounds because of its anti-inflammatory properties.

Sweet goldenrod is used as an astringent and as a calmative. The tea made from the dried leaves and flowers is an aromatic beverage and can be used to improve the taste of other medicinal preparations. Native Americans applied lotions made from goldenrod flowers to bee stings.

Stachys officinalis
BETONY

Also known as Lousewort, Purple betony, Wood betony, Bishop's wort and Devil's plaything. From the family Lamiaceae.

This attractive plant, native to Europe, is still found growing wild in Britain.

Betony certainly merits inclusion in the herb garden, but is thought by some to be one of the plant world's frauds. There are so many conflicting stories, all of which are well worth hearing. I leave it to you to decide what is fact or fiction.

The ancient Egyptians were the first to attribute magical properties to Betony. In England, by the 10th century, the Anglo-Saxons had it as their most important magical plant, claiming it as effective against the Elf sickness. In the 11th century it was mentioned in the *Lacnunga* as a beneficial medicinal plant against the Devilish affliction of the body. Later, Gerard wrote in his *Herbal*, "Betony is good for them that be subject to the falling sickness," and went on to describe its many virtues, one of them being as "a remedy against the biting of mad dogs and venomous serpents."

In the 18th century it was still used in the cure of diverse afflictions, including headaches and drawing out splinters, as well as used in herbal tobacco and snuff. Today, Betony retains an important place in folk medicine, though its true value is seriously questioned. We owe the name to the Romans, who called the herb first *Bettonica* and then *Betonica*.

 varieties

Stachys officinalis
Betony
Hardy perennial. Ht. 24 in., spread 10 in. Dense spikes of pink or purple flowers from late spring through summer. Square hairy stems bear aromatic, slightly hairy, round, lobed leaves. Zone 4.

Stachys officinalis 'Alba'
White Betony
Hardy perennial. Ht. 24 in., spread 10 in. White flowers from late spring through summer. Zone 4.

 cultivation

Propagation
Seed
Grows readily from seed, which it produces in abundance. Sow in late summer or spring in planting position and cover very lightly with soil. Alternatively, sow seeds in trays and prick out seedlings into small pots when large enough to handle.

Division
Divide roots of established plants in spring or fall, replant at a distance of 12 in. from other plants. Alternatively, pot using a standard seed compost mixed in equal parts with composted fine bark.

Pests and Diseases
Apart from the occasional caterpillar, which can be picked off, this plant is pest and disease free.

Maintenance
Spring Sow seeds. Divide established plants.
Summer Plant out spring seedlings.
Fall Cut back flowering stems, save seeds, divide established plants.
Winter No protection needed.

Garden Cultivation
A very accommodating plant, it will tolerate most soils, but prefers some humus. Flourishes in sun or shade, and in fact it will put up with all but the deepest of shade. A wild plant, but it has for centuries been grown in cottage gardens.

other uses

The fresh plant provides a yellow dye. A hair rinse, good for highlighting graying hair, can be made from an infusion of the leaves.

 ## warning

Care must be taken if it is taken internally because in any form the root can cause vomiting and violent diarrhea.

Betony leaves

 ## medicinal

Today opinions differ as to its value. Some authorities consider it is only an astringent while others believe it is a sedative. It is however now chiefly employed in herbal smoking mixtures and herbal snuffs. As an infusional powder, it is used to treat diarrhea, cystitis, asthma and neuralgia. Betony tea is invigorating, particularly if prepared in a mixture with other herbs. In France it is recommended for liver and gall bladder complaints.

Dried leaves, flowers and root of betony

In the wild flower garden it is a very colorful participant and establishes well either in a mixed bed or in grassland. It is also an excellent plant for the woodland garden.

Harvesting
Collect leaves for drying before flowering in late spring and early summer. Use leaves fresh either side of flowering.

Pick flowers for drying and for use in potpourri just as they start to open. Collect through flowering season to use fresh.

Collect and save seed in early fall. Store in a dry, dark container.

 ## container growing

Betony grows to great effect in half a beer barrel and combines well with other wild flowers such as poppies, oxeye daisy, chamomile. Use a soil-based compost mixed in equal parts with composted fine bark. I do not advise it for growing indoors or in small containers.

STEVIA

Also known as Sweet leaf, Yerba dulce, Honeyleaf and Caa'-ehe. From the family Asteraceae.

This fascinating and controversial subtropical and tropical herb is indigidous to South and Central America where it has been used for hundreds of years. In the 16th century the invading Spaniards noticed that the Guarani Indians of Paraguay were using this herb not only to sweeten their drinks, but also in herbal remedies and for making snacks. The Indians had many local names for stevia, one of which was Caa'-ehe; this and all the other local names have some form of reference to the sweetness of the leaf. In 1931 two French chemists, Bridel and Lavieille, extracted "stevioside" from the leaf, a compound which is 300 times sweeter than sucrose, which is now being used in many countries throughout the world.

 ## varieties

Stevia rebaudiana
Stevia
Subtropical evergreen perennial, grown as an annual in cold climates. Ht. and spread 18 in. Clusters of small white flowers in late summer, early fall. Mid-green, oval leaves with serrated edges, which have an intense sugary taste, with a licorice aftertaste. Warmer zones.

 ## cultivation

Propagation
Seed
Sow fresh seeds in spring into prepared module plug trays or small pots using a standard seed compost mixed in equal parts with perlite. Cover the seeds with perlite. Place under protection at 65°F (18°C); germination is erratic. As soon as the first few seeds emerge, remove from the heat, keep the container warm and the remaining seeds may germinate over the next few months. Once the seedlings are large enough, pot using a soil-based potting compost mixed in equal parts with composted fine bark.

Cuttings
This is by far the most reliable method of propagation for this herb. Take semiripe cuttings from non-flowering shoots in early summer and place into prepared module plug trays using a seed compost mixed in equal parts with propagating bark. Place in a warm environment (bottom heat is not necessary), and it should root within 2 weeks. Once rooted, pot using the same methods as for seed-raised plants.

Pests and Diseases

This herb, when grown in the tropics, rarely suffers from pests and diseases. In cold climates it is difficult to winter as it is prone to mildew and rot, especially if overwatered. If it is grown under protection in spring and summer, make sure that the leaves do not become scorched and watch out for greenfly, especially on new growth. If the infestation becomes invasive, spray with an insecticidal soap following the manufacturer's instructions.

Maintenance

Spring Sow seeds.
Summer Take cuttings.
Fall Bring plants inside to protect from frost.
Winter Cut back on the watering of container plants in cool and cold climates.

Garden Cultivation

Outside the tropics this herb can only be grown as an annual in the garden. Plant in full sun—it will not tolerate shade—in a light fertile soil that does not dry out in summer. If you know your soil is prone to drying, after planting add a good deep mulch, preferably leaf mold or well-rotted compost.

Harvesting

Pick the leaves to use fresh as required from spring until late summer. Pick the leaves for drying in early summer.

 container growing

Stevia is ideally suited for growing in a container. Plant in a soil-based potting compost mixed in equal parts with composted fine bark. Place the container in a warm sunny position. Water and feed regularly throughout the growing season. In the fall, in cold and cool climates, bring the container into a warm greenhouse, sunroom or well-lit windowsill. Cut back the plant to 4 in. and reduce the watering to minimal, but not totally dry. Reintroduce watering and move up one size of pot in the spring. Place the container outside once all frosts have passed.

 medicinal

For today's society this herb has phenomenal potential in the treatment of obesity, high blood pressure and for those, such as diabetics, who require a natural sweetener and for those on a low carbohydrate diet. Due to lack of clinical trials it is not yet recognized; however, there is currently lots of different scientific research being carried out worldwide and I would not be surprised to find it being included in many herbal preparations in the near future.

 warning

This herb is banned for sale as a food or food ingredient in the United Kingdom and European Union. In the United States it can only be sold as a dietary supplement and not as a sweetener.

Stevia rebaudiana under cultivation

 culinary

I have read many arguments regarding the safety of stevia in food production, and they have left me puzzled and frustrated. The Japanese, who have banned all artificial sweeteners, have been using stevia as a commercial sweetener for the past 30 years without a single case of documented stevia toxicity or adverse reaction, yet it has been banned by U.S. and European agencies, although the U.S. Food and Drug Administration has agreed that it can be used as a food supplement in the home.

The leaves can be used fresh or dried; they have a very, very sweet, slightly licorice flavor. The flavor and intensity of the sugar content can vary due to growing position, sun strength, watering and age of plant. To test how strong the fresh leaves are, place a minute amount on the end of your tongue; this will immediately indicate strength. Alternatively, take one leaf, pour over 1 cup of boiled water, let it stand for 10 minutes, then taste the water with a teaspoon. If not sweet enough for your taste or recipe add another leaf, reheat the water to just below boiling, let it stand for a further 10 minutes, then taste again. Repeat this until you get the flavor you want. Always start with a few leaves because you can add but you cannot take away once you have created a sweet water. Once you have the flavor you require you can then use this sweet water in drinks, with fruit, water ices and other desserts.

Sutherlandia frutescens
CANCER BUSH

Also known as Kankerbos, Kankerbossie, Unwele, Phetola Mukakana and Lerumo-lamadi. From the family Papilionaceae.

The first time I saw this plant flower I knew that it was special, however I had no idea how special until I heard the BBC world news in November 2001, when it was proclaimed as a beneficial herb in the treatment of AIDS. This native of South Africa is regarded as the most profound and multi-purpose of their native medicinal plants. It has been used for centuries as a medicine; the Zulu sangomas, or traditional healers, know it as *unwele*, "the great medicine," which they used to ward off the effects of the devastating 1918 influenza pandemic that claimed 20 million lives worldwide. The Afrikaaners call it the *kanker-bossie* or cancer bush, because of its properties in treating people suffering with internal cancers and wasting.

 varieties

Sutherlandia frutescens
Cancer Bush
Evergreen tender shrub. Ht. up to 4 ft., spread 3 ft. Bright scarlet flowers, from early to midsummer, which grow in terminal clusters and are followed by inflated seed pods that are pale green, ripening to beige, tinged with red, in which there are small flat black seeds. Each gray/silver slightly hairy leaf is divided into 13–21 leaflets. Zone 9.

 cultivation

Propagation
Seed
The cancer bush self-seeds readily around the garden. However, as with many herbs that do this, it does need encouragement when grown under controlled conditions in a greenhouse or cold frame. Sow either in the fall using fresh seed, or in the following spring with dried seeds. Prepare the seeds in exactly the same way as the seeds of sweet peas, as they are from the same botanical family. Prior to sowing, scarify the seeds lightly by rubbing them gently on sandpaper and then soak them overnight in hand-hot water. Finally sow the prepared seed into plug modules or small pots, using a standard seed compost mixed in equal parts with perlite. Cover the seeds with just perlite as this helps prevent damping off. Place under protection at 60°F (15°C); germination takes 2 to 3 weeks. When sowing in the fall, winter the seedlings in a frost-free environment. Once the seedlings are large enough, pot using a soil-based compost mixed in equal parts with river sand. Harden off prior to planting in the garden or before growing on in a container. Plants raised from seed will take 3 years before they flower.

Cuttings
Take cuttings from nonflowering shoots from April until June. Put into prepared plug modules or very small pots, using a standard seed compost mixed in equal parts with perlite. Place the cuttings in a warm position or on a propagator at 60°F (15°C); rooting takes 2–3 weeks. Once roots have established, pot using a soil-based potting compost mixed in equal parts with river sand.

CANCER BUSH

Sutherlandia frutescens

Pests and Diseases

The plant is quite pest resistant in the garden. When container grown, however, it can be prone to red spider mite *(Tetranychus urticae)*. The best way to control this is to use a biological predator *Phytoseiulus persimilis,* which feeds on the eggs and the active stages of red spider mite. This predator does not work well in cold weather, therefore use from late spring until early fall, well before the first frosts.

Container plants in the winter can suffer from powdery mildew, usually due to poor air circulation and the root ball being too dry. It can also suffer from downy mildew, which again is especially a problem in cold damp falls where the air circulation is stagnant and the plant's leaves have not been picked up. To prevent both of these mildews, check the plants regularly, and lift the container off the floor onto bricks, to stop osmosis from the damp floor. Check the watering regularly to make sure that the root ball is just damp but not overdry or sodden and, if the leaves do drop, make sure that they are removed and not left to rot on the surface of the pot.

Maintenance

Spring Sow seeds.
Summer Harvest leaves. Take cuttings.

Fall Harvest leaves and seeds. Bring in containers.
Winter Protect from frosts. Check air circulation.

Garden Cultivation

This stunning plant makes a very good focal point in the garden. In the northern hemisphere and areas where the night temperature falls constantly below 50°F (10°C), it can only be grown as an annual, or as a container plant that is sunk into the border for the growing season and lifted in the fall before the first frosts. With either method, plant in full sun in any good fertile, free-draining soil. The Cancer bush, once established, is fast growing; it is not particularly long lived, approximately 5 years, so it is worth taking cuttings each summer as insurance.

Harvesting

The leaves are harvested in summer and then dried for medicinal use.

 ## companion planting

The cancer bush is a member of the legume (pea) family. Plants of this family fix atmospheric nitrogen via their roots in the soil, which then becomes a benefit for other plants.

 ## container growing

This herb grows happily in containers; use a soil-based potting compost mixed in equal parts with river sand. Water regularly and feed weekly with a liquid fertilizer throughout the growing season. In winter, in cool and cold climates, cut back on the watering and place in a frost-free environment that has good air circulation.

 ## medicinal

The cancer bush is a traditional Cape remedy that is taken as a bitter tonic and used for numerous conditions including chickenpox, piles, backache and rheumatism.

In 2001 The Medical Research Council of South Africa performed clinical trials to assess the immune-boosting properties of the cancer bush to support the anecdotal evidence that this plant can improve the quality of life of thousands of people both with HIV and full-blown AIDS. A multidisciplinary team headed by Dr. Nigel Gericke, a botanist, medical doctor and indigenous plant specialist, found that *Sutherlandia* contained a powerful combination of molecules which have been identified and used in the treatment of patients with cancer, tuberculosis, diabetes, schizophrenia and clinical depression, and as an antiretroviral agent.

 ## warning

This herb should be taken under supervision only.

Seed pods

Symphytum
COMFREY

Also known as Knitbone, Boneset, Bruisewort, Knitback, Church bells, Abraham, Isaac-and-Jacob (from the variation in flower color) and Saracen's root. From the family Boraginaceae.

Native to Europe and Asia, it was introduced into America in the 17th century, where it has naturalized.

Traditionally known as Saracen's root, common comfrey is believed to have been brought to England by the Crusaders, who had discovered its value as a healing agent with mucilaginous secretions strong enough to act as a bone-setting plaster, which gave it the nickname Knitbone.

The Crusaders passed it to monks for cultivation in their monastic herb gardens, dedicated to the care of the sick.

Elizabethan physicians and herbalists were never without it. A recipe from that time is for an ointment made from comfrey root boiled in sugar and licorice, and mixed with coltsfoot, mallow and poppy seed. People also made comfrey tea for colds and bronchitis.

Symphytum ibericum

But times have changed. Once the panacea for all ills, comfrey is now under suspicion medicinally as a carcinogen. In line with its common name "Bruisewort," research in the United States has shown that comfrey breaks down red blood cells. At the same time, the Japanese are investigating how to harness its beneficial qualities; there is a research program into the high protein and vitamin B content of the herb.

Symphytum x *uplandicum*

Symphytum officinale
Comfrey (Wild or Common)
Hardy perennial. Ht. and spread 3 ft. White/purple/pink flowers in summer. This is the best medicinal comfrey and can also be employed as a liquid feed, although the potassium content is only 3.09 percent compared to 7.09 percent in 'Bocking 14.' It makes a first-class composting plant, as it helps the rapid breakdown of other compost materials. Zone 5.

Symphytum x uplandicum
Russian Comfrey
Hardy perennial. Ht. 3 ft., spread indefinite. Pink/purple flowers in summer. Green lance-shaped leaves. This is a hybrid that occurred naturally in Upland, Sweden. It is a cross between *S. officinale*, the herbalist's comfrey, and *S. asperum*, the blue-flowered, prickly comfrey from Russia. A very attractive form is *S.* x *uplandicum* 'Variegatum', with cream and green leaves. Zone 5.

Symphytum x uplandicum 'Bocking 4'
Hardy perennial. Ht. 3 ft., spread indefinite. Flowers near to violet in color, in spring and early summer. Thick, solid stems. Large green lance-shaped leaves. Not a particularly attractive plant but it contains almost 35 percent total protein, the same percentage as in soya beans. Comfrey is an important animal feed in some parts of the world, especially in Africa. Zone 5.

Symphytum x uplandicum 'Bocking 14'
Hardy perennial. Ht. 3 ft., spread indefinite. Mauve flowers in spring and early summer. Thin stems. Green oval leaves, tapering to a point. This variety has the highest potash content, which makes it the best for producing liquid manure. Zone 5.

 ## varieties

Symphytum 'Hidcote Blue'
Comfrey Hidcote Blue
Hardy perennial. Ht. 20 in., spread 24 in. Pale blue flowers in spring and early summer. Green lance-shaped leaves. Very attractive in a large border. Zone 5.

Symphytum ibericum
Dwarf Comfrey
Hardy perennial. Ht. 10 in., spread 40 in. Yellow/white flowers in spring. Green lance-shaped leaves. An excellent groundcover plant, having foliage through most winters. This comfrey contains little potassium and no allantoin, the crucial medicinal substance. Zone 5.

cultivation

Propagation

Seed
Not nearly as reliable as root cutting or division. Sow in spring or fall in either seed or plug trays. Germination slow and erratic.

Root Cuttings
In spring, dig up a piece of root, cut into ¾ in. sections, and put these small sections into a prepared plug or seed tray.

Division
Use either the double spade method or simply dig up a chunk in the spring and replant it elsewhere.

Pests and Diseases

Sometimes suffers from rust and powdery mildew in late fall. In both cases cut the plant down and burn the contaminated leaves.

Maintenance

Spring Sow seeds. Divide plants. Take root cuttings.
Summer Cut back leaves for composting, or to use as a mulch around other herbs in the growing season.
Fall Sow seeds.
Winter None needed.

Garden Cultivation

Fully hardy in the garden, all the comfreys prefer sun or semishade and a moist soil, but will tolerate most conditions. The large tap root can cause problems if you want to move the plant. When doing this make sure you dig up all the root because any left behind will reappear later.

Harvesting

Cut leaves with shears from early summer to the fall to provide foliage for making liquid feed. Each plant is able to give four cuts a year if well fed. Cut leaves for drying before flowering.

Dig up roots in the fall for drying.

Liquid Manure

Use either *S.* x *uplandicum* or *S.* x *uplandicum* 'Bocking 14' to make a quickly available source of potassium for the organic gardener. One method of extracting it is to put 14 lb. of freshly cut comfrey into a 24 gallon tapped, fiberglass water barrel. Do not use

Powdery mildew on comfrey leaf

metal as rust will add toxic quantities of iron oxide to the liquid manure. Fill up the barrel with rain or tap water and cover with a lid to exclude the light. In about 4 weeks a clear liquid can be drawn off from the tap at the bottom. Ideal feed for tomatoes, onions, gooseberries, beans and all potash-hungry crops. It can be used as a foliar feed.

The disadvantage of this method is that the liquid stinks, because comfrey foliage is about 3.4 percent protein, and when proteins break down they smell.

An alternative is to bore a hole into the side (just above the bottom) of a plastic trash can. Stand the container on bricks, so that it is far enough off the ground to allow a dish to be placed under the hole. Pack it solid with cut comfrey, and place something (a heavy lump of concrete) on top to weigh down the leaves. Cover with lid, and in about 3 weeks a black liquid will drip from the hole into a dish.

This concentrate can be stored in a screw-top bottle if you do not want to use it immediately. Dilute it 1 part to 40 parts water, and if you plan to use it as a foliar feed, strain it first.

 ## container growing

Comfrey is not suitable for growing indoors, but it can be grown on a patio as long as the container is large enough. Situate in partial shade and give plenty of water in warm weather.

 ## culinary

Fresh leaves and shoots were eaten as a vegetable or salad and there is no reason to suppose that it is dangerous to do so now, although it may be best to err on the side of caution until suspicions are resolved (see "Warning" below).

 ## medicinal

Comfrey has received much attention in recent years, both as a valuable healing herb, a source of vitamin B12 and self-proliferate allantoin, and as a potential source of protein.

Comfrey is also useful as a poultice for varicose ulcers and a compress for varicose veins, and it alleviates and heals minor burns.

 ## warning

Comfrey is reported to cause serious liver damage if taken in large amounts over a long period of time.

 ## other uses

Boil fresh leaves for golden fabric dye (see also pages 288–289).

Comfrey is a good feed for racehorses and helps cure laminitis. For curing septic sores on animals, make a poultice between clean pieces of cotton and tie to the affected places.

Comfrey dye

Tagetes lucida

WINTER TARRAGON

Also known as Mexican tarragon, Spanish tarragon and Sweet mace. From the family Asteraceae.

The first time I saw winter tarragon was over 15 years ago in Florida, where I found it on sale in a garden center. Until then I had never seen an edible *Tagetes* and was amazed by the power and the anise flavor of the leaves, which proved to be great in cooking.

Winter tarragon is indigenous to southern and central Mexico. Historically it is said that the Aztecs used it to flavor *chocólatl*, a coca-based drink and it is still popular today with the Tarahumara Indians of Chihuahua. It is revered by the modern Huichol Indians as a shamanic trance "tobacco," which is used in their religious rituals.

 ## varieties

Tagetes lucida
Winter Tarragon, Mexican Tarragon
Tender herbaceous perennial, usually grown as an annual. Ht. 32 in. in warm climates only, spread 18 in. Sweetly scented yellow flowers in late summer. Rarely flowers in cold temperatures. Narrow lance-shaped aromatic mid-green toothed leaves, which have strong aniseed scent and flavor. This herb, in cool climates, dies back in early spring, reappearing in early summer. All zones.

Tagetes patula
Wild Mexican marigold, French marigold
Half-hardy annual. Ht. 4 ft., spread 18 in. Clusters of single yellow flowers midsummer until first frosts. Aromatic, deeply divided, lightly toothed mid-green leaves. This species is said to deter nematodes in the soil, and whitefly from tomatoes. The leaves have been used to flavor food; medicinally it is a diuretic and it improves the digestion. Externally it has been used to treat sore eyes and rheumatism. The flowers have been used to feed poultry and to color dairy produce and textiles. All zones.

 ## cultivation

Propagation
Seed
Sow the seeds in early spring into prepared seed or plug module trays, using a standard seed compost mixed in equal parts with perlite. Place under protection at 68°F (20°C); germination takes 14–21 days. Once the seedlings are large enough, pot into a soil-based compost mixed in equal parts with river sand. Alternatively sow in late spring, into prepared open ground, when the air temperature does not fall below 50°F (10°C) at night; germination takes 2–4 weeks.

Cuttings
Take tip cuttings in early summer, place the cutting into prepared plug module trays using a standard seed compost, mixed in equal parts with perlite. Place in a warm environment until rooted, about 2–3 weeks. Once fully rooted, pot into a soil-based compost mixed in equal parts with river sand.

236 THE COMPLETE HERB BOOK

WINTER TARRAGON

Pests and Diseases

Rarely suffers from pests. In cold, damp climates it will die back in late winter; make sure at this time of year that the leaves do not become too damp because this could rot the crown. If you notice mildew, cut off all the remaining growth, raise the container up onto some bricks and put in a well aired, frost-free place.

Maintenance

Spring Sow seeds. Cut back any winter growth.
Summer Take cuttings.
Fall Lift garden plants and bring in containers once the night temperature falls below 50°F (10°C).
Winter Cut back the watering to minimal.

Garden Cultivation

It can only be grown successfully outside all year round in a tropical or subtropical climate. In cooler climates it must be grown as an annual or lifted in winter. Plant in a well-drained fertile soil in a sunny position.

Harvesting

The leaves can be picked as required throughout the growing season for using fresh. Alternatively pick in midsummer for drying.

container growing

Winter tarragon is ideal for growing in a container in cool and cold climates. Pot using a soil-based compost mixed in equal parts with river sand. Once the night temperature falls below 10°C (50°F), bring the container into a frost-free environment and cut back on watering to minimal but not totally dry. Repot each spring, after removing any winter growth. Only repot one size up at a time as this herb likes being pot-bound.

medicinal

The leaves of this herb are used as a relaxant and to treat diarrhea, indigestion, malaria and feverishness. It also has the reputation of being a very good hangover cure.

other uses

Burnt leaves make a good insect repellent.
The juice from crushed leaves when applied to ticks makes them easy to remove.

warning

Not to be taken medicinally when pregnant or breast-feeding. If taken in excess it can cause hallucinations.

Tagetes patula

culinary

Winter tarragon makes a good substitute for French tarragon (*Artemisia dracunculus*), not only in winter, when French tarragon has died back into the ground, but also where it is difficult to grow i.e., in humid climates. The leaves of this tarragon are much stronger and more anise than the French variety so use with care until you get used to it.

Chicken and Winter Tarragon Parcel
Serves 2

2 skinless organic chicken breasts
2 cloves of garlic, peeled and sliced
6 x 4 in. sprigs of winter tarragon, leaves removed and chopped
3 tablespoons butter
²⁄₃ cup white wine
Extra-wide tin foil

Preheat the oven to 425°F/220°C.
Cut two pieces of tin foil 14 x 20 in. Place them on top of each other. Then fold in half and seal the two long sides leaving the top open. Place the chicken breasts in the foil bag, with the garlic, chopped tarragon and butter. Check the sides of the bag are well sealed then pour in the white wine and seal the top. Place this on a baking tray and put in the preheated oven for 25 minutes. Once cooked, place the foil bag onto a plate or serving dish before opening to catch all the juices. Serve with baked potatoes and a crisp green salad.

Tanacetum balsamita
ALECOST

Also known as Costmary, Bible leaf, English mace and Sweet Mary. From the family Asteraceae

The first syllable in the common name, "alecost," is derived from the use to which its scented leaves and flowering tops were used in the Middle Ages, namely to clear, preserve and impart an astringent minty flavor to beer. The word "cost" derives from kostos, the Greek for spicy, so therefore "alecost" literally means a spicy herb for ale. With the demise of its use in beer it has now become a rare plant in Europe, however in North America it can be found as a garden escapee growing wild in the Eastern and mid-West states.

 ## varieties

Tanacetum balsamita
Alecost
Perennial. Ht. 3 ft. and spread 18 in. Clusters of small white yellow-eyed daisy flowers from July–September. Oblong, silver/green mint-scented leaves. Zones 6–9.

Tanacetum balsamita subsp. balsamitoides
Camphor plant
Perennial. Ht. 3 ft. and spread 18 in. Clusters of small white yellow-eyed daisy flowers from July–September. Oblong, silver/green camphor-scented leaves. Zones 6–9.

cultivation

Propagation
Seed
Although possible, as it is difficult to obtain viable seed, I recommend raising this plant from division.

Division
Divide established plants in spring or early fall. Either plant out directly into the prepared garden or pot into individual pots using a potting compost mixed in equal parts with composted fine bark. If you have a very wet cold soil, it is better to winter fall-divided plants in pots, in a cold frame or cold greenhouse.

Pests and Diseases
Both species rarely suffer from pest or diseases.

Maintenance
Spring Divide established plants.
Summer Dead head flowers.
Fall Cut back the flowers. Divide established plants.
Winter Tidy up dead leaves as these will spread disease if left to rot. Protect pot-grown plants from excessive wet.

Garden Cultivation
Both species will adapt to most conditions. However they prefer a fertile well-drained soil. Plant at a distance of 2 ft. from other plants and, if possible, in a sunny position because when planted in shade they will not flower.

Harvesting
Pick alecost leaves for culinary use throughout the growing season. For drying, pick the leaves in late spring, before flowering, which is when the leaves have the best sweet scent.

 ## container growing

This herb is not ideal for growing in containers all year round, as it grows tall and rapidly outgrows its pot, requiring regular repotting throughout the growing season.

 ## culinary

Alecost leaves have a sharp bitter tang that can be overpowering, so use sparingly. Add finely chopped leaves to carrots, salads, game, poultry, stuffings and fruit cakes.

 ## medicinal

Traditionally a tea made from the leaves of this herb was used to ease the pain of childbirth. It was also used as a tonic for colds, inflammation of mucus membranes, stomach upsets and cramps.
  Rub a fresh leaf of alecost on a bee sting or horsefly bite to relieve the pain.

 ## other uses

The leaves and flowers can be used in home brewing to clear, flavor and preserve the beer. Dried leaves make a good addition to potpourri, they can also be added to linen bags where they not only smell good but act as a good moth repellent.
  Fresh or dried leaves of alecost can be added to baths for a refreshing soak.

 ## warning

Do not use Camphor in any culinary dishes.

Tanacetum cinerariifolium
PYRETHRUM

Also known as Dalmatian pellitory. From the family Asteraceae.

This plant is a native of Croatia and can be found growing wild in the hills above the Adriatic sea. It is now cultivated commercially in many parts of the world, including Japan, South Africa and parts of central Europe for its insecticidal properties. Originally the insecticide was known as Dalmatian insect powder because for many hundreds of years the eastern coast of the Adriatic was known as Dalmatia. The insecticide is now known as Pyrethrum and can be found in many proprietary products.

 ## varieties

Tanacetum cinerariifolium (Chrysanthemum cinerariifolium)
Hardy perennial. Ht. 12–15 in., spread 8 in. Daisy-like flower, white petals with a yellow center. Leaves green/gray, finely divided, with white down on the underside. Zone 6.

Tanacetum coccineum (Chrysanthemum roseum)
Hardy perennial. Ht. 12–24 in., spread 12 in. Large flowerhead, which can be white or red, and sometimes tipped with yellow. Very variable under cultivation. Vivid green leaves. Native of Iran. It was known as Persian insect powder, but it is not as strong as *T. cinerariifolium*, so it fell out of favor. An attractive garden plant. Zone 5.

 ## cultivation

Propagation
Seeds
In spring sow into a prepared seed or plug tray and cover with perlite. Germination is easy and takes 14–21 days. In late spring, when the young plants are large enough and after a period of hardening off, plant into a prepared site in the garden 6–12 in. apart.

Division
Established clumps can be dug up in the spring or fall and divided.

Pests and Diseases
Mostly free from pests and diseases.

Maintenance
Spring Sow seed. Divide established plants.
Summer Deadhead flowers to prolong season if not collecting seed.
Fall Divide established plants if necessary.
Winter Fully hardy.

Garden Cultivation
Pyrethrum likes a well-drained soil in a sunny spot; it is drought tolerant and fully hardy in most winters.

Harvesting
The flowerheads are collected just as they open and dried gently. When they are quite dry, store away from light. The insecticide is made from the powdered dried flower.

 ## container growing

This herb is very well suited for growing in containers, especially terracotta. Use a soil-based compost mixed in equal parts with composted fine bark. Water well during the summer months, but be stingy with the liquid fertilizer, otherwise the leaves will become green and it will stop flowering.

 ## medicinal

This herb is rarely used medicinally. Herbalists have found the roots to be a remedy for certain fevers. Recent research has shown that the flowerheads possess a weak antibiotic.

 ## other uses

This is a useful insecticide because it is relatively non-toxic to mammals and does not accumulate in the environment or in the bodies of animals. However it can cause allergic reactions, and in very high doses can damage the central nervous and immune system. It acts by paralyzing the nervous system of the insects, and can kill pests living on the skin of man and animals. Sprinkle the dry powder from the flowers to deter all common insects, pests, bed bugs, cockroaches, flies, mosquitoes, aphids and ants. Traditionally the dried flowers were mixed with methylated spirits and water and used as a garden spray. When buying it in a proprietary product, do read the instructions carefully as Pyrethrum is harmful to many beneficial pollinating insects.

⚠ warning

When used as an insecticide, it can kill helpful insects and fish, as well as pests. Can cause contact dermititis.

Tanacetum vulgare

TANSY

Also known as Bachelor's buttons, Bitter buttons, Golden buttons, Stinking Willy, Hind heel and Parsley fern. From the family Asteraceae.

Tansy is a native to Europe and Asia, and it has managed to become naturalized elsewhere, especially in North America.

The name derives from the Greek *athanasia*, meaning "immortality." In ancient times it was used in the preparation of the embalming sheets and rubbed on corpses to save them from earthworms or corpse worm.

varieties

Tanacetum vulgare
Tansy
Hardy perennial. Ht. 3 ft., spread 1–2 ft. and more. Yellow button flowers in late summer. The aromatic leaf is deeply indented, toothed and fairly dark green. Zone 3.

Tanacetum vulgare var. crispum
Curled Tansy
As *T. vulgare* except ht. 2 ft., and the aromatic leaf is crinkly, curly and dark green. Zone 3.

Tanacetum vulgare 'Isala Gold'
Tansy Isala Gold
As *T. vulgare* except ht. 2 ft., and the leaf is golden in color. Zone 3.

Tanacetum vulgare 'Silver Lace'
Tansy 'Silver Lace'
As *T. vulgare* except ht. 2 ft., and the leaf starts off white-flecked with green, progressing to full green. If, however, you keep cutting it, some of the variegation can be maintained. Zone 3.

cultivation

Propagation
Seed
Sow the small seed in spring or fall in a prepared seed or plug tray using a standard seed compost, and cover with perlite. Germination takes 10–21 days. Plant 18 in. apart when the seedlings are large enough to handle. If sown in the fall, protect over winter.

Division
Divide root runners in either spring or fall.

Pests and Diseases
Aphids are the only real problem for tansy.

Maintenance
Spring Sow seed. Divide established clumps.
Summer Cut back after flowering to maintain shape and color.
Fall Divide established clumps. Sow seeds.
Winter The plant is fully hardy and dies back into the ground for winter.

Garden Cultivation
Tansy needs to be positioned with care as the roots spread widely. The gold and variegated forms are much less invasive and very attractive in a semishaded border. They tolerate most conditions provided the soil is not completely wet.

Harvesting
Pick leaves as required. Gather flowers when open.

container growing

Because of its antisocial habit, container growing is recommended. Use a soil-based compost and a large container, water throughout the growing season, and only feed about twice during flowering. In winter keep on the dry side in a cool place.

medicinal

Can be used by trained herbalists to expel roundworm and threadworm. Use tansy tea externally to treat scabies, and as a compress to bring relief to painful rheumatic joints.

warning

Use tansy only under medical supervision. It is a strong emmenagogue, provoking the onset of a period, and should not be used during pregnancy. An overdose of tansy oil or tea can be fatal.

other uses

Rub into the coat of your dog or cat to prevent fleas. Hang leaves indoors to deter flies. Put dried sprigs under carpets. Add to insect-repellent sachets. Sprinkle chopped leaves and flowers to deter ants and mice. It produces a yellow/green woollen dye.

Tanacetum vulgare 'Isala Gold'

Tanacetum parthenium
FEVERFEW

Also known as Featherfew in America and Febrifuge. From the family Asteraceae.

The common name suggests that this herb was used in the treatment of fevers, and the old herbalists even call it febrifuge; however, strange as it may seem, the herb was hardly ever employed for this purpose. In the 17th century, Culpeper advised its use for pains in the head and colds, and nowadays it is used in the treatment of migraines.

Feverfew in sachets makes a good moth repellant

Harvesting
Pick the leaves before flowering to use fresh or to dry. Pick the flower heads just as they open for drying.

 ## varieties

Tanacetum parthenium (Chrysanthemum parthenium)
Feverfew
Hardy herbaceous perennial. Ht. up to 4 ft., spread 18 in. Clusters of small white yellow-eyed daisy flowers from early summer until the first frosts. The leaf is mid-green, lobed and divided with lightly serrated edges.

Tanacetum parthenium 'Aureum'
Golden Feverfew.
Hardy herbaceous perennial. Ht. 8–18 in., spread 18 in. Clusters of small white yellow eyed daisy flowers from early summer until the first frosts. The leaf is golden, lobed and divided with lightly serrated edges. Excellent edging plant.

 ## cultivation

Propagation
Seed
The fine, thin and fairly small seeds tend to stick together, especially if they are damp. Mix the seed with a small amount of perlite or dry sand prior to sowing. Sow seeds in the fall or spring, into prepared pots or plug modules using a standard seed compost; do not cover. Place in a cold frame, germination 2–4 weeks. Fall sowings, winter in the cold frame. Plant when large enough to handle 12 in. apart.

Cuttings
Take stem cutting in summer, making sure there are not flowers on the cutting material.

Division
Divide established plants in the fall or spring, replanting into a prepared site.

Pests and Diseases
Aphids are the only real problem for Feverfew.

Maintenance
Spring Sow seeds.
Summer As flowering finishes, cut back to restore shape and minimize self-seeding. Take stem cuttings.
Fall Divide established plants. Sow seeds.
Winter No need for protection, frost hardy.

Garden Cultivation
Plant in a well-drained fertile soil in a sunny position. Feverfew is drought tolerant and will adapt to most soils and conditions, however if planted in shade they are unlikely to flower. Golden feverfew can suffer from sun scorch; if this occurs cut back and the new growth will be unaffected.

 ## container growing

Both forms of feverfew look attractive in containers. Use a soil based compost mixed in equal parts with composted fine bark.

 ## culinary

The young leaves can be added to salads; however, they have a very bitter taste so use sparingly.

 ## medicinal

Feverfew is a renowned remedy for certain types of migraines. Because they are so bitter, place 2–3 fresh leaves in between slices of bread. This will make them more palatable. Do not take for a prolonged period and do not overeat.

 ## other uses

A decoction made from the leaves is a good basic household disinfectant. The dried leaves, placed in a sachet, make a good moth repellent.

 ## warning

One side effect associated with taking feverfew is ulceration of the mouth.

DANDELION

Taraxacum

Also known as Pee in the bed, Lions teeth, Fairy clock, Clock, Clock flower, Clocks and watches, Farmers clocks, Old mans clock, One clock, Wetweed, Blowball, Cankerwort, Lionstooth, Priests crown, Puffball, Swinesnout, White endive, Wild endive and Piss-a-beds. From the family Asteraceae.

Dandelion is one of nature's great medicines and it really proves that a weed is only a plant out of place! It is in fact one of the most useful of herbs. It has become naturalized throughout the temperate regions of the world and flourishes on nitrogen-rich soils in any situation to a height of 6,500 ft.

There is no satisfactory explanation why it is called dandelion, dents lioness, tooth of the lion in medieval Latin, and *dent de lion* in French. The lion's tooth may be the tap root, the jagged leaf or the flower parts.

The Arabs promoted its use in the 11th century. By the 16th it was well established as an official drug. The apothecaries knew it as *Herba taraxacon* or *Herba urinari*, and Culpeper called it piss-a-beds, all referring to its diuretic qualities.

 varieties

Taraxacum officinale agg.
Dandelion
Perennial. Ht. 6–9 in. Large, brilliant yellow flowers 2 in. wide, spring to fall. The flower heads as they turn to seed form a fluffy ball (dandelion clock). Leaves oblong with a jagged edge. Zone 3.

Taraxacum kok-saghyz Rodin
Russian Dandelion
Perennial. Ht. 12 in. Similar to the above. Extensively cultivated during the World War II: latex was extracted from the roots as a source of rubber. Zone 3.

Taraxacum mongolicum
Chinese Dandelion
Perennial. Ht. 10–12 in. Similar to the above. Used to treat infections, particularly mastitis. Zone 3.

 cultivation

Propagation
Seed
Grow as an annual to prevent bitterness developing in the plant. Sow seed in spring on the surface of pots or plug trays. Do not use seed trays as the long tap root makes it difficult to prick out. Cover with a fine layer of perlite. Germination will be in 3–6 weeks, depending on seed freshness and air temperature. Plant when large enough to handle.

Root
In spring and fall, sections of the root can be cut and put in pots, seed trays or plug trays. Each piece will sprout again, just like comfrey.

Pests and Diseases
Dandelion is rarely attacked by either pest or disease.

Maintenance
Spring Sow seeds for use as a fall salad herb. Take root cuttings.
Summer Continually pick off the flower buds if you are growing dandelion as a salad crop.
Fall Put an up-turned flowerpot over some of the plants to blanch them for fall salads. Sow seed for spring salad crop. Take root cuttings.
Winter No protection is needed. For salad crops,

however, if temperatures fall below 15°F (−10°C), cover with a frost cloth or 3 in. of straw or bracken to keep the leaves sweet.

Garden Cultivation

If the dandelion was a rare plant, it would be thought a highly desirable garden species, for the flowers are most attractive, sweet smelling and a brilliant yellow, and then form the delightful puff balls. Up to that point all is fine. But then the wind disperses the seed all over the garden. And it is very difficult to eradicate when established since every bit of root left behind produces another plant. So, it finds no favor at all with gardeners.

In general, details on how to grow dandelions are superfluous. Most people only want to know how to get rid of them. The easiest time to dig up the plants completely is in the early spring.

Harvesting

Pick leaves as required to use fresh, and flowers for wine as soon as they open fully. Dig up roots in the fall for drying.

Dandelion wine

 ## container growing

Dandelions do look attractive growing in containers, especially in window boxes, if you can stand neighbors' remarks. But in all seriousness the containers will need to be deep to accommodate the long tap root.

 ## medicinal

It is one of the most useful medicinal plants, as all parts are effective and safe to use. It is regarded as one of the best herbal remedies for kidney and liver complaints. The root is a mildly laxative, bitter tonic, valuable in treating dyspepsia and constipation. The leaves are a powerful diuretic. However, unlike conventional diuretics, dandelion does not leach potassium from the body as its rich potassium content replaces what the body loses.

The latex contained in the leaves and stalks is very effective in removing corns and in treating warts and verrucas. Apply the juice from the plant daily to the affected part.

The flowers can be boiled with sugar for coughs, but honey has a greater medicinal value.

 ## other uses

As a herbal fertilizer, dandelion has a good supply of copper. Pick three plants completely: leaves, flowers and all. Place in a bucket, pour over 3½ cups of boiling water, cover and allow to stand for 30 minutes. Strain through an old pair of pantyhose or something similar. This fertilizer will not store.

A dye, yellow-brown in color, can be obtained from the root and dandelions are excellent food for domestic rabbits, guinea pigs and gerbils.

There is one thing for which they are useless, however—flower arrangements. As soon as you pick them and put them in water, their flowers close tight.

 ## culinary

Both the leaves and root have long been eaten as a highly nutritious salad. In the last century, cultivated forms with large leaves were developed as a fall and spring vegetable. The leaves were usually blanched in the same way as endive. Dandelion salad in spring is also considered a blood cleanser, owing to its diuretic and digestive qualities. The leaves are very high in vitamins A, B, C and D; the A content being higher than that of carrots.

The flowers make an excellent country wine and dandelion roots provide, when dried, chopped and roasted, the best-known substitute for coffee.

Dandelion and Bacon Salad

Serves 4

½ lb. young dandelion leaves
¼ lb. streaky bacon, diced
½ in. slice white bread, cubed
4 tablespoons olive or walnut oil
1 tablespoon white wine vinegar
1 clove garlic, crushed
Salt and freshly ground pepper
Oil for cooking

Wash and dry the leaves and tear into the salad bowl. Make a vinaigrette using olive oil and vinegar, and season to taste, adding a little sugar if desired. Fry the bacon, crushed garlic and bread in oil until golden brown. Pour the contents of the pan over the leaves and turn the leaves until thoroughly coated. Add the vinaigrette and toss again. Serve at once.

Teucrium chamaedrys L.

WALL GERMANDER

Also known as Ground oak and Wild germander. From the family Lamiaceae.

This attractive plant, native of Europe, is now naturalized in Britain and other countries in the temperate zone. It is found on dry limy/alkaline soils.

The Latin *Teucrium* is said to have been named after Teucer, first king of Troy. It is the ancient Greek word for "ground oak," its leaves resembling those of the oak tree.

In medieval times, it was a popular strewing herb and a remedy for dropsy, jaundice and gout. It was also used in powder form for treating head colds, and as a snuff.

Pests and Diseases
Wall germander rarely suffers from pests or diseases.

Maintenance
Spring Sow seeds. Take softwood cuttings. Trim established plants and hedges. Divide established plants.
Summer Trim plants after flowering, take semi-hardwood cuttings.
Fall Trim hedges.
Winter Protect when temperatures drop below 23°F (−5°C).

Garden Cultivation
Wall germander needs a well-drained soil (slightly alkaline) and a sunny position. It is hardier than lavender and cotton lavender, and makes an ideal hedging or edging plant. To make a good dense hedge, plant at a distance of 6 in. If you clip the hedge in spring and fall to maintain its shape, you will never need to cut it hard back.

It can also be planted in rockeries, and in stone walls where it looks most attractive. During the growing season it does not need extra water, even in hot summers, nor does it need extra protection in cold winters.

Harvesting
For drying for medicinal use, pick leaves before flowering, and flowering stems when the flowers are in bud.

 ## varieties

Teucrium chamaedrys
Wall Germander
Evergreen hardy perennial. Ht. 18 in., spread 8 in. Pink flowers from midsummer to early fall. The leaves are mid-green and shaped like miniature oak leaves with crumpled edges. Zone 6.

Teucrium fruticans
Tree Germander
Evergreen hardy perennial. Ht. 3–6 ft., spread 6–12 ft. Blue flowers in summer. The leaves are aromatic, gray/green with a white underside. Zone 8.

Teucrium x lucidrys
Hedge Germander
Evergreen hardy perennial. Ht. 18 in., spread 8 in. Pink flowers from midsummer to early fall. The leaves are dark green, small, shiny and oval. When rubbed, they smell pleasantly spicy. Zone 5.

 ## cultivation

Propagation
Seed
Sow the small seeds in spring. Use a prepared seed or plug tray and a standard seed compost mixed in equal parts with composted fine bark. Cover with perlite. Germination can be erratic—from 2–4 weeks. When the seedlings are large enough to handle, plant in a prepared site 8 in. apart.

Cuttings
This is a better method of propagating germander. Take softwood cuttings from the new growth in spring, or semihardwood in summer. Ensure compost does not dry out or become sodden.

Division
The teucriums produce creeping rootstock in the spring and are easy to divide. Dig up the plants, split them in half, and replant in a chosen site.

 ## container growing

Looks good in containers. Use a soil-based compost mixed in equal parts with composted fine bark. Only feed in the flowering season. Keep on the dry side in winter.

 ## culinary

Used extensively in the flavoring of liqueurs.

 ## medicinal

Its herbal use today is minor. However, there is a revival of interest, and some use it as a remedy for digestive and liver troubles, anemia and bronchitis.

Teucrium scorodonia

WOOD SAGE

Also known as Gypsy sage, Mountain sage, Wild sage and Garlic sage. From the family Lamiaceae.

This plant is a native of Europe and has become naturalized in Britain and other countries in the temperate zone.

There is not much written about wood sage apart from the fact that, like alecost, it was used in making ale before hops were introduced. However, Gertrude Jekyll recognized its value, and with renewed interest in her gardens comes a revival of interest in wood sage.

 ## varieties

Teucrium scorodonia
Wood Sage
Hardy perennial. Ht. 12–24 in., spread 10 in. Pale greenish-white flowers in summer. Soft green heart-shaped leaves, which have a mild smell of crushed garlic. Zone 6.

Teucrium scorodonia 'Crispum'
Curly Wood Sage
Hardy perennial. Ht. 14 in., spread 12 in. Pale greenish-white flowers in summer. The leaves are soft, oval and olive green with a reddish tinge to their crinkled edges. Whenever it is on show it causes much comment. Zone 6.

 ## cultivation

Propagation
Wood sage can be propagated by seed, cuttings or division. Curly wood sage can only be propagated by cuttings or division.

Seed
Sow the fairly small seed under protection in the fall or spring, in a prepared seed or plug tray. Use a standard seed compost mixed in equal parts with composted fine bark, and cover with perlite. Germination can be erratic, taking from 2–4 weeks. When the seedlings are large enough to handle, pot and winter under cover in a cold frame. In the spring, after a period of hardening off, plant in a prepared site in the garden at a distance of 10 in.

Cuttings
Take softwood cuttings from the new growth in spring, or semihardwood cuttings in summer.

Division
Both wood sages produce creeping rootstock. In the spring they are easy to divide.

Pests and Diseases
In the majority of cases, it is free from pests and diseases.

Maintenance
Spring Sow seeds. Divide established plants. Take softwood cuttings.
Summer Take semihardwood cuttings.

Fall Sow seeds.
Winter No need for protection, the plants die back for the winter.

Garden Cultivation
It grows well in semishaded situations, but also thrives in full sun on sandy and gravelly soils. It will adapt quite happily to clay and heavy soils, but not produce such prolific growth.

Harvesting
Pick young leaves for fresh as required.

 ## container growing

I have grown curly wood sage most successfully in containers. The plain wood sage does not look quite so attractive. Use a soil-based compost mixed in equal parts with composted fine bark, and plant in a large container—its creeping rootstock can too easily become pot-bound. Only feed twice in a growing season, otherwise the leaves become large, soft and floppy. When the plant dies back, put it somewhere cool and keep it almost dry.

 ## medicinal

Wood sage has been used to treat blood disorders, colds and fevers, and as a diuretic and wound herb.

 ## culinary

The leaves of ordinary wood sage have a mild garlic flavor. When young and tender, the leaves can be added to salads for variety. But use sparingly as they are slightly bitter.

Thymus
THYME

From the family Lamiaceae.

This is a genus comprising numerous species that are very diverse in appearance and come from many different parts of the world. They are found as far afield as Greenland and Western Asia, although the majority grow in the Mediterranean region.

This ancient herb was used by the Egyptians in oil form for embalming. The Greeks used it in their baths and as an incense in their temples. The Romans used it to purify their rooms, and most probably its use spread through Europe as their invasion train swept as far as Britain. In the Middle Ages, drinking it was part of a ritual to enable one to see fairies, and it was one of many herbs used in nosegays to purify the odors of disease. Owing to its antiseptic properties, judges also used it along with rosemary to prevent jail fever.

Thymus vulgaris

Mixed thymes

 varieties

There are so many species of thyme that I am only going to mention a few of interest. New ones are being discovered each year. They are eminently collectable. Unfortunately their names can be unreliable, a nursery preferring its pet name or one traditional to it, rather than the correct one.

Thymus caespititius
Caespititius Thyme
Evergreen hardy perennial. Ht. 4 in., spread 8 in. Pale pink flowers in summer. The leaves narrow, bright green and close together on the stem. Makes an attractive low-growing mound, good between paving stones. Zone 7.

Thymus camphoratus
Camphor Thyme
Evergreen half-hardy perennial. Ht. 12 in., spread 8 in. Pink/mauve flowers in summer, large green leaves smelling of camphor. Makes a beautiful compact bush. Zone 7.

Thymus cilicicus
Sicily Thyme
Evergreen hardy perennial. Ht. 2 in., spread 8 in. Pink flowers in summer. The leaves are bright green, narrow and pointed, growing close together on the stem with an odd celery scent. Makes an attractive low-growing mound, and is good between paving stones. Zone 9.

Thymus citriodorus
Lemon Thyme
Evergreen hardy perennial. Ht. 12 in., spread 8 in. Pink flowers in summer. Fairly large green leaves with a strong lemon scent. Excellent culinary thyme, combines well with many chicken or fish dishes. Zone 6.

Thymus citriodorus 'Golden King'
Golden King Thyme

Evergreen hardy perennial. Ht. 12 in., spread 8 in. Pink flowers in the summer. Fairly large green leaves variegated with gold, strongly lemon-scented. Excellent culinary thyme, combines well with many dishes, like chicken, fish and salad dressing. Zone 6.

Thymus citriodorus 'Silver Queen'
Silver Queen Thyme

Evergreen hardy perennial. Ht. 12 in., spread 8 in. Pink flowers in the summer. Fairly large leaves, gray with silver variegation, a strong lemon scent. Excellent culinary thyme, combines well with many dishes, like chicken and salad dressing. Zone 6.

Thymus Coccineus Group
Coccineus Thyme

Also known as creeping red thyme. Evergreen hardy perennial, prostrate form, a creeper. Red flowers in summer. Green small leaves. Decorative, aromatic and good groundcover. Zone 4.

Thymus comosus

Evergreen hardy perennial. Ht. 4 in., spread 8 in. Attractive clusters of pink flowers in summer. Small mid-green round leaves. Excellent for growing in gravel. Zone 5.

Thymus doerfleri
Doerfleri Thyme

Evergreen half-hardy perennial. Ht. 1 in., spread 8 in. Mauve/pink flowers in summer, gray, hairy, thin leaves, which are mat forming. Decorative thyme, good for rockeries, hates being wet in winter. Originates from the Balkan Peninsula. Zone 8.

Thymus herba-barona

Thymus 'Jekka'

Thymus doerfleri 'Bressingham'
Bressingham Thyme

Evergreen hardy perennial. Ht. 1 in., spread 8 in. Mauve/pink flowers in summer. Thin, green, hairy leaves, which are mat forming. Decorative thyme, good for rockeries, hates being wet in winter. Zone 8.

Thymus 'Doone Valley'
Doone Valley Thyme

Evergreen hardy perennial. Ht. 3 in., spread 8 in. Purple flowers in summer. Round variegated green and gold leaves with a lemon scent. Very decorative, can be used in cooking if nothing else is available. Zone 7.

Thymus 'Fragrantissimus'
Orange-Scented Thyme

Evergreen hardy perennial. Ht. 12 in., spread 8 in. Small pale pink/white flowers in summer. The leaves are small, narrow, grayish/green, and smell of spicy orange. Combines well with stir-fry dishes, poultry—especially duck—and even molasses pudding. Zone 6.

Thymus herba-barona
Caraway Thyme

Evergreen hardy perennial. Ht. 1 in., spread 8 in. Rose-colored flowers in summer. Dark green small leaves with a unique caraway scent. Good in culinary dishes especially stir-fry and meat. It combines well with beef. Zone 4.

Thymus 'Jekka'
Jekka's Thyme

Evergreen hardy perennial. Ht. 4 in., spread 12 in. Clusters of small pink and white flowers in early summer. Prolific mid-green aromatic leaves. Spreading habit. Good culinary flavor. Zone 6.

Thymus polytrichus subsp. *britannicus*
Wild Creeping Thyme

Also known as mother of thyme and creeping thyme.

Evergreen hardy perennial. Ht. 1 in., spread 8 in. Pale mauve flowers in summer. Small dark green leaves which, although mildly scented, can be used in cooking. Wild thyme has been valued by herbalists for many centuries. Zone 4.

Thymus 'Porlock'
Porlock Thyme

Evergreen hardy perennial. Ht. 12 in., spread 8 in. Pink flowers in summer. Fairly large green leaves with a mild but definite thyme flavor and scent. Excellent culinary thyme. Medicinal properties are antibacterial and antifungal. Zone 4.

Thymus pseudolanuginosus
Woolly Thyme

Evergreen hardy perennial. Ht. 1 in., spread 8 in. Pale pink/mauve flowers for most of the summer. Gray hairy mat-forming leaves. Good for rockeries and in stone paths or walls. Dislikes wet winters. Zone 5.

Thymus pulegioides
Broad-Leaved Thyme

Evergreen hardy perennial. Ht. 3 in., spread 8 in. Pink/mauve flowers in summer. Large round dark green leaves with a strong thyme flavor. Good for culinary uses, excellent for groundcover and good in hanging baskets. Zone 4.

Thymus pulegioides 'Aureus'
Golden Thyme

Evergreen hardy perennial. Ht. 12 in., spread 8 in. Pale pink/lilac flowers. Green leaves that turn gold in summer, good flavor, combining well with vegetarian dishes. Zone 6.

Thymus pulegioides 'Bertram Anderson'
Bertram Anderson Thyme

Evergreen hardy perennial. Ht. 4 in., spread 8 in. Pink/mauve flowers in summer. More of a round mound than 'Archer's Gold' and the leaves are slightly rounder with a more even golden look to the leaves. Decorative and culinary, it has a mild thyme flavor. Zone 6.

Thymus 'Redstart'
Redstart Thyme

Evergreen hardy perennial. Ht. 2 in., spread 8 in.. Bright red flowers in summer. Small dark green round leaves. Decorative, aromatic and good groundcover. Zone 4.

Thymus serpyllum var. albus
Creeping White Thyme
Evergreen hardy perennial, prostrate form, a creeper. White flowers in summer. Bright green small leaves. Decorative aromatic and good groundcover. Zone 4.

Thymus serpyllum 'Annie Hall'
Annie Hall Thyme
Evergreen hardy perennial, prostrate form, a creeper. Pale pink flowers in summer. Small green leaves. Decorative, aromatic and good groundcover. Zone 4.

Thymus serpyllum 'Goldstream'
Goldstream Thyme
Evergreen hardy perennial, prostrate form, a creeper. Pink/mauve flowers in summer. Green/gold variegated small leaves. Decorative, aromatic and good groundcover. Zone 4.

Thymus serpyllum 'Lemon Curd'
Lemon Curd Thyme
Evergreen hardy perennial, prostrate form, a creeper. White/pink flowers in summer. Bright green lemon-scented small leaves. Decorative, aromatic and good groundcover. Can be used in cooking if nothing else available. Zone 4.

Thymus serpyllum 'Minimalist'
Minimalist Thyme
Evergreen hardy perennial, prostrate form, a creeper. Pink flowers in summer. Tiny leaves, very compact. Decorative, aromatic and good groundcover. Ideal for growing between pavings and alongside paths. Zone 4.

Thymus 'Redstart'

Thymus comosus

Thymus serpyllum 'Pink Chintz' AGM
Pink Chintz Thyme
Evergreen hardy perennial, prostrate form, a creeper. Pale pink flowers in summer. Grey green small hairy leaves. Decorative, aromatic, good groundcover. Does not like being wet in winter. Zone 4.

Thymus serpyllum 'Rainbow Falls'
Rainbow Falls Thyme
Evergreen hardy perennial, prostrate form, a creeper. Purple flowers in summer. Variegated green/gold small leaves. Decorative, aromatic and good groundcover. Zone 4.

Thymus serpyllum 'Russetings'
Russetings Thyme
Evergreen hardy perennial, prostrate form, a creeper. Purple/mauve flowers in summer. Small green leaves. Decorative, aromatic and good groundcover. Zone 4.

Thymus serpyllum 'Snowdrift'
Snowdrift Thyme
Evergreen hardy perennial, prostrate form, a creeper. Masses of white flowers in summer. Small green round leaves. Decorative, aromatic and good groundcover. Zone 4.

Thymus vulgaris
Common (Garden) Thyme
Evergreen hardy perennial. Ht. 12 in., spread 8 in. Mauve flowers in summer. Thin green aromatic leaves. This is the thyme everyone knows. Use in stews, salads, sauces etc. Medicinal properties are antibacterial and antifungal. Zone 4.

Thymus vulgaris 'Silver Posie'
Silver Posie Thyme
Evergreen hardy perennial. Ht. 12 in., spread 8 in. Pale pink/lilac flower. The leaves have a very pretty

grey/silver variegation with a tinge of pink on the underside. This is a good culinary thyme and looks very attractive in salads. Zone 4.

Thymus zygis
Zygis Thyme
Evergreen half-hardy perennial. Ht. 12 in., spread 8 in. White attractive flowers. Small thin grey/green leaves which are aromatic. This is an attractive thyme which is good for rockeries. Originates from Spain and Portugal, therefore does not like cold wet winters. Zone 7.

Upright Thymes
Up to 12 in.:
T. caespititius, T. cilicicus Boiss. & Bail., T. Jekka, T. pulegioides 'Bertram Anderson'

12 in. and above:
T. camphoratus, T. citriodorus, T. 'Fragrantissimus', T. 'Porlock', T. vulgaris

Creeping Thymes
T. Coccineus Group, T. doerfleri, T. 'Doone Valley', T. Herba-barona, T. pseudolanuginosus and all T. serpyllum.

 ## cultivation

Propagation
To maintain the true plant, it is better to grow the majority of thymes from softwood cuttings. Only a very few, such as T. vulgaris and T. 'Fragrantissimus,' can be propagated successfully from seed.

Seed
Sow the very fine seed in early spring using the cardboard technique (see page 265) on the surface of prepared trays (seed or plug), using a standard seed compost mixed in equal parts with composted fine bark. Give a bottom heat of 60–70°F1 (5–21°C). Do not cover. Keep watering to the absolute minimum, as these seedlings are prone to damping off disease. When the young plants are large enough and after a period of hardening off, plant out in the garden in late spring/early summer, 9–15in. apart.

Cuttings
Thymes are easily increased by softwood cuttings from new growth in early spring or summer. The length of

the cutting should be 2–3 in. Use a standard seed compost mixed in equal parts with composted fine bark. Winter the young plants under protection and plant the following spring.

Division
Creeping thymes put out aerial roots as they spread, which makes them very easy to divide in late spring.

Layering
An ideal method for mature thymes that are getting a bit woody. Use either the strong branch method of layering in early autumn or mound layer in early spring.

Pests and Diseases
Being such an aromatic plant, it does not normally suffer from pests but, if the soil or compost is too rich, thyme may be attacked by aphids. Treat with a liquid horticultural soap. All varieties will rot if they become too wet in a cold winter.

Maintenance
Spring Sow seeds. Divide established plants. Trim old plants. Layer old plants.
Summer Take cuttings of nonflowering shoots. Trim back after flowering.
Autumn Protect tender thymes. Layer old plants.
Winter Protect containers and only water if absolutely necessary.

Garden Cultivation
Thymes need to be grown in poor soil, in a well-drained bed to give their best flavour. They are drought-loving plants and will need protection from cold winds, hard and wet winters. Sow seed when the soil has warmed and there is no threat of frost. Thin on average to 8 in. apart.

It is essential to trim all thymes after flowering; this not only promotes new growth, but also stops the plant from becoming woody and sprawling in the wrong direction.

In very cold areas grow it in the garden as an annual or in containers and then winter with protection.

Harvesting
As thyme is an evergreen it can be picked fresh all year round provided you are not too greedy. For preserving, pick before it is in flower. Either dry the leaves or put them in a vinegar or oil.

 container growing

All varieties suit being grown in containers. They like a free-draining poor soil (low in nutrients); if grown in a rich soil they will become soft and the flavour will be impaired. Use a soil-based compost mixed in equal parts with composted fine bark; water sparingly, keeping the container bordering on dry, and in winter definitely dry – only watering if absolutely necessary, when the leaves begin to lose too much color. Feed only occasionally in the summer months. Put the container in a sunny spot, which will help the aromatic oils come to the leaf surface and impart a better flavour. Trim back after flowering to maintain shape and promote new growth.

 medicinal

Thyme has strong antiseptic properties. The tea makes a gargle or mouthwash, and is excellent for sore throats and infected gums. It is also good for hangovers.

The essential oil is antibacterial and antifungal and used in the manufacture of toothpaste, mouthwash, gargles and other toilet articles. It can also be use to kill mosquito larvae. A few drops of the oil added to the bath water helps ease rheumatic pain, and it is often used in liniments and massage oils.

 warning

Although a medical dose drawn from the whole plant is safe, any amount of the volatile oil is toxic and should not be used internally except by prescription. Avoid altogether if you are pregnant.

 culinary

Thyme is an aid to digestion and helps break down fatty foods. It is one of the main ingredients of bouquet garni; it is good, too, in stocks, marinades and stews; and a sprig or two with half an onion makes a great herb stuffing for chicken.

Poached Trout with Lemon Thyme
Serves 4

4 trout, cleaned and gutted
Salt
6 peppercorns (whole)
4 fresh bay leaves
1 small onion cut into rings
1 lemon
1 sprig lemon thyme
1 tablespoon chopped lemon thyme leaves
½ cup white wine
2 tablespoons fresh snipped garlic chives
⅓ cup butter

Place the trout in a large frying pan. Sprinkle with salt and add the peppercorns. Place one bay leaf by each trout. Put the onion rings on top of the trout, cut half the lemon into slices and arrange this over the trout, add the thyme sprig, and sprinkle some of the chopped thyme leaves over the whole lot. Pour in the wine and enough water just to cover the fish. Bring it to the boil on top of the stove and let it simmer uncovered for 6 minutes for fresh trout, 20 minutes for frozen.

Mix the remaining chopped lemon thyme and garlic chives with the butter in a small bowl. Divide this mixture into 4 equal portions. When the trout are cooked lift them out gently, place on plates with a slice of lemon and the herb butter on the top. Serve with new potatoes.

Trapaeolum majus
NASTURTIUM

Also known as Garden nasturtium, Indian cress and Large cress. From the family Tropaeolaceae.

Nasturtiums are native to South America, especially Peru and Bolivia, but are now cultivated worldwide.

The generic name, *Tropaeolum*, is derived from the Latin *tropaeum*, meaning "trophy" or "sign of victory." After a battle was finished, a tree-trunk was set up on the battlefield and hung with the captured helmets and shields. It was thought that the round leaves of the nasturtium looked like shields and the flowers like blood-stained helmets.

It was introduced into Spain from Peru in the 16th century and reached London shortly afterwards. When first introduced it was known as *Nasturcium indicum* or *Nasturcium peruvinum*, which is how it got its common name Indian cress. The custom of eating its petals, and using them for tea and salads, comes from the Orient.

 varieties

Tropaeolum majus
Nasturtium
Half-hardy annual. Ht. and spread 12 in. Red/orange flowers from summer to early fall. Round, mid-green leaves. All zones.

***Tropaeolum majus* Alaska Series**
Nasturtium Alaska (Variegated)
Half-hardy annual. Ht. and spread 12 in. Red, orange and yellow flowers from summer to early fall. Round, variegated (cream and green) leaves. All zones.

***Tropaeolum majus* 'Peaches & Cream'**
Nasturtium Peaches & Cream
Half-hardy annual. Ht. 8 in., spread 12 in. Cream and orange flowers from summer to early fall. Round, mid-green leaves. All zones.

A few special species of interest:

Tropaeolum peregrinum
Canary Creeper
Tender perennial. Climber: Ht. 6 ft. Small, bright yellow flowers with two upper petals that are much larger and fringed from summer until first frost. Gray/green leaves with five lobes. In cool areas, best grown as an annual. Zone 9.

Tropaeolum polyphyllum
Hardy perennial. Ht. 2–3 in., spread 12 in. or more. Fairly small yellow flowers from summer to early fall. Leaves gray/green on trailing stems. A fast-spreading plant once established. Looks good on banks or hanging down walls. Zone 8.

Tropaeolum speciosum
Flame Creeper
Hardy perennial. Climber: Ht. 9 ft. Scarlet flowers in summer followed by bright blue fruits surrounded by deep red calyxes in the fall. Leaves green with six lobes. This very dramatic plant should be grown like honeysuckle with its roots in the shade and head in the sun. Zone 8.

Tropaelolum majus 'Peaches & Cream'

cultivation

Propagation

Seed

The seeds are large and easy to handle. To have plants flowering early in the summer, sow in early spring under protection directly into prepared pots or cell trays using a standard seed compost, and cover lightly with compost. Plugs are ideal, especially if you want to introduce the young plants into a hanging basket; otherwise use small pots to allow more flexibility before planting. When the seedlings are large enough and there is no threat of frosts, plant into a prepared site in the garden, or into containers.

Cuttings

Take cuttings of the perennial varieties in the spring from the new soft growth.

Pests and Diseases

Aphids and caterpillars of cabbage white butterfly and its relatives may cause a problem. If the infestation is light, the fly may be brushed off or washed away with soapy water.

Maintenance

Spring Sow seed early under protection, or after frosts in the garden.
Summer Deadhead flowers regularly to prolong the flowering season.
Fall Dig up dead plants.
Winter Plan next year.

Garden Cultivation

Nasturtiums prefer a well-drained, poor soil in full sun or partial shade. If the soil is too rich, leaf growth will

Trapaeolum majus

be made at the expense of the flowers. They are frost-tender and will suffer if the temperature falls below 40°F (4°C).

As soon as the soil has begun to warm and the frosts are over, nasturtiums can be sown directly into the garden. Sow individually 8 in. apart. For a border full of these plants, sow 6 in. apart. Claude Monet's garden at Giverny in France has a border of nasturtiums sprawling over a path that looks very effective.

Harvesting

Pick the flowers for fresh use only; they cannot be dried.

Pick the seed pods just before they lose their green color (for pickling in vinegar).

Pick the leaves for fresh use as required. They can be dried, but personally I don't think it is worth it.

 ## companion planting

This herb attracts blackfly away from vegetables such as cabbage and broad beans. It also attracts hoverflies, whose larvae attack aphids. Further, it is said to repel whitefly, woolly aphids and ants. Altogether it is a good tonic to any garden.

 ## container growing

This herb is excellent for growing in pots, tubs, window boxes and hanging baskets. Use a standard potting compost mixed in equal parts with composted fine bark. Do not feed, because all you will produce are leaves not flowers, but do keep well watered, especially in hot weather.

 ## medicinal

This herb is rarely used medicinally, although the fresh leaves contain vitamin C and iron as well as an antiseptic substance, which is at its highest before the plant flowers.

 ## warning

Use the herb with caution. Do not eat more than ½ oz at a time or 1 oz. per day.

 ## culinary

I had a group from the local primary school around the farm to talk about herbs. Just as they were leaving I mentioned that these pretty red flowers were now being sold in supermarkets for eating in salads. When a little boy looked at me in amazement, I suggested he try one. He ate the whole flower without saying a word. One of his friends said, "What does it taste like?" With a huge smile he asked if he could pick another flower for his friend, who ate it and screamed, "Pepper pepper...." The seeds, flowers and leaves are all now eaten for their spicy taste. They are used in salads also as an attractive garnish. The pickled flower buds provide a good substitute for capers.

Nasturtium Cream Cheese Dip

¼ lb. cream cheese
2 teaspoons tender nasturtium leaves, chopped
3 nasturtium flowers

Blend the cream cheese with the chopped leaves. Put the mixture into a bowl and decorate with the flowers. Eat this mixture as soon as possible because it can become bitter if left standing.

NETTLE

Also known as Common nettle, Stinging nettle, Devil's leaf and Devil's plaything. From the family Urticaceae.

This plant is found all over the world. It is widespread on wasteland, especially on damp and nutrient-rich soil.

The generic name *Urtica* comes from the Latin *uro*, meaning "I burn." The Roman nettle *Urtica pilulifera* originally came to Britain with the invading Roman army. The soldiers used the plants to keep themselves warm. They flogged their legs and arms with nettles to keep their circulation going.

The use of nettles in the making of fabric goes back for thousands of years. Nettle cloth was found in a Danish grave of the later Bronze Age, wrapped around cremated bones. It was certainly made in Scotland as late as the 18th century. The Scottish poet, Thomas Campbell, wrote then of sleeping in nettle sheets in Scotland and dining off nettle tablecloths. Records show that it was still being used in the early 20th century in Tyrol.

In the Middle Ages it was believed that nettles marked the dwelling place of elves and were a protection against sorcery. They were also said to prevent milk from being affected by house trolls or witches.

Settlers in New England in the 17th century were surprised to find that this old friend and enemy had crossed the Atlantic with them. It was included in a list of plants that sprang up unaided. Before World War II, vast quantities of nettles were imported to Britain from Germany. During the war there was a drive to collect as much of the homegrown nettle as possible. The dark green dye obtained from the plant was used as camouflage, and chlorophyll was extracted for use in medicines.

 varieties

Urtica dioica
Stinging Nettle
Hardy perennial. Ht. 5 ft., spread infinite on creeping rootstock. The male and female flowers are on separate plants. The female flowers hang down in clusters, the male flower clusters stick out. The color for both is a yellowish green. The leaves are green toothed and have bristles. This is the variety that can be eaten when young. Zone 3.

Urtica pilulifera
Roman Nettle
Hardy perennial. Ht. 5 ft., spread infinite on creeping rootstock. This looks very similar to the common stinging nettle, but its sting is said to be more virulent. Zone 3.

Urtica urens
Small Nettle
Hardy annual. Ht. and spread 12 in. The male and female flowers are in the same cluster and are a greenish white in color. The green leaves are deeply toothed and have bristles. Zone 3.

Urtica urentissima
Devil's Leaf
This is a native of Timor and the sting said to be so virulent that its effects can last for months and may even cause death. A plant of interest, but not for the garden. Zone 3.

Urtica dioica in flower

NETTLE

cultivation

Propagation

Seed
Nettles can be grown from seed sown in the spring. But I am sure any of your friends with a garden would be happy to give you a root.

Division
Divide established roots early in spring before they put on much leaf growth, and the sting is least strong.

Pests and Diseases
Rarely suffers from pests and disease (at least none subject to eradication!).

Maintenance
Spring Sow seeds, divide established plants.
Summer Cut plants back if they are becoming invasive.
Fall Cut back the plants hard into the ground.
Winter No need for protection, full hardy.

Garden Cultivation
Stinging nettles are the scourge of the gardener and the farmer and the pest of children in summer, but are very useful in the garden, attracting butterflies and moths, and making an excellent caterpillar food. They will grow happily in any soil. It is worth having a natural corner in the garden where these and a few other wildflowers can be planted.

Harvesting
Cut young leaves in early spring for use as a vegetable.

medicinal

The nettle has many therapeutic applications but is principally of benefit in all kinds of internal hemorrhages, as a diuretic in jaundice and hemorrhoids, and as a laxative. It is also used in dermatological problems including eczema.

Nettles make a valuable tonic after the long winter months when they provide one of the best sources of minerals. They are an excellent remedy for anemia. Their vitamin C content makes sure that the iron they contain is properly absorbed.

Nettle hair conditioner

other uses

Whole plants yield a greenish/yellow woollen dye.

Traditionally the old gardeners used nettles to make a spray to get rid of aphids, especially blackfly. They soaked the nettles in rain water for a period of time, then used the steeped water to spray the infected plants. It was also said to be a good plant tonic.

Nettles have a long-standing reputation for preventing hair loss and making the hair soft and shiny. They also have a reputation for eliminating dandruff.

Nettle Rinse and Conditioner
Use this as a final rinse after washing your hair, or massage it into your scalp and comb through the hair every other day. Store it in a small bottle in the refrigerator.

1 big handful-size bunch of nettles
2 cups water

Wear rubber gloves to cut the nettles. Wash thoroughly and put the bunch into an enamel saucepan with enough cold water to cover. Bring to the boil, cover and simmer for 15 minutes. Strain the liquid into a jug and allow to cool.

warning

Do not eat old plants uncooked; they can produce kidney damage and symptoms of poisoning. The plants must be cooked thoroughly to be safe.

Handle all plants with care; they do sting.

culinary

Nettles are an invaluable food, rich in both vitamins and minerals.

In spring the fresh leaves may be cooked and eaten like spinach, made into a delicious soup, or drunk as a tea.

When cooked, I am pleased to say, nettles lose their sting.

Nettle Soup
Serves 4

½ lb. young nettle leaves
¼ cup oil or butter
1 small onion, chopped
½ lb. cooked potatoes, peeled and diced
3 cups pints milk
1 teaspoon each (mix, fresh, chopped) sweet marjoram, sage, lemon thyme
2 teaspoons fresh chopped lovage
2 tablespoons, cream and French parsley, chopped, optional

Pick only the fresh young nettle leaves, and wear gloves to remove from stalks and wash them. Heat the oil in a saucepan, add the chopped onions, slowly sweat them until clear. Then add the nettles and stew gently for about a further 10 minutes. Add the chopped potatoes, all the herbs and the milk and simmer for a further 10 minutes. Allow to cool then put all the ingredients into a food processor and blend. Return to a saucepan over gentle heat. Add a swirl of cream to each bowl and sprinkle some chopped French parsley over the top. Serve with French bread.

Valeriana officinalis

VALERIAN

Also known as All heal, Set all, Garden heliotrope, Cut finger, and Phu. From the family Valerianaceae.

This herb is indigenous to Europe and West Asia and is now naturalized in North America. It can be found in grasslands, ditches, damp meadows and close to streams. The name may come from the Latin *valere*, "to be healthy," an allusion to its powerful medicinal qualities. The root is the medicinal part of this herb which, when dug up, literally stinks, hence another of its common names "phu." But to cats the scent of this herb is sheer elixir, even more than catmint *(Nepeta cateria)*, and it is said the Pied Piper of Hamelin carried the root to entice the cats to eat the rats of Hamelin. A tincture of valerian was employed in World Wars I and II to treat shellshock and nervous stress.

 varieties

Valeriana officinalis
Valerian
Hardy herbaceous perennial. Ht. up to 4½ ft., spread 3ft. Clusters of small, sweetly scented white flowers that are often tinged with pink in summer. Leaves are mid-green, deeply divided and toothed around the edges. Short conical rootstock which, when broken or cut, exudes a strong, rather unpleasant aroma. Zone 5.

Other varieties of special interest and well worth looking out for are:

Valeriana jatamansii (Valeriana wallichii)
Spikenard, Nard, Indian Valerian, Tagara
Hardy herbaceous perennial. Ht. 4–10 in. and spread 18 in. Clusters of small white flowers in summer. Mid-green, toothed, heart-shaped leaves. In India the roots are used medicinally to treat hysteria, hypochondria and as a tranquilizer, and an essential oil is extracted from the sweet-smelling roots for use in perfumery. I was given this plant by Roy Lancaster, the well-known plantsman, who collected it in 1978 on one of his expeditions to the Himalayas. It has happily adapted to our climate. He grows his plant, from which he gave me a cutting, in the garden and I am growing it in a container using a soil-based compost mixed with 25 percent horticultural grit. This herb is often confused with, and medicinally substituted for, *Nardostachys grandiflora* (see below). Zone 5.

Nardostachys grandiflora
Nard, Spikenard, Musk Root
Hardy herbaceous perennial. Ht. and spread 10–12 in. Clusters of small pink to pale purple flowers in summer. Narrow, basal, lance-shaped, mid-green leaves. The roots of this plant have a sweet musk scent. This herb is a member of the Valerianaceae family, and often confused with *Valeriana jatamansii*. It is indigenous to the alpine Himalayas and has been used for thousands of years as a nervine tonic. It is mentioned in the Song of Solomon and was the substance used to anoint the feet of Jesus at the Last Supper. Zone 7.

VALERIAN

Valeriana jatamansii

 cultivation

Propagation
Seed
In spring, sow the fairly small seeds into prepared seed or module plug trays, using a standard seed compost. Press the seeds into the soil, cover with perlite. Do not cover with soil as this will delay germination. Place in a cold frame or cold greenhouse. Germination takes 3–4 weeks. Plant when large enough to handle, 24 in. apart.

Division
Divided established plants in the fall, or early spring, using two forks back to back, replanting into a well-prepared site.

Pests and Diseases
Valerians rarely suffer from pests and diseases.

Maintenance
Spring Sow seeds. Divide established plants.
Summer Cut back after flowering to prevent self-seeding.
Fall Divide established plants if required.
Winter A very hardy plant, does not need protection.

Garden Cultivation
The roots of this herb like to be kept cool and damp in summer, so plant in any soil that does not dry out in high summer, in sun or partial shade. Choose the position in your garden with care and remember, if you have to move the plant, that the scent of the broken roots will attract all the neighborhood cats.

Harvesting
Dig up the roots of a second- or third-year plant. Wash and remove the pale fibrous root. Cut the root into manageable slices for drying.

 companion planting

It is said that valerian makes a good companion plant when planted near vegetables; the roots release phosphorus and stimulate earthworm activity.

 container growing

Valerian can be grown in a container, but make sure that it is large enough to accommodate the root system. Use a soil-based potting compost. Position the container in partial shade so that the compost does not dry out. Water regularly throughout the growing season, especially in summer. Divide the plants each fall; this will prevent the roots rotting in the pots in wet winters.

 medicinal

This herb has been used for thousands of years as a sedative and relaxant. The dried roots are prepared into tablets, powder, capsules or tinctures which are then used as a safe, nonaddictive relaxant that reduces nervous tension and anxiety and promotes restful sleep.

This is an extremely useful herb for treating anxious or restless pets. I have had a number of cats and dogs and one dog in particular, Hampton, hated going in the car. After treating him with a few drops of valerian tincture, diluted in some water, prior to the journey he became much less frightened and slept peacefully throughout the journey, which made the family holiday even more enjoyable. I have also used it with the cats, especially if one had been injured in a fight, before cleaning their wounds or taking them to the vet for treatment. Cats are notoriously fussy about their food, but adore valerian which they find very soothing. Make a decoction by crushing 1 teaspoon of dried root, which is then added to 3½ cups of cold water. Leave for 24 hours. Strain the decoction into a clean, sterilized bottle. This will keep for 48 hours in a refrigerator. For a medium-sized, stressed or anxious cat, add 3 drops of the decoction to a small amount of water, which they will drink with relish.

 other uses

An infusion of the root sprayed onto the soil is said to attract earthworms. The root has been used as a bait in rat traps and to catch wild cats. Add the mineral-rich leaves to the compost heap.

 warning

Do not take for an extended period. Do not take during pregnancy.

Verbena officinalis
VERVAIN

Verbena officinalis

Also known as Holy herb, Simpler's joy, Pigeon's grass, Burvine, Wizard's herb, Herba sacra, Holy plant, European vervain, Enchanter's plant and Herba the cross. From the family Verbenaceae.

This herb is a native of Mediterranean regions. It has now become established elsewhere within temperate zones and, for that matter, wherever the Romans marched.

It is a herb of myth, magic and medicine. The Egyptians believed that it originated from the tears of Isis. The Greek priests wore amulets made of it, as did the Romans, who also used it to purify their altars after sacrifice. The Druids used it for purification and for making magic potions.

Superstition tells that when you pick vervain, you should bless the plant. This originates from a legend that it grew on the hill at Calgary, and was used to staunch the flow of Christ's blood at the Crucifixion.

In the Middle Ages it was an ingredient in a holy salve, a powerful protector against demons and disease: "Vervain and Dill hinders witches from their will."

Garden Cultivation
Vervain can be sown direct into the garden in the spring in a well-drained soil and a sunny position. It is better to sow or plant in clumps because the flower is so small that otherwise it will not show to advantage. But beware its capacity to self-seed.

Harvesting
Pick leaves as required. Cut whole plant when in bloom. Dry leaves or whole plant if required.

 ## container growing

Vervain does nothing for containers, and containers do nothing for vervain.

 ## medicinal

Vervain has been used traditionally to strengthen the nervous system, dispel depression and counter nervous exhaustion. It is also said to be effective in treating migraines and headaches of the nervous and bilious kind.

Chinese herbalists use a decoction to treat suppressed menstruation, and for liver problems and urinary tract infections.

 ## culinary

In certain parts of France, a tea is made from the leaves. Use with caution.

 ## warning

Avoid during pregnancy.

 ## varieties

Verbena officinalis
Vervain
Hardy perennial. Ht. 2–3 ft., spread 1 ft. or more. Small pale lilac flowers in summer. Leaves green, hairy and often deeply divided into lobes with curved teeth. This plant is not to be muddled with lemon verbena (*Aloysia triphylla*). Zone 4.

 ## cultivation

Propagation
Seed
Sow the small seeds in early spring in a prepared seed or plug tray using a standard seed compost. Cover with perlite. No need for extra heat. When the seedlings are large enough, and after hardening off, plant in a prepared site, 1 ft. apart.

Division
An established plant can be divided either in the spring or fall. It splits easily with lots of roots.

Pests and Diseases
If soil is too rich or high in nitrates, aphids can attack.

Maintenance
Spring Sow seeds. Divide established plants.
Summer Cut back after flowering to stop it self-seeding.
Fall Divide established plants.
Winter No need for protection; fully hardy.

Viola tricolor

HEARTSEASE

Also known as Wild pansy, Field pansy, Love lies bleeding, Love in idleness, Herb trinity, Jack behind the garden gate, Kiss me behind the garden gate, Kiss me love, Kiss me love at the garden gate, Kiss me quick, Monkey's face, Three faces under a hood, Two faces in a hood and Trinity violet. From the family Violaceae.

Heartsease is a wild flower in Europe and North America, growing on wasteland and in fields and hedgerows.

In the Middle Ages, due to the influence of Christianity and because of its tricolor flowers—white, yellow and purple—heartsease was called Trinitaria or Trinitatis Herba, the herb of the Blessed Trinity.

In the traditional language of flowers, the purple form meant memories, the white loving thoughts, and the yellow, souvenirs.

Viola tricolor

 varieties

Viola arvensis
Field Pansy
Hardy perennial. Ht. 2–4 in. The flowers are predominantly white or creamy, and appear in early summer. The green leaves are oval with shallow, blunt teeth. Zone 4.

Viola lutea
Mountain Pansy
Hardy perennial. Ht. 3–8 in. Single-colored flowers in summer vary from yellow to blue and violet. The leaves are green and oval near the base of the stem, narrower further up. Zone 4.

Viola tricolor
Heartsease
Hardy perennial, often grown as an annual. Ht. 6–12 in. Flowers from spring to fall. Green and deeply lobed leaves. Zone 4.

 cultivation

Propagation
Seed
Sow seeds under protection in the fall, either into prepared seed, plug trays or pots using a standard seed compost. Do not cover the seeds. No bottom heat required. Winter the seedlings in a cold frame or cold greenhouse. In the spring harden off and plant out at a distance of 6 in. apart.

Maintenance
Spring Sow seed.
Summer Deadhead flowers to maintain flowering.
Fall Sow seed for early spring flowers.
Winter No need to protect.

Garden Cultivation
Heartsease will grow in any soil, in partial shade or sun. Sow the seeds from spring to early fall where they are to flower. Press into the soil but do not cover.

Harvesting
Pick the flowers fully open from spring right through to late fall. Use fresh or for drying. The plant has the most fascinating seed capsules, each capsule splitting into three. The best time to collect seeds is midday when the maximum number of capsules will have opened.

 container growing

Heartsease look very pretty in any kind of container. Pick off the dead flowers as this appears to keep the plant flowering for longer.

 medicinal

An infusion of the flowers has long been prescribed for a broken heart. Less romantically, it is also a cure for bedwetting. An ointment made from it is good for eczema and acne and also for curing milk rust and cradle cap. Herbalists use it to treat gout, rheumatoid arthritis and respiratory disorders. An infusion of heartsease leaves added to bath water has proved beneficial to suffers of rheumatic disease.

 warning

In large doses, it may cause vomiting.

 other uses

Cleansing the skin and shampooing thinning hair.

 culinary

Add flowers to salads and to decorate sweet dishes.

Viola

VIOLET

From the family Violaceae.

There are records of sweet violets growing during the first century AD in Persia, Syria and Turkey. It is a native not only of these areas but also of North Africa and Europe. Violets have been introduced elsewhere and are now cultivated in several countries for their perfume.

This charming herb has been much loved for over 2,000 years and there are many stories associated with it. In a Greek legend, Zeus fell in love with a beautiful maiden called Io. He turned her into a cow to protect her from his jealous wife Hera. The earth grew violets for Io's food, and the flower was named after her.

The violet was also the flower of Aphrodite, the goddess of love, and of her son, Priapus, the god of gardens. The ultimate mark of the reverence in which the Greeks held sweet violet is that they made it the symbol of Athens.

For centuries perfumes have been made from the flowers of sweet violet mixed with the violet-scented roots of orris, and the last half of the 19th century saw intense interest in it— acres were cultivated to grow it as a market garden plant. Its main use was as a cut flower. No lady of quality would venture out without wearing a bunch of violets. It was also customary in gardens of large country houses to move the best clump of violets to a cold frame in late fall to provide flowers for the winter.

varieties

Viola odorata
Sweet Violet
Also known as garden violet. Hardy perennial. Ht. 3 in., spread 6 in. or more. Sweet-smelling white or purple flowers from late winter to early spring. Heart-shaped leaves form a rosette at the base, from which long-stalked flowers arise. *Viola odorata* is one of the few scented violets. It has been hybridized to produce Palma violets, with a single or double flower, in a range of rich colors. A recent revival in interest in this plant means it is being offered again by specialist nurseries. Zone 5.

Viola reichenbachiana
Wood Violet
Hardy perennial. Ht. 1–8 in., spread 6 in. or more. Pale lilac/blue flowers in early spring. Leaves are green and heart-shaped. The difference between this plant and the common dog violet is the flowering time; there is also a slight difference in flower color but it is difficult to discern. Zone 5.

Viola riviniana
Common Dog Violet
Also known as blue mice, hedging violet, horse violet and pig violet. Hardy perennial. Ht. 1–8 in., spread 6 in. or more. Pale blue/lilac flowers in early summer. Leaves are green and heart-shaped. This violet does not grow runners. Zone 5.

cultivation

Propagation
Seed
The small seed should be sown in early fall in prepared seed or plug trays. Use a soil-based seed compost; I have found violets prefer this. Water and cover with a layer of compost, and finally cover with a

sheet of glass or plastic. Put the trays either in a corner of the garden or in a cold frame (because the seeds germinate better if they have a period of stratification, though it will still be erratic). In the spring when the seedlings are large enough to handle, prick out into pots. If grown in cells allow a period of hardening off. Plant as soon as temperatures have risen at a distance of 12 in.

Cuttings
These can be taken from the parent plant, with a small amount of root attached, in early spring and rooted in cell trays, using a standard seed compost mixed in equal parts with composted fine bark. Harden off and plant into a prepared site in the garden in late spring when they are fully rooted. Water in well.

When using runners to propagate this plant, remove them in late spring and replant in a prepared site in the garden, 12 in. apart. Plant them firmly in the ground, making sure that the base of the crowns are well-embedded in the soil; water well.

Runners can be grown on in pots in early fall. Remove a well-rooted runner and plant in a pot of a suitable size. Overwinter in a cool greenhouse, watering from time to time to prevent red spider mite. Bring into the house in the spring to enjoy the flowers. After flowering, plant in the garden in a prepared site.

Division
Divide well-established plants as soon as flowering is over in early summer. It is a good idea to plant three crowns together for a better show and as an insurance policy against damage when splitting a crown. Replant in the garden in exactly the same way as for runners.

Pests and Diseases
The major pest for container-grown violets in warm weather is red spider mite. A good way to keep this at bay is to spray the leaves with water. If it is persistent, use a liquid insecticidal soap as per the manufacturer's instructions.

In propagating violets, the disease you will most probably come across is black root rot, which is encouraged by insufficient drainage in the compost.

Young plants can also be affected by damping off root rot, which is caused usually by too much water and insufficient drainage.

Maintenance
Spring Take cuttings from established plants. Remove

Viola riviniana

runners, pot or replant in the garden.
Summer Divide well-established plants, and replant.
Fall Sow seed. Pot root runners for wintering under cover.
Winter Feed the garden with well-rotted manure.

Garden Cultivation
Violets thrive best in a moderately heavy, rich soil in a semißshaded spot. If you have a light and/or gravelly soil, it is a good idea to add some texture—a mulch of well-rotted manure—the previous fall. In spring dig the manure in.

Plant in the garden as soon as the frosts have finished, allowing 12 in. between plants. When they become established, they quickly create a carpet of lovely sweet-smelling flowers. There is no need to protect any of the above-mentioned violets, they are fully hardy.

Harvesting
Pick the leaves in early spring for fresh use or for drying.
Gather the flowers just when they are opening, for drying or crystallizing.
Dig up the roots in the fall to dry for medicinal use.

 container growing

Violets make good container plants. Use a soil-based compost mixed in equal parts with composted fine bark. Give them a liquid feed of fertilizer (following the manufacturer's instructions) after flowering. During the summer months, place the container in partial shade. In winter they do not like heat, and if it is too warm they will become weak and fail to flower. So, it is most important that they are in a cool place with temperatures no higher than 45°F (7°C). There must also be

VIOLET

good air circulation, and watering should be maintained on a regular basis.

 culinary

The flowers of sweet violet are well known in crystallized form for decorating cakes, desserts, ice-cream and homemade sweets. They are also lovely in salads, and make an interesting oil—use an almond oil as base.

The flowers of common and dog violet can also be added to salads and used to decorate desserts. Their flavor is very mild in comparison to sweet violet, but they are just as attractive.

 medicinal

Only sweet violet has been used medicinally. Various parts are still used, most commonly, the rootstock. It is an excellent, soothing expectorant and is used to treat a range of respiratory disorders, such as bronchitis, coughs, whooping cough and head colds. It also has a cooling nature and is used to treat hangovers.

Made into a poultice, the leaves soothe sore, cracked nipples. Also they have a reputation for treating tumors, both benign and cancerous. Strong doses of the rhizome are emetic and purgative.

The flowers have a reputation for being slightly sedative and so can be helpful in cases of anxiety and insomnia.

 other uses

The flowers of sweet violets are used in potpourri, floral waters and perfumes.

Sweet violet perfume

CHASTE TREE

Vitex agnus-castus

Also known as Monks pepper, Lygos, Hemptree, Agnus castus, Abraham's tree and Chaste berry. From the family Verbenaceae.

This aromatic shrub, indigenous to the Mediterranean and Central Asia, has been used medicinally for thousands of years. The first known records of its medical use were made in the fourth century BC by Hippocrates; he used it to treat female disorders, particularly the diseases of the uterus. Historically the Christian monks used to chew the leaves and grind the dried berries over their food to reduce their libido. Agnus castus translates as "chaste lamb," which is the Christian symbol of purity. In Germany in the 20th century Dr. Gerhard Madaus conducted scientific research into the plant's effects on the female hormonal system. He subsequently developed a medicine made from the dried berries called "Agnolyt," which is still available today.

 varieties

Vitex agnus-castus
Chaste tree
Deciduous shrub. Ht. and spread 15 ft. Upright panicles of fragrant, tubular violet blue or pink flowers in late summer until mid-fall, which are followed by small round orange/red fruit. Dark green, aromatic leaves are divided into five or seven lance-shaped leaflets. Zone 7.

 cultivation

Propagation
Seed
The best time to sow the seeds is in the late fall when they are fresh. Sow into prepared plug module trays or small containers using a standard seed compost mixed in equal parts with perlite. Once the seedlings are large enough to handle, pot using a standard potting compost mixed in equal parts with composted fine bark. Place the container in a frost-free environment for the winter. Do not think it is dead when all you are left with is a twig for the first winter; new shoots will appear in the spring if you do not overwater. It will flower in the fourth or fifth summer.

Cuttings
The easiest and the most reliable method of propagation is by softwood cuttings taken in the late spring/early summer from nonflowering shoots. Prepare module plug trays or a small pot using a standard seed compost mixed in equal parts with perlite. Place the cuttings in a sheltered, warm environment; they do not need bottom heat. Once rooted, pot in exactly the same way as the seedlings and again winter in a frost-free environment. It will flower in the second or third summer.

Pests and Diseases
As the whole plant is aromatic, it is rarely attacked by pests. Overwatering of young container plants can cause rotting in winter, especially in cold and cool climates.

Maintenance
Spring Prune back last year's growth to 2 in.
Summer Take cuttings in early summer.
Fall Sow seeds.
Winter Protect from excessive wetness.

CHASTE TREE

Garden Cultivation

This most attractive aromatic shrub is worthy of a place in the garden: it smells good, looks good and does you good—what more can you ask of a plant? Plant in a fertile soil; it will tolerate dry soils, moist soils but not cold, heavy clay soils. When living in cold areas, plant against a warm, sunny wall; the wall will help cut down the rainfall by 25 percent and give added protection and warmth in winter. Allternatively, plant in full sun in a sheltered position. It will not tolerate shade.

Harvesting

The leaves are picked in early summer for use fresh or for drying. Stems are cut in late summer or fall and are dried. Roots are lifted, from plants over 5 years old in late summer and fall and dried. The fruits are harvested in the fall for use fresh or for drying. However this plant rarely sets fruit in cool or cold climates.

 ## companion planting

Good late nectar plant for butterflies, which is therefore beneficial for late pollination.

 ## container growing

From experience I know that this plant adapts happily to being grown in a container. Use a soil-based compost mixed in equal parts with composted fine bark. Feed the container throughout the growing season with a liquid feed following the manufacturer's instructions. In winter allow the plant to drop its leaves,

then clear away any fallen debris to prevent disease. Place the container in a sheltered spot. In wet conditions raise the pot on bricks so it does not become waterlogged.

 ## medicinal

Vitex agnus-castus is one of the most important herbs for treating menstrual and menopausal problems and infertility. The key part of the plant used is the berries, which are taken in tablet or tincture form. It is used to regulate the hormones, for increasing female fertility, for regulating irregular periods and during the menopause to balance the hormones. It is also used to relieve spasms of pain, especially PMS, and to treat migraines and acne associated with the menstrual cycle.

 ## other uses

The flowers are used in the making of perfume. A yellow dye is obtained from the leaves, the seed and the roots.

 ## warning

Do not take excessive doses. Do not take *Vitex agnus-castus* during pregnancy. Do not take when taking any other product or drug that affects the female hormone system, such as HRT or the contraceptive pill.

Vitex agnus-castus

 ## culinary

The small aromatic fruit when dried is often used as a pepper subsitute; the flavor is milder and spicier. Today, it is rare to find chaste tree berries in recipes, although they can appear in a Moroccan spice mixture called *ras el hanout*, which translates as "top (or head) of the shop," referring to the best combination of spices the seller can provide.

Ras el Hanout

No two recipes for this combination of spices are the same.

1 tablespoon dried chaste berries
2 cinnamon sticks, broken into several pieces
1 tablespoon cloves
1 tablespoon coriander seeds
1 tablespoon cumin seeds
1 tablespoon fenugreek
1 tablespoon fennel seeds
1 oz. dried Damask rose petals; these are
   available in Middle Eastern food stores

Place all the ingredients in a heavy-based metal frying pan and place over a low heat. Do not let them burn, but cook until the seeds begin to pop in the pan. As soon as they start, shake or toss gently, cook for a further minute, then allow to cool slightly. Remove all the ingredients from the frying pan and grind the mixture in a coffee grinder, mini food processor or pestle and mortar. Store in an airtight container in a cupboard, and use this mixed spice within 2 weeks with meat, vegetable and rice dishes.

Zingiber officinale
GINGER

Also known as Sweet ginger, Ginger root, Shunthi, and Adrak. From the family Zingiberaceae.

Ginger is a very ancient herb. Confucius (551–479 BC) was known to have eaten fresh ginger with every meal as a digestive and carminative, and it has been used in India from the Vedic period (1500 BC) when it was called Maha-aushadhi, which means "the great medicine." Together with black pepper, ginger was one of the most commonly traded spices during the 13th and 14th centuries. Arabs carried the rhizomes on their voyages to East Africa and Zanzibar to plant at coastal settlements. During this time in England, ginger was sought after, and one pound in weight of ginger was equivalent to the cost of a sheep.

Zingiber officinale roots

varieties

Zingiber officinale
Ginger
Tropical, subtropical, deciduous perennial. Ht. 5 ft., spread indefinite. The yellow/green flowers, with a deep purple and cream lip in summer, grow on a single stem and are followed by red fleshy fruits, each having three chambers containing several small black seeds. Commercially cultivated plants are often sterile. Aromatic long, mid-green, lance-shaped leaves. The root is a thick branching rhizome. Zone 9.

cultivation

Propagation
Seed
Rarely grown from seed as root cuttings are very simple and quick.

Cuttings
Unless you live in the tropics, the best source for fresh ginger root is from a good greengrocer. However, be aware that the quality can be variable. For example, air-freighted rhizomes can be often killed by the cold temperatures or they may have been treated with chemicals to inhibit sprouting. Choose a fresh, plump, juicy-looking root with a stout horn-like growing bud. Fill a pot with seed compost mixed in equal parts with vermiculite. Slice the root 2 in. below the bud, place in the container with the bud facing up, gently push the root into the compost, being careful not to break the bud. The compost should just cover the bud. Place the pot in a plastic bag and seal; put in a warm place or on a propagator at 68°F (20°C). In about 3 weeks, maybe longer depending on the warmth, shoots will emerge. As soon as they do, remove the plastic bag. Keep the container warm and out of direct sunlight until the plant is fully established. Then place in one size larger pot, using a soil-based potting compost mixed in equal parts with composted fine bark.

Division
Divide established plants in the spring. Use a spade to remove a clump, which includes some rhizomes, from the established plant in the garden, replanting into a prepared site in the garden. Alternatively, for container-raised plants, ease off some rhizomes either by hand or using two small forks, repotting into a container that

is just big enough. Use a soil-based potting compost mixed in equal parts with composted fine bark.

Pests and Diseases

Red spider mite can be an occasional problem in older plants: regular misting and keeping the leaves well-washed will reduce this. If it gets out of hand, use an insecticidal soap following the manufacturer's instructions. If you live in the northern hemisphere you might find it difficult to overwinter plants due to the low light levels.

Maintenance

Spring Take cuttings from fresh roots. Divide established plants.
Summer Feed container-grown plants regularly.
Fall Harvest roots, cut back on watering container-raised plants.
Winter Protect from frost. Minimum temperature 68°F (20°C).

Garden Cultivation

When grown outdoors in the tropics, it needs a minimum annual rainfall of 60 in., temperatures of 86°F (30°C) or over, a short dry season and a deep, fertile soil. It usually takes 5–9 months to produce a crop.

Zingiber officinale

In the northern hemisphere it is best grown as a container plant either indoors, in a sunroom or a heated greenhouse. However it rarely flowers outside of the tropics.

Harvesting

Outside the tropics one can only produce a small amount of fresh rhizome. The rhizome can be harvested in late fall. The leaves can be used as a flavoring; pick as required throughout the growing season. A fresh rhizome can be stored in the refrigerator for up to 2 weeks. Freshly grated ginger can be frozen.

 ## container growing

Container-raised plants do not produce much useful rhizome, although you can use the leaves in the kitchen for flavoring foods. Grow your plant in a soil-based potting compost mixed in equal parts with composted fine bark. In summer keep the compost damp and warm, place the container in a slightly shaded position and feed during the growing season weekly with a general-purpose liquid fertilizer. In dry weather, plants will benefit from being lightly misted with rainwater daily. In the fall cut back on the watering, keeping the plant fairly dry over the winter at a minimum of 68°F (20°C).

 ## medicinal

Ancient Indian and Chinese herbalists used this herb for many aliments. It has a wide range of demonstrated health-giving properties; it both stimulates the heart and settles the stomach. It will improve your digestion and circulation, reduce any inflammatory process in your body and improve the absorption of anything you eat. Ginger works best when treating post-operative nausea and morning sickness, although its effectiveness in treating sea-sickness and other forms of motion sickness is questioned by some scientists, and I personally can vouch that it did not help me.

Fresh rhizomes are said to help to reduce inflammation in conditions like osteo- and rheumatoid arthritis. In Ayurvedic medicine it is used as a cure for cholera, anorexia and "inflamed liver."

 ## culinary

When you buy fresh ginger, choose roots, which are often called "hands," that are plump, not shriveled. Fresh ginger, peeled and ground or grated into a pulp, is used in many types of curries and spicy foods. In India it is used in curries, in China it is often used with seafood and mutton, in Japan it is pickled and is known as *gari* and *beni-shoga* and eaten with sushi. In European cooking, ginger is mainly used in sweet preparations, spiced breads, biscuits and cakes. Many countries make liqueurs and drinks from the root; the Europeans make ginger beer and green ginger wine, and in China they make a liqueur called Canton, to name just a few.

Salmon, Watercress and Fresh Ginger

Serves 2
I love the combination of fish and ginger. Here is a very simple recipe that does not fail.

2 fillets of salmon, boned
1 tablespoon grated ginger
1 clove of garlic, finely choped
1 tablespoon chopped coriander leaf
Half a fresh lemon
I bunch of watercress, washed and chopped
Olive oil and balsamic vinegar dressing
*   (3 tablespoons olive oil, 1 tablespoon vinegar)*
2 pieces of foil large enough to encapsulate the
*   salmon fillets.*

Preheat the oven to 400°F/200°C.
Place the fillets of fresh salmon onto an individual piece of foil, sprinkle each fillet with the ginger, garlic and coriander and finish with the lemon juice. Wrap loosely with the foil, bake in the oven for about 14 minutes or until the fresh fish is cooked. Serve on the watercress that has been drizzled with an oil and balsamic vinegar dressing.

PROPAGATION

One of the great joys of gardening is propagating your own plants. Success is dependent on adequate preparation and the care and attention you give during the critical first few weeks. The principles remain the same, but techniques are constantly changing. There is always something new to discover.

The three main methods of propagating new plants are by seed, cuttings and layering.

This chapter provides general, step-by-step instructions for each of these methods. As there are always exceptions to a rule, please refer also to the propagation section under each individual herb.

Misting unit

seed

Sowing Outside
Most annual herbs grow happily, propagated year after year from seed sown directly into the garden. There are two herbs worth mentioning where that is not the case—sweet marjoram, because the seed is so small that it is better started in a pot; and basil because, in damp northern climates, the young seedlings are likely to rot.

In an average season, the seed should be sown in mid-to late spring after the soil has been prepared and warmed. Use the arrival of weed seedlings in the garden as a sign that the temperature is rising.

Herbs will survive in a range of different soils. Most culinary herbs originate from the Mediterranean so their preference is for a sandy free-draining soil. If your soil is sticky clay do not give up; give the seeds a better start by adding a fine layer of river sand along the drill when preparing the seed bed.

Preparation of Seed Bed
Before starting, check your soil type (see pages 268–269), making sure that the soil has sufficient food to maintain a seed bed. Dig the bed over, mark out a straight line with a piece of string secured tightly over each row, draw a shallow drill, ¼–½ in. deep, using the side of a fork or hoe, and sow the seeds thinly, 2 or 3 every 2 in. Do not overcrowd the bed, otherwise the seedlings will grow leggy and weak and be prone to disease.

Protected Sowing
Starting off the seeds in a greenhouse or on a windowsill gives you more control over the warmth and moisture they need, and enables you to begin propagating earlier in the season.

Nothing is more uplifting than going into the greenhouse on a cold and gloomy late-winter morning and seeing all the seedlings emerging. It generates enthusiasm for spring.

Preparation of Seed
Most seeds need air, light, the right temperature and moisture to germinate. Some have a long dormancy period before they are ready to germinate, and some have hard outer coats and need a little help to get going. Here are two techniques.

Scarification
If left to nature, seeds that have a hard outer coat would take a long time to germinate. To speed up the process, rub the seed between 2 sheets of fine sandpaper. This weakens the coat of the seed so that moisture essential for germination can penetrate.

Stratification (Vernalization)
Some seeds need a period of cold (from 1 to 6 months) to germinate. Mix the seed with damp sand and place in a plastic bag in the refrigerator or freezer. After 4 weeks sow on the surface of the compost and

cover with perlite. My family always enjoys this time of year. They go to the freezer to get the ice cream and find herb seed instead.

Preparation of Seed Container

One of the chief causes of diseased compost is a dirty propagation container. To minimize the spread of disease, remove any "tidemarks" of compost, soil or chemicals around the insides of the pots and seed trays. Wash and scrub them thoroughly with dishwashing liquid, rinse with water and give a final rinse with disinfectant. Leave for 24 hours before reuse. Old compost also provides ideal conditions for damping off fungi and fungus gnats. To avoid cross-infection always remove spent compost from the greenhouse or potting shed.

Compost

It is always best to use a sterile seed compost. Ordinary garden soil contains many weed seeds that could easily be confused with the germinating herb seed. The compost used for most seed sowing is a standard seed compost mixed in equal portions with composted fine bark and, unless stated otherwise within the specific herb section, this is the mix to use. However, for herbs that prefer a freer-draining compost, or for those that require stratification outside, I advise using a mix of 25 percent standard seed compost, 50 percent composted fine bark and 25 percent horticultural grit. And if you are sowing seeds that have a long germination period, use a soil-based seed compost.

Sowing in Seed Trays

To prepare, fill a clean seed tray with compost up to ½ in. below the rim and firm down with a flat piece of wood. Do not press too hard as this will over-compress the compost and restrict drainage, which may in turn encourage damping off disease and attack by fungus gnats.

The gap below the rim is essential, as it prevents the surface-sown seeds and compost being washed over the edge when watering, and it allows room for growth when you are growing under glass.

Water the prepared tray using a fine rose on the watering can. Do not overwater. The compost should be damp, not soaking. After an initial watering, water as little as possible, but never let the surface dry out. Once the seed is sown, lack of moisture can prevent germination and kill the seedlings, but too much water excludes oxygen and encourages damping-off fungi and root rot. Be sure to use a fine rose on the watering can so as not to disturb the seed.

Sowing Methods

There are three main methods, the choice dependent on the size of the seed. They are, in order of seed size, fine to large:

1 Scatter on the surface of the compost, and cover with a fine layer of perlite.

2 Press into the surface of the compost, either with your hand or a flat piece of wood the size of the tray, and cover with perlite.

3 Press down to one seed's depth and then cover with compost.

The Cardboard Trick

When seeds are too small to handle, you can control distribution by using a thin piece of cardboard (cereal boxes are good), cut to 4 in. x 2 in., and folded down the middle.

Place a small amount of seed into the folded card and gently tap it over the prepared seed tray. This technique is especially useful when sowing into plug trays (see below).

Sowing in Plug (Module) Trays (Multi-cell Trays)

These plug trays are a great invention. The seed can germinate in its own space, get established into a strong seedling, and make a good root ball. When potting, the young plant remains undisturbed and will continue growing, rather than coming to a halt because it has to regenerate roots to replace those damaged in pricking out from the seed tray. This is very good for plants like coriander, which hate being transplanted and tend to bolt if you move them. Another advantage is that as you are sowing into individual cells, the problem of overcrowding is cut to a minimum, and damping-off disease and fungus gnats are easier to control. Also, because seedlings in plugs are easier to maintain, planting or potting is not so critical.

Plug trays come in different sizes; for example, you can get trays with very small holes of ½ in. x ½ in. up to trays with holes of 1¼ in. x 1¼ in. To enable a reasonable time lapse between germination and potting, I recommend the larger.

When preparing these trays for seed sowing, make sure you have enough space, otherwise compost seems to land up everywhere. Prepare the compost and fill the tray right to the top, scraping off surplus compost with a piece of wood level with the top of

the holes. It is better not to firm the compost down. Watering settles the compost enough to allow space for both the seed and the top dressing of perlite.

For the gardener-in-a-hurry there are available in good garden centers ready-prepared propagation trays, which are plug trays already filled with compost. All you have to do is water and add the seed.

The principles of sowing in plug trays are the same as for trays. Having sown your seed, DO label the trays clearly with the name of the plant, and also the date. The date is useful as one can check their late or speedy germination. It is also good for record keeping, if you want to sow them again next year, and helps with organizing the potting.

Seed Germination

Seeds need warmth and moisture to germinate.

The main seed sowing times are fall and spring. This section provides general information, with the table below providing a quick guide to germination. Any detailed advice specific to a particular herb is provided in the A-Z of Herbs section.

Quick Guide to Temperatures for Germination of Different Seeds

Hot 80–90°F (27–32°C)
Rosemary

Warm 60–70°F (15–21°C)
Most plants, including those from the Mediterranean, and chives and parsley.

Cool 40–50°F (4–10°C)
Lavenders (old lavender seed will need a period of stratification before sowing).

Stratification
Arnica (old seed), sweet woodruff, yellow iris, poppy, soapwort, sweet cicely, hops (old seed), sweet violet.

Need Light (i.e., do not cover)
Chamomile, foxglove, thyme, winter savory, poppy and sweet marjoram.

In a cold greenhouse, a heated propagator may be needed in early spring for herbs that germinate at warm to hot temperatures. In the house you can use a shelf near a radiator (never on the radiator), or any warm room in the house, perhaps the furnace room.

Darkness does not hinder the germination of most herbs (see the table above for exceptions), but if you put your containers in an airing cupboard YOU MUST CHECK THEM EVERY DAY. As soon as there is any sign of life, place the trays in a warm light place, but not in direct sunlight.

Hardening Off

When they are large enough to handle, prick out seed tray seedlings and pot them individually. Allow them to root fully.

Test plug tray seedlings by giving one or two a gentle tug. They should come away from the cells cleanly, with the root ball. If they do not, leave for another few days.

When the seedlings are ready, harden them off gradually by leaving the young plants outside during the day. Once weaned into a natural climate, either plant them directly into a prepared site in the garden, or into a larger container for the summer.

cuttings

Taking cuttings is sometimes the only way to propagate some herbs, including those that do not flower such as chamomile 'Treneague,' and variegated forms, such as tricolor sage.

Taking cuttings is not as difficult as some people suggest, and even now I marvel at how a mere twig can produce roots and start the whole life cycle going again.

There are four types of cutting used in herb growing:

1 Softwood cuttings taken in spring

2 Semihardwood cuttings taken in summer

3 Hardwood cuttings taken in the fall

4 Root cuttings, which can be taken in spring and fall.

For successful softwood cuttings it is worth investing in a heated propagator, which can be placed either in a greenhouse or on a shady windowsill. For successful semiripe, hardwood and root cuttings, a shaded cold frame can be used.

Softwood Cuttings

Softwood cuttings are taken from the new lush green growth of most perennial herbs between spring and midsummer, a few examples being balm of Gilead, bergamot, the chamomiles, the mints, prostanthera, the rosemarys, the scented geraniums, the thymes, curly wood sage and wormwood. Check under the individual herb entries in the A–Z section for more specific information.

1 The best way to get a plant to produce successful rooting material is to prune it vigorously in winter (which will encourage rapid growth when the temperature rises in the spring), and to take cuttings as soon as there is sufficient growth.

2 Fill a pot, seed tray, or plug tray with cutting compost—a standard seed compost mixed in equal portions with composted fine bark. It is important to use a well-draining medium rather than standard potting mixes as, without root systems, cuttings are prone to wet rot. Firm the compost to within ¾ in. of the rim. If space is limited or pots are unavailable, you can put several cuttings in damp sphagnum moss (rolled up firmly in a plastic strip and held in place by a rubber band or string) until the roots form.

3 Collect the cuttings in small batches in the morning. Choose sturdy shoots with plenty of leaves. Best results come from nonflowering shoots with the base leaves removed. Cut the shoot with a knife, not scissors. This is because scissors tend to pinch or seal the end of the cutting, thus hindering rooting.

4 Place the cutting at once in the shade in a plastic bag or a bucket of water. Softwood cuttings are extremely susceptible to water loss; even a small loss will hinder root development. If the cuttings cannot be dealt with quickly, keep them cool (e.g., in the crisper of your refrigerator) to prevent excessive water loss.

5 To prepare the cutting material, cut the base of the stem ¼ in. below a leaf joint, to leave a cutting of roughly 4 in. long.

6 If the cutting material has to be under 4 in., take the cutting with a heel. Remove the lower leaves and trim the tail that is left from the heel.

7 Trim the stem cleanly before a node, the point at which a leaf stalk joins the stem. Remove the leaves from the bottom third of the cutting, leaving at least two or three leaves on top. The reason for leaving leaves on cuttings is that the plant feeds through them as it sets root. Do not tear off the base leaves as this can cause disease; use a knife and gently cut them off.

8 Make a hole with a dibble in the compost and insert the cutting up to its leaves. Make sure that the leaves do not touch or go below the surface of the compost; they will rot away and may cause a fungus condition, which can spread up the stem and to other cuttings. Do not overcrowd the container or include more than one species, because quite often they take different times to root. (For instance, keep box and thymes separate.)

Hormone rooting-powders that some gardeners use contain synthetic plant hormones and fungicide and are **not** for the organic grower; following my detailed instructions you should find them unnecessary. However, they may help with difficult cuttings. The cutting should be dipped into the rooting-powder just before inserting into the compost.

9 Label and date the cuttings clearly, and only water the compost from above if necessary (the initial watering after preparing the container should be sufficient). Keep out of direct sunlight in hot weather. In fact, if it is very sunny, heavy shade is best for the first week.

Either place in a heated or unheated propagator, or cover the pot or container with a plastic bag supported on a thin wire hoop (to prevent the plastic touching the leaves), or with an upturned plastic bottle with the bottom cut off. If you are using a plastic bag, make sure you turn it inside out every few days to stop excess moisture from condensation dropping onto the cuttings.

10 Spray the cuttings every day with water for the first week. Do this in the morning, never at night. Do not test for rooting too early by tugging the cutting up, as you may disturb it at a crucial time. A better way to check for new roots is to look underneath the container. Average rooting time is 2–4 weeks.

The cutting medium is low in nutrients, so give a regular foliar feed when the cutting starts to root.

11 Harden off the cuttings gradually when they are rooted. Bring them out in stages to normal sunny, airy conditions.

12 Pot them using a prepared potting compost once they are weaned. Label and water well after transplanting.

13 About 4–5 weeks after transplanting, when you can see that the plant is growing away, pinch out the top center of the young cutting. This will encourage the plant to bush out, making it stronger as well as fuller.

14 Allow to grow on until a good-size root ball can be seen in the pot—check occasionally by gently removing the plant from the pot—then plant.

Semihardwood Cuttings or Greenwood Cuttings

Usually taken from shrubby herbs such as rosemary and myrtle towards the end of the growing season (from midsummer to mid-fall). Use the same method (steps 2–8) as for softwood cuttings, with the following exceptions:

2 The compost should be freer-draining than for softwood cuttings, as semihardwood cuttings will be left for longer (see 10 below). Make the mix equal parts a standard seed compost and perlite.

9 Follow step 9 for softwood cuttings, but place the pot, seed tray or plug tray in a cold greenhouse, cold frame, cool sunroom, or on a cold windowsill in a garage, not in a propagator, unless it has a misting unit.

10 Average rooting time for semihardwood cuttings is 4–6 weeks. Follow step 10 except for the watering schedule. Instead, if the fall is exceptionally hot and the compost or cuttings seem to be drying out, spray once a week. Again, do this in the morning, and be careful not to overwater.

11 Begin the hardening off process in the spring after

the frosts. Give a foliar feed as soon as there is sufficient new growth.

Hardwood Cuttings

Taken mid- to late fall in exactly the same way as softwood cuttings steps 2–8, but with a freer-draining compost of equal parts, a standard seed compost and perlite. Keep watering to the absolute minimum. Winter in a cold frame, greenhouse or sunroom. Average rooting time can take as long as 12 months.

Root Cuttings

This method of cutting is suitable for plants with creeping roots, such as bergamot, comfrey, horseradish, lemon balm, mint, soapwort and sweet woodruff.

1 Dig up some healthy roots in spring or fall.

2 Fill a pot, seed tray or plug tray with cutting compost—made from equal parts a standard seed compost and perlite—firmed to within 1¼ in. of the rim. Water well and leave to stand while preparing your cutting material.

3 Cut 1½–3 in. lengths of root that carry a growing bud. It is easy to see the growing buds on the roots of mint.

Taking a root cutting

This method is equally applicable for all the varieties mentioned above as suitable for root propagation, with the exception of comfrey and horseradish, where one simply slices the root into sections, 1½–3 in. long, using a sharp knife to give a clean cut through the root. Do not worry, each will produce a plant! These cuttings lend themselves to being grown in plug trays.

4 Make holes in the compost with a dibble. If using pots or seed trays these should be 1–2½ in. apart. Plant the cutting vertically.

5 Cover the cutting with a small amount of compost, followed by a layer of perlite.

6 Label and date. This is most important because you cannot see what is in the container until the plant begins to grow and it is all too easy to forget what you have planted.

7 Average rooting time is 2–3 weeks. Do not water until roots or top growth appears. Then apply liquid feed.

8 Slowly harden off the cuttings when rooted.

9 Pot in a potting compost once they are weaned. Label and water well after transplanting. You can miss this stage out if you have grown the root cuttings in plug trays.

10 About 2–3 weeks after transplanting, when you can see that the plant is growing away, pinch out the top center of the young cutting. This encourages the plant to bush out, making it stronger as well as fuller.

11 Allow to grow on until a good-size root ball can be seen in the pot. Plant in the garden when the last frosts are over.

layering

If cuttings are difficult to root you can try layering, a process that encourages sections of plant to root while still attached to the parent. Bay, rosemary and sage are good examples of plants that suit this method.

1 Prune some low branches off the parent plant during the winter season to induce vigorous growth and cultivate the soil around the plant during winter and early spring by adding peat and grit to it.

2 Trim the leaves and side shoots of a young vigorous stem for 4–24 in. below its growing tip.

3 Bring the stem down to ground level and mark its position on the soil. Dig a trench at that point, making one vertical side 4–6 in. deep, and the other sloping toward the plant.

4 Roughen the stem at the point where it will touch the ground.

5 Peg it down into the trench against the straight side, then bend the stem at right angles behind the growing tip, so that it protrudes vertically. Then return the soil to the trench to bury the stem. Firm in well.

6 Water well using a watering can and keep the soil moist, especially in dry periods.

7 Sever the layering stem from its parent plant in the fall if well rooted, and 3–4 weeks later nip out the growing tip from the rooted layer to make plant bush out.

Planting a root cutting

8 Check carefully that the roots have become well established before lifting the layered stem. If necessary, leave for a further year.

9 Replant either in the open ground or in potting compost mixed in equal parts with composted fine bark. Label and leave to establish.

Mound Layering

A method similar to layering, this not only creates new growth but also improves the appearance of old plants. This is particularly suitable for sages and thymes, which can grow woody in the center.

1 In the spring, pile soil mixed with composted fine bark and a soil-based potting compost over the bare woody center until only the young shoots show.

2 By late summer, roots will have formed on many of these shoots. They can be taken and planted in new locations as cuttings or by root division.

3 The old plant can then be dug up and disposed of.

Seedling with roots being transplanted

PLANNING YOUR HERB GARDEN

Herbs are so versatile that they should appeal to anyone, be they a cook, a lover of salads, or just someone wanting to enjoy the rich scents of plants and watch the butterflies collecting nectar from the flowers. And there are herbs for every space; they will grow in a window-box or in a pot on a sunny window ledge; and some can be grown indoors as houseplants as well as outside in gardens, small or large.

The best way to grow herbs is the organic way. Quite apart from the fact that if you use natural products, the soil remains clean and free from chemical pollutants, in organic herb gardens there is no chance of contaminating a plant before you eat it. Organic methods also attract bees and other insects to the garden, which in turn helps maintain the healthy natural balance of predator and pest.

A collection of herbs in containers

conditions

As herbs are basically wild plants tamed to fit a garden, it makes sense to grow them in conditions comparable with their original environment. This can be a bit difficult, for they come from all over the world. As a general rule, many culinary herbs come from the Mediterranean and prefer a dry sunny place. But herbs are adaptable and they do well outside their native habitat, provided you are aware of what they prefer.

choosing the site

Before planning your site, it is worth surveying your garden in detail. Start by making a simple plan and mark on it north and south. Show the main areas of shade—a high fence, a neighboring house, any high trees, noting whether the trees are deciduous or evergreen. Finally, note any variations in soil type—wet, dry, heavy, etc. Soil is one of the most important factors and will determine the types of herb you can grow.

use

Next, decide what you want from your herb garden. Do you want a retreat away from the house? Or a herb garden where the scents drift indoors? Or do you want a culinary herb garden by the kitchen door?

style

Then think about what shape or style you want the garden to take. Formal herb gardens are based on patterns and geometric shapes. Informal gardens are a free-for-all, with species and colors all mixed together. Informal gardens may look unplanned, but the best that I know have been well planned. For some ideas, look at the gardens on pages 272–281.

Detailed planning is worth doing, even if it is just to check the height and spread of the plant. I know only too well how misleading it can be buying plants from a garden center—they are all neat, uniform and fairly small. After hearing me give a talk, one woman asked if she should remove the lovage she had just planted in the front of her rockery as I had just explained that it grew to 6 ft. high and at least 3 ft. wide.

The plants have to be accessible, either for using fresh or to harvest, so paths are a good idea. They also introduce patterns to the design and can help to define its shape. For convenience, herbs should be no more than 30 in. from a path, and ideally the beds no more than 3–4 ft. wide. If they are more than 4 ft. wide, insert stepping stones to improve access.

preparing the site

Having chosen your sites, and what to do, you really have got to condition your soil.

Eliminate Weeds

If you do this at the start, you will not have the hassle of trying to remove quack grass, bindweed or ground elder. (By the way, ground elder was a herb...! It was said to have been used by the Romans to feed their livestock. So the next time you are grappling with this weed, you can thank your ancestors.)

Weeds do not emerge until the spring, and continue well into the season. If you wish to get rid of them successfully, it is best to cover the plot with black plastic the previous fall. Dig a shallow trench around the area and bury the sides of the plastic in it to keep it secure. Starved of light, weeds will eventually give up.

This will take until the following spring, so if you do not like the sight of the black plastic, position a few paving stones (taking care not to make any holes because the weeds will find them and come through), cover the plastic with bark, and place terracotta pots planted with herbs on top of the stones.

If you do not have the patience, use a weedkiller instead, which is not organic. You could use a glyphosate herbicide product or weedkiller. It is effective against all plants, so do not get it on any you wish to keep.

check the soil

The soil is the engine of your garden so it is important to know your soil type and whether it is acidic, neutral or alkaline. This will help you choose the correct herbs for your garden and also to produce a bountiful crop.

Soil Type

Soil is made up of the following mineral elements, sand, clay and silt. The soil's texture can be best described in terms of its proportions of these components, loam containing a mixture of all three. Limy soils also contain calcium carbonate or lime. Stones in the soil will increase drainage, so very stony soils can be drought-prone.

Texture Testing

Take a handful of soil from the garden: what does it feel like? Sandy soil will feel gritty and run through your fingers; clay is sticky and when you close your hand it makes a solid lump. Pure silt soil is rare, it occurs on river flood plains and has a slightly soapy feel and when you close your hand it does not stick together. If the soil froths when placed in a jar of vinegar, then it contains free calcium carbonate or limestone.

Clay Soil

This soil is made up of tiny particles that stick together when wet, making the soil heavy. When dry, they set rock hard. Because it retains water and restricts air flow around roots, it is often known as a "cold soil." It may have a natural reserve of plant food, but even so work compost into the first few inches to help get the plant

Assessing the position of herbs before planting

established and improve drainage. If you do this every year, it will gradually become easier to cultivate. My nursery is on heavy clay and when planting out herbs that prefer a free-draining soil, I add some sharp sand to the site when preparing it. Herbs that like these conditions are the bergamots *(Monarda)*, the comfreys *(Symphytum)*, the mints *(Mentha)*, and wormwood *(Artemisia absinthium)*.

Sandy Soil

This is a very well-drained soil, so much so that plant foods are quickly washed away, but it warms up quickly in the spring. For fleshy herbs you will need to build the soil up with compost to help retain moisture and stop the leaching of nutrients. But the Mediterranean herbs will thrive on this soil. Herbs that like sandy soils are arnica *(Arnica montana)*, borage *(Borago officinalis)*, the chamomile family *(Chamaemelum)*, evening primrose *(Oenothera missouriensis)*, the fennel family *(Foeniculum)*, the lavender family *(Lavandula)*, the marjoram family *(Origanum)*, tarragon *(Artemisia dracunculus)*, the thyme family *(Thymus)*, and winter savory *(Satureja montana)*.

Silt Soil

This type of soil is similar to clay but needs a soil test before you start to determine the correct course of action as the soil pH can be acidic or alkaline. It is important not to work a silt soil in wet conditions as it can take a long time to recover. The beauty of a silt soil is that it allows you to grow the widest range of herbs. Depending on the pH you can grow mint *(Mentha)*, French tarragon, wormwood *(Artemisia)*, sages *(Salvia)* and rosemarys *(Rosmarinus)* and oreganos *(Origanum)*. However, you may require extra grit for both lavenders *(Lavandula)* and thymes *(Thymus)*.

Loam Soil

This soil is a mixture of clay and sand. It contains a good quantity of humus and is rich in nutrients. There are various types of loam: heavy, which contains more clay than loam and becomes wet in winter and spring; light loam, which has more sand than clay and is the very best for herbs; and medium loam, which is an equal balance of clay and sand.

Herbs that like these conditions are the basil family *(Ocimum)*, bay *(Laurus nobilis)*, betony *(Bettonica officinalis)*, caraway *(Carum carvi)*, catmint *(Nepeta racemosa)*, chervil *(Anthriscus cerefolium)*, chives *(Allium schoenoprasum)*, coriander *(Coriandrum sativum)*, dill *(Anethum graveolens)*, lady's mantle *(Alchemilla mollis)*, lovage *(Levisticum officinale)*, parsley *(Petroselinum crispum)*, rue *(Ruta graveolens)*, and the sage family *(Salvia)*.

Soil pH

Find out whether your soil is acidic or alkaline. Herbs generally do best in a soil between pH 6.5 and 7.5 (fairly neutral). To measure the pH of your soil buy a reliable soil-testing kit from any good garden center, or contact your local agriculture office.

Acid soil (pH 0–6.5)

The soils in this category, on a sliding scale from acidic to nearly neutral, are sphagnum moss peat, sandy soil, coarse loam soil, sedge peat and heavy clay.

Plants that will tolerate these conditions are arnica (*Arnica montana*), dandelion (*Taraxacum officinale*), comfrey (*Symphytum officinale*), foxglove (*Digitalis purpurea*), honeysuckle (*Lonicera periclymenum*), pennyroyal (*Mentha pulegium*), sorrel (Rumex rugosus), buckler-leaf sorrel (*Rumex scutatus*), and sweet cicely (*Myrrhis odorata*).

Alkaline soil (pH 7.7–14)

The soils in this category tend to contain lime and are of a fine loam. Some plants become stunted and leaves go yellowish in color, because the minerals, especially iron, become locked away. If you find the plants are not thriving, I recommend a raised bed where you can introduce the soil you require.

Herbs that like these conditions are the box family (*Buxus sempervirens*), catnip (*Nepeta cataria*), chicory (*Cichorium intybus*), cowslip (*Primula veris*), hyssop (*Hyssopus officinalis*), juniper (*Juniperus communis*), lily of the valley (*Convallaria majalis*), lungwort (*Pulmonaria officinalis*), the marjoram family (*Origanum*), the pink family (*Dianthus*), the rosemary family (*Rosmarinus*), and salad burnet (*Sanguisorba minor*).

Altering the pH

A reading that approaches either end of the pH scale indicates that the soil will tend to lock up the nutrients necessary for good growth. If it is very acidic, add lime in the late fall to raise the pH. Fork the top 4 in. of the soil and dress with lime. Clay soils need a good dressing, but don't over-lime sandy soils. It should not be necessary to do this more than once every 3 years

Soil tester

unless your soil is very acidic. Never add lime at the same time as manure, garden compost or fertilizer, as a chemical reaction can occur which will ruin the effects of both. As a general rule, either add lime 1 month before, or 3 months after manuring, and 1 month after adding fertilizers. If the soil is alkaline, dress it every fall with well-rotted manure to a depth of 2–4 in., and dig over in the spring.

Digging and Improving the Soil

Check the ground has good drainage especially in winter and early spring.

A clay soil restricts air circulation around the roots, which not only restricts the growth but also means that the soil stays cold, which delays spring growths and germination. To help lighten the soil dig in some leaf mold, or if it is just a small area, some composted fine bark, prior to planting. Check that the ground can retain some moisture during the growing season. If the soil is sandy, it may dry out in summer, so again, dig in some well-rotted manure or garden compost.

Dig the site over. If the soil is heavy it's best to dig in early winter, so that the frosts can break up the clods of earth. If the soil is light, early spring is best, allowing the soil some protection during the winter against leaching of the nutrients. For all soils, it is beneficial to lay a good layer of well-rotted manure or garden compost over the surface in winter and dig it in the following spring; they benefit from a good digging in the spring.

laying paths

No matter whether you are planning a formal or informal herb garden, you will need paths. There are a number of choices.

Grass

A grass path is quite easy to achieve and looks very attractive. Another plus point is the minimal cost. Make it at least as wide as your lawn mower, otherwise you will be cutting it on your hands and knees with shears. It is a good idea to edge the path either with wood, metal or, more attractively, with bricks, laid on their side end to end. Disadvantages to this kind of path are that it needs mowing and will not take heavy traffic.

Gravel

Gravel paths really do lend themselves to being planted with herbs. Be sure to prepare them well, otherwise a water trap will form and the plants would be better off being aquatic.

First remove the top soil carefully. Then dig out to a depth of 12 in., putting the soil to one side. It is advisable to put a wooden edge between the soil of the garden or lawn and the new path. This will stop the soil falling into the path, and keep the edge neat. Fill the newly formed ditch with 6 in. of hard core (rubble). Mix the top soil with peat, bark and grit in the ratio 3:1:1:1, and put this mix on top of the hard core to a depth of 3 in. Finish with 3 in. gravel or pea gravel. There are many colors of gravel available; most large garden centers stock a good range, or if you have a quarry nearby it is worth investigating. Roll the path before planting. Herbs that will grow happily in gravel are creeping or upright thymes, winter savory, and pennyroyal. The disadvantage of gravel is that you will find that weeds will recur, so be diligent.

Bricks

These paths have become very fashionable. There is now a subtle range of colors available, and varied and original patterns can be made. For standard-size bricks, dig out to a depth of 4 in. As with the gravel path, include a wooden edge. Spread 2 in. of sharp sand over the base; level and dampen. Lay the brick on top of the sand in the desired pattern, leaving $1/8$–$1/4$ in. gap between the bricks.

Settle them in, using a mallet or a hired plate vibrator. To plant the path with herbs, leave out one or two bricks, filling the gaps later with compost and planting them when the path has settled. When the

Raised bed

whole path has been laid, spread the joints with a mix 4:1 of fine dry sand and cement, and brush it in. The mixture will gradually absorb the moisture from the atmosphere, so setting the brick.

Paving Stones

These can take up a lot of space and are expensive. Garden centers now stock a large range in various colors and shapes. Also try home improvement stores; you may get a better deal, especially if you require large quantities. Paving stones are ideal for the classic checkerboard designs and the more formal designs.

To lie flush with the ground, dig out the soil to the depth of the slab plus 2 in. Put 2 in. of sharp sand onto the prepared area, level off and lay the slabs on top, tapping them down, and making sure they are level. If the chosen area is already level and you want the slabs to be a little higher, then lay them directly in position with only a small layer of sand underneath.

planting the garden

The planning and hard preparation work are done, so now for the fun part. If this is a new garden, it is worth laying the plants out on top of the prepared ground first, walking round and getting an overall view. Make any changes to the design now, rather than later. Having satisfied yourself, dig adequate holes to accommodate the plants, adding extra sharp sand or grit if necessary. Firm in, and water well. Now you can enjoy watching your garden grow.

alternative planting

Raised Beds

If your soil is difficult, or if you wish to create a feature, raised beds are a good solution. Also, plants in raised beds are easier to keep under control and will not

Hampton, me and parsley

wander so much around the rest of the garden. Finally, they are more accessible for harvesting and stand at an ideal height for those in wheelchairs.

I consider the ideal height for a raised bed to be between 12 in. and 30 in. If you raise it over 3 ft. high you will need some form of foundation for the retaining walls, to prevent them keeling over with the weight of the soil. Retaining walls can be made out of old railway ties, logs cut in half, old bricks, or even red bricks—leave the odd one out and plant a creeping thyme in its place.

For a 12 in. raised bed, first put a layer of hard core on top of the existing soil to a depth of 3 in., followed by a 3 in. layer of gravel, and finally 6 in. of topsoil mix—1 part composted fine bark, 1 part grit or sharp sand, with 3 parts topsoil.

Lawns

Many herbs are excellent groundcover but, as I have already mentioned under chamomile, beware of doing too large an area to begin with. It can be an error costly in both time and money. Small areas filled with creeping herbs give great delight to the unsuspecting visitor who, when walking over the lawn, discovers a pleasant aroma exuding from their feet!

I know it is repetitious, but those of you who are gardeners will understand why I say again, "Prepare your site well." This is the key to many good gardens. Given a typical soil, prepare the site for the lawn by digging the area out to a depth of 12 in. and prepare in exactly the same way as the raised bed: 3 in. hard core, 3 in. gravel, 6 in. topsoil mix—this time, 1 part composted fine bark, 2 parts sharp sand, 3 parts top soil. Apart from chamomile, other plants that can be used are Corsican mint (Mentha requinni), planted 4 in. apart, or creeping thymes—see pages 246–248 for varieties—and plant them 9 in. apart.

HERB GARDENS

first herb garden

The gardens I have designed can be followed religiously, or adapted to meet your personal tastes, needs, and of course space. It is with this last requirement in mind that I have specifically not put the exact size into the design and concentrated on the shape, layout and the relationship between plants. I hope these plans give you freedom of thought and some inspiration.

When planning your first herb garden, choose plants you will use and enjoy. I have designed this garden in exactly the same way as the one at my herb farm. Much as I would love to have a rambling herb garden, I need something practical and easy to manage, because the nursery plants need all my attention.

It is also important that the herbs are easy to get at, so that I can use them every day. By dividing the garden up into four sections and putting paving stones around the outside and through the middle, it is easy to maintain and provides good accessibility.

For this garden, I have chosen a cross-section of herbs with a bias toward culinary use, because the more you use and handle the plants, the more you will understand their habits. There is much contradictory advice on which herb to plant with which but much of these are old wives' tales.

There are only a few warnings I will give: Do not plant dill and fennel together because they intermarry and become fendill, losing their unique flavors in the process. Equally, do not plant dill or coriander near wormwood as it will impair their flavor. Also, different mints near each other cross-pollinate and over the years will lose their individual identity. Finally, if you plan to collect the seed from lavenders, keep the species well apart. Aside from that, if you like it, plant it.

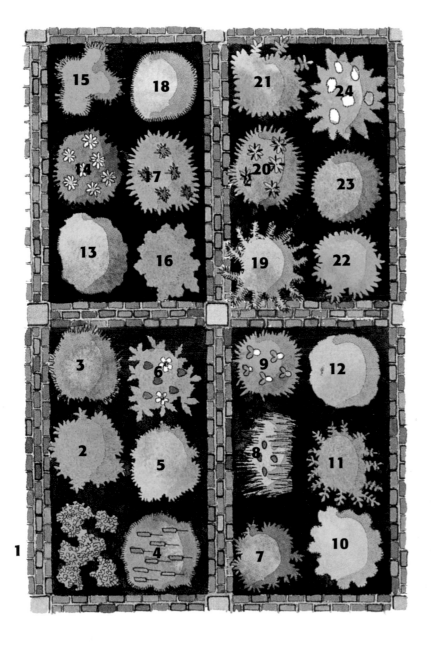

1   Parsley *Petroselinum crispum*
2   Pineapple Mint *Mentha suaveolens* 'Variegata'
3   Fennel *Foeniculum vulgare*
4   Lavender Munstead *Lavandula angustifolia* 'Munstead'
5   Greek Oregano *Origanum vulgare* subsp. *hirtum* 'Greek'
6   Alpine Strawberry *Fragaria vesca*
7   Purple Sage *Salvia officinalis* 'Purpurascens'
8   Chives *Allium schoenoprasum*
9   Heartsease *Viola tricolor*
10 Golden Curly Marjoram *Origanum vulgare* 'Aureum Crispum'
11 Salad Burnet *Sanguisorba minor*
12 Lemon Thyme *Thymus citriodorus*
13 Garden Thyme *Thymus vulgaris*
14 Roman Chamomile *Chamaemelum nobile*
15 Rock Hyssop *Hyssopus offinialis* subsp. *aristatus*
16 Buckler-Leaf Sorrel *Rumex scutatus*
17 Bergamot *Monarda didyma*
18 Dartington Curry Plant *Helichrysum italicum* 'Dartington'
19 Rosemary *Rosmarinus officinalis*
20 Borage *Borago officinalis*
21 Variegated Lemon Balm *Melissa officinalis* 'Aurea'
22 Apple Mint *Mentha suaveolens*
23 Winter Savory *Satureja montana*
24 Chervil *Anthriscus cerefolium*

herb bath garden

This may seem a bit eccentric to the conventially minded, but when my back is aching after working in the nursery, and I feel that unmentionable age, and totally exhausted, there is nothing nicer than lying in a herb bath and reading a good book.

The herbs I use most are thyme, to relieve an aching back, lavender, to give me energy, and eau-de-cologne to knock me out. Simply tie up a bunch of your favorite herbs with string, attach them to the hot water tap and let the water run. The scent of the plants will invade both water and room. Alternatively, put some dried herbs in a muslin bag and drop it into the bath.

Remember when planting this garden to make sure that the plants are accessible. Hops will need to climb up a fence or over a log. Again, quite apart from the fact that the herbs from this garden are for use in the bath, they make a very aromatic garden in their own right. Position a seat next to the lavender and rosemary so that when you get that spare 5 minutes, you can sit in quiet repose and revel in the scent.

1 Lavender Seal *Lavandula* x *intermedia* 'Seal'
2 Lemon Verbena *Aloysia triphylla*
3 Benenden Blue Rosemary *Rosmarinus officinalis* var. *angustissimus* 'Benenden Blue'
4 Gold Sage *Salvia officinalis* icterina
5 Valerian *Valeriana officinalis*
6 Bronze Fennel *Foeniculum vulgare* 'Purpureum'
7 Tansy *Tanacetum vulgare*
8 Golden Lemon Thyme *Thymus citriodorus* 'Golden Lemon'
9 Double-Flowered Chamomile *Chamaemelum nobile* 'Flore Pleno'
10 Houseleek *Sempervivum tectorum*
11 Black Peppermint *Mentha* x *piperita*
12 Orange-scented Thyme *Thymus* 'Fragrantissimus'
13 Meadowsweet *Filipendula ulmeria*
14 Fennel *Foeniculum vulgare*

15 Pennyroyal *Mentha pulegium*
16 Creeping Hops *Humulus lupulus*
17 French Lavender *Lavandula stoechas*
18 Bay *Laurus nobilis*
19 Roman Chamomile *Chamaemelum nobile*
20 Lemon Balm *Melissa officinalis*
21 Porlock Thyme *Thymus* 'Porlock'
22 Prostrate Rosemary *Rosmarinus officinalis* Prostratus Group
23 Golden Marjoram *Origanum vulgare* 'Aureum'
24 Eau de Cologne Mint *Mentha* x *piperita* f. *citrata*
25 Comfrey *Symphytum officinale*
26 Lady's Mantle *Alchemilla mollis*
27 Yarrow *Achillea millefolium*
28 Lavender Grappenhall *Lavandula* x *intermedia* 'Pale Pretender'
29 Silver Posie Thyme *Thymus vulgaris* 'Silver Posie'

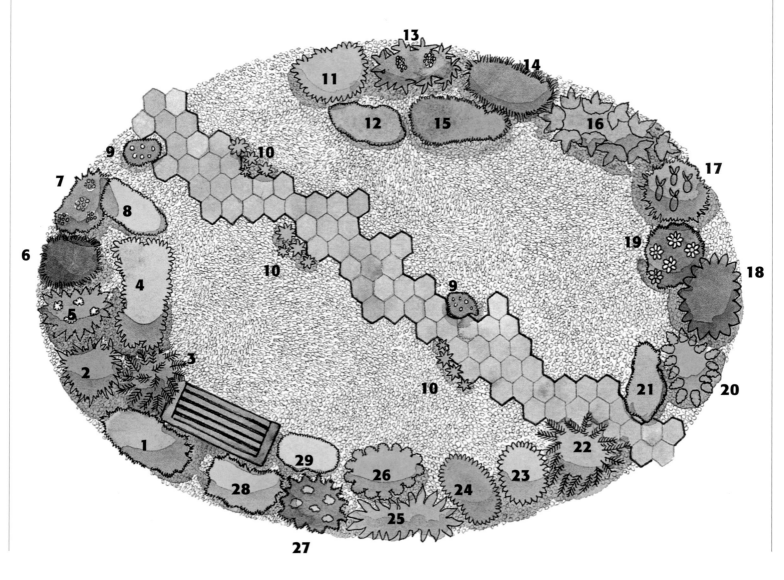

aromatherapy herb garden

One of the things I enjoy about growing herbs is the scent. Aroma is very evocative, and aromatherapy is growing in importance today. This garden has been designed not to create one's own oils, which is a complex process, but to have those aromas around that help our everyday lives, and to make an attractive garden, as the plants all have useful qualities apart from their aroma. The sweet marjoram, basil, thyme, fennel and rosemary are excellent culinary herbs. The chamomile and lemon balm make good herbal teas to help one relax.

I have placed paving stones in the garden to make access to the plants easier. However, when this garden becomes established, the stones will barely show.

I include a list of the herbs in this garden with the properties of the essential oil.

Herb	Properties of the Essential Oil
1 Sweet Basil *Ocimum basilicum*	Concentration
2 Bergamot *Monarda fistulosa*	Uplifting
3 Roman Chamomile *Chamaemelum nobile*	Relaxing
4 Fennel *Foeniculum vulgare*	Antitoxic
5 Rose Geranium *Pelargonium graveolens*	Relaxing
6 Hyssop *Hyssopus officinalis*	Sedative
7 Juniper *Juniperus communis*	Stimulant
8 Lemon Balm *Melissa officinalis*	Antidepressant
9 Lavender *Lavandula angustifolia*	Soothing
10 Rosemary *Rosmarinus officinalis*	Invigorating
11 Sweet Marjoram *Origanum majorana*	Calming
12 Thyme *Thymus vulgaris*	Stimulant

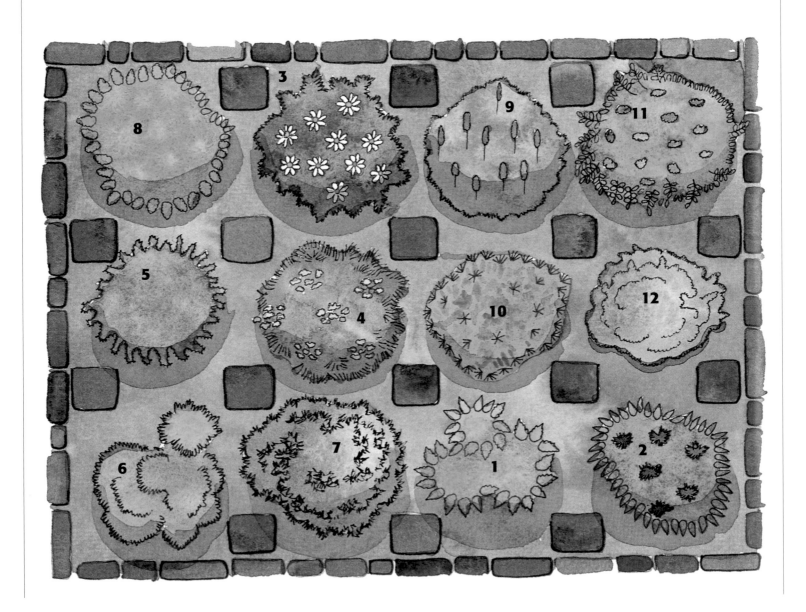

white herb garden

This garden gave me great pleasure to create. For me, it is a herb garden with a different perspective.

It has a row of steps going from the road to the front door of the house. Either side of the steps is a dwarf white lavender hedge. In spring before the lavender, and just before the lily of the valley are in flower, the sweet woodruff gives a carpet of small white flowers. This is the start of the white garden, which then flowers throughout the year through to the fall. It is a most attractive garden with a mixture of scents, foliage and flowers.

This planting combination can easily be adapted to suit a border. Even though it is not a conventional herb garden, all the herbs can be used in their traditional way. The garlic chives with baked potatoes, the horehound for coughs, the chamomile to make a soothing tea, and the lavender to make lavender bags or to use in the bath.

The great thing about a garden like this is that it requires very little work to maintain. The hedge is the only part that needs attention—trim in the spring and after flowering in order to maintain its shape.

1   Dwarf White Lavender *Lavandula angustifolia* 'Nana Alba'
2   Sweet Woodruff *Galium odoratum*
3   Bergamot Snow Maiden *Monarda* 'Schneewittchen'
4   Jacob's Ladder (white) *Polemonium caeruleum* subsp. *caeruleum* f. *album*
5   Yarrow *Achillea millefolium*
6   Foxgloves (white) *Digitalis purpurea* f. *albiflora* (POISONOUS)
7   Roman Chamomile *Chamaemelum nobile*
8   Lily of the Valley *Convallaria majalis* (POISONOUS)
9   White Thyme *Thymus serpyllum* var. *albus*
10 White Hyssop *Hyssopus officinalis* f. *albus*
11 Snowdrift Thyme *Thymus serpyllum* 'Snowdrift'
12 Garlic Chives *Allium tuberosum*
13 Pyrethrum *Tanacetum cinerariifolium*
14 Sweet Cicely *Myrrhis odorata*
15 Valerian *Valeriana officinalis*
16 White Horehound *Marrubium vulgare*
17 Prostanthera *Prostanthera cuneata*

salad herb garden

Herbs in salads make the difference between boring and interesting; they add flavor, texture and color (especially the flowers).

Included in the design is a selection of salad herbs and salad herb flowers. There are two tall herbs in the middle, chicory and red orach (blue and red), which are planted opposite each other. Also, I have positioned the only other tall plant—borage—on the outside ring, opposite the chicory so that the blue flowers together will make a vivid splash. To make access easy, there is an inner ring of stepping stones.

The herbs chosen are my choice and can easily be changed if you want to include a particular favorite. Remember to look at the heights; for instance, do not plant angelica in the outside circle because it will hide anything in the inner circle. Equally, in the inner circle make sure you do not plant a low growing plant next to a tall spreading herb because you will never find it.

This whole design can be incorporated in a small garden or on the edge of a vegetable garden to give color throughout the growing season. As the majority of these herbs are annuals or die back into the ground, the fall is an ideal time to give the garden a good feed by adding well rotted manure. This will encourage lots of leaves from the perennial herbs in the following season, and give a good kick start to the annuals when they are planted out in the following spring.

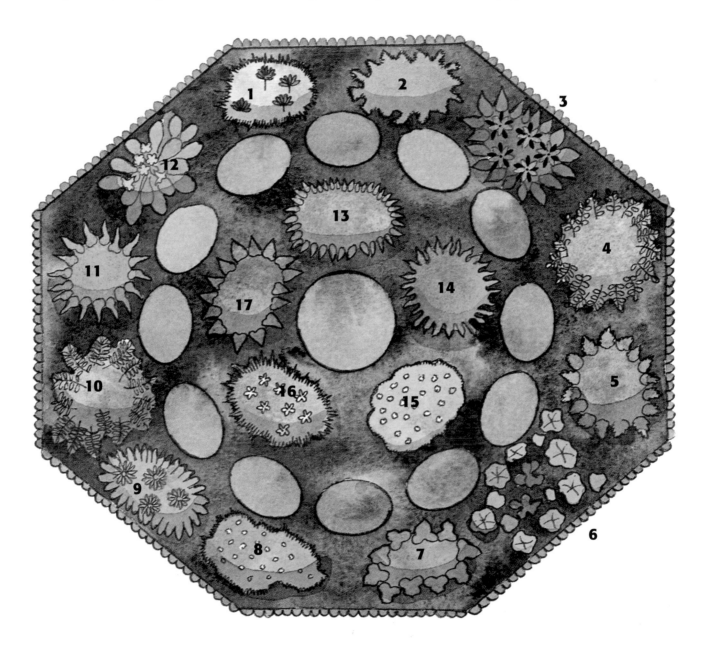

1 Chives *Allium schoenoprasum*	7 Buckler-Leaf Sorrel *Rumex scutatus*	13 Spearmint *Mentha spicata*
2 Caraway *Carum carvi*	8 Hyssop *Hyssopus officinalis*	14 Chicory *Cichorium intybus*
3 Borage *Borago officinalis*	9 Pot Marigold *Calendula officinalis*	15 Lemon Thyme *Thymus citriodorus*
4 Salad Burnet *Sanguisorba minor*	10 French Tarragon *Artemisia dracunculus*	16 Garlic Chives *Allium tuberosum*
5 French Parsley *Petroselinum crispum* French	11 Salad Rocket *Eruca vesicaria* subsp. *sativa*	17 Red Orach *Atriplex hortensis* var. *rubra*
6 Nasturtium *Tropaeolum majus*	12 Cowslips *Primula veris*	

medicinal herb garden

I would like this garden, not just for its medicinal use, but for the tranquility it would bring. The choice of herbs is not only for internal use but for the whole being. I can imagine sitting on the seat watching the dragonflies playing over the pond.

Some of the herbs included are certainly not for self-administration, for instance blue flag iris, but this is a beautiful plant and would look most attractive with the meadowsweet and the valerian. Chamomile, peppermint, dill and lemon balm are easy to self-administer with care as they all make beneficial teas.

One should not take large doses just because they are natural, as some are very powerful. I strongly advise anyone interested in planting this garden to get a good herbal medicine book, see a fully trained herbalist, and always consult your doctor about a particular remedy.

1   Blue Flag Iris *Iris versicolor*
2   Meadowsweet *Filipendula ulmaria*
3   Valerian *Valeriana officinalis*
4   Horseradish *Armoracia rusticana*
5   Sage *Salvia officinalis*
6   Lady's Mantle *Alchemilla mollis*
7   Rosemary *Rosmarinus officinalis*
8   Dill *Anethum graveolens*
9   Chamomile *Chamaemelum nobile*
10 White Horehound *Marrubium vulgare*
11 Comfrey *Symphytum officinale*
12 Feverfew *Tanacetum parthenium*
13 Heartsease *Viola tricolor*
14 Lemon Balm *Melissa officinalis*
15 Garlic *Allium sativum*
16 Black Peppermint *Mentha x piperita*
17 Fennel *Foeniculum vulgare*
18 Pot Marigold *Calendula officinalis*
19 Lavender Seal *Lavandula x intermedia* 'Seal'
20 Garden Thyme *Thymus vulgaris*
21 Houseleek *Sempervivum tectorum*

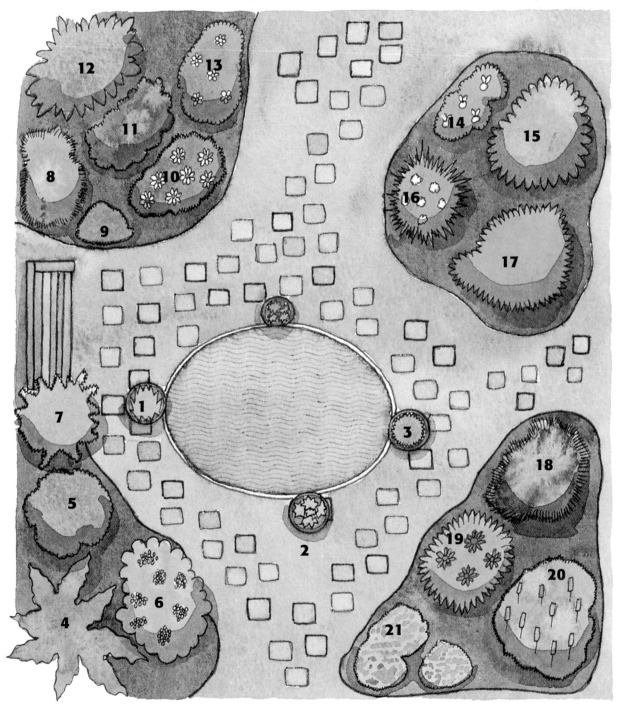

cook's herb garden

The best site for a culinary herb bed is a sunny area accessible to the kitchen. The importance of this is never clearer than when it is raining. There is no way that you will go out and cut fresh herbs if they are a long way away and difficult to reach. Another important factor is that the sunnier the growing position, the better the flavor of the herbs. This is because the sun brings the oils to the surface of the leaf of herbs such as sage, coriander, rosemary, basil, oregano and thyme.

The cook's herb garden could be made in the ground or in containers. If it is to be in the ground, make sure that the site is very well drained. Position a paving stone near each herb so that it can be easily reached for cutting, weeding and feeding and also to help contain the would-be rampant ones, such as the mints, which might otherwise take over.

Alternatively, the whole design could be adapted to be grown in containers. I have chosen only a few of the many varieties of culinary herbs. If your favorite is missing, either add it to the design or substitute it for one of my choice.

1	Ginger Mint *Mentha x gracilis*
2	Chervil *Anthriscus cerefolium*
3	Coriander *Coriandrum sativum*
4	French Parsley *Petroselinum crispum* French
5	Chives *Allium schoenoprasum*
6	Corsican Rosemary *Rosmarinus officinalis* var. *angustissimus* 'Corsican Blue'
7	Garden Thyme *Thymus vulgaris*
8	Angelica *Angelica archangelica*
9	Fennel *Foeniculum vulgare*
10	Winter Savory *Satureja montana*
11	Greek Basil *Ocimum minimum* 'Greek'
12	Buckler-Leaf Sorrel *Rumex scutatus*
13	Bay *Laurus nobilis*
14	Sweet Cicely *Myrrhis odorata*
15	Garlic *Allium sativum*
16	Greek Oregano *Origanum vulgare* subsp. *hirtum* 'Greek'
17	French Tarragon *Artemisia dracunculus*
18	Lovage *Levisticum officinale*
19	Garlic Chives *Allium tuberosum*
20	Lemon Balm *Melissa officinalis*
21	Moroccan Mint *Mentha spicata* var. *crispa* 'Moroccan'
22	Dill *Anethum graveolens*
23	Parsley *Petroselinum crispum*
24	Lemon Thyme *Thymus citriodorus*
25	Sweet Marjoram *Origanum majorana*

natural dye garden

There has been a marked increase of interest in plants as a dye source, which is not surprising since they offer a subtle range of rich colors.

This garden includes a representative selection of those dyes that can be easily grown. It is designed with separate beds because you will need a fairly large quantity of each herb to produce the dye, and the beds make it easy to harvest the leaves, flowers and roots. You should allow sufficient space between the beds for access and maintenance.

The eight herbs I have selected give a broad range of colors. As the marigolds and the parsley are shortlived you may like to replace them with woad or even nettles to experiment with other colors. For more choice of plants, see the section on natural dyes, pages 288–289.

When choosing which plant goes where, the only important consideration is that the elder will grow into a fairly large tree, so plant it where it will not get in the way of the other plants or spoil the sightlines of your garden. In the present design, you will note that all, with the exception of the elder, die back into the ground in winter. Fall is therefore an ideal time to give all the herbs, including the elder, a good mulch of well-rotted manure.

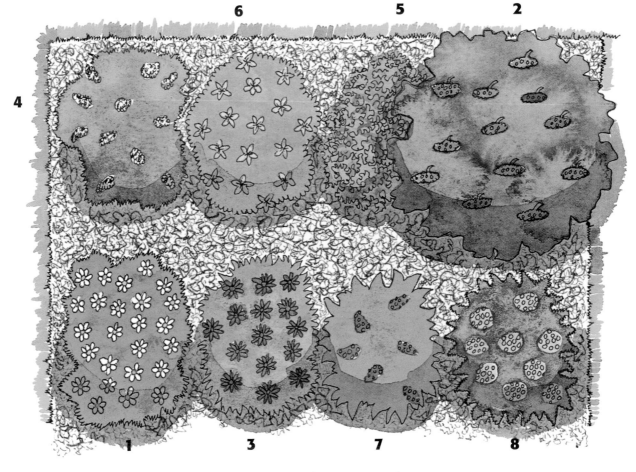

Herb	Part	Mordant	Color
1 Dyers Chamomile *Anthemis tinctoria*	Flowers	Alum	Bright yellow
	Flowers	Copper	Olive
2 Elder *Sambucus nigra*	Leaves	Alum	Green
	Berries	Alum	Violet/purple
3 Marigold *Calendula officinalis*	Petals	Alum	Pale yellow
4 Meadowsweet *Filipendula ulmaria*	Roots	Alum	Black
5 Parsley *Petroselinum crispum*	Fresh leaves	Alum	Cream
6 St. John's Wort *Hypericum perforatum*	Flowers	Alum	Beige
7 Sorrel *Rumex acetosa*	Whole plant	Alum	Pale dirty yellow
8 Tansy *Tanacetum vulgare*	Flowers	Alum	Yellows

potpourri garden

Home-made potpourri are warm, not flashy in color, and the aroma is gentle.

This garden is planted with herbs that can be dried and used in the making of potpourri. The leaves and petals should be harvested, dried and stored as described under Harvesting, pages 284–285. There is also further information under the individual species.

Position this garden in full sun to make the oils come to the surface of the leaves and get the benefit of the aroma. Also, as it has turned out to be a fairly tender garden, the soil will need a little bit of extra attention to ensure that it is very well drained. There are also some herbs that will need lifting in the autumn—lemon verbena, pineapple sage, and the scented geranium 'Attar of Roses.' Equally, if you live in a damp, cold place, the myrtle and lavender dentata will need protection. When planting, note that I have put the honeysuckle in the corner to give it a wall or fence to climb up.

1	Southernwood *Artemisia abrotanum*	7	Orange-Scented Thyme *Thymus* 'Fragrantissimus'	13	Lavender Dentata *Lavandula dentata*
2	Marjoram Golden Curly *Origanum vulgare* 'Aureum Crispum'	8	Pineapple Sage *Salvia elegans* 'Scarlet Pineapple'	14	Myrtle *Myrtus communis*
3+18	Double-Flowered Chamomile *Chamaemelum nobile* 'Flore Pleno'	9	Orris *Iris* 'Florentina'	15	Rock Hyssop *Hyssopus officinalis* subsp. *aristatus*
4	Honeysuckle *Lonicera periclymenum*	10	Alecost *Tanacetum balsamita*	16	Benenden Blue Rosemary *Rosmarinus officinalis* var. *angustissimus* 'Benenden Blue'
5	Lemon Verbena *Aloysia triphylla*	11	Scented Geranium *Pelargonium* 'Attar of Roses'	17	Pinks, Doris *Dianthus* 'Doris'
6	Bergamot *Monarda didyma*	12	Caraway Thyme *Thymus herba-barona*	19	Oregano *Origanum vulgare*

roman herb garden

Over the years I have been asked by several schools to supply a list and simple plan of plants that would have been used in a Roman herb garden. This design makes use of a few of the many herbs used by the Romans. The circular hedge is a slight cheat, as Lavender Hidcote, with its flowers of a deep purple/blue, is, of course, a modern cultivar. I have chosen it because, being a small growing lavender, it is easy to maintain. To be strictly correct use *Lavandula angustifolia*, which grows much bigger. As the wormwood, elecampane, myrtle and catmint can grow to a good size, I have positioned them outside the circle to give them room to spread.

Whatever your personal preference, no good Roman would have been without his houseleek to protect him from witches, lightning and fire. Caraway was also said to give protection from witches and won its place, too, both as a fine culinary herb and as an ingredient in love potions to prevent a loved one leaving. Equally, no Roman herb garden would be complete without a bay tree, the leaves of which they used to crown their victorious soldiers. It reminded them of home and also harked back to an earlier heroic civilization—the roof of Apollo's temple at Delphi was made entirely of bay leaves. Finally, Romans would have added lavender to their baths at the end of a busy day to help them relax.

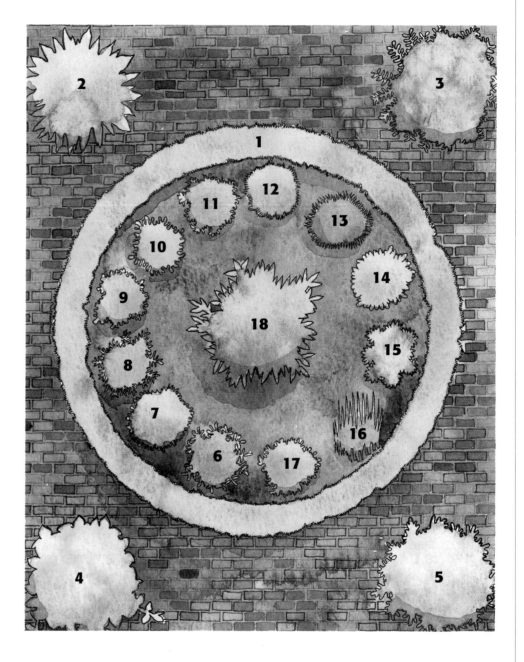

1   Lavender Hidcote *Lavandula angustifolia* 'Hidcote'
2   Wormwood *Artemisia absinthium*
3   Catmint *Nepeta cataria*
4   Elecampane *Inula helenium*
5   Myrtle *Myrtus communis*
6   Welsh Onion *Allium fistulosum*
7   Coriander *Coriandrum sativum*
8   Licorice *Glycyrrhiza glabra*
9   Winter Savory *Satureja montana*
10 Caraway *Carum carvi*
11 Parsley *Petroselinum crispum*
12 Rue *Ruta graveolens*
13 Creeping Pennyroyal *Mentha pulegium*
14 Hyssop *Hyssopus officinalis*
15 Dill *Anethum graveolens*
16 Alecost (Costmary) *Tanecetum balsmita*
17 Houseleek *Sempervivum tectorum*
18 Bay *Laurus nobilis*

HERBS IN CONTAINERS

In all the years I have been growing herbs I have only found a very, very few that cannot be grown in containers. In the A-Z section of this book I have given details not only about each herb and what size container best suits it, but also where to place it. This section provides more general information and advice on container growing that is applicable to most herbs.

Back row, left to right: **Lungwort,** *Pulmonaria officinalis,* **Prostanthera** *Prostanthera ovalifolia,* **Variegated Box,** *Buxus sempervirens* 'Elegantissimus', **Rosemary Benenden Blue,** *Rosmarinus officinalis* 'Benenden Blue', **Box,** *Buxus sempervirens*; front row, left to right: **Marjoram Golden Curly,** *Origanum vulgare* 'Aureum', **Rue Jackman's Blue,** *Ruta Graveolens* 'Jackman's Blue', **Old Warrior** *Artemisia pontica*

containers

* Choose the container to suit the plant. If it is a tall plant make sure the container has a base wide enough to prevent it toppling over, even if placed outside in a high wind.
* A collection of containers is sometimes much easier to look after than a window box, and you can give each herb its own individual bit of tender loving care.
* If using unconventional containers—old watering cans, sinks, a half beer barrel—make sure they have drainage holes, and gravel or broken pots in the bottom of the container to stop the holes clogging up.

hanging baskets

Herbs can suit hanging baskets, but the position is crucial. They dislike high wind and full sun all day. Also, they are mostly fast growers and if too cramped or over- or under-watered they will drop their leaves. They also benefit from being picked regularly, which is not always possible in a hanging basket.

I can recommend the following: double-flowered chamomile, creeping thymes, prostrate rosemary, catmint, creeping savory, golden marjoram, dwarf marjoram, pineapple mint, pennyroyal and maiden pinks—to name but a few. Other candidates can be found in the A to Z section.

Preparation of Hanging Baskets
* Line the basket with sphagnum moss followed by a layer of black plastic with holes punched in it.
* Fill the basket half full with compost. Position the plants, trailers at the side, taller, more upright herbs in the middle. Do not overcrowd.
* Fill up with compost. Water in well. Let it drain before hanging on a secure hook or bracket.
* Check hanging position for accessibility. In the height of the season you will need to water at least night and morning. Make sure that it cannot fall on anyone's head.

composts and organic fertilizers

Choosing the right compost is essential for healthy plants.

Own Soil-Based Mix

If you wish to make a soil-based compost of your own this recipe is fairly reliable.

4 parts good weed-free garden top soil
3 parts well rotted garden compost
3 parts of either coir or wood fiber or composted fine bark, all of which must be moistened prior to mixing with the other ingredients.
1 part sharp river sand.

Fertilizer

When making your own compost you will need to add a fertilizer either in granule form or as a liquid feed. Add at the rate that the manufacturers recommend. You can buy organic fertilizers from garden centers and hardware stores. The following organic fertilizers are ideal to be added to potting or seed-sowing composts.

Liquid Seaweed

This contains small amounts of nitrogen, phosphorous, potassium and it is also rich in trace elements. It not only makes a good soil feed but as the elements are easily taken in by the plant, it can also be sprayed on as a foliar feed.

Calcified Seaweed

This contains calcium magnesium, sodium and numerous trace elements. It is ideal for adding to seed compost. Add according to the manufacturer's instructions.

Ready-Made Potting and Seed Composts

Multipurpose Potting Compost

This is usually a peat-based compost with added nutrients. However, the nutrients are too strong for seed sowing and not enough for potting. Therefore I advise you to use a seed compost for seed sowing and a good peat-free potting compost for all your potting needs.

Peat-Free Composts

These are now readily available. Over the past three decades I have trialed everything here on my herb farm from composted duck manure to bark, coir and green waste.

Coir

This is a by-product of coconuts. Its main advantage is that it is very light. However, the main disadvantages are that it dries out very quickly, and it leaches the fertilizer. For this reason it is worth looking out for coir mixed with clay, which acts as a buffer and stops the fertilizer from disappearing, and it also stops the compost drying out too fast.

Clockwise: *Symphytum* 'Goldsmith'; *Primula veris*; *Viola rumiana* Purpurea Group; *Alchemilla conjuncta*

Composted bark

This is a byproduct of the wood industry. It is available in many sizes and shapes. For potting and container growing it is essential to get bark that has been properly composted for an adequate length of time. This is because newly harvested bark will not only burn the roots and stems of young plants, it will also take the nutrients from the plant and the compost as it starts to decompose.

Composted wood fiber

This is another byproduct of the wood industry and is now becoming readily available. The advantages are that it is very light and absorbent and behaves well in containers. The disadvantage is that it has to be heat treated, which puts up the cost and is not particularly environmentally friendly.

Green waste

This is a byproduct of city waste. Many local councils now sell green waste and many composts now include this. The advantage is that it is environmentally friendly; the disadvantages are the consistency of the contents and, if it has not been correctly composted, you can have an invasion of compost fly. There can be a certain amount of heavy metal waste within the compost, which can cause the plants to become distorted.

Maintenance

Spring This is the time of year to pot plants if necessary. A good sign of when they need this is that the roots are truly protruding from the bottom of the container. Use a pot next size up. Carefully remove the plant from its old pot. Give it a good tidy up—remove any weed and dead leaves. If it is a perennial, trim the growing tip to promote new bushy growth. Place gravel or other drainage material in the bottom of the container and keep the compost sweet by adding a tablespoon of granulated charcoal. As soon as the plant starts producing new growth or flowers, start feeding regularly with liquid seaweed.

Summer Keep a careful eye on the watering; make sure the pots do not dry out fully. Move some plants out of the midday sun. Deadhead any flowers. Feed with liquid seaweed, on average once a week. Remove any pest-damaged leaves.

Fall Cut back the perennial herbs. Weed containers and at the same time remove some of the top compost and redress. Bring any tender plants inside before the frosts. Start reducing the watering.
Winter Protect all container-grown plants from frosts. If possible, move into a cold greenhouse or sunroom. If weather is very severe, cover the containers in a layer of sacking. Keep watering to the absolute minimum.

HARVESTING

The more you pick, the healthier the plant. People are told that if their chives start to flower they will have no more fresh leaves until the following year. Rubbish! Pick some of the flowers to use in salads and, if the plant is then cut back to within 1½ in. of the ground and given a good feed of liquid fertilizer, it will produce another crop of succulent leaves within a month. Keep two chive plants: one for flowering and one for harvesting.

Herbs can be harvested from very early on in their growing season. This encourages the plant to produce vigorous new growth. It allows the plant to be controlled both in shape and size. Most herbs reach their peak of flavor just before they flower. Snip off suitable stems early in the day before the sun is fully up, or even better on a cloudy day (provided it is not too humid). Cut whole stems rather than single leaves or flowers. Always use a sharp knife, sharp scissors or hand pruners, and cut lengths of 2–3 in. from the tip of the branch, this being the new soft growth. Do not cut into any of the older, woody growth. Cut from all over the plant, leaving it looking shapely. Pick herbs which are clean and free from pests and diseases; they should not be discolored or damaged in any way. If herbs are covered in garden soil, sponge them quickly and lightly with cold water, not hot, as this will draw out the oils prematurely. Pat dry as quickly as possible. Keep each species separately so that they do not contaminate each other.

harvesting

Annual Herbs
Most can be harvested at least twice during a growing season. Cut them to within 4–6 in. of the ground, and feed with liquid fertilizer after each cutting.

Do not cut the plants too low in the first harvesting as they will not be able to recover in time to give a further cutting later on. Give annuals their final cut of the season before the first frosts; they will have stopped growing some weeks before.

Perennial Herbs
In the first year of planting, perennials will give one good crop; thereafter it will be possible to harvest two or three times during the growing season. Do not cut into the woody growth unless deliberately trying to prevent growth; again, cut well before frosts as cutting late in the season may weaken plants and inhibit them from surviving the winter. There are of course exceptions; sage is still very good after frosts, and both thyme and golden marjoram (with some protection) can be picked gently even in midwinter.

Flowers and Seeds
Pick flowers for drying when they are barely opened. Seed should be collected as soon as you notice a change in color of the seed pod; if when you tap the pod a few scatter on the ground, it is the time to gather them. Seeds ripen very fast, so watch them carefully.

Roots
These are at their peak of flavor when they have completed a growing season. Dig them through the fall as growth ceases. Lift whole roots with a garden fork, taking care not to puncture or bruise the outer skin. Wash them free of soil. Cut away any remains of top growth and any fibrous off-shoots. For drying cut large, thick roots in half lengthways and then into smaller pieces for ease.

drying

The object of drying herbs is to eliminate the water content of the plant quickly and, at the same time, to retain the essential oils. It looks pretty to have bunches of herbs hanging up in a kitchen but most of the flavor will be lost quickly. Herbs need to be dried in a warm, dark, dry and well-ventilated place. The faster they dry, the better retained are the aromatic oils. Darkness helps to prevent loss of color and unique flavors. The area must be dry, with a good air flow, to hasten the drying process and to discourage mold.

Suitable places for drying herbs include:
* an airing cupboard
* attic space immediately under the roof (provided it does not get too hot)
* in the oven at low temperature and with the door

ajar (place the herbs on a brown piece of paper with holes punched in it and check regularly that the herbs are not over-heating)

* a plate-warming compartment
* a spare room with curtains shut and door open.

The temperature should be maintained at slightly below body temperature, between 70–90°F/21–33°C.

Herbs should always be dried separately from each other, especially the stronger-scented ones like lovage. Spread them in a single layer on trays or slatted wooden racks covered with muslin or netting. The trays or frames should be placed in the drying areas so that they have good air circulation. Herbs need to be turned over by hand several times during the first two days.

Roots require a higher temperature—from 120–140°F/50–60°C. They are quicker and easier to dry in an oven and require regular turning until they are fragile and break easily. Specific requirements are given for each herb in the A–Z section.

Seeds should be dried without any artificial heat and in an airy place. Almost-ripe seed heads can be hung in paper bags (plastic causes them to sweat) so the majority of seeds will fall into the bag as they mature. They need to be dried thoroughly before storing and the process can take up to 2 weeks.

TIP An alternative method for flowers, roots or seed heads is to tie them in small bundles of 8 to 10 stems. Do not pack the stems too tightly together, as air needs to circulate through and around the bunches. Then hang them on coathangers in an airy, dark room until they are dry.

The length of drying time varies from herb to herb, and week to week. The determining factor is the state of the plant material. If herbs are stored before drying is complete, moisture will be reabsorbed from the atmosphere and the herb will soon deteriorate. Leaves should be both brittle and crisp. They should break easily into small pieces but should not reduce to a powder when touched. The roots should be brittle and dry right through. Any softness or sponginess means they are not sufficiently dry and, if stored that way, will rot.

a quick method of herb drying

Microwave manufacturers have said it takes 3 to 4 minutes to dry thoroughly 10 sprigs of any herb! I have tried. It is easy to overdry and cook the leaves to the point of complete disintegration. I have found that small-leaved herbs such as rosemary and thyme take

Parsley stored in a bag for freezing, together with ice cubes for convenience

about 1 minute, while the larger, moist leaves of mint dry in about 3 minutes. Add an eggcupful of water to the microwave during the process. And be warned! Sage can ignite….

storing

Herbs lose their flavor and color if not stored properly. Pack the leaves or roots, not too tightly, into a dark glass jar with an air-tight screw top. Label with name and date. Keep in a dark cupboard; nothing destroys the quality of the herb more quickly at this stage than exposure to light.

After the initial storing, keep a check on the jars for several days. If moisture starts to form on the inside of the container, the herbs have not been dried correctly. Return them to the drying area and allow further drying time.

Most domestic herb requirements are comparatively small so there is little point in storing large amounts for a long time. The shelf life of dried herbs is only about 1 year so it is sufficient to keep enough just for the winter.

Dried herbs are usually three to four times more powerful than fresh. When a recipe calls for a tablespoon of a fresh herb and you only have dried, use a teaspoonful.

TIP If you have large, dark jars, thyme and rosemary can be left on the stalk. This makes it easier to use them in casseroles and stews and to remove before serving.

freezing herbs

Freezing is great for culinary herbs as color, flavor and the nutritional value of the fresh young leaves are retained. It is becoming an increasingly popular way to preserve and store culinary herbs, being quick and easy. I believe it is far better to freeze herbs such as fennel, dill, parsley, tarragon and chives than to dry them.

Pick the herbs and, if necessary, rinse with cold water, and shake dry before freezing, being careful not to bruise the leaves. Put small amounts of herbs into labeled plastic bags, either singly, or as a mixture for bouquet garnis. Either have a set place in the freezer for them or put the bags into a container, so that they do not get damaged with the day-to-day use of the freezer.

There is no need to thaw herbs before use; simply add them to the cooking as required. For chopped parsley, freeze the bunches whole in bags and, when you remove them from the freezer, crush the parsley in its bag with your hand. Do not be distracted in this task or you will have a herb that has thawed and is a limp piece of greenery. This technique is good for all fine-leaved herbs.

Another way to freeze herbs conveniently is to put finely chopped leaves into an ice-cube tray and top them up with water. The average cube holds 1 tablespoon of chopped herbs mixed with 1 teaspoon of water.

TIP The flowers of borage and the leaves of the variegated mints look very attractive when frozen individually in ice-cubes for drinks or fruit salads.

HERB OILS, VINEGARS & PRESERVES

Many herbs have antiseptic and antibacterial qualities, and were used in preserving long before there were cookbooks. Herbs aid digestion, stimulate appetite and enhance the flavor of food. I hope the following recipes will tempt you, because a variety of herb oils and vinegars can lead to the creation of unusual and interesting dishes. Herbs can make salad dressings, tomato-based sauces for pasta dishes, marinades for fish and meat, and can act as softening agents for vegetables, introducing a myriad of new tastes and flavors. They also make marvelous gifts.

Basil oil, coriander seed vinegar and coriander oil

herb oils

These can be used in salad dressings, in marinades, sauces, stir-fry dishes and sautéing. Find some interesting bottles with pleasing shapes.

To start with, you need a clean glass jar, large enough to hold 1½ cups with a screw top.

Basil oil

This is one of the best ways of storing and capturing the unique flavor of basil.

4 tablespoons basil leaves
1½ cups olive or sunflower oil

Pick over the basil, remove the leaves from the stalks, and crush them in a mortar. For Greek basil, with its small leaves, simply crush in the mortar. Pound very slightly. Add a little oil and pound gently again. This bruises the leaves, so releasing their own oil into the oil. Mix the leaves with the rest of the oil and pour into a wide-necked jar, seal tightly and refrigerate. Shake it every other day; and, after 2 weeks, strain through muslin into a decorative bottle and add a couple of fresh leaves of the relevant basil. This helps to identify the type of basil used and also looks fresh and enticing. Label.

Adapt for dill, fennel (green), sweet marjoram, rosemary and garden or lemon thyme.

Garlic also makes a very good oil. Use 4 cloves of garlic, peeled and crushed, and combined with the oil.

Bouquet Garni Oil

I use this oil for numerous dishes.

1 tablespoon sage
1 tablespoon lemon thyme
1 tablespoon Greek oregano
1 tablespoon French parsley
1 bay leaf
1½ cups olive or sunflower oil

Break all the leaves and mix them in a mortar, pounding lightly. Add a small amount of the oil and mix well, allowing the flavors to infuse. Pour into a wide-necked jar with the remaining oil. Cover and leave on a sunny windowsill for 2–3 weeks. Shake or stir the jar every other day. Strain through muslin into an attractive bottle. If there is room, add a fresh sprig of each herb used.

sweet oils

Good with fruit dishes, marinades and puddings. Use almond oil, which combines well with scented flowers such as pinks, lavender, lemon verbena, rose petals and scented geraniums. Make as for savory oils above. Mix 4 tablespoons of torn petals or leaves with 1½ cups almond oil.

spice oils

Ideal for salad dressings, they can be used for sautéing and stir-frying too. The most suitable herb spices are: coriander seeds, dill seeds and fennel seeds. Combine 2 tablespoons of seeds with 1½ cups olive or sunflower oil, having first pounded the seeds gently to crush them in a mortar and mixed them with a little of the oil. Add a few of the whole seeds to the oil before bottling and labeling. Treat as for savory oils and store.

herbal vinegars

Made in much the same way as oils, they can be used in gravies and sauces, marinades and salad dressings.

10 tablespoons chopped herb, such as basil, chervil, dill, fennel, garlic, lemon balm, marjoram, mint, rosemary, savory, tarragon or thyme
1½ cups white wine or cider vinegar

Pound the leaves gently in a mortar. Heat half the vinegar until warm but not boiling, and pour it over the herbs in the mortar. Pound further to release the flavors of the herb. Leave to cool. Mix this mixture with the remaining vinegar and pour into a wide-necked bottle. Seal tightly. Remember to use an acid-proof lid (lining the existing lid with greaseproof paper is a way around this). Put on a sunny windowsill and shake each day for 2 weeks. Test for flavor; if a stronger taste is required, strain the vinegar and repeat with fresh herbs. Store as is or strain through double muslin and rebottle. Add a fresh sprig of the chosen herb to the bottle for ease of identification.

To Save Time
1 bottle white wine vinegar (1½ cups)
4 large sprigs herb
4 garlic cloves, peeled

Pour off a little vinegar from the bottle and push in 2 sprigs of herb and the garlic cloves. Top up with the reserved vinegar if necessary. Reseal the bottle and leave on a sunny windowsill for 2 weeks. Change the herb sprigs for fresh ones and the vinegar is now ready to use.

Seed Vinegar
Make as for herb vinegar, but the amounts used are 2 tablespoons of seeds to 2 cups white wine or cider vinegar. Seeds that make well-flavored vinegars include dill, fennel and coriander.

Floral Vinegar
Made in the same way, these are used for fruit salads and cosmetic recipes. Combine elder, nasturtiums, sweet violets, pinks, lavender, primrose, rose petals, rosemary or thyme flowers in the following proportions:

10 tablespoons torn flower heads or petals
1½ cups white wine vinegar

Pickled Horseradish
As a child I lived in a small village in the West of England where an old man called Mr Bell sat outside his cottage crying in the early fall. It took me a long time to understand why—he was scraping the horseradish root into a bowl to make pickle. He did this outside because the fumes given off by the horseradish were so strong that they made one's eyes water.

Wash and scrape the skin off a good-sized horseradish root. Mince in a food processor or grate it (if you can stand it!). Pack into small jars and cover with salted vinegar made from 1 teaspoon salt to 1 cup cider or white wine vinegar. Seal and leave for 4 weeks before using.

Pickled Nasturtium Seeds
Poor man's capers!
Pick nasturtium seeds while still green. Steep in brine made from ½ cup salt to 3½ cups water for 24 hours. Strain the seeds and put 2 tablespoons of seeds into a small jar. Into a saucepan add 1 clove of peeled garlic, 1 teaspoon black peppercorns, 1 teaspoon dill seeds and 1 tablespoon English mace leaves and enough white wine vinegar to fill the jar. Slowly bring to simmering point. Then strain the vinegar and pour over the seeds. Seal the jars with acid-proof lids and leave for about 4 weeks. After opening, store in the refrigerator, and use the contents quickly.

savory herb jelly

Use the following herbs: sweet marjoram, mints (all kinds), rosemary, sage, summer savory, tarragon and common thyme.
Makes 2 x 12 oz. jars.

2 lb. tart cooking apples or crabapples, roughly chopped, cores and all
3 cups water
2 cups sugar
2 tablespoons wine vinegar

2 tablespoons lemon juice
1 bunch herbs, approx ½ oz.
4 tablespoons chopped herbs

Put the apples into a large pan with the bunch of herbs and cover with cold water. Bring to the boil and simmer until the apples are soft, which may take roughly 30 minutes. Pour into a jelly bag and drain overnight.

Measure the strained juice and add 2 cups sugar to every 2 cups fluid. Stir over gentle heat until the sugar has dissolved. Bring to the boil, stirring, and boil until setting point is reached. This takes roughly 20–30 minutes. Skim the surface scum and stir in the vinegar and lemon juice and the chopped herbs. Pour into jars, seal and label before storing.

sweet jellies

Follow the above recipe, omitting the vinegar and lemon juice, and instead adding ½ cup water. The following make interestingly flavored sweet jellies: bergamot, lavender flower, lemon verbena, scented geranium, sweet violet and lemon balm.

preserves

Coriander Chutney
Makes 2 x 1 lb. jars.

2 lb. cooking apples, peeled, cored and sliced
1 lb. onions, peeled and roughly chopped
2 cloves garlic, peeled and crushed
1 red and 1 green pepper, deseeded and sliced
3 cups red wine vinegar
1 lb. soft brown sugar
½ tablespoon whole coriander seeds
6 peppercorns tied securely in a piece of muslin
6 all-spice berries
2 oz. root ginger, peeled and sliced
2 tablespoons coriander leaves, chopped
2 tablespoons mint, chopped

Combine the apples with the onions, garlic and peppers in a large, heavy saucepan. Add the vinegar and bring to the boil, simmering for about 30 minutes until all the ingredients are soft. Add the brown sugar and the muslin bag of seeds and berries. Then add the ginger. Heat, gently stirring all the time, until the sugar has dissolved, and simmer until thick; this can take up to 60 minutes. Stir in the chopped coriander and mint and spoon into hot, sterilized jars. Seal and label when cool.

NATURAL DYES

fabric

Any natural material can be dyed; some are more tricky than others. It just takes time and practice. In the following sections I will explain the techniques connected with dying wool, the most reliable and easiest of natural materials. Silk, linen and cotton can also be dyed, but are more difficult.

Herbs have been used to dye cloth since the earliest records. In fact, until the 19th century and the birth of the chemical industry, all dyes were "natural." Then the chemical process, offering a larger range of colors and a more guaranteed result, took over. Now, once again, there is a real demand for more natural products and colors, which has resulted in a revival of interest in plants as a dye source.

The most common dyeing herbs are listed in the dye chart. You will notice that yellows, browns and grays are predominant. Plenty of plant material will be required so be careful not to overpick in your own garden (and please do not pick other people's plants without permission! I plead from personal experience). To begin with, keep it simple. Pick the flowers just as they are coming out, the leaves when they are young and fresh and a good green; dig up roots in the fall and cut them up well before use.

preparation

First time, this is a messy and fairly lengthy process, so use a utility room, or clear the decks in the kitchen and protect all areas. Best of all keep it away from the home altogether. Some of the mordants used for fixing dye are poisonous, so keep them well away from children, pets and food.

The actual dyeing process is not difficult, but you will need space, and a few special pieces of equipment:

1 large stainless steel vessel, such as a preserving can (to be used as the dye-bath)
1 stainless steel or enamel bucket and bowl
1 pair of tongs (wooden or stainless steel; to be used for lifting)
1 measuring jug
1 pair rubber gloves essential for all but Jumblies—
"Their heads are green and their hands are blue, And they went to sea in a sieve."
Pestle and mortar
Thermometer
Water; this must be soft, either rainwater or filtered
Scales

Dyeing comprises four separate tasks:

* Preparation of the material (known as scouring)

* Preparation of the mordant

* Preparation of the dye

* Dyeing process

preparation of the material (scouring)

Prepare the wool by washing it in a hot solution of soap flakes or a proprietary scouring agent in order to remove any grease. Always handle the wool gently. Rinse it several times, squeezing (gently) between each rinse. On the final rinse add ¼ cup of vinegar.

The flowers of St. John's Wort produce a beige dye

preparation of the mordant

Mordants help "fix" the dye to the fabric. They are available from chemists or dye suppliers. The list below includes some of the more common. Some natural dyers say that one should not use mordants, but without them the dye will run very easily.

Alum: Use 2 tablespoons to 18 oz. dry wool
This is the most useful of mordants, its full title being potassium aluminum sulfate. Sometimes potassium hydrogen tartrate, cream of tartar, is added (beware! this is not the baking substance) in order to facilitate the process and brighten the color.

Iron: Use ½ tablespoon to 18 oz. dry wool
This is ferrous sulfate. It dulls and deepens the colors. It is added in the final process after first using the mordant Alum. Remove the wool before adding the iron, then replace the wool and simmer until you get the depth of color required.

Copper: Use 1 tablespoon to 18 oz. dry wool
This is copper sulfate. If you mix with 1¼ cup of vinegar when preparing the mordant it will give a blue/green tint to colors.
WARNING: Wear gloves; copper is poisonous.

Chrome: Use 1 tablespoon to 18 oz. dry wool
This is bichromate of potash and light-sensitive, so keep it in the dark. It gives the color depth, makes the colors fast, and gives the wool a soft, silky feel.
WARNING: Wear gloves; chrome is poisonous.

* Dissolve the mordant in a little hot water.

* Stir into 5 gallons of hot water 122°F (50°C).

* When thoroughly dissolved immerse the wet, washed wool in the mixture. Make sure it is wholly immersed.

* Slowly bring to the boil and simmer at 180–200°F (82–94°C) for an hour.

* Remove from the heat. Take the wool out of the water and rinse.

preparation of the dye

No two batches of herbal dye will be the same. There are so many variable factors—plant variety, water, mordant, immersion time.

The amount of plant material required for dyeing is very variable. A good starting ratio is 18 oz. of mordanted wool in skeins to 18 oz. plant material.

* Chop or crush the plant material.

* Place loosely in a muslin or nylon bag and tie securely.

* Leave to soak in 5 gallons of soft, tepid water overnight.

* Slowly bring the water and herb material to the boil.

* Reduce heat and simmer at 180–200°F (82–94°C) for as long as it takes to get the water to the desired color. This can take from 1 to 3 hours.

* Remove the pan from the heat, remove the herb material, and allow the liquid to cool to hand temperature.

dyeing process

* Gently add the wool.

* Bring the water slowly to the boil, stirring occasionally with the wooden tongs.

* Allow to simmer for a further hour.

* Remove pan from the heat and leave the wool in the dye-bath until cold, or until the color is right.

* Remove the wool with the tongs and rinse in tepid water until no color runs out.

* Give a final rinse in cold water.

* Dry the skeins of wool over a rod or cord, away from direct heat. Tie a light weight to the bottom to stop the wool kinking during the drying process.

dye chart

Common Name	Botanical Name	Part Used	Mordant	Color
Comfrey	*Symphytum officinale*	Leaves and stalks	Alum	Yellows
Chamomile, Dyers	*Anthemis tinctoria*	Flowers	Alum	Yellows
Chamomile, Dyers	*Anthemis tinctoria*	Flowers	Copper	Olives
Elder	*Sambucus nigra*	Leaves	Alum	Greens
Elder	*Sambucus nigra*	Berries	Alum	Violets/Purple
Goldenrod	*Solidago canadensis*	Whole plant	Chrome	Golden Yellows
Horsetail	*Equisetum arvense*	Stems and leaves	Alum	Yellows
Juniper	*Juniperus communis*	Crushed berries	Alum	Yellows
Marigold	*Calendula officinalis*	Petals	Alum	Pale Yellow
Meadowsweet	*Filipendula ulmaria*	Roots	Alum	Black
Nettle	*Urtica dioica*	Whole plant	Copper	Grayish-green
St. John's Wort	*Hypericum perforatum*	Flowers	Alum	Beiges
Sorrel	*Rumex acetosa*	Whole plant	Alum	Dirty yellow
Sorrel	*Rumex acetosa*	Roots	Alum	Beige/pink
Tansy	*Tanacetum vulgare*	Flowers	Alum	Yellows
Woad	*Isatus tinctoria*	Leaves	Sodium dithionite, ammonia	Blues

PESTS & DISEASES

Herbs suffer from few pests and diseases, and in fact many of them can be used in the vegetable garden to protect other crops. Even so, always be on the lookout, as, in early stages of attack, they can often be dealt with by methods other than the dreaded spray gun.

general methods of control

Biological Control
Many biological control methods are now available commercially. When you plant in the open, harmful pests are mostly kept under control by predators. However, in the enclosed environment of the greenhouse, the natural balance can break down. All biological control methods are relatively expensive when compared with the chemical alternatives, and nearly all are dependent on warm temperatures to work efficiently.

Organic Sprays
If all else fails, there are now organic sprays for pests such as aphids and whitefly, which can be purchased at any good garden center or hardware store. Make sure that it is an organic spray with the recognized organic symbol. I use a liquid insecticidal soap, which is then mixed with rainwater and sprayed on infestations of whitefly or aphids. It is harmless to ladybirds, bees and other large insects. There are no organic fungicides on the market. Traditionally the old gardeners used homemade sprays made from many different herbs to control mildew and "dampening off."

Companion Planting
I believe that certain plants can assist other plants to thrive when planted together. Fragrant herbs such as hyssop, thyme, marjoram, chives and parsley are beneficial in maintaining the health of a vegetable garden. There are no scientific records to back this up, but a number of gardeners have reported improvements in the general health of their vegetables when they are interplanted with these herbs. Many herbs act as an insect repellent when they are grown near other plants, one reason being the strong scent that they give off. The most effective ones are tansy, pennyroyal, nasturtiums, stinging nettle, garlic, chives, hyssop, wormwood and southernwood.

Chemicals for Control of Pests and Diseases
I realize that some people need to use chemicals. However, most herbs can be grown very successfully without, and if the herbs are being used as a food crop, it is worth taking that little bit of extra care.

When selecting chemicals, choose the one appropriate to the problem. Follow the manufacturer's instructions carefully and keep them with the bottle for future reference. Store the bottle after use in a secure cupboard, locked well away from animals and children.

pests

There are many, many pests in the garden, and I have only mentioned the few that are known to affect herbs in general.

Aphids: Greenfly, Blackfly, Black Bean Aphid

From early spring in the greenhouse, and later outside, keep a watch for greenfly. If you see a few, kill them! If there are a lot, spray them with an insecticidal soap, following the manufacturer's instructions.

With blackfly, do exactly the same. Do not use a high-pressure hose as you will damage the plant. If it is a potted plant, such as nasturtiums, wash them off gently under the tap; otherwise spray with an insecticidal soap, as above.

Carrot Root Fly

The grub of this fly tunnels into the roots of plants during early summer, so herbs such as those from the Umbelliferous family, which have a long tap root, are at risk. The first sign of attack will be the yellowing of the leaves and stunted growth. Parsley may be particularly vulnerable, and in this case the plant should be pulled up and destroyed to get rid of the pests. However, large herbs should overcome attacks, so just pick off dead leaves and boost the plant by feeding with liquid seaweed.

A preventative method is to put a 30 in. plastic barrier around the crop during mid-spring, or cover with a frost cloth while the plants are young. Sowings after midsummer miss the first generation.

Caterpillars: Cabbage White

These are attracted to herbs with large leaves, such as horseradish, in late spring through to early fall. Check weekly, and simply pick them off by hand and destroy. Early in the season, when the plants are small, a frost cloth is a good barrier.

Leaf Miners

These grubs are sometimes a problem on lovage, wild celery, certain sorrels and various mints. They eat inside the leaf, creating winding tunnels in the leaves

Aphids

like little silver tracks, which are clearly visible. Watch for the first tunnels, pick off the affected leaves and destroy them. If left, the tunnels will extend into broad dry patches, and complete leaves will wither away.

Red Spider Mite

The spider mites like hot, dry conditions and can become prolific in a glasshouse. Look out for early signs of the pests such as speckling on the upper surfaces of the leaves. Look under the leaf with a magnifying glass and you will see these minute red spiders. Another tell-tale sign is the cobwebs. At first sight, either use insecticidal soap in the form of a spray, or the natural predator *Phytoseiulus persimilis*, following the instructions that will come with them. Do not use both.

Rosemary Beetle

This small, shiny, metallic dark green beetle, which is distinguished by the five purple strips on each wing case has become prevalent since I originally wrote this book 15 years ago. They eat the leaves and growing tips of lavender, rosemary, thyme and sage.
The easiest way to get rid of this pest is to hand-pick and destroy the beetles and larvae when found.

Scale Insects

These are often noticeable as immobile, waxy, brown/yellow, flat, oval lumps gathered on the backs of leaves or on the stems of bay trees. These leaves also become covered with sticky black sooty mold. Rub off the scales gently before the infestation builds up. Alternatively, spray with an insecticidal soap, following the manufacturer's instructions.

Slugs

These can only be elimimated by hand or by setting out beer traps, or even better a size 10 boot. There is a microscopic nematode that can be used as a form of biological control and infects the slugs with a bacterium that stops them feeding within a week, it actually kills them in two. This is an expensive way of getting rid of them, but worth it to protect your specimen plants.

Vine Weevil

These can be a major pest. Look out for them in the spring and early fall. In the ground or in pots you may see horrid white grubs with orange heads. The parent is a small nocturnal beetle with a weevil's nose. The grubs eat the roots of plants; the beetles eat leaves, especially those of vines. I have tried various organic methods of eradication, from repotting 10,000 plants to check and get rid of the grubs, to watering with nematodes (eelworms) in the fall. This is a form of biological control in which the worms destroy the vine weevil grubs. The soil temperature must be above 41°F (5ºC) for them to work.

Whitefly

Under protection in the glasshouse this can be a problem, less so outside. It is essential to act immediately. One method is to introduce the natural predator *Encarsia formosa*, a minute parasitic wasp that lays its eggs in the whitefly larvae, which are usually found attached to the underside of the leaves.

Scale insect

Unfortunately, these parasites need warm temperatures to multiply so they cannot be successfully used in early spring or fall. Alternatively, spray with an insecticidal soap and repeat 7 days later.

diseases

Mint Rust (and Other Similar Rusts)

Plants affected by rust should be dug up and thrown away. Alternatively, you can, in the fall, put straw around the affected plants and set it alight. This will actually sterilize the soil and the plant. Comfrey also suffers from a rust disease. Here the best answer is to keep the plant clipped. Cut off leaves every 4 weeks and keep well fed with manure and compost.

Powdery Mildew

This common fungal disease can occur when the conditions are hot and dry, and the plants are overcrowded. Prevent it by watering well during dry spells, following the recommended planting distances, and clearing away any fallen leaves in the fall. Adding a mulch in the fall or early spring also helps. If your plant does suffer, destroy all the affected leaves.

Powdery mildew

YEARLY CALENDAR

As any gardener knows, you cannot be precise. Each year is different—wetter, windier, hotter, drier, colder than the last. This calendar can be used as a general guide. You can adjust what you do according to your first and last frost dates, or if you live in a particularly hot region, you may have to pay more attention to watering for much of the year.

midwinter

This is one of the quietest times. Keep an eye on the degrees of frost and protect tender herbs with an extra layer of frost cloth or mulch if necessary. With (one hopes) everything quiet, this is a good time to plan any additions or changes to the herb garden—like constructing new paths, steps, arches etc. It is also the time to order seeds for spring sowing.

Fresh Herbs Available
With a little bit of protection in the garden, bay, hyssop, rosemary, sage, winter savory, thyme, lemon thyme, chervil, parsley, celery leaf.

Cultivation
Seed with Heat
Parsley.

Seed Outside in the Garden
If not sown in the fall, sow sweet cicely, sweet woodruff, cowslip, to enable a period of stratification.

Force in Boxes in the Greenhouse
Chives, mint, tarragon.

Force outside
Sea kale.

Containers
Keep watering to a minimum. Clean old pots ready for spring potting.

Garden
Nothing to do other than keep an eye on the garden to ensure no damage is being caused by the weather.

late winter

As the days begin to lengthen, and if the weather is not too unpleasant, this is a good time to have the final tidy up before the busy season starts. If you want to get an early start in the garden and you have prepared a site the previous fall, cover the soil now with black plastic. It will warm up the soil and force any weeds.

Fresh Herbs Available
With a little bit of protection in the garden: bay, hyssop, rosemary, sage, winter savory, thyme, lemon thyme, chervil, parsley.
  Chives start to come up if they are under protection, and mint can be available if forced.

Cultivation

Seed with Heat
Borage, dill, parsley.

Seed in Cold Greenhouse
Chervil.

Division
Herbaceous perennial herbs can be divided now, as long as they are not too frozen and are given added protection after replanting. Chives, lemon balm, pot marjoram, mints, oregano, broad-leafed sorrel, tarragon.

Containers
As the containers have been brought in for the winter, new life may be starting. Dust off, and slowly start watering. Not too much.

Garden
Check that any dead or decaying herbaceous growth is not damaging plants. Check for wind and snow damage.

early spring

Spring is in the air, everything is Go. Even with a cold start to spring it is still worth getting started, even if the worst comes to the worst and the seed has to be sown again in a month. Gradually uncover tender plants outside and look for hopeful signs of life. Give them a gentle tidy.

Fresh Herbs Available

Angelica, lemon balm, bay, chives, fennel, hyssop, mint, parsley, peppermint, pennyroyal, rue, sage, savory, sorrel, thyme.

Cultivation

Seed with Heat

Amaranth, celery leaf, beetroot, purslane, shiso, borage, fennel, coriander, sweet marjoram, rue and basil—once conditions start to warm up a little.

Seed in Cold Greenhouse

Chervil, chives, dill, lemon balm, lovage, parsley, sage, summer savory, sorrel.

Seed Outside in the Garden

Chervil, chives, parsley (cover with cloches), chamomile, tansy, caraway, borage, fennel.

Check seeds that have been left outside from the previous fall for the purpose of stratification. If they are starting to germinate, move them into a cold greenhouse.

Root Cuttings

Mint, tarragon, bergamot, chamomile, hyssop, tansy, sweet woodruff, sweet cicely.

Division

Mint, tarragon, wormwood, lovage, rue, sorrel, lemon balm, salad burnet, camphor plant, thyme, winter savory, marjoram, alecost, horehound, pennyroyal.

Layering

This is a good time to start mound layering on old sages or thymes.

Containers

Tidy up all the pots, trim old growth to maintain shape. Start liquid feeding with seaweed. Repot if necessary. Pot new plants into containers for display later in the season.

Garden

Clear up all the winter debris, fork the garden over and give a light dressing of bonemeal. If your soil is alkaline, and you gave it a good dressing of manure in the fall, now is the time to dig it well in.

Remove black plastic, weed and place a cloche over important sowing sites a week before sowing to raise the soil temperature and keep it dry.

A few weeks into spring, if the major frosts are over, you can cut lavender back and into shape. This is certainly advisable for plants 2 years old and older. Give them a good mulch. Equally, sage bushes of 2 years and older would benefit from a trim—not hard back because sage does not recover well when cut into the old wood. Cut back elder and rosemary; neither minds a hard cutting back, in fact, quite often they benefit from it. Transplant the following if they need it: alecost, chives, mint, balm, pot marjoram, sorrel, horehound and rue.

mid-spring

Suddenly there are not enough hours in the day. This is the main time for sowing outdoors, as soon as soil conditions permit. It is also now possible to prune back to strong new shoots the branches of any shrubs that have suffered in winter.

Fresh Herbs Available

Angelica, balm, bay, borage, caraway, chervil, chives, fennel, hyssop, lovage, pot marjoram, mints, parsley, pennyroyal, peppermint, rosemary, sage, winter savory, sorrel, thyme, tarragon, lemon thyme, celery leaf, lemon grass.

Cultivation

Seed with Heat

Basil.

Seed in Cold Greenhouse

Borage, chervil, coriander, dill, fennel, lemon balm, lovage, pot marjoram, sweet marjoram, sage, summer savory, winter savory, sorrel, buckler-leaf sorrel, horehound, rue, bergamot, caraway, garden thyme.

Seed Outside in the Garden

Parsley, chives, hyssop, caraway, pot marigold, mustard.

Seedlings

Prick out previously sown seeds, pot on, or harden off before planting out.

Softwood Cuttings

Rue, mint, sage, southernwood, winter savory, thymes, horehound, lavender, rosemary, cotton lavender, curry.

Root Cuttings

Sweet cicely, fennel, mint.

Division

Pennyroyal, chives, lady's mantle, salad burnet, tarragon, last year's lemon grass.

Containers

You should be able to put all containers outside now; keep an eye on the watering and feeding.

Garden

This is a busy time in the garden. If all the frosts have finished, the following will need cutting and pruning into shape: bay, winter savory, hyssop, cotton lavender, lavenders, rue especially variegated rue, southernwood and thymes.

late spring

Everything should be growing quickly now. The annuals will need thinning; tender and half-hardy plants should be hardened off under a cold frame or beside a warm wall. A watch must be kept for a sudden late frost; Sir Basil is especially susceptible. Move container specimens into bigger pots or top dress with new compost.

Fresh Herbs Available

Nearly all varieties.

Cultivation

Seed Outside in the Garden

Keep sowing beetroot, coriander, dill, chervil, parsley, sweet marjoram, basil, and any other annuals you require to maintain crop.

Seedlings

Prick out and pot or plant any of the previous month's seedlings.

Softwood Cuttings

Marjorams, all mints, oregano, rosemarys, winter savory, French tarragon, all thymes.

Containers

These should now be looking good. Keep trimming to maintain shape; water and feed regularly.

Garden

Trim southernwood into shape.

Harvesting

Cut second-year growth of angelica for candying. Cut thyme before flowering for drying.

Allium schoenoprasum 'Forescate'
Pink chives

early summer

This is a great time in the herb garden. All planting is now completed. Plants are beginning to join up so that little further weeding will be needed. Many plants are now reaching perfection.

Fresh Herbs Available
All.

Cultivation
Seed Outside in the Garden
Basil, borage, chives, coriander, dill, fennel, sweet marjoram, summer savory, winter savory, mustard, amaranth, sea fennel and any others you wish to replace, or keep going.

Cuttings
With all the soft new growth available this is a very busy time for cuttings. Make sure you use material from non-flowering shoots.

Softwood Cuttings
All perennial marjorams, all mints, all rosemary, all sage, variegated lemon balm , tarragon (French), all thymes.

Division
Thymes.

Layering
Rosemary.

Containers
Plant annual herbs into containers to keep near the kitchen. Basil, sweet marjoram, etc.

Garden
If you must plant basil in the garden, do it now. Nip out the growing tips of this year's young plants to en-courage them to bush out.

Trim cotton lavender hedges if flowers are not required and to maintain their shape; clip box hedges and topiary shapes as needed. A new herb garden should be weeded thoroughly to give the new plants the best chance.

Harvesting
Cut second-year growth of angelica for candying. Cut sage for drying.

midsummer

The season is on the wane, the early annuals and biennials are beginning to go over. It is already time to think of next year and to start collecting seeds. Take cuttings of tender shrubs as spare shoots become available.

Borago officinalis

Fresh Herbs Available
All.

Cultivation
Seed Outside in the Garden
Chervil, angelica (if seed is set), borage, chervil, coriander, dill, lovage, parsley.

Softwood Cuttings
Wormwood, scented geraniums, lavenders, thymes.

Layering
Rosemary.

Containers
Keep an eye on the watering as the temperatures begin to rise.

Garden
Cut all lavenders back after flowering to maintain shape. If this is the first summer of the herb garden and the plants are not fully established it is important to make sure they do not dry out, so water regularly. Once established many are tolerant of drought.

Harvesting
Drying
Lemon balm, horehound, summer savory, hyssop, tarragon, thyme, lavender.

Dyeing and Potpourri
Lavender, rosemary.

Seed
Caraway, angelica.

late summer

Traditionally a time for holidays, but it is also a time to harvest and preserve many herbs for winter use. Collect and dry material for potpourri, and collect seeds for sowing next year.

Fresh Herbs Available
All.

Cultivation
Seed Outside in the Garden or Greenhouse
Angelica, coriander, dill, lovage, parsley, winter savory.

Softwood Cuttings
Bay, wormwood, rosemary, thymes, lavenders, scented geraniums, balm of Gilead, pineapple sage, myrtles.

Containers
If you are going away, make sure you ask a friend to water your containers for you.

Garden
Give box, cotton lavender, and curry their second clipping and trim any established plants that are looking unruly. Maintain watering of the new herb garden and keep an eye on mints, parsley, and comfrey, which need water to flourish. There is no real need to feed if the ground has been well prepared, but if the plants are recovering from a pest attack they will benefit from a foliar feed of liquid seaweed.

Harvesting
Drying
Thyme, sage, clary sage, marjoram, lavender.

Freezing
The mints, pennyroyal.

Oils
Basil.

Seed
Angelica, anise, caraway, coriander, cumin, chervil, dill, fennel.

early fall

Shortly after the start of fall, basil should be taken up and leaves preserved. Line out semiripe cuttings of box, cotton lavenders, etc, in cold frames, under cloches or in plastic tunnels for hedge renewal in the spring.

Fresh Herbs Available
Lemon balm, basil, bay, borage, caraway, chervil, chives, clary sage, fennel, hyssop, pot marigold, marjoram, the mints, parsley, pennyroyal, peppermint, rosemarys, sages, winter savory, sorrels, the thymes.

Cultivation
Seed Outside in the Garden or Greenhouse
Angelica, chives, coriander, parsley, winter savory.

Softwood and Semiripe Cuttings
Rosemary, the thymes, tarragon, the lavenders, rue, the cotton lavenders, the curry plants, box.

Division
Bergamot.

Containers
As it becomes colder, take in all containers, and protect tender plants like bay trees, myrtles, scented geraniums, lemon grass and cardamom.

Garden
Give the shrubby herbs their final clipping (bay, lavender, etc.). Do not leave it too late or the frost could damage the new growth.
　　Put basil into glasshouse or kitchen. Top dress bergamots if they have died back.
　　If lemon verbena is to be kept outside make sure it is getting adequate protection.

Harvesting
Drying or Freezing
Dandelion (roots), parsley, marigold, clary sage, peppermint.

Seed
Angelica, anise, caraway, chervil, fennel.

mid-fall

The best time in all but the coldest areas to plant hardy perennial herbs.

Fresh Herbs Available
Basil, bay, borage, chervil, fennel, hyssop, marigold, marjoram, parsley, rosemary, sage, winter savory, sorrel, the thymes.

Cultivation
Seed with Heat
Parsley.

Seed Outside in the Garden
Catmint, chervil, wormwood, chamomile, fennel, angelica.

Softwood and Semiripe Cuttings
Bay, elder, hyssop, cotton lavender, southernwood, lavenders, the thymes, curry, box.

Root Cuttings
Tansy, pennyroyal, the mints, tarragon.

Division
Alecost, the marjorams, chives, lemon balm, lady's mantle, hyssop, bergamot, camphor plant, lovage, sorrel, sage, oregano, pennyroyal.

Containers
Start reducing the watering.

Garden
Clear the garden and weed it well. Cut down the old growth and collect any remaining seed heads. Cut back the mints, trim winter savory and hyssop. Give them all a leaf mold dressing. Dig up and remove the annuals, dill, coriander, borage, summer savory, sweet marjoram, and the second-year biennials, parsley, chervil, rocket etc. Protect with plastic or a frost cloth any herbs to be used fresh through the winter, like parsley, chervil, lemon thyme, salad burnet. Dig up some French tarragon, pot up in trays for forcing and protection.
　　Check the pH of alkaline soil every third year. Dress with well-rotted manure to a depth of 2–4 in. and

Calendula officinalis

leave the digging until the following spring. Dig over heavy soils; add manure to allow the frost to penetrate.

late fall

The days are getting shorter and frosts are starting. The garden can be tidied up and planting of hardy herbaceous herbs can continue as long as soil remains unfrozen and in a workable condition.

Fresh Herbs Available
Basil, bay, hyssop, marjoram, mint, parsley, rosemary, rue, sage, thyme.

Cultivation
Seed
Sow the following so that they can get a good period of stratification: arnica (old seed), sweet woodruff, yellow iris, poppy, soapwort, sweet cicely, hops (old seed), sweet violet.
　　Sow in trays, cover with glass and leave outside in a cold frame or corner of the garden where they cannot get damaged.

Containers
Cut back on all watering of container-grown plants. Give them all a prune, so that they go into rest mode for the winter.

Garden
This is the time for the final tidy up. Cut back the remaining plants, lemon balm, alecost, horehound, and give them a dressing of leaf mold. Give the elders a prune. Dig up a clump of mint and chives, put them in pots or trays and bring them into the greenhouse for forcing for winter use.

early winter

This is the start of the quiet time in the herb garden.

Fresh Herbs Available
Bay, hyssop, marjoram, oregano, mint (forced), parsley, chervil, rosemary, rue, sage, thyme, winter tarragon.

Garden
Even though the garden is entering its dormancy period it does not mean you can put your feet up and watch television.
　　Remove all the dead growth that falls into other plants, add more protective layers if needed. Wrap terracotta or stone ornaments in sacking if you live in extremely cold conditions and bring terracota pots indoors, as frost will cause them to crack. Bring bay trees in if the temperature drops too low. Keep an eye on the plants you are forcing in the greenhouse. You will need your fresh herbs to complete a Christmas feast.

climate

Climate is a major factor in determining what plants you can grow successfully. Most perennials are hardy, but those that are Mediterranean in origin (over half of those mentioned in this book) can suffer due to their shallow roots. Plants such as bay, rosemary and the thymes may therefore be affected in prolonged wet and cold winters.

On the other hand, perennial herbs grown from bulbs can suffer from warm winters as the plants need to hibernate (die back) during the winter months to give the plant time to rest and regenerate.

I have indicated the hardiness of each herb in the A–Z section. The following are the minimum temperatures that the plant can withstand for short periods without serious damage.

Half-hardy (Tender) 32°F (0°C)
Hardy 23°F (−5°C) to 5°F (−15°C)
Fully hardy below 5°F (−15°C)

I have also indicated the northern cold-hardiness of each herb by giving the USDA hardiness zone for North American readers. Consult a zone map to find the zone where you live, and choose plants accordingly.

An important climatic factor that must be taken into consideration are your frost dates. These dates are important when planting out annuals, and when harvesting both perennials and annuals. The seedlings of annual plants, if planted out too early, are most likely to be killed by a late frost, and very tender plants like basil can be killed if the night temperature falls to below 39°F (4°C).

For harvesting perennial herbs you should ensure that your last cutting is at least one month before the first winter frost, otherwise the severed stems will not have enough time to heal and the frost may damage or even kill the plant.

In my region, the last frost in spring is toward the end of April, and the first serious frost starts at the end of October; therefore I do not start planting annuals until the beginning of May and complete any harvesting of perennials by mid-September to be on the safe side. As a precaution I advise that you keep a roll of frost cloth available. This is a marvelous material that can make all the difference between death and survival when placed over young plants if an unexpected late frost occurs at the beginning of your season.

If your climate is not suitable for a particular herb, I suggest that you grow it either in a pot or as an annual rather than struggle each winter to keep the plant alive.

Angelica archangelica

In some regions of the world, of course, some herbs suffer more from summer heat than winter cold. You'll learn from experience that these herbs die back in summer and may recover in the fall, or they may be short-lived in your area and need frequent replacement.

botanical names

The herbs in the A–Z section have been listed alphabetically by their botanical (Latin) name; also given is the family name and the other species within that genus that also have herbal properties. I know this can be very confusing, so I will explain.

Plants are usually listed in reference books under their botanical names. This is because one plant may have several common names, as you will see when reading the A–Z section. For instance elder is also known as dogtree, Judas tree, score tree, God's stinking tree, black elder, European elder, and ellhorne. Even greater confusion can occur when a common name in different parts of the world refers to a different plant. For instance, in England meadowsweet *(Filipendula ulmaria)* is often called queen of the meadow, while in America queen of the meadow is gravelroot or Joe Pye weed *(Eupatorium purpureum)*.

Latin is the universal language for naming plants. The system used today is known as the Binomial System and was devised by the famous 18th-century Swedish botanist Carl Linnaeus (1707–1778). In this system, each plant is classified by using two words in Latin form, usually printed in italics. The first word is the name of the genus (e.g., *Thymus*) and the second the specific epithet (e.g., *vulgaris*); together they provide a universally recognized name (e.g., *Thymus vulgaris*).

The Binomial system of classification has been developed so that all living things are divided into a multibranched family tree according to their characteristics. Plants are gathered into particular families according to their anatomy (see table). A family may contain just one of a few genera, e.g., Family Cannabaceae, which contains the cannabis and hops genera, or many (e.g., Asteraceae) of which there are over 800 genera, including *Achillea*, *Arnica* and *Artemisia* to name a few, and over 13,000 species.

Wild plants are bred for the garden to make them more suitable for cultivation, to give them more aromatic leaves or flowers, for example. This can be done either by selection from seedlings or by spotting a mutation. Such plants are known as cultivars (a combination of "cultivated varieties"). Propagation from these varieties is normally done by cuttings or division. Cultivars are given vernacular names, which are printed within quotes, e.g., *Thymus* 'Doone Valley', to distinguish them from wild varieties in Latin form appearing in italics, i.e., *Thymus pulegioides*. Sexual crosses between species, usually of the same genus, are known as hybrids and are indicated by a multiplication sign e.g., *Mentha* x *piperita*.

For each of the herbs in the A–Z section, the following information is given at the beginning of each entry.
Genus (Botanical Name) Thymus
Common name Thyme
Other common names
Family name Lamiaceae

In a following section entitled "varieties" I list a selection of other species of the same genus that have similar herbal properties. In that section the following information is given as appropriate:

Botanical name Thymus vulgaris
Common name Common Thyme
Other names Garden Thyme

Finally, a problem that seems to be getting worse: many plants, including herbs, are undergoing reclassification, and long-established names are being changed. This is the result of scientific studies and research whereby it is found either that a plant has been incorrectly identified or that its classification has changed. In this book I have used the latest information available, found in the *RHS Plant Finder*, but I am aware that within the next few years there are going to be yet more changes. Where there has been a recent change in the botanical name, and the previous name is still used or well-known, this is shown in brackets.

Lamiaceae
FAMILY

Thymus
GENUS

Mentha
GENUS

Lavandula
GENUS

Thymus pulegioides
SPECIES

Thymus vulgaris
SPECIES

Thymus pulegioides 'Aureus'
CULTIVAR

Thymus vulgaris 'Silver Posie'
CULTIVAR

glossary

Analgesic A substance that relieves pain.

Annual A plant that completes its life-cycle from germination to flowering and death in one growing season.

Antidote A substance that counteracts or neutralizes a poison.

Apothecary An old term for a person who prepared and sold drugs and administered to the sick.

Aromatherapy The use of essential oils in the treatment of medical problems and for cosmetic purposes.

Astringent A substance that contracts the tissues of the body, checking discharges of blood and mucus.

Atropine An alkaloid obtained from members of the Solanaceae family.

Biennial A plant that produces roots and leaves in the first growing season, then flowers, seeds and dies by the end of the second.

Bolting What happens when a plant produces flowers and seeds prematurely.

Bulbil A small bulb rising above the ground in the axil of a leaf or bract.

Carminative A substance that allays pain and relieves flatulence and colic.

Columnar Column-shaped.

Cultivar A cultivated or horticultural variety of a species that may have originated either in the wild or in cultivation.

Deciduous Describes a plant that loses its leaves annually at the end of the growing season.

Decoction An extract of a herb (when the material is hard and woody, i.e., root, wood, bark, nuts) obtained by boiling a set weight of plant matter in a set volume of water for a set time. An average decoction would be 1 oz. of herb to 2 cups water, brought to the boil and simmered for 10–15 minutes. The decoction should be strained while still hot.

Diuretic A substance that increases the frequency of urination.

Emetic A substance that induces vomiting.

Essential oil A volatile oil obtained from a plant by distillation, having a similar aroma to the plant itself.

Frost cloth There are many different manufactured forms of this light, woven fleece. When used to cover crops it protects them from frost, wind, hail, birds, rabbits and other pests that eat or chew the leaves. It allows a light transmission of around 85 percent and can be permeated by rain.

Genus A group of species with common botanical features.

Globose Spherical, globe-like.

Herbaceous Relating to plants that are not woody and that die down at the end of each growing season.

Herbicide A substance that kills plants.

Homeopathy A system of medicine pioneered by Samuel Hahnemann, based on the supposition that minute quantities of a given substance, such as that of a medicinal plant, will cure a condition that would be caused by administering large quantities of the same substance.

Infusion An infusion is made by pouring a given quantity of boiling water over a given weight of soft herbal material (leaves or petals) and infusing. An average infusion would be 1 oz. dried herb or 3 oz. fresh herb to 2 cups boiling water. Leave the infusion to steep covered for 10–15 minutes before straining.

Knot garden A decorative formal garden popular in the 16th century and normally consisting of very low hedges in geometric patterns.

Leaf mold Partially decomposed leaves.

Mordant A substance used in dyeing that, when applied to the fabric to be dyed, reacts chemically with the dye, fixing the color.

Mulch A substance spread around a plant to protect it from weeds, water loss, heat or cold, and in some cases to provide nutrient material. Materials ranging from sawdust and pine needles to black plastic can be used as mulches; leaves and old straw are most commonly employed. Mulches should only be applied to moist soil.

Perennial A plant that survives for 3 or more years.

Perlite Expanded volcanic rock. It is inert, sterile and has a neutral pH value (i.e., it is neither acidic nor alkaline).

Rhizome A swollen underground stem that stores food and from which roots and shoots are produced.

Runner A trailing shoot that roots where it touches the ground.

Salve A soothing ointment.

Saponin A substance that foams in water and has a detergent action.

Shrub A perennial plant with woody stems growing from or near the base.

Species A natural group of plants composed of similar individuals which produce similar offspring when grown from seed—but usually include minor variations.

Stamen The pollen-producing part of the plant.

Stigma The part of a pistil (the female organs of a flower) that accepts the pollen.

Tap root The main root, which grows larger than any of the secondary roots and is usually swollen with food.

Thymol A bactericide and fungicide found in several volatile oils.

Tincture A solution that has been extracted from plant material after macerating in alcohol or alcohol/water solutions.

Tisane A drink made by the addition of boiling water to fresh or dried unfermented plant material.

Topiary The art of cutting shrubs and small trees into ornamental shapes.

Umbel An inflorescence with stalked flowers arising from a single point.

Vermifuge A substance that expels or destroys worms.

Vulnerary A preparation useful in healing wounds.

further reading

Encyclopedia of Herbs and Herbalism ed. Malcolm Stuart, Black Cat, 1979

Encyclopedia of Medicinal Plants Andrew Chevallier, Dorling Kindersley, 1996

Encyclopedia of Medicinal Plants Roberto Chiej, Macdonald, 1984

Evening Primrose Oil Judy Graham, Thorsons, 1984

HDRA Encyclopedia of Organic Gardening Dorling Kindersley, 2001

Herbal John Gerard, 1636; Bracken Books, 1985

Home Herbal Penelope Ody, Dorling Kindersley, 1995

Medicinal Plants of South Africa Ben-Erik van Wyk, Bosh van Oudtshoorn, Nigel Gericke, Briza Publications, 1997

Modern Herbal A.M. Grieve, Peregrine, 1976

Organic Gardening, Month by Month Guide to Lawrence D. Hills, Thorsons, 1983

RHS Encyclopedia of Gardening Dorling Kindersley, 4th edition 2007

RHS Encyclopedia of Herbs Deni Bown, Dorling Kindersley, 1995

RHS Plant Finder Dorling Kindersley, published annually

Seeds Jekka McVicar, Kyle Cathie, 2001

Information from *The Complete New Herbal*, ed. Richard Mabey, is reproduced by permission of Gaia Books Ltd.

bibliography

Complete Book of Herbs Lesley Bremness, Dorling Kindersley, 1988

Complete Herbal Culpeper, J. Gleave & Son, 1826

Complete New Herbal, The ed. Richard Mabey, Penguin, 1988

Complete Cookery Course Delia Smith, BBC Books, 1982

English Man's Flora, The Geoffrey Grigson, Paladin, 1975

Herb Book, The Arabella Boxer & Philippa Black, Octopus, 1980

Herb Book, The John Lust, Bantam, 1974

Herb Gardening at its Best Sal Gilbertie with Larry Sheehan, Atheneum/smi, 1978

Allium schoenoprasum f. *albiflorum* in bud

INDEX

Photographic acknowledgments

All photographs by Jekka McVicar except:

Maxine Adcock/Science Photo Library: 97 (left); Steve Baxter: 92, 104 (right); Pat Behnke/Alamy: 68; Bickwinkel/Alamy: 16 (left), 135 (top), 238; Richard Bloom/Garden Picture Library: 101 (top); Mark Bolton/Garden Picture Library: 140 (right); Christopher Burrows/Alamy: 182 (left); David Chapman: 1, 25 (bottom); Torie Chugg: 20 (left), 22 (left), 26 (left), 66 (left), 138, 156, 184, 247 (top); Cubolmages srl/Alamy: 69 (bottom); Humberto Olarte Cupas/Alamy: 263 (bottom left); Eising/StockFood: 261 (right); Fenix rising/Alamy: 161 (bottom left), 231 (left); Neil Hardwick/Alamy: 259 (top); David Hoffman Photo Library/Alamy: 73 (right); Holmes Garden Photo/Alamy: 261 (bottom left); Michelle Garratt: 13 (right), 15, 19, 21, 23, 25 (right), 27, 30 (right), 31 (right), 35, 37, 39, 43, 45 (bottom), 47, 49 (right), 51, 57, 63 (right), 65 (right), 67 (bottom & right), 70 (right), 71, 75 (right), 81, 83, 85, 89 (right), 98 (right), 103 (right), 111 (top right), 113, 115, 117 (bottom right), 119 (bottom right), 125 (right), 127 (bottom right), 129 (bottom right), 131 (bottom right), 133 (top right), 137, 139 (bottom), 143, 145, 147 (top & bottom right), 148 (right), 150 (bottom right), 153, 157, 159, 163, 165 (bottom right), 167 (top right), 170 (top & bottom right), 171, 178, 179 (bottom right), 183, 189 (left), 190 (right), 196 (right), 199 (bottom right), 205, 207 (right), 212 (top right), 213, 215 (top right), 217, 219 (bottom right), 220 (bottom right), 223 (bottom right), 225 (right), 229 (bottom right), 235 (bottom right), 241 (right), 243, 245 (bottom right), 249, 251 (right), 253, 255 (bottom right), 257 (bottom right), 259 (bottom right), 284, 285, 286; John Glover/Alamy: 18 (left), 87 (left); Geoff Hayes: 21 (left), 29 (left), 30 (left), 31 (left), 52, 66 (right), 78 (right), 79 (bottom), 84 (right), 102 (bottom), 111 (bottom), 112, 114, 120 (left), 126, 129 (top left), 130, 131 (left), 139 (top), 142 (right), 146, 147 (bottom left), 152 (right), 158 (bottom right), 165 (left), 168 (top left), 172 (left), 174, 188, 190 (bottom left), 193, 206, 207 (bottom left), 208 (bottom left), 209 (top right), 212 (bottom), 216 (left), 218 (left), 219 (top right, bottom left), 220 (top left), 224 (right), 226 (right), 235 (top), 246 (right), 252 (top), 254; Will Heap: 33 (right), 41 (left), 55, 59 (right), 69 (top), 77 (right), 87 (right), 91 (right), 93 (bottom), 95 (bottom), 97 (right), 101 (right), 105, 107 (right), 109 (right), 118 (bottom right), 134 (bottom), 149 (right), 161 (top right), 173 (top), 175 (bottom left), 185 (right), 187, 189 (right), 200 (bottom right), 227 (bottom), 229 (top left), 231 (right), 237 (right), 265, 267, 270, 271, 290, 291, 292, 293, 294, 295, 299; D. Hurst/Alamy: 95 (top); John La Gette/Alamy: 214; Sally Maltby: 13 (left), 50 (right), 75 (left), 99, 108 (left), 191 (bottom right), 198 (bottom right), 225 (bottom left), 239, 241 (left), 256 (top right), 264 and artwork from pages 272–281; Mediacolor's/Alamy: 16 (right), 20 (right), 124; Manda Nicholls/Alamy: 90 (right); Clive Nichols/Garden Picture Library: 28 (right); Ron Niebrugge/Alamy: 17; Organica/Alamy: 18 (right), 116 (bottom), 229 (top right); Organics image library/Alamy: 89 (left), 216 (right); Photo Dinodia/Garden Picture Library: 93 (top); Howard Rice/Garden Picture Library: 233 (right); Scherer, Tim/StockFood: 263 (right); Derek St. Romaine: 268, 282, 283, 296; Friedrich Strauss/ Garden Picture Library: 123 (bottom right); Chris & Tilde Stuart/FLPA: 233 (top left); Sara Taylor: 72 (bottom right); TH Foto/Alamy: 195 (top right); Paul Thompson Images/Alamy: 262; Rob Walls/Alamy: 118 (top); Dave Watts/ Alamy: 215 (bottom left); Woodystock/ Alamy: 136 (right); Konrad Zelazowski/Alamy: 228